T0345055

Agricultural Productivity
and Producer Behavior

National Bureau of
Economic Research
Conference Report

Agricultural Productivity and Producer Behavior

Edited by **Wolfram Schlenker**

The University of Chicago Press

Chicago and London

The University of Chicago Press, Chicago 60637
The University of Chicago Press, Ltd., London
© 2019 by the National Bureau of Economic Research, Inc.
Published 2019
Printed in the United States of America

28 27 26 25 24 23 22 21 20 19   1 2 3 4 5

ISBN-13: 978-0-226-61980-4 (cloth)
ISBN-13: 978-0-226-61994-1 (e-book)
DOI: https://doi.org/10.7208/chicago/9780226619941.001.0001

Library of Congress Cataloging-in-Publication Data

Names: Schlenker, Wolfram, editor.
Title: Agricultural productivity and producer behavior / edited by
    Wolfram Schlenker.
Other titles: National Bureau of Economic Research conference report.
Description: Chicago : University of Chicago Press, 2019. | Series:
    National Bureau of Economic Research conference report | Includes
    index.
Identifiers: LCCN 2019024315 | ISBN 9780226619804 (cloth) | ISBN
    9780226619941 (ebook)
Subjects: LCSH: Agricultural productivity—Congresses. | Agricultural
    productivity—United States—Congresses. | Agricultural subsidies—
    Congresses. | Agricultural subsidies—United States—Congresses.
Classification: LCC S494.5.P75 A373 2019 | DDC 338.1/6—dc23
LC record available at https://lccn.loc.gov/2019024315

♾ This paper meets the requirements of ANSI/NISO Z39.48-1992
(Permanence of Paper).

Relation of the Directors to the Work and Publications of the National Bureau of Economic Research

1. The object of the NBER is to ascertain and present to the economics profession, and to the public more generally, important economic facts and their interpretation in a scientific manner without policy recommendations. The Board of Directors is charged with the responsibility of ensuring that the work of the NBER is carried on in strict conformity with this object.

2. The President shall establish an internal review process to ensure that book manuscripts proposed for publication DO NOT contain policy recommendations. This shall apply both to the proceedings of conferences and to manuscripts by a single author or by one or more co-authors but shall not apply to authors of comments at NBER conferences who are not NBER affiliates.

3. No book manuscript reporting research shall be published by the NBER until the President has sent to each member of the Board a notice that a manuscript is recommended for publication and that in the President's opinion it is suitable for publication in accordance with the above principles of the NBER. Such notification will include a table of contents and an abstract or summary of the manuscript's content, a list of contributors if applicable, and a response form for use by Directors who desire a copy of the manuscript for review. Each manuscript shall contain a summary drawing attention to the nature and treatment of the problem studied and the main conclusions reached.

4. No volume shall be published until forty-five days have elapsed from the above notification of intention to publish it. During this period a copy shall be sent to any Director requesting it, and if any Director objects to publication on the grounds that the manuscript contains policy recommendations, the objection will be presented to the author(s) or editor(s). In case of dispute, all members of the Board shall be notified, and the President shall appoint an ad hoc committee of the Board to decide the matter; thirty days additional shall be granted for this purpose.

5. The President shall present annually to the Board a report describing the internal manuscript review process, any objections made by Directors before publication or by anyone after publication, any disputes about such matters, and how they were handled.

6. Publications of the NBER issued for informational purposes concerning the work of the Bureau, or issued to inform the public of the activities at the Bureau, including but not limited to the NBER Digest and Reporter, shall be consistent with the object stated in paragraph 1. They shall contain a specific disclaimer noting that they have not passed through the review procedures required in this resolution. The Executive Committee of the Board is charged with the review of all such publications from time to time.

7. NBER working papers and manuscripts distributed on the Bureau's web site are not deemed to be publications for the purpose of this resolution, but they shall be consistent with the object stated in paragraph 1. Working papers shall contain a specific disclaimer noting that they have not passed through the review procedures required in this resolution. The NBER's web site shall contain a similar disclaimer. The President shall establish an internal review process to ensure that the working papers and the web site do not contain policy recommendations, and shall report annually to the Board on this process and any concerns raised in connection with it.

8. Unless otherwise determined by the Board or exempted by the terms of paragraphs 6 and 7, a copy of this resolution shall be printed in each NBER publication as described in paragraph 2 above.

Contents

Acknowledgments   ix

Introduction   1
Wolfram Schlenker

1.   **Heterogeneous Yield Impacts from Adoption of Genetically Engineered Corn and the Importance of Controlling for Weather**   11
Jayson L. Lusk, Jesse Tack, and Nathan P. Hendricks

2.   **Impacts of Climate Change and Extreme Weather on US Agricultural Productivity: Evidence and Projection**   41
Sun Ling Wang, Eldon Ball, Richard Nehring, Ryan Williams, and Truong Chau

3.   **Farming under Weather Risk: Adaptation, Moral Hazard, and Selection on Moral Hazard**   77
Hsing-Hsiang Huang and Michael R. Moore

4.   **Intranational Trade Costs, Reallocation, and Technical Change: Evidence from a Canadian Agricultural Trade Policy Reform**   125
Mark Brown, Shon M. Ferguson, and Crina Viju-Miljusevic

5.   Electricity Prices, Groundwater, and Agriculture:
          The Environmental and Agricultural Impacts of
          Electricity Subsidies in India   157
          Reena Badiani-Magnusson and Katrina Jessoe

6.   Estimating the Impact of Crop Diversity on
          Agricultural Productivity in South Africa   185
          Cecilia Bellora, Élodie Blanc, Jean-Marc Bourgeon,
          and Eric Strobl

7.   Crop Disease and Agricultural Productivity:
          Evidence from a Dynamic Structural Model of
          Verticillium Wilt Management   217
          Christine L. Carroll, Colin A. Carter,
          Rachael E. Goodhue, and C.-Y. Cynthia Lin Lawell

8.   Willingness to Pay for Low Water Footprint Foods
          during Drought   251
          Hannah Krovetz, Rebecca Taylor,
          and Sofia B. Villas-Boas

          Contributors   293
          Author Index   297
          Subject Index   303

Acknowledgments

To promote economic research on agricultural productivity growth, the National Bureau of Economic Research (NBER), with the generous financial support of the Economic Research Service at the United States Department of Agriculture as well as the Giannini Foundation of Agricultural Economics at the University of California, convened a Universities Research Conference in May 2017. This book consists of eight chapters that were presented at the conference and assigned a discussant. I wanted to especially thank the discussants for the time they took to prepare their comments. These comments were essential in revising the presented papers before they became book chapters. The discussants of the following chapters were, respectively, Michael J. Roberts (University of Hawaii at Manoa), Ximing Wu (Texas A&M University), Joshua Woodard (Cornell University), Paul Rhode (University of Michigan and NBER), Nicholas Ryan (Yale University and NBER), Eyal Frank (University of Chicago), Paul T. Scott (New York University), and Dmitry Taubinsky (University of California, Berkeley, and NBER). Kelsey Jack (Tufts University and NBER) and Thibault Fally (University of California, Berkeley, and NBER) also served as discussants for two additional papers. Comments by two anonymous referees who reviewed the entire book are also gratefully acknowledged.

Introduction

Wolfram Schlenker

Agriculture historically employed a large share of the overall population. For example, as recently as 1800, more than half the population in most European countries were working in agriculture (Allen 2000). With the start of the industrial revolution and the accompanying mechanization, labor shifted out of agriculture. Still, throughout the 19th century and the beginning of the 20th century, increases in agricultural production were mainly driven by an increase in the growing area, whereas yields (output per area) were rather constant. Figure I.1 displays US corn yields from 1866 to 2016. Yields were flat until roughly 1950, when the Green Revolution led to a robust and persistent positive trend in average yields through 2016. The yield trend is added as a dashed black line showcasing the switch from constant average yields prior to 1950 toward a rather smooth constant upward trend following 1950. The steady growth in productivity is remarkable: US agriculture exhibited one of the highest postwar productivity growth rates of 1.6 percent per year, only surpassed by communications (Jorgenson and Gollop 1992).

On the other hand, the thick dashed line in figure I.1 displays the trend in the variability of yields around the trend—specifically, the trend in absolute yield deviations from the yield trend. When average yields started to increase, so did yield shocks (deviation from the average). The United States had tremendous technological progress in average yields, which increased by a factor of six between 1950 and 2016. At the same time, there was no prog-

Wolfram Schlenker is a professor at the School of International and Public Affairs and the Earth Institute at Columbia University and a research associate of the National Bureau of Economic Research.

For acknowledgments, sources of research support, and disclosure of the author's material financial relationships, if any, please see https://www.nber.org/chapters/c13939.ack.

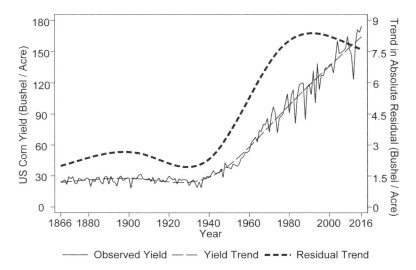

Fig. I.1   US corn yields (1866 to 2016)

Notes: This figure displays US corn yields (bushel/acre) for the years 1866 to 2016 from the National Agricultural Statistics Service (NASS). The solid line shows realized yields in each year. The dashed line shows the trend in yields. The thick dashed line shows the trend in the absolute residual, where the scale is given on the right vertical axis. All trends are estimated using restricted cubic splines with five knots, which are local third-order approximations.

ress in determining how well plants can withstand year-to-year shocks. The coefficient of variation—that is, the standard deviation of the fluctuation around the mean divided by the mean—remained rather constant. Empirical studies therefore often focus on relative yield deviations in a log model, as yield deviations are constant in relative terms.

A similar trend break from flat average yields to monotonically increasing average yields and an accompanying increase in yield variability hold for other crops and other countries, although the point at which the break occurs might differ, as might the slope.

Studying growth in agricultural productivity is still crucial, as it has important implications for food prices and food security across the globe. This book examines specific aspects of the observed productivity growth in agriculture, highlighting how modern breeding methods, pest control, irrigation, or biodiversity influence productivity and how climate change might hinder such productivity growth. Government policies in the form of trade policy and crop insurance are shown to have an effect on farm productivity.

Recent data on agricultural production is available for the entire globe: figure I.2 shows total global production of the four basic staple commodities following Roberts and Schlenker (2013). The graph shows global production quantities for the four basic staple commodities—maize (corn), wheat, rice, and soybeans—that account for 75 percent of the calories that humans

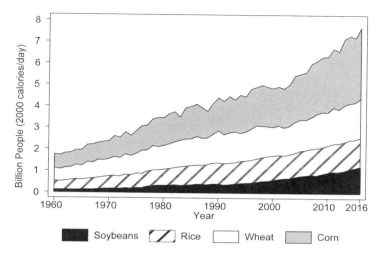

Fig. I.2   Global caloric production of basic staple commodities

Notes: This figure displays global production of the four staple commodities (corn, wheat, rice, and soybeans) that are responsible for 75 percent of the calories humans consume. Both the FAO as well as the FAS of the United States Department of Agriculture (USDA) give estimates of the total amount of production for various crops from 1960 onward. The graph uses data from the USDA Foreign Agricultural Statistics Service and converts them into the number of people who could be fed 2,000 calories per day (see table I.1).

Table I.1   **Caloric conversion factors**

Crop	People fed
Maize/corn	3.34
Wheat	2.99
Rice	2.84
Soybeans	4.51

Notes: Table lists caloric conversion factors for various crops. The numbers are taken from Williamson and Williamson (1942) and converted so the right column gives the caloric equivalent for a metric ton of a crop—that is, how many people could be fed 2,000 calories per day for a year, or 0.73 million calories.

consume, either directly or indirectly when they are used as feedstock for animals. Individual production quantities are multiplied by the number of calories that each metric ton of a particular crop generates. Table I.1 lists the caloric conversion factors for each crop, which are taken from Williamson and Williamson (1942) and converted into how many people could be fed by one metric ton on a 2,000-calorie-per-day diet for 365 days. The resulting unit, number of people fed for a year, is easier to interpret than trillions of calories. Obviously, a 2,000-calorie-per-day diet that is solely based on eating corn and nothing else would not be healthy or nutritiously balanced. The graph relies on data from the Foreign Agricultural Service (FAS) through

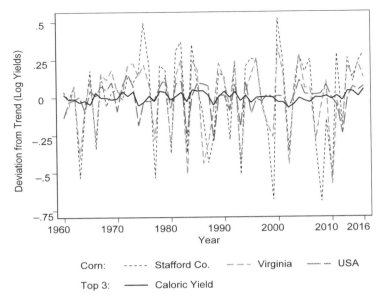

Fig. I.3   Smoothing of idiosyncratic production shocks across globe

Notes: This figure displays yield shocks (log deviations from a quadratic trend) at various geographic scales from 1960 to 2016. Idiosyncratic shocks average out for larger geographic scales. Yield shocks for Stafford County, Virginia, are shown in gray. It is the US county with the smallest corn-growing area (1,686 acres on average) that reports yields every year from 1960 to 2016. Yield shocks for Virginia are shown as a gray dashed line, while the long-dashed line shows shocks for aggregate US corn yields. Finally, the solid line shows yield shocks by aggregating global caloric production from corn, wheat, and rice (see figure I.2) and dividing it by the combined growing area.

2016. The global total is slightly higher in the Food and Agricultural Organization (FAO) data, which covers more countries than the FAS data.

Global production for soybeans is extremely smooth, as idiosyncratic production shocks average out. The lines for wheat and rice have slightly more year-to-year variability around the trend, but most of the year-to-year variability is observed for corn. The reason is that more than 40 percent of global corn production is located in the United States—predominantly in the Corn Belt, which is susceptible to common weather shocks.

The importance of trade in smoothing out production shocks is further demonstrated in figure I.3, which plots yield shocks—that is, deviations in log yields (production per unit area) from a quadratic time trend on various geographic scales. Stafford County, Virginia, is the county with the smallest growing area that continuously reports corn yields from 1960 to 2016. The growing area averaged 1,686 acres in those 51 years, which is almost exactly twice the area of Central Park in New York City. Annual yield shocks are shown with a small dotted line and exceed −0.6 (a decline of more than

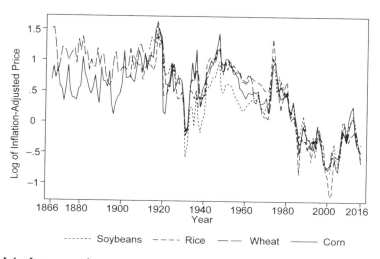

Fig. I.4   Log crop prices

Notes: This figure displays the log of inflation-adjusted prices from 1866 to 2016. The mean of log prices from 1960 to 2016 is set to zero. Nominal prices were downloaded from the NASS and adjusted to real dollars using the Minneapolis Federal Reserve's long-term consumer price index. Price series were normalized by subtracting the mean from 1960 to 2016.

60 log points). The largest decline during the time period is −0.69. When corn yields are averaged over the state of Virginia, the variability starts to decline but is still significant, as farms in Virginia face correlated weather shocks. The long-dashed line in figure I.3 displays aggregate corn yields for the entire United States. While there are years with significant yield declines, most notably 1988 and 2012, log yield deviations never exceed −0.3. Finally, the solid line shows global caloric yields for the three largest staple commodities (corn, wheat, and soybeans) by dividing the aggregate caloric production quantity from figure I.2 by the combined growing area. Soybeans were excluded, as the growing area was not reported in the FAS data. The variability of aggregate global caloric yield shock is much lower. The largest negative shock was −0.069—that is, one-tenth the size of the maximum shock for Stafford County, Virginia.

While aggregate production variability of the four staple commodities is limited, prices can vary substantially. Figure I.4 shows commodity prices in real terms. The figure shows log prices to show relative deviations. It normalizes log prices by subtracting the mean from 1960 to 2016, the same time period for which global production data are available in previous figures. The first noteworthy fact is that limited aggregate global production shocks imply much larger swings in prices, suggesting that demand is highly inelastic. Second, prices are highly correlated, as they are substitutes on the margin. Third, prices have generally followed a downward trend since the middle of the 20th century, when the Green Revolution led to a sustained increase in agricultural productivity. This trend seems to stop with the onset of the 21st century, although it is too early to tell from the graph whether recent price drops will revert to the previous downward trend or whether factors (climate change, emerging countries that switch to a more meat-heavy diet that requires more calories, and biofuel mandates) have led to a breakpoint where demand increases start to outpace supply increases. When prices tripled in the early 2000s, they were still low in real terms by historic standards.

One of the "fathers" of the Green Revolution, Norman Borlaug, was awarded the 1970 Nobel Peace Prize for his contribution to ending world hunger by boosting agricultural productivity around the globe and making basic calories cheaper. Will productivity continue to increase through the adoption of new technologies or cropping practices? Will it be limited through climate change or policies that encourage maladaptation? The remaining chapters examine various aspects. The first two chapters examine long-term drivers of agricultural productivity growth—specifically, the adoption of hybrid corn and changes in climatic factors.

Lusk, Tack, and Hendricks (2018) examine in chapter 1 the effect of genetically engineered (GE) corn on yields using a panel of county-level corn yields in the United States from 1980 to 2015 that is matched with adaptation rates of GE corn. The authors find that the adoption of GE corn has increased average yields by 17 percent if the adoption rate goes from zero to 100 percent. At the same time, it did not increase the resilience to heat or water stress. The gains in average yields are spatially heterogeneous and are correlated with soil quality, suggesting that productivity enhancements are not uniform. Since the adoption rate has trended upward over time, the authors emphasize the importance of controlling for time trends as well as weather, which trended over the same time period.

Wang et al. (2018) model in chapter 2 the effect of climate change on US agricultural productivity using a stochastic frontier approach for the last half century (1960 to 2010). Similar to the previous chapter, the authors document spatially heterogeneous trends in weather. "Bad" weather, as measured by the temperature humidity index (heat waves) or the Oury drought index, is pushing yields inside the production possibility frontier. The authors do not model individual crops but rather state-level aggregate output and how individual variables (e.g., heat wave and droughts) push observed output inside the frontier. The effect of medium-term climate change on the production efficiency under climate change is simulated, which is generally negative but spatially heterogeneous with the largest decrease in efficiency in the Delta region.

The next three chapters examine how farmers adjust production practices to changing governmental regulations—specifically, crop insurance (chapter 3), transport subsidies (chapter 4), and electricity subsidies (chapter 5).

Chapter 3 by Huang and Moore (2018) looks at farmer responses to the US federal crop insurance program—specifically, whether preplanting precipitation, which influences soil moisture and possible planting dates, influences the insurance coverage. The US crop insurance program is highly subsidized, as premiums are not sufficient to cover average payouts. The authors address the US Farm Bill's temporary introduction of the Supplemental Revenue Assistance Program in 2008—that is, halfway through their sample period. This policy lowered farmer deductibles and moved from insurance of individual crops to a combined insurance for all crops grown on a farm. The policy change gave farmers an incentive to change their crop mix as well as their insurance coverage. The chapter utilizes detailed data for each 1 × 1 mile section in four states—Illinois, Iowa, Nebraska, and North Dakota—from 2001 to 2014. The observed behavioral response is more pronounced in the drier states of Nebraska and North Dakota, where soil moisture at planting is crucial. The federal crop insurance program is found to lead to moral hazard and impair farmers' optimal responses.

Brown, Ferguson, and Viju-Miljusevic (2018) examine in chapter 4 the role of trade subsidies on productivity measures. The authors were able to gain access to microlevel census data on farm outcomes to study the issue of trade access and transportation cost. They examine the removal of a 700-million-a-year freight subsidy in Canada and find that farmers further from a port, who face longer transportation routes, saw a bigger wedge between the world price that is paid at the port and the realized price at the farm gate (net of transportation cost). In the short term, the shift from low-value to high-value crops as well as adoption of new seed varieties is driven by changes in existing farms and not by acreage changes between farms. In the long term, the opposite is true: most of the observed changes in technology can be explained by shifts in acreages to farms that utilize these technologies more.

Badiani-Magnusson and Jessoe (2018) study groundwater usage in Indian districts in chapter 5, utilizing changes in state-level electricity subsidies. The chapter uses a panel setting to control for district and year fixed effects (and controlling for weather and state elections in another specification). The authors find that changes in electricity subsidies impact aggregate water use, which in turn impacts agricultural output. While irrigation water use increases agricultural productivity, it depletes aquifers for the future. This problem is amplified when electricity prices are kept artificially low through subsidies.

The final three chapters of the book study the effects of specific farm practices on agricultural productivity and consumer demand. These include crop diversification (chapter 6), disease management (chapter 7), and water-saving methods (chapter 8).

Bellora et al. (2018) use an innovative microlevel data set to examine whether crop diversity has an effect on agricultural productivity. Ecologists have long emphasized that fields that grow a diverse set of crops will produce higher biomass than monocultures. This finding has been confirmed in field experiments of grasslands. The authors obtain field-level data for South Africa that is merged with satellite data on the Normalized Difference Vegetation Index (NDVI). Most research to date focused on developing countries, so it is informative to see whether similar results hold in emerging economies. The benefits of crop diversity might be different, for example, because the beneficial effect of diversity on pest suppression is different in places that use a different amount of pesticides. The authors have only one observation per field and therefore have to control for various other controls. They include farm fixed effects to compare fields of different diversity within farms and find that more diverse fields are more productive.

Chapter 7 by Carroll et al. (2018) examines the benefits of pest control on agricultural productivity in a dynamic model, highlighting that contamination not only impacts the current crop but also has implications for future plantings, as the pest stays in the soil. There is an intertemporal externality, as contamination in the current period impacts pest outcomes and profits in future periods, as well as supply-chain externality, as seed companies might deliver seeds that are contaminated, and testing for the pest is costly. A dynamic model that incorporates these linkages is developed. The authors apply their model to the case of *Verticillium dahliae*, a fungus that gets spread through spinach seeds and impacts lettuce, which is grown year-round in Monterey County, California. The county accounts for a significant share of total US lettuce production. Data on pesticides used to fumigate fields as well as cropping choices are merged. The structural model reveals that growing spinach is less desirable than what can be explained by its price for the current period—a consequence of the negative effects of possibly contaminated seeds on future productivity.

Finally, in chapter 8, Krovetz, Taylor, and Villas-Boas (2018) conduct an online experiment to elicit the willingness to pay for water-saving technologies for four water-intensive crops: avocados, almonds, lettuce, and tomatoes. The average water use for almonds is approximately one gallon for each almond. The authors find an implicit willingness to pay about 12 cents per gallon of water saved. On the other hand, informing consumers about the drought conditions in California did not statistically significantly increase the willingness to pay, possibly because they were already aware of it. The study finds that consumers would respond to a label about the water technology used, similar to the USDA organic seal.

Together, the following eight chapters demonstrate that there are both technological as well as policy choices that impact agricultural productivity and that consumers have preferences over the technology that is used to grow a crop.

References

Allen, R. C. 2000. "Economic Structure and Agricultural Productivity in Europe, 1300–1800." *European Review of Economic History* 4 (1): 1–25.

Badiani, R., and K. Jessoe. 2018. "Electricity Prices, Groundwater, and Agriculture: The Environmental and Agricultural Impacts of Electricity Subsidies in India." In *Agricultural Productivity and Producer Behavior*, edited by W. Schlenker. Chicago: University of Chicago Press. This volume.

Bellora, C., É. Blanc, J.-M. Bourgeon, and E. Strobl. 2018. "Estimating the Impact of Crop Diversity on Agricultural Productivity in South Africa." In *Agricultural Productivity and Producer Behavior*, edited by W. Schlenker. Chicago: University of Chicago Press. This volume.

Brown, M., S. M. Ferguson, and C. Viju-Miljusevic. 2018. "Intranational Trade Costs, Reallocation and Technical Change: Evidence from a Canadian Agricultural Trade Policy Reform." In *Agricultural Productivity and Producer Behavior*, edited by W. Schlenker. Chicago: University of Chicago Press. This volume.

Carroll, C. L., C. A. Carter, R. E. Goodhue, and C.-Y. C. Lin Lawell. 2018. "Crop Disease and Agricultural Productivity: Evidence from a Dynamic Structural Model of Verticillium Wilt Management." In *Agricultural Productivity and Producer Behavior*, edited by W. Schlenker. Chicago: University of Chicago Press. This volume.

Huang, H.-H., and M. R. Moore. 2018. "Farming under Weather Risk: Adaptation, Moral Hazard, and Selection on Moral Hazard." In *Agricultural Productivity and Producer Behavior*, edited by W. Schlenker. Chicago: University of Chicago Press. This volume.

Jorgenson, D. W., and F. M. Gollop. 1992. "Productivity Growth in U.S. Agriculture: A Postwar Perspective." *American Journal of Agricultural Economics* 74 (3): 745–50.

Krovetz, H., R. Taylor, and S. B. Villas-Boas. 2018. "Willingness to Pay for Low Water Footprint Foods during Drought." In *Agricultural Productivity and Producer Behavior*, edited by W. Schlenker. Chicago: University of Chicago Press. This volume.

Lusk, J. L., J. Tack, and N. P. Hendricks. 2018. "Heterogeneous Yield Impacts from Adoption of Genetically Engineered Corn and the Importance of Controlling for Weather." In *Agricultural Productivity and Producer Behavior*, edited by W. Schlenker. Chicago: University of Chicago Press. This volume.

Roberts, M. J., and W. Schlenker. 2013. "Identifying Supply and Demand Elasticities of Agricultural Commodities: Implications for the US Ethanol Mandate." *American Economic Review* 103 (6): 2265–95.

Wang, S. L., E. Ball, R. Nehring, R. Williams, and T. Chau. 2018. "Impacts of Climate Change and Extreme Weather on U.S. Agricultural Productivity: Evidence and Projection." In *Agricultural Productivity and Producer Behavior*, edited by W. Schlenker. Chicago: University of Chicago Press. This volume.

Williamson, L., and P. Williamson. 1942. "What We Eat." *Journal of Farm Economics* 24 (3): 698–703.

1

Heterogeneous Yield Impacts from Adoption of Genetically Engineered Corn and the Importance of Controlling for Weather

Jayson L. Lusk, Jesse Tack, and Nathan P. Hendricks

Although agriculture has historically experienced one of the highest rates of productivity growth in the US economy (Jorgenson, Gollop, and Fraumeni 1987), there is evidence that agricultural productivity growth is beginning to slow (Alston, Andersen, and Pardey 2015; Alston, Beddow, and Pardey 2009; Ray et al. 2012). The decline in productivity growth has coincided with concerns about food price spikes, social instability, food insecurity, population growth, drought, and climate change (Bellemare 2015; Ray et al. 2013; Roberts and Schlenker 2013; Schlenker and Roberts 2009; Tack, Barkley, and Nalley 2015a,b). This confluence of problems has prompted interest in determining whether certain technologies can promote gains in crop yields, and none has been more controversial than biotechnology.

Many previous studies have investigated whether adoption of genetically engineered (GE) crops has increased yield (e.g., see reviews in Fernandez-Cornejo et al. 2014; Klümper and Qaim 2014; NASEM 2016), and the consensus from the microlevel data and experimental studies is that adoption of GE crops, particularly insect-resistant Bt varieties targeting the corn borer, have generally been associated with higher yield. However, ample skepticism remains, with high-profile popular publications purporting that GE crops have failed to live up to their promise of yield increases (e.g., Foley 2014; Gurian-Sherman 2009; Hakim 2016).

Jayson L. Lusk is distinguished professor and head of the Department of Agricultural Economics at Purdue University.

Jesse Tack is an associate professor in the Department of Agricultural Economics at Kansas State University.

Nathan P. Hendricks is an associate professor in the Department of Agricultural Economics at Kansas State University.

For acknowledgments, sources of research support, and disclosure of the authors' material financial relationships, if any, please see http://www.nber.org/chapters/c13940.ack.

A variety of factors might explain the divergence in views about the yield effects of GE crops, but one of the main issues is that adoption of GE crops does not appear to have had much effect on trend yields when investigating national-level yield data (Duke 2015), nor do yield trends appear much different in developed countries that have and have not adopted GE varieties (Heinemann et al. 2014). As the NASEM (2016, 66) put it, "The nation-wide data on maize, cotton, or soybean in the United States do not show a significant signature of genetic-engineering technology on the rate of yield increase." This raises the question of whether the yield-increasing effects of GE crops observed in particular locations and experiments can be generalized more broadly and, if so, whether the impact on crop yields varies spatially.

In this chapter, we show that simple analyses of yield trends mask important weather-related factors that influence the estimated effect of GE crop adoption on yield. Our analysis couples county-level data on corn yields from 1980 to 2015 and state-level adoption of GE traits with data on weather variation and soil characteristics. Using state-level adoption data does not induce measurement-error bias because state-level aggregate adoption is necessarily uncorrelated with the deviation of a particular county's adoption from the state-level aggregate. Using state-level adoption data does induce serial correlation of the error term, which we address with two-way clustering.

A number of important findings emerge from our analysis. First, changes in weather and climatic conditions confound yield effects associated with GE adoption. Without controlling for weather, adoption of GE crops appears to have little impact on corn yields; however, once temperature and precipitation controls are added, GE adoption has significant effects on corn yields. Second, the adoption of GE corn has had differential effects on crop yields in different locations even among corn-belt states. However, we find that ad hoc political boundaries (i.e., states) do not provide a credible representation of differential GE effects. Rather, alternative measures based on soil characteristics provide a broad representation of differential effects and are consistent with the data. In particular, we find that the GE effect is much larger for nonsandy soils with a larger water-holding capacity. Overall, our studies show that GE adoption has increased yields by approximately 18 bushels per acre on average, but this effect varies spatially across counties ranging from roughly five to 25 bushels per acre. Finally, we do not find evidence that adoption of GE corn has led to lower yield variability, nor do we find that current GE traits mitigate the effects of heat or water stress.

The adoption of GE crops does not necessarily imply that farmers perceived yield benefits, because there are several other benefits associated with the adoption of GE crops—primarily through a reduction in the cost of production. The nonyield benefits have come in the form of labor savings, reduced insecticide use, and improved weed and pest control, which has facilitated the ability to adopt low- and no-till production methods, alter crop rotations, and utilize higher planting densities (Chavas, Shi, and Lauer 2014; Fernandez-Cornejo et al. 2014; Klümper and Qaim 2014; Perry, Moschini, and Hennessy 2016; Perry et al. 2016). Revealed preferences of US farmers indicate producer benefits over and above the substantially higher price of GE corn relative to conventional corn (Shi, Chavas, and Stiegert 2010). The rapid adoption of GE corn by farmers also provides evidence of these benefits. GE corn was first grown commercially in the United States in 1996. In just four years, a quarter of the corn acres were planted with a GE trait, and in less than 10 years, adoption had spread to more than half the US corn acres. In 2016, 92 percent of US corn acres were planted with GE corn, with 81 percent of the total GE corn acreage being planted with "stacked" varieties that are both insect resistant and herbicide tolerant. It is also important to recognize that GE crops can increase production through the expansion of designated crop-planting areas (i.e., the extensive margin) because greater yields and lower costs of production provide incentives to expand crop production (Barrows, Sexton, and Zilberman 2014).

Nonetheless, discussion of yield impacts of GE crops remains at the forefront of public discussions about whether and to what extent biotechnology can contribute to food security and help mitigate the effects of climate change. In response to the finding that GE adoption does not appear to alter national-level yield trends, NASEM (2016, 16) recommended that research "should be conducted that isolates effects of the diverse environmental and genetic factors that contribute to yield." Our objective here is to help fill this gap in the literature.

The next section reviews some of the research on the yield effects of GE crops, and we delineate our contribution to the literature. The third and fourth sections discuss the data and methods, followed by the presentation of results. The last section concludes.

1.1 Background

GE crops currently on the market do not increase yield per se. However, they can reduce the gap between actual and potential yield by reducing the adverse effects of weeds and insects (NASEM 2016). It is also possible that crops with GE traits can reduce yields if introduced into less productive varieties not ideally suited to a particular growing region (Chavas, Shi, and Lauer 2013).

Figure 1.1 shows the national trend in US corn yield and the adoption of GE corn from 1980 to 2016. The figure suggests, in the words of Duke (2014, 653), that "yields have continued to increase at the same rate as before introduction [of GE crops]." Leibman et al. (2014) similarly investigated aggregate yields and found after adoption of GE corn a small (0.5 bushels/acre) trend increase; however, no tests of statistical significance were performed.

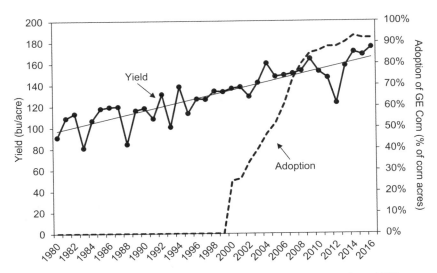

Fig. 1.1   Trend in national US corn yield and adoption of GE corn from 1980 to 2016. Circles represent observed yields, the solid line represents linear yield trend, and the dashed line represents percentage of corn acres planted with GE corn.

Source: Data are from USDA National Agricultural Statistics Service (NASS).

These sorts of aggregate comparisons make no attempt to control for potentially confounding factors such as weather, which could have coincidentally been worse in the 1980s before the adoption of GE corn. Controlling for weather in a national-level trend analysis is difficult due to the nonlinear impacts of weather on yield and highly spatially heterogeneous weather conditions within the country. This motivates the use of disaggregate data to test the impact of GE adoption on yields.

These aggregate investigations can be contrasted with the large literature from agronomic experimental studies that attempt to hold constant many factors such as location and germplasm. Nolan and Santos (2012) summarize the results of more than 30 such studies mainly published between 2000 and 2003. None of the reviewed studies report a statistically significant negative effect associated with Bt GE corn, and nearly all reported positive yield effects associated with the Bt GE trait, with yield gains as high as 19 percent. In their analysis, Nolan and Santos (2012) combined data sets from multiple experiments conducted by 10 different state agricultural extension services from 1997 to 2009. They found, after controlling for weather, agronomic inputs, management, and soil characteristics, that planting of Bt GE corn led to yield gains of around 14 bushels per acre, although when the only GE trait present was herbicide tolerance, yield was unaffected or slightly negative. Despite finding that yield was affected by location, weather, and soil characteristics, the authors did not investigate whether these factors inter-acted with the GE effect (i.e., whether GE yield gains were higher or lower in different locations, in different weather patterns, or in different soils).

As shown by Chavas, Shi, and Lauer (2013), however, there is likely ample heterogeneity in the effects of GE adoption on mean yield and yield variance. Using experiment data from agricultural experiment stations in Wisconsin from 1990 to 2010, Chavas, Shi, and Lauer (2013) found that GE traits had variable effects on corn yields, depending on the type of GE trait introduced and how long the trait had been used in production, with mean yields significantly increasing relative to conventional non-GE corn for some traits (namely, Bt targeted at the European corn borer) but not oth-ers (namely, herbicide-tolerant-only GE corn and GE corn with Bt targeted only at corn rootworm). Additional analysis of the same data by Chavas, Shi, and Lauer (2013) suggests that some of the yield gains attributable to GE hybrids were a result of improvements in non-GE germplasm and the wider availability of higher-quality germplasm. However, regardless of the GE trait analyzed, the authors found a consistent effect on yield variance, with GE crops reducing the variance of corn yields. The authors conclude that GE crops have helped farmers reduce their risk exposure.

As was the case in Nolan and Santos (2012), Chavas, Shi, and Lauer (2013) did not investigate whether the yield effects of GE traits were affected by location, management practices, soil type, and so on. However, there are reasons to believe the potential yield effects of GE adoption are not uniform across location or time. Currently available GE traits rely on Bt to provide protection against the European corn borer and/or corn rootworm, and/or tolerance to certain herbicides (primarily glyphosate). While there are fewer agronomic reasons to suggest that herbicide tolerance would con-vey significant yield benefits, insect resistance can plausibly lower the gap between potential and realized yield. As discussed by Nolan and Santos (2012), conventionally applied insecticides only provide 60 percent to 80 percent protection against corn borer and rootworm, whereas Bt provides near 100 percent protection. As such, the effect of Bt GE corn relative to con-ventional corn depends on pest pressure. It has long been known that corn borer and corn rootworm pressures are affected by soil characteristics and weather (e.g., Beck and Apple 1961; Huber, Neiswander, and Salter 1928; Turpin and Peters 1971; MacDonald and Ellis 1990), and prior research has hinted at the fact that yield effects of Bt corn might depend on soil charac-teristics via their effects on insect populations (Ma, Meloche, and We 2009). Pest pressure is also likely to vary spatially according to the density of corn production, which depends on soil and climatic conditions.

In a paper most similar to the present inquiry, Xu et al. (2013) used aggre-gate, nonexperimental data and found that GE adoption led to a 19.4 bushel per acre increase in corn yields in the central Corn Belt (Illinois, Indiana, and Iowa). What explains the contrast between the apparent lack of impact of GE adoption in aggregate trend yields shown in figure 1.1 and the results from Xu et al. (2013)? There are a variety of possibilities. For example, Xu et al. (2013) look at county (rather than national) yields, and they control for confounding factors related to weather and fertilizer use. However, it is unclear from Xu et al. (2013) what the impacts are of ignoring these factors. Moreover, these authors only considered limited geographic heterogeneity (they only explored central Corn Belt to noncentral Corn Belt), and they did not consider other factors like soil characteristics or how weather and soil characteristics may influence GE-adoption effects on yield. In addition, the authors did not consider the effects of GE adoption on yield variability.

Another confounding factor that exists when exploring national yield trends is the fact that the number of acres planted to corn has increased significantly over the same period of time that GE traits have been adopted. For example, in the 10 years from 1980 to 1989 prior to adoption of GE corn, 75.7 million acres of corn were planted on average each year in the United States. By contrast, in the most recent 10-year period from 2007 to 2016, during a period of near full adoption of GE traits, on average 91.2 million acres of corn were planted each year in the United States, a 20.5 percent increase. Some of the acreage expansion is a result of GE adoption, as GE traits have increased the viability of continuous corn (planting corn after corn rather than rotating with soybeans; Chavas, Shi, and Lauer 2014), a practice that has historically been associated with significant yield drag (Gentry, Ruffo, and Below 2013). Ethanol policies, among other factors, also led to a dramatic increase in corn prices over the period of GE corn adoption, which both increased the prevalence of continuous corn (Hendricks, Smith, and Sumner 2014) and led to the expansion of corn onto acres that would previously have been considered marginal lands. Combined, these factors suggest that national corn yields would have been higher in recent years had it not been for the expansion of corn acreage.

1.2   Data

We utilize a large panel of roughly 28,000 yield observations spanning 819 counties from 1980 to 2015. We chose 1980 as the starting point for the time series, as this gives us a roughly equal number of years pre- and post-GE adoption, which started in 1996. Roughly 13,000 (45 percent) of the yield observations correspond to the pre-GE period. These data were collected via USDA NASS Quick Stats and correspond to total production divided by harvested acres in each county. As in Xu et al. (2013), we omit any county where (i) more than 10 percent of harvested cropland is irrigated or (ii) yield data was reported for less than two-thirds of the pre-GE years or two-thirds of the post-GE years. Figure 1A.1 in the appendix to this chapter shows that there exists extensive cross-sectional and temporal variation of yields. Note that all tables and figures with a leading S are contained in the accompanying supplementary material.

The limiting factor for the cross-sectional (spatial) representation of the data is the availability of GE adoption data. We utilize the same NASS data as Xu et al. (2013), which reports GE adoption at the state-year level for 13 states: Illinois, Indiana, Iowa, Kansas, Michigan, Minnesota, Missouri, Nebraska, North Dakota, Ohio, South Dakota, Texas, and Wisconsin. These data were first recorded in 2000 for all but North Dakota and Texas, which were recorded starting in 2005, several years after adoption had already started to occur in some areas. We interpolate missing data using predictions from a generalized linear model with a binomial family and a logit link function. A pooled model with state fixed effects provides similar predictions as separate models for each state. We use the latter here. Our interpolation procedure follows the seminal work of Griliches (1957), who modeled the diffusion of hybrid corn seed as logistic growth. Figure 1A.2 provides the observed adoption data in addition to the predictions from both models used to interpolate missing values. Table 1A.1 provides summary statistics for both the observed and observed-plus-interpolated GE adoption rate variables. Figure 1A.3 provides a spatial map of the in-sample counties studied in the analysis.

While our analysis focuses on identifying the effects of GE adoption on corn yields, it is likely that one must control for several sources of confounding factors in practice. For example, if the post-1996 period of adoption coincided with an abnormal run of good or bad weather conditions, then failure to control for weather could bias the estimate of the GE effect. Recent evidence suggests that this can be an important consideration for crop yield analyses (Tack, Barkley, and Nalley 2015a,b). We use the same weather data as in Schlenker and Roberts (2009), updated to 2015 to control for the influence of weather on corn yields. Daily outcomes on minimum and maximum temperatures at the county level are interpolated within each day using a sinusoidal approximation and are then used to construct three degree-day variables: between 0°C and 10°C, between 10°C and 29°C, and above 29°C. Along with cumulative precipitation, these variables are aggregated across March–August. Figure 1A.4 shows that there is extensive variation both cross-sectionally and over time for these variables.

Soil characteristic data are from the gSSURGO (Gridded Soil Survey Geographic) database created by NRCS (Natural Resources Conservation Service) and were also used in Hendricks (2016). Soils are aggregated to the county level using only the area in the county classified as cropland according to the National Land Cover Database. One measure of soil quality that we consider is water-holding capacity (measured in mm), which is the total volume of plant-available water that the soil can store within the root zone and is calculated as a weighted average across the county. Figure 1A.7 provides a spatial map of the water-holding capacity across counties, which has a wide range from near zero to just over 300 mm and a sample average value of 216 mm. Another measure we consider is a grouping of soil types based on the soil texture of the county. This is calculated as the dominant soil texture classification within the county and includes nine different soil types: clay, clay-loam, loam, loamy-sand, sand, sandy-loam, silt-loam, silty-clay, and silty-clay-loam. Figure 1A.8 provides a spatial map of these soil types by county.

1.3   Empirical Model

We assume that the effect of GE adoption on corn yields is identified using the regression model

$$y_{ist} = \alpha + \delta A_{it}^* + f(\mathbf{x}_{ist}, \boldsymbol{\gamma}) + \varepsilon_{ist},$$

where y_{ist} are corn yields (bushels/acre) in county i, state s, and year t. The variable A_{it}^* is the unobserved GE adoption rate at the county-year level and is measured as the fraction of acreage planted to GE varieties. The parameter of interest is δ, which measures the effect of GE adoption on corn yields. We discuss the implications of only observing adoption rates at the state-year level in the next section. We also include a vector of control variables $\mathbf{x}_{ist}$ that include county-level fixed effects, state-level trend variables, and weather variables measured at the county-year level.

Our identification comes from two different sources of variation. First, the effect is identified from differences in yield over time as GE adoption has increased, controlling for state-specific yield trends and weather. Second, the effect is identified from differences in yields from the county-specific average—adjusted for the state-specific trend—between counties that had different levels of GE adoption.

One potential concern is that GE adoption could be endogenous— counties with larger increases in yield adopted GE more rapidly. Our primary source of variation in GE adoption—before and after the introduction of GE technology—is exogenous because the introduction of GE varieties was driven by supply of the technology rather than farmer demand. A more likely source of endogeneity is that counties with greater (or smaller) increases in yields had more rapid early adoption. To test if this endogeneity affects our results, we present a robustness check, where all periods during diffusion are omitted from the sample so that we only exploit yield differences before and after the introduction of the GE technology. An alternative strategy is to include year fixed effects so that our source of identification is the change in yields between counties with different changes in adoption rates of GEs. We do not include year fixed effects in our preferred specification because it precludes the use of exogenous preadoption data as a counterfactual for postadoption data. Including year fixed effects also exploits a narrow source of variation in GE adoption.

1.3.1   State-Level Adoption Rates

One of the main concerns in identifying δ is that data on GE adoption are only available at the state level, thus the variable that we observe is A_{st}. This can be cast as a nonclassical measurement-error problem, where the true, unobserved measure A_{it}^* is related to our observed measure A_{st} by

$$A_{it}^* = A_{st} + v_{it},$$

where v_{it} denotes the difference between the county-specific adoption and the state-level aggregate adoption. Substituting this expression into the regression model and rearranging gives

$$y_{ist} = \alpha + \delta A_{st} + f(\mathbf{x}_{ist}, \gamma) + u_{ist}$$

$$u_{ist} = \delta v_{it} + \varepsilon_{ist}.$$

The error term u_{ist} is a composite random variable. Note that this source of measurement error is nonclassical in the sense that it does not induce bias in our estimate of δ because the measurement error is uncorrelated with the observed state-level adoption. The state-level aggregate adoption in each year is uncorrelated—by definition—with the deviation of a particular county's adoption from the state-level aggregate.

However, the measurement error does induce serial correlation of the error terms on a subsample of the data. Some counties are likely to lead or lag the state-level adoption rate in all periods of technology diffusion, resulting in serial correlation of the errors. Note that measurement error is only a concern during the period of adoption when $A_{st} \in (0,1)$, since A_{it}^* and A_{st} are necessarily both equal to zero prior to adoption and both equal to one at full adoption. Thus the measurement error induces serial correlation in the errors only when both periods are in the adoption phase of the data.

We use the two-way clustering approach of Cameron, Gelbach, and Miller (2012) to account for multiple sources of correlation in the errors. The first dimension of clustering is accomplished by using a county-by-adoption-phase grouping scheme such that each county is split into two groups, one when GE adoption equals zero and another when adoption is positive. This clustering accounts for potential serial correlation resulting from the measurement error of the state-level adoption variable. The second dimension of clustering is by year in order to account for the presence of spatial correlation in the errors (ε_{ist}) driven by the spatial similarity of residual weather shocks not accounted for in the model across counties within each year. We interpret this approach as being robust to heteroscedasticity, spatial correlation of the error terms across counties, and serial correlation of the errors within each county both within and outside of the adoption period.

1.3.2   Importance of Controlling for Weather

It is worth noting that the need to control for weather is important if the exposure differs between the pre- and post-GE subsamples in the data (or if weather was relatively good or bad in counties that adopted more rapidly). In theory, if one were to observe a large enough frequency of weather outcomes in both periods such that average weather exposures were similar, then one would not need to control for its influence. In practice, weather may bias coefficients in samples where the number of time periods is not large. We investigate this possibility by comparing precipitation and extreme heat exposure (degree-days above 29°C) in both periods—that is, pre- and post-1996. For each county, we calculate the percentage difference in the average precipitation and extreme heat variables across periods and report these values in figures 1A.5 and 1A.6. Precipitation was roughly 4 percent higher in the post-GE period on average across counties. However, this masks a large amount of heterogeneity, as county-level differences ranged from −15 to 21 percent. Similarly, the occurrence of extreme heat exhibited a large amount of heterogeneity, as differences as large as −63 and 22 percent spanned an average value of −20 percent. This suggests that controlling for weather is important and must be done at a local level. It would not likely be properly accounted for using spatially aggregated measures of weather shocks at the regional or national level or using crude measures such as year fixed effects.

1.3.3   Heterogeneous Yield Response

We also consider models of the form

$$y_{ist} = \alpha + \delta_g A_{st} + f(\mathbf{x}_{ist}, \boldsymbol{\gamma}) + u_{ist},$$

where we are now allowing the parameter of interest δ to vary across different subsections of the data represented by groupings g. We interact the GE adoption variable with the weather variables that are a subset of the variables in $\mathbf{x}_{ist}$ to investigate whether GE varieties are more or less susceptible to certain weather outcomes. We also consider several models of cross-sectional heterogeneity, each based on a different assignment of the county to a group. The first utilizes a grouping based on the state each county is in, while the other two assign each county to a group based on measures of soil quality. The first measure of soil quality defines groups based on the percentiles of the observed water-holding capacity variable: 0–10th, 10th–25th, 25th–50th, 50th–75th, 75th–90th, and 90th–100th. The second defines groups based on the dominant soil texture in each county.

1.4   Results

We report estimates for three classes of models in this section. The first section provides estimates for a class of models that assume a homogeneous

Table 1.1   **Regression results: Impacts of GE adoption on corn yield (bushels/acre)**

	Model 1	Model 2	Model 3	Model 4	Model 5
Variables					
GE adoption rate	43.36***	−7.648	6.547	18.15***	18.26***
	[7.116]	[11.17]	[12.15]	[6.546]	[6.748]
Time trend		2.000***	1.506***	1.008***	0.943***
		[0.393]	[0.413]	[0.206]	[0.208]
Precipitation (mm)				1.652***	1.596***
				[0.363]	[0.363]
Precipitation squared (mm^2)				−0.0146***	−0.0142***
				[0.00328]	[0.00327]
Degree-days 0°–10°C				0.0216	0.0181
				[0.0262]	[0.0263]
Degree-days 10°–29°C				0.0159	0.0176
				[0.0155]	[0.0143]
Degree-days above 29°C				−0.590***	−0.591***
				[0.0868]	[0.0808]
County fixed effects	N	N	Y	Y	Y
State-specific trends	N	N	N	N	Y
R-squared	0.171	0.234	0.649	0.781	0.792
Out-of-sample RMSE (% reduction)	—	3.89	32.8	46.9	48.8
Observations	28,628	28,628	28,628	28,628	28,628
Counties	819	819	819	819	819
Years	36	36	36	36	36

Notes: The reported coefficient estimate for the time trend variable under model 5 is the simple average of the state-specific estimates. The out-of-sample prediction comparison reports the percentage reduction in the root-mean-squared prediction error (RMSE) for each model compared to the baseline model 1 that does not include any control variables. Each model is estimated 1,000 times, where each iteration randomly selects 80 percent of the sample observations. Relative performance is measured according to the accuracy of each model's prediction for the omitted 20 percent of the data. Two-way clustered standard errors by year and county adoption are reported in square brackets, and *, **, and *** denote statistical significance at the 10 percent, 5 percent, and 1 percent levels, respectively.

GE effect across counties. The second class of models maintains this homogeneity assumption but reports estimates for models of the higher-order moments of the corn-yield distribution. The final class of models relaxes the homogeneity assumption and allows the GE effect to vary across weather outcomes and county groupings. All models are estimated using ordinary least squares with dummy variables as the fixed effects and standard errors clustered using the two-way approach previously discussed.

1.4.1   Homogeneous GE Effect

Table 1.1 reports parameter estimates for five models that sequentially include additional control variables. In the absence of any controls, the estimated GE effect is 43 bushels per acre. However, it is clear that this estimate is confounded by the absence of a trend variable, which, when included, changes the estimate to–8 bushels per acre. This sensitivity is expected, as the

increase in GE adoption has coincided with many other production innovations that have increased productivity over time. Failure to account for this
source of variation in the data confounds the estimate. The next model adds
county fixed effects to the model, and the estimate becomes positive but is
not statistically significantly different from zero at conventional levels. In
addition, the estimate of the time trend parameter is also sensitive to the
inclusion of these fixed effects as it decreases from 2 to 1.5 bushels per acre
per year. It is clear that controlling for county-specific time-invariant yield
drivers such as soil quality is an important consideration for estimating
productivity gains. The next model includes the precipitation and weather
variables, and again we see a sensitivity of the estimates as the GE effect
increases and becomes statistically significant at the 1 percent level. ·

Note that adding the weather variables nearly triples the estimate of the
GE effect and reduces the standard error by half. Adding the weather variables also reduces the trend coefficient to one bushel per acre per year, implying that the trend increase in yield was much smaller before the introduction
of GE varieties after we account for weather conditions.

The final model allows the time trend parameters to vary across states,
and we find that the GE estimate has stabilized across this additional gener-
alization. Both the in-sample fit and the out-of-sample prediction accuracy
of the models steadily increases as we include additional control variables
in the model. Further supporting this finding that control variables matter,
we reject the null of equality for the state-specific trend estimates (p-value =
0.000) and reject the null that the weather variable estimates are jointly zero
(p-value = 0.000). Thus under an assumption of a homogenous GE effect,
we find that the introduction of GE corn has increased yields by approximately 18 bushels per acre. This represents a roughly 17 percent increase in
yields relative to the five-year average yield prior to the introduction of GE
traits.

We also estimated alternative specifications that exploit different sources
of variability in GE adoption. First, we removed all observations during
the diffusion process—defined as adoption greater than 0 and less than
0.85—so that we only exploit variation in GE adoption before and after the
introduction of the technology. This specification exploits variation in GE
adoption that is more plausibly exogenous, but we reduce the sample size to
17,424. The effect of GE adoption on yield is larger at 28 bushels per acre
(p-value = 0.013), but the standard error increases to 11.24.

Our second specification adds year fixed effects to the main specification.
The effect of GE adoption on yield decreases to eight bushels per acre and
lacks statistical significance (p-value = 0.555) with a standard error of 13.92.
As mentioned previously, the specification with year fixed effects exploits a
small amount of cross-sectional variation in GE adoption, which leads to
an imprecise estimate.

We also consider specifications that only use a subset of years in the data to better understand our primary source of identification. When we omit years for which the national adoption rate exceeded 50 percent (i.e., 2005 to 2014), the effect of GE adoption is 31 bushels per acre (p-value = 0.013). If we instead omit years when national adoption is between 0 and 50 percent (i.e., 1996 to 2004), the effect of GE adoption is 24 bushels per acre (p-value = 0.028). However, when we omit years when national adoption was zero (i.e., 1980 to 1995), the effect of GE adoption drops substantially to two bushels per acre (p-value = 0.79; standard error = 9.1). These results indicate that our estimate of the effect of GE adoption in our preferred specification is identified primarily from the inclusion of preadoption data that permits a credible estimation of yield trends prior to adoption. Overall, these alternative specifications provide evidence that endogenous selection into early- versus late-adoption cohorts does not substantially bias the results.

We also consider robustness to a model that includes solar radiation as an additional control, as recent literature has suggested that this can confound trend estimation for US corn (Tollenaar et al. 2017), but find little concern here, as the GE adoption estimate is 17.5 bushels per acre (p-value = 0.022) under this alternative. Finally, it is possible that GE adoption coincided with large expansions and/or retractions of acreage to/from marginal land within each county. While we cannot observe this directly in these data, we can omit annual observations for each county that are more or less than one standard deviation away from county-specific sample averages of harvested acreage. This effectively produces a subset of data (25 percent fewer observations) that experiences smaller year-to-year acreage variations, and we find a similar estimate of 14.8 bushels per acre (p-value = 0.012).

1.4.2   Higher-Order Moment Effects of GE

We next consider whether GE adoption has influenced the higher-order moments of the corn-yield distribution using a moments-model approach (Antle 1983, 2010; Just and Pope 1978). Specifically, we estimate both the variance and skewness of the yield distribution using the squared and cubed residuals from the preferred model from the previous section (table 1.1, model 5). These transformed residuals are then regressed on the same set of covariates as the preferred model. Under expectation of the dependent variable, these models provide linkages between the GE adoption and control variables on the variance and skewness of the yield distribution.

The parameter estimates for these models are reported in table 1A.2. We find no evidence that GE adoption has affected the variance or skewness of the yield distribution, as the estimates are not statistically significant at standard levels. However, taken in conjunction with the results revealing increases in mean yields, our results suggest that GE adoption has led to a reduction in yield risk, as it has increased yields without a proportionate increase in the standard deviation—that is, the coefficient of variation has decreased. Importantly, the estimate for the time trend variable implies an increase in yield variance over time, suggesting that it is an important control variable for studies to consider when estimating yield risk implications of GE. Although not reported here, when the time trends are dropped from the model, the estimate of the GE effect on yield variance becomes positive and significant at the 105 level (p-value = 0.096).

1.4.3   Heterogeneous GE Effect

Results for joint hypothesis tests for the heterogeneous models are reported in table 1A.3, where the p-values correspond to a null hypothesis of a homogenous GE effect. The first three models explore interactions between the weather variables and GE adoption. We find no evidence of these interactions for precipitation alone, temperature alone, or precipitation and temperature combined. Thus we conclude that while ignoring weather severely biases the estimated effect of GE corn adoption, the performance of GE varieties is not likely dependent on particular weather outcomes occurring. One reason for this result is that the initial GE traits focused on insect resistance and herbicide tolerance rather than developing traits to improve drought or heat tolerance. In the future, GE traits may focus more on drought and heat so that our result may not continue to hold (Marshall 2014).

The next set of heterogeneity models that we consider assign each county to a particular group. We first use state boundaries to define the grouping and estimate the heterogeneous effects by interacting dummy variables for each state with the GE adoption variable. We fail to reject the null of a homogeneous effect at standard significance levels (p-value = 0.1117); however, figure 1A.9 provides a spatial map of these estimates and suggests that there are potentially large differences in effects across regions. A simple average of the estimates is 19.1, and they range from 5.5 to 27.5 bushels per acre.

To further explore potential spatial heterogeneities, we assign each county to one of six groups based on the soil's water-holding capacity. The groups correspond to different percentiles of the empirical distribution of observed values (1: 0th–10th percentile, 2: 10th–25th percentile, 3: 25th–50th percentile, 4: 50th–75th percentile, 5: 75th–90th percentile, and 6: 90th–100th percentile). We interact dummy variables for each group with the GE adoption variable, and we find evidence that this pattern of spatial heterogeneity is supported by the data, as a joint hypothesis test suggests rejecting the null of a homogeneous effect at standard significance levels (p-value = 0.0000). The parameter estimates are reported in table 1A.4, and figure 1.2 provides a spatial map of the impacts by county. The county-level estimates have an average value of 18.4, and they range from 12.5 to 25.1 bushels per acre. It is clear from the map that there exists substantial within-state variation of the GE effect that the state-specific heterogeneity model is not capable of capturing. Figure 1A.10 plots the range of county-level GE effects within each state along with the average value within that state and shows that there exists a broad range of more than 10 bushels per acre within most states. This

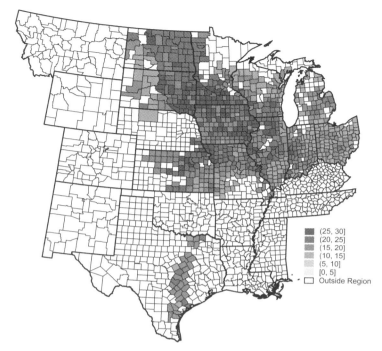

(25, 30]
(20, 25]
(15, 20]
(10, 15]
(5, 10]
[0, 5]
Outside Region

Fig. 1.2   mpacts of GE corn adoption (bushels/acre) by counties' soil water-holding capacities. Each county is assigned to one of six groups based on the soil's water-holding capacity, and a separate GE impact is estimated for each group. Estimated impacts are then binned according to values in the figure legend.

insight is consistent with the state-specific model's failure to reject the null of a homogeneous effect, as the spatial heterogeneities are being driven not by ad hoc political boundaries but rather by the localized growing conditions.

The final model that we consider further supports this insight and suggests that soil texture is also an important dimension for understanding heterogeneous GE effects. We assign each county to one of nine groups based on the dominant soil texture: clay, clay-loam, loam, loamy-sand, sand, sandy-loam, silt-loam, silty-clay, silty-clay-loam. We interact dummy variables for each group with the GE adoption variable, and we find evidence that this pattern of spatial heterogeneity is supported by the data, as a joint hypothesis test suggests rejecting the null of a homogeneous effect at standard significance levels (p-value $= 0.0001$). The parameter estimates are reported in table 1A.4, and figure 1.3 provides a spatial map of the impacts by county. The county-level estimates have an average value of 18.3, and they range from 3.9 to 24.0 bushels per acre. We again find that there exists substantial within-state variation of the GE effect that the state-specific heterogeneity model is not capable of capturing as shown in figure 1A.10.

The location of greater yield impacts from GE adoption corresponds gen-

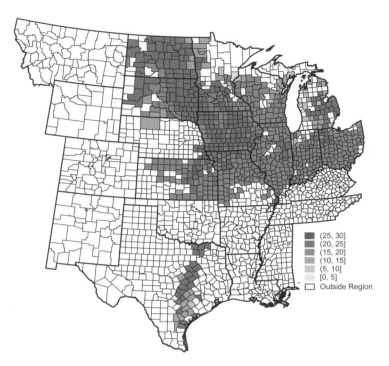

Fig. 1.3   Impacts of GE corn adoption (bushels/acre) by counties' soil types. Each county is assigned to one of nine groups based on the soil's texture, and a separate GE impact is estimated for each group. Estimated impacts are then binned according to values in the figure legend.

erally with the location of greater utilization of Bt traits (see Hutchison et al. 2010). As mentioned earlier, research from experimental plots has generally found greater yield benefits from Bt traits than herbicide-resistant traits. There are a couple reasons soil characteristics might be driving greater adoption of Bt traits. First, corn borer and corn rootworm pressures are affected by soil characteristics (e.g., Beck and Apple 1961; Huber, Neiswander, and Salter 1928; Turpin and Peters 1971; MacDonald and Ellis 1990). Second, areas with better soil characteristics have a greater concentration of corn production resulting in greater pest pressure.

1.5   Conclusion

There is considerable interest, both within the academic community and among the broader public, in the effects of GE crop adoption. In particular, the effect of GE crop adoption on yield has been the subject of much debate, perhaps because of relationships between yield and environmental outcomes via land use and because of the implications for food security.

Numerous experiments have found that GE traits have tended to reduce the gap between actual and potential corn yields (Fernandez-Cornejo et al. 2014; Klümper and Qaim 2014; NASEM 2016); however, experimental studies often generate significantly higher yields than farmers actually experience (Lobell, Cassman, and Field 2009). Moreover, aggregate yield trends in the United States appear, at first blush, relatively stable before and after adoption of GE corn.

This chapter sought to identify whether, in fact, for corn "the nationwide data . . . in the United States do not show a significant signature of genetic-engineering technology on the rate of yield increase," as was indicated by NASEM (2016). Using corn-yield panel data corresponding to roughly 28,000 US county-years before and after adoption of GE corn, a simple model only including a time trend confirms NASEM's assertion, as the effect of GE adoption appears, if anything, to have had a negative effect on yields. However, subsequent analysis reveals that this simple model is biased. After controlling for weather and soil characteristics and assuming a homogeneous effect of adoption, we find that adoption of GE corn has led to an approximate 17 percent increase in corn yields. We also find significant heterogeneity in the yield effect that is related not to state boundaries but rather to soil characteristics. On average, adoption of GE corn has led to an 18.5 bushel per acre increase in yield, but the effects range from 12.5 to 25.1 bushels per acre depending on soil characteristics. We conjecture that the variation across soil types may be related to differences in insect pressure.

While we found important soil-GE adoption interactions, there were no significant interactions related to weather. The findings suggest that the current GE traits have not led to more resilience to heat or water stresses. Moreover, while we find that the variance in corn yield has increased over time, adoption of GE corn has not lowered the variance. Nonetheless, if, as our results show, adoption of GE corn increases yield without affecting variance, the coefficient of variation on yields has fallen as a result of GE corn adoption. This suggests that GE corn is less risky, as, for example, the actuarially fair price of insurance to indemnify a given yield falls as the coefficient of variation falls.

Our study has a number of limitations. As we discussed, the available adoption data only exist at the state level. We showed that this produces a type of measurement-error problem that can lead to serially correlated errors—an issue we address using the two-way clustering approach of Cameron, Gelbach, and Miller (2012). There are other issues that have likely affected national-level yields, such as the move toward more continuous corn and other factors that have led to the expansion of corn acres. The adoption of GE crops may have also led to an expansion of corn acres on more marginal land that decreased county average yield. We partially addressed this problem by limiting our analysis to only those counties that reported yield data for at least two-thirds of the years before and after GE adoption, but an altogether different sort of analysis that moves from our primal production function approach to a structural model that relates planting decisions to input and output prices would likely be required to fully address the issue. To the extent that adoption of GE crops did reduce county average yields through an expansion of growing area, our estimate reflects this effect and understates the impact of GE on field-level corn yields. It would also be of interest to conduct the sort of analysis performed here using data, for example, from the European Union, where there has been little to no adoption of GE corn. Such an approach would permit a truer difference-in-difference estimate of the effect of GE corn adoption.

A final important caveat to be noted is that the estimated effects of GE corn adoption depend critically on the available GE technologies. Genetic engineering is not a single "thing." In the case of our data, GE corn is one of four types: herbicide tolerant, Bt corn-borer tolerant, Bt root-worm tolerant, or stacked varieties that include combinations of the previous three types. Geneticists and plant scientists are continually working on new genetic modifications that could further reduce the gap between actual and potential yield or even increase potential yields. For example, Kromdijk et al. (2016) recently genetically engineered a tobacco plant to improve the efficiency of photosynthesis, which increased potential yields by about 20 percent. Other research has focused on genetic pathways to increasing nitrogen utilization (McAllister, Beatty, and Good 2012). Whether these additional GE crop technologies can live up to the "hype" of increasing crop yields remains to be seen. However, if and when these biotechnologies arrive, it will be important to closely scrutinize whether they substantively affect real-world farm yields, just as this study has attempted to do with the first generations of GE corn.

Appendix

Table 1A.1   **Summary statistics for raw and interpolated state-level GE adoption rates, 1980–2015**

Site		Mean	Std. dev.	Min.	Max.	Obs.
All states	Raw	0.349	0.395	0.00	0.98	419
	Interpolated	0.322	0.377	0.00	0.98	481
Illinois	Raw	0.322	0.381	0.00	0.93	33
	Interpolated	0.294	0.370	0.00	0.93	37
Indiana	Raw	0.289	0.366	0.00	0.88	33
	Interpolated	0.262	0.354	0.00	0.88	37
Iowa	Raw	0.368	0.399	0.00	0.95	33
	Interpolated	0.341	0.385	0.00	0.95	37
Kansas	Raw	0.381	0.408	0.00	0.95	33
	Interpolated	0.353	0.394	0.00	0.95	37
Michigan	Raw	0.312	0.371	0.00	0.93	33
	Interpolated	0.284	0.359	0.00	0.93	37
Minnesota	Raw	0.387	0.409	0.00	0.93	33
	Interpolated	0.360	0.394	0.00	0.93	37
Missouri	Raw	0.341	0.373	0.00	0.93	33
	Interpolated	0.315	0.360	0.00	0.93	37
Nebraska	Raw	0.388	0.413	0.00	0.96	33
	Interpolated	0.360	0.399	0.00	0.96	37
North Dakota	Raw	0.391	0.462	0.00	0.97	28
	Interpolated	0.357	0.414	0.00	0.97	37
Ohio	Raw	0.252	0.338	0.00	0.86	33
	Interpolated	0.228	0.327	0.00	0.86	37
South Dakota	Raw	0.437	0.446	0.00	0.98	33
	Interpolated	0.409	0.429	0.00	0.98	37
Texas	Raw	0.360	0.425	0.00	0.91	28
	Interpolated	0.327	0.378	0.00	0.91	37
Wisconsin	Raw	0.319	0.369	0.00	0.92	33
	Interpolated	0.293	0.357	0.00	0.92	37

Table 1A.2   **Regression results: Impacts of GE adoption on variance and skewness of corn yields**

	Variance	Skewness
Variables		
GE adoption rate	−95.18	1526.6
	[166.1]	[10927.8]
Time trend	9.086**	−134.0
	[4.588]	[306.5]
Precipitation (mm)	−22.46***	−352.3
	[7.371]	[503.8]
Precipitation squared (mm^2)	0.187***	3.344
	[0.0498]	[4.773]
Degree-days 0°–10°C	0.689	−22.56
	[0.512]	[50.22]
Degree-days 10°–29°C	−0.375	−8.051
	[0.354]	[24.25]
Degree-days above 29°C	4.955**	104.7
	[1.940]	[183.8]
County fixed effects	Y	Y
State-specific trends	Y	Y
R-squared	0.134	0.034
Observations	28,628	28,628
Counties	819	819
Years	36	36

Notes: The reported coefficient estimates for the time trend variable in both models is the simple average of the state-specific estimates. Two-way clustered standard errors by year and county adoption are reported in square brackets, and *, **, and *** denote statistical significance at the 10 percent, 5 percent, and 1 percent levels, respectively.

Table 1A.3   **Joint hypothesis tests for the heterogeneous GE effect models**

Null hypothesis	*p*-value
Weather interaction model	
All weather/GE interactions are equal to zero.	0.3344
All precipitation/GE interactions are equal to zero.	0.4538
All temperature/GE interactions are equal to zero.	0.6672
State-specific GE effect	
All state-specific GE effects are equal.	0.1117
GE effect varies by soil water-holding capacity	
All GE effects for each group are equal.	0.0000
GE effect varies by soil type	
All GE effects for each group are equal.	0.0001

Notes: The reported *p*-values correspond to the joint hypothesis of a homogenous GE effect using two-way clustered standard errors by year and county adoption.

Table 1A.4   Regression results: Heterogeneous impacts of GE adoption by soil type

Variables	Model 1	Model 2
(GE adoption rate) × (<10th percentile water-holding capacity)	12.50* [7.070]	
(GE adoption rate) × (10th–25th percentile water-holding capacity)	18.68*** [6.971]	
(GE adoption rate) × (25th–50th percentile water-holding capacity)	14.12** [6.805]	
(GE adoption rate) × (50th–75th percentile water-holding capacity)	15.69** [6.941]	
(GE adoption rate) × (75th–90th percentile water-holding capacity)	21.84*** [6.866]	
(GE adoption rate) × (>90th percentile water-holding capacity)	25.13*** [7.002]	
(GE adoption rate) × (clay soil)		24.01* [12.31]
(GE adoption rate) × (clay-loam soil)		19.46*** [7.385]
(GE adoption rate) × (loam soil)		22.35*** [6.861]
(GE adoption rate) × (loamy-sand soil)		7.537 [7.329]
(GE adoption rate) × (sand soil)		3.911 [7.955]
(GE adoption rate) × (sandy-loam soil)		12.56* [7.436]
(GE adoption rate) × (silt-loam soil)		16.41** [6.934]
(GE adoption rate) × (silty-clay soil)		14.79** [7.490]
(GE adoption rate) × (silty-clay-loam soil)		22.99*** [7.382]
Simple average of GE effects	17.99*** [6.735]z	16.00** [6.963]
R-squared	0.7929	0.7927
Out-of-sample RMSE (% reduction)	−50.1	−50.0
Observations	28,628	28,628
Counties	819	819
Years	36	36

Notes: Both models include a full set of controls: weather variables, county fixed effects, and state-specific linear trends. The out-of-sample prediction comparison reports the percentage reduction in the root-mean-squared prediction error (RMSE) for each model compared to a baseline model that does not include any control variables and assumes a homogeneous GE effect. Each model is estimated 1,000 times, where each iteration randomly selects 80 percent of the sample observations. Relative performance is measured according to the accuracy of each model's prediction for the omitted 20 percent of the data. Two-way clustered standard errors by year and county adoption are reported in square brackets, and *, **, and *** denote statistical significance at the 10 percent, 5 percent, and 1 percent levels, respectively.

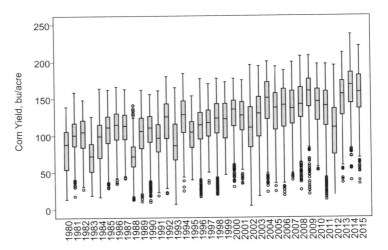

Fig. 1A.1 Spatial and temporal variation of yields. We observe yields at the county-year level and construct boxplots for each year. Each box is defined by the upper and lower quartile, with the median depicted as a horizontal line within the box. The endpoints for the whiskers are the upper and lower adjacent values, which are defined as the relevant quartile +/− three-halves of the interquartile range, and circles represent data points outside of the adjacent values.

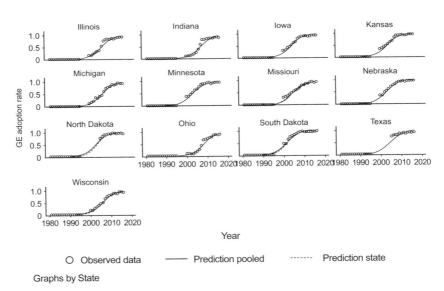

Fig. 1A.2 Observed and interpolated values for state-level GE adoption rates. The dots represent observed data, and the lines denote interpolated (predicted) values for the rates using two different. We interpolate missing data using predictions from a generalized linear model with a binomial family and a logit link function. The "prediction pooled" model pools all states and includes state fixed effects, while the "prediction state" model estimates a separate model for each state.

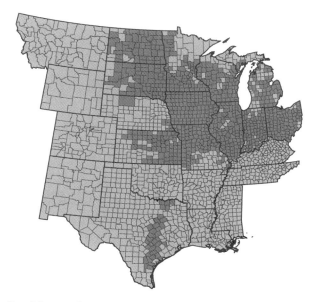

Fig. 1A.3 Spatial map of counties included in analysis. In-sample counties are dark gray.

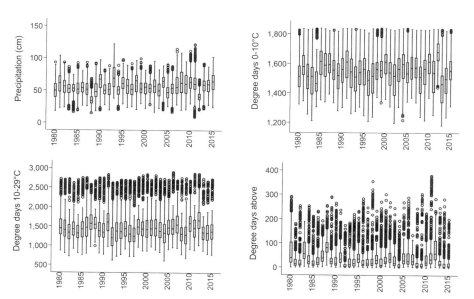

Fig. 1A.4 Spatial and temporal variation of weather variables. We observe the weather variables at the county-year level and construct boxplots for each year. Each box is defined by the upper and lower quartile, with the median depicted as a horizontal line within the box. The endpoints for the whiskers are the upper and lower adjacent values, which are defined as the relevant quartile +/− three-halves of the interquartile range, and circles represent data points outside of the adjacent values.

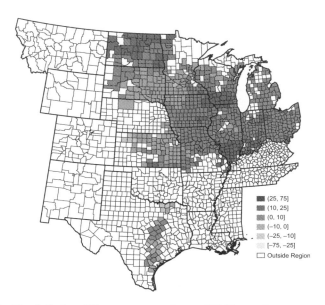

Fig. 1A.5 Precipitation difference, pre- and post-GE. For each county, we calculate the average of the observed cumulative growing season precipitation across years in the pre- and post-GE periods. We report the percentage change of the latter over the former here.

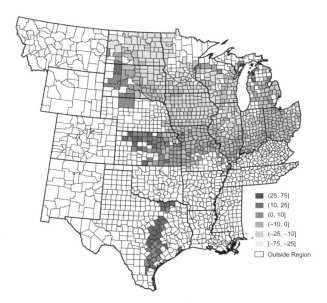

Fig. 1A.6 Extreme heat difference, pre- and post-GE. For each county, we calculate the average of the observed cumulative growing season degree-days over 29°C across years in the pre- and post-GE periods. We report the percentage change of the latter over the former here.

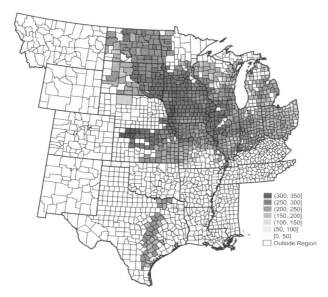

Fig. 1A.7   Spatial map of water-holding capacity (mm). For each county, we observe the total volume of plant-available water that the soil can store within the root zone.

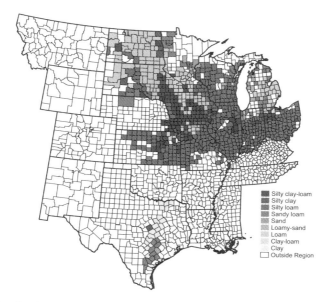

Fig. 1A.8   Spatial map of soil types. For each county, we observe the most common soil texture.

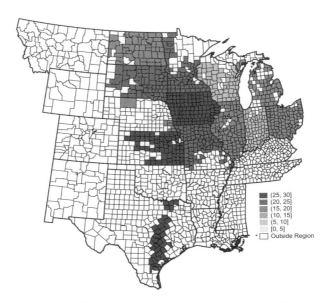

■	(25, 30]
■	(20, 25]
■	(15, 20]
■	(10, 15]
░	(5, 10]
░	[0, 5]
□	Outside Region

Fig. 1A.9   Impacts of GE corn adoption (bushels/acre) by state. The parameter of interest in the regression model measuring the impact of GE adoption on yield is allowed to vary by state. Estimated impacts are then binned according to values in the figure legend.

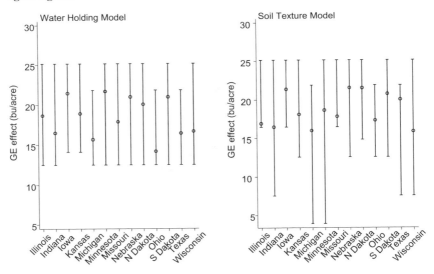

Fig. 1A.10   Impacts of GE corn adoption (bushels/acre) by counties' water-holding capacity and soil texture reported for each state. County-level estimates from figures 1A.2 and 1A.3 are reported by state. The vertical bars are the distance between the highest and lowest value within each state. Dots denote the average of the county-level estimates within each state.

References

Alston, J. J., M. A. Andersen, and P. G. Pardey. 2015. "The Rise and Fall of U.S. Farm Productivity Growth, 1910–2007." Working Paper, Department of Applied Economics, University of Minnesota, Staff Paper P15-02. http://ageconsearch.umn.edu//handle/200927.

Alston, J. M., J. M. Beddow, and P. G. Pardey. 2009. "Agricultural Research, Productivity, and Food Prices in the Long Run." *Science* 325 (5945): 1209–10.

Antle, J. 1983. "Testing the Stochastic Structure of Production: A Flexible Moment-Based Approach." *Journal of Business and Economic Statistics* 1 (3): 192–201.

Antle, J. 2010. "Asymmetry, Partial Moments, and Production Risk." *American Journal of Agricultural Economics* 92:1294–1309.

Barrows, G., S. Sexton, and D. Zilberman. 2014. "The Impact of Agricultural Biotechnology on Supply and Land-Use." *Environment and Development Economics* 19 (6): 676–703.

Beck, S. D., and J. W. Apple. 1961. "Effects of Temperature and Photoperiod on Voltinism of Geographical Populations of the European Corn Borer, Pyrausta Nubilalis." *Journal of Economic Entomology* 54 (3): 550–58.

Bellemare, M. F. 2015. "Rising Food Prices, Food Price Volatility, and Social Unrest." *American Journal of Agricultural Economics* 97 (1): 1–21.

Cameron, A. C., J. B. Gelbach, and D. L. Miller. 2012. "Robust Inference with Multiway Clustering." *Journal of Business and Economic Statistics* 29 (2): 238–49.

Chavas, J. P., G. Shi, and J. Lauer. 2014. "The Effects of GM Technology on Maize Yield." *Crop Science* 54 (4): 1331–35.

Duke, S. O. 2015. "Perspectives on Transgenic, Herbicide-Resistant Crops in the USA almost 20 Years after Introduction." *Pest Management Science* 71:652–57.

Fernandez-Cornejo, J., S. Wechsler, M. Livingston, and L. Mitchell. 2014. *Genetically Engineered Crops in the United States.* Economic Research Report Number 162, USDA Economic Research Service, February. https://www.ers.usda.gov/web docs/publications/err162/43668_err162.pdf.

Foley, J. 2014. "GEs, Silver Bullets and the Trap of Reductionist Thinking." Ensia .com, February 25, 2014. http://ensia.com/voices/GEs-silver-bullets-and-the-trap -of-reductionist-thinking/.

Gentry, L. F., M. L. Ruffo, and F. E. Below. 2013. "Identifying Factors Controlling the Continuous Corn Yield Penalty." *Agronomy Journal* 105 (2): 295–303.

Griliches, Z. 1957. "Hybrid Corn: An Exploration in the Economics of Technological Change." *Econometrica* 25 (4): 501–22.

Gurian-Sherman, D. 2009. "Failure to Yield: Evaluating the Performance of Genetically Engineered Crops." Union of Concerned Scientists, April 2009. http://www .ucsusa.org/sites/default/files/legacy/assets/documents/food_and_agriculture /failure-to-yield.pdf.

Hakim, D. 2016. "Doubts about the Promised Bounty of Genetically Modified Crops." *New York Times*, October 29. http://www.nytimes.com/2016/10/30 /business/GE-promise-falls-short.html?_r=0.

Heinemann, J. A., M. Massaro, D. S. Coray, S. Z. Agapito-Tenfen, and J. D. Wen. 2014. "Sustainability and Innovation in Staple Crop Production in the US Midwest." *International Journal of Agricultural Sustainability* 12 (1): 71–88.

Hendricks, N. P. 2016. "The Economic Benefits from Innovations to Reduce Heat and Water Stress in Agriculture." Working Paper. https://nphendricks.com/.

Hendricks, N. P., A. Smith, and D. A. Sumner. 2014. "Crop Supply Dynamics and the Illusion of Partial Adjustment." *American Journal of Agricultural Economics* 96 (5): 1469–91.

Huber, L. L., C. R. Neiswander, and R. M. Salter. 1928. "The European Corn Borer and Its Environment." Bulletin 429. December 1928. Wooster, OH: Ohio Agricultural Experiment Station.

Hutchison, W. D., E. C. Burkness, P. D. Mitchell, R. D. Moon, T. W. Leslie, S. J. Fleischer, M. Abrahamson, et al. 2010. "Areawide Suppression of European Corn." *Science* 330 (6001): 222–25.

Jorgenson, D., F. Gollop, and B. Fraumeni. 1987. *Productivity and U.S. Economic Growth.* Cambridge, MA: Harvard University Press.

Jorgenson, D., M. Ho, and K. Stiroh. 2005. *Productivity: Information Technology and the American Growth Resurgence.* Cambridge, MA: MIT Press.

Just, R. E., and R. D. Pope. 1978. "Stochastic Specification of Production Functions and Economic Implications." *Journal of Econometrics* 7 (1): 67–86.

Klümper, W., and M. Qaim. 2014. "A Meta-analysis of the Impacts of Genetically Modified Crops." *PLoS One* 9 (11): p.e111629.

Kromdijk, J., K. Głowacka, L. Leonelli, S. T. Gabilly, M. Iwai, K. K. Niyogi, and S. P. Long. 2016. "Improving Photosynthesis and Crop Productivity by Accelerating Recovery from Photoprotection." *Science* 354 (6314): 857–61.

Leibman, M., J. J. Shryock, M. J. Clements, M. A. Hall, P. J. Loida, A. L. McClerren, Z. P. McKiness, J. R. Phillips, E. A. Rice, and S. B. Stark. 2014. "Comparative Analysis of Maize (Zea Mays) Crop Performance: Natural Variation, Incremental Improvements and Economic Impacts." *Plant Biotechnology Journal* 12 (7): 941–50.

Lobell, D. B., K. G. Cassman, and C. B. Field. 2009. "Crop Yield Gaps: Their Importance, Magnitudes, and Causes." *Annual Review of Environment and Resources* 34 (1): 179–204.

Ma, B. L., F. Meloche, and L. Wei. 2009. "Agronomic Assessment of Bt Trait and Seed or Soil-Applied Insecticides on the Control of Corn Rootworm and Yield." *Field Crops Research* 111 (3): 189–96.

MacDonald, P. J., and C. R. Ellis. 1990. "Survival Time of Unfed, First-Instar Western Corn Rootworm (Coleoptera: Chrysomelidae) and the Effects of Soil Type, Moisture, and Compaction on Their Mobility in Soil." *Environmental Entomology* 19 (3): 666–71.

Marshall, A. 2014. "Drought-Tolerant Varieties Begin Global March." *Nature Biotechnology* 32 (4): 308.

McAllister, C. H., P. H. Beatty, and A. G. Good. 2012. "Engineering Nitrogen Use Efficient Crop Plants: The Current Status." *Plant Biotechnology Journal* 10 (9): 1011–25.

NASEM (National Academies of Sciences, Engineering, and Medicine). 2016. *Genetically Engineered Crops: Experiences and Prospects.* Washington, DC: National Academies. DOI: 10.17226/23395.

Nolan, E., and P. Santos. 2012. "The Contribution of Genetic Modification to Changes in Corn Yield in the United States." *American Journal of Agricultural Economics* 94 (5): 1171–88.

Perry, E. D., F. Ciliberto, D. A. Hennessy, and G. Moschini. 2016. "Genetically Engineered Crops and Pesticide Use in US Maize and Soybeans." *Science Advances* 2 (8): e1600850.

Perry, E. D., G. Moschini, and D. A. Hennessy. 2016. "Testing for Complementarity: Glyphosate Tolerant Soybeans and Conservation Tillage." *American Journal of Agricultural Economics* 98 (3): 765–84.

Ray, D. K., N. D. Mueller, P. C. West, and J. A. Foley. 2013. "Yield Trends Are Insufficient to Double Global Crop Production by 2050." *PLoS One* 8 (6): e66428.

Ray, D. K., N. Ramankutty, N. D. Mueller, P. C. West, and J. A. Foley. 2012. "Recent Patterns of Crop Yield Growth and Stagnation." *Nature Communications* 3:1293.

Roberts, M. J., and W. Schlenker. 2013. "Identifying Supply and Demand Elasticities of Agricultural Commodities: Implications for the US Ethanol Mandate." *American Economic Review* 103 (6): 2265–95.

Schlenker, W., and M. J. Roberts. 2009. "Nonlinear Temperature Effects Indicate Severe Damages to US Crop Yields under Climate Change." *Proceedings of the National Academy of Sciences* 106 (37): 15594–98.

Shi, G., J. P. Chavas, and K. Stiegert. 2010. "An Analysis of the Pricing of Traits in the US Corn Seed Market." *American Journal of Agricultural Economics* 92 (5): 1324–38.

Tack, J., A. Barkley, and L. L. Nalley. 2015a. "Effect of Warming Temperatures on US Wheat Yields." *Proceedings of the National Academy of Sciences* 112 (22): 6931–36.

Tack, J., A. Barkley, and L. L. Nalley. 2015b. "Estimating Yield Gaps with Limited Data: An Application to United States Wheat." *American Journal of Agricultural Economics* 97 (5): 1464–77.

Tollenaar, M., J. Fridgen, P. Tyagi, P. W. Stackhouse Jr., and S. Kumudini. 2017. "The Contribution of Solar Brightening to the US Maize Yield Trend." *Nature Climate Change* 7 (4): 275–78.

Turpin, F. T., and D. C. Peters. 1971. "Survival of Southern and Western Corn Rootworm Larvae in Relation to Soil Texture." *Journal of Economic Entomology* 64 (6): 1448–51.

Xu, Z., D. A. Hennessy, K. Sardana, and G. Moschini. 2013. "The Realized Yield Effect of Genetically Engineered Crops: US Maize and Soybean." *Crop Science* 53 (3): 735–45.

2

Impacts of Climate Change and Extreme Weather on US Agricultural Productivity
Evidence and Projection

Sun Ling Wang, Eldon Ball, Richard Nehring, Ryan Williams, and Truong Chau

In the past four decades, the frequency of adverse weather events has increased (Parry et al. 2007; IPCC 2007; Hatfield et al. 2014). Bad weather can result in higher unit-production costs when producers try to mitigate heat stress on animals or drought effects on crops. It can also widen the distance between observed production and the feasible production frontier and lower productivity estimates. According to USDA's US agricultural productivity statistics (USDA-ERS 2017), in 2015, farm output was more than 2.7 times its 1948 level. With little growth in input use, the growth of total factor productivity (TFP) accounted for nearly all output growth during that period. However, TFP growth rates fluctuate considerably from year to year in response to transitory events (see Wang et al. 2015 for discussion), mostly adverse weather. Since there is a growing consensus that climate change is occurring and the average daily temperature and the frequency of extreme

Sun Ling Wang is an economist in the Resource and Rural Economics Division of the Economic Research Service (ERS), US Department of Agriculture (USDA).

Eldon Ball is a former program leader in the Resource and Rural Economics Division of the ERS, USDA. He is currently with the Department of Agricultural and Resource Economics, University of Maryland.

Richard Nehring is an agricultural economist in the Resource and Rural Economics Division of the ERS, USDA.

Ryan Williams is a geographic information system analyst at the ERS, USDA.

Truong Chau is an economist in the Office of Technical and Regulatory Analysis (OTRA) of the Public Service Commission of the District of Columbia.

We thank Wolfram Schlenker, Ximing Wu, Marcel Aillery, two anonymous reviewers of this book chapter, and participants at the NBER Understanding Productivity Growth in Agriculture Conference for their valuable comments and suggestions. The findings and conclusions in this publication are those of the authors and should not be construed to represent any official USDA or US Government determination or policy. This research was supported by the USDA's Economic Research Service (ERS). For acknowledgments, sources of research support, and disclosure of the authors' material financial relationships, if any, please see http://www.nber.org/chapters/c13944.ack.

weather are likely to increase in the future (IPCC 2007; EPA 2018; NASA 2018), the likely effects of climate change or weather fluctuations on agricultural productivity have gained much attention in recent studies.

In the literature, "weather" is usually used to denote short-term variations in temperature or precipitation, while "climate change" refers to changes in average levels of weather outcomes (e.g., degree of temperature) that cover a long period of time. While climate change and weather variation are two different issues, one phenomenon of climate change is the increasing frequency of weather shocks (extreme weather). Therefore, it is critical to consider the case of extreme weather in addressing the effect of climate on agricultural productivity.

There are three major streams of literature studying the relationship between climate change / weather effect and economic activities. One body of work focuses on biophysical impacts through examining the relationship between climatic factors and individual commodity production or productivity, such as weather and crop yield or livestock production (e.g., St-Pierre, Cobanov, and Schnitkey 2003; Schlenker and Roberts 2009; Lobell, Schlenker, and Costa-Roberts 2011; Paltasingh, Goyari, and Mishra 2012; Mukherjee, Bravo-Ureta, and Vries 2012; Hatfield et al. 2014; Key and Sneeringer 2014; Burke and Emerick 2016). A second body of work focuses on adaptive response at the individual/firm level through evaluating how an individual farm/firm/person reacts to climatic impacts, such as a farmer's behavior under uncertainty (risk management, see Schimmelpfennig 1996; Kim and Chavas 2003; Di Falco and Veronesi 2013; Yang and Shumway 2015.) The third stream of literature addresses impacts at a regional/national/sectoral scale, considering both biophysical effects and adaptation or other economic impacts (e.g., land values, see Mendelsohn, Nordhaus, and Shaw 1994; agricultural profit, see Deschênes and Greenstone 2007; economic growth, see Dell, Jones, and Olken 2012). They are usually done by quantifying the effects of climate/weather changes on aggregate economic performance using country- and regional-level data (e.g., Mendelson, Nordhaus, and Shaw 1994; Sachs and Warner 1997; Dell, Jones, and Olken 2009, 2012) or sectoral data (e.g., Malcom et al. 2012; Hatfield et al. 2014; Marshall et al. 2015; Liang et al. 2017).

In the literature on identifying climatic impacts on aggregate economic performance, researchers either employ an empirical approach based on historical data or utilize simulation techniques to project economic responses to climate/weather shocks based on baseline projections and scenario analysis, especially in agricultural studies. While projecting climatic impacts can be useful for informing policy or making policy recommendations, empirical studies can help identify the relationship between climate/weather and economic activities and provide statistical evidence in explaining economic phenomena. Empirical studies can rely on either time-series data or cross-sectional data. The advantage of using time-series data is that they capture the impacts of climate change and the farmers' adaption to these changes over time. Nevertheless, they could fail to capture varied effects across regions. Notwithstanding, while the cross-sectional data approach contains information on geospatial differences, the statistical results may be biased if regionally specific characteristics are not taken into account, such as irrigation areas (Schlenker, Hanemann, and Fisher 2006). Panel data, on the other hand, can both preserve desired features of time-series and cross-sectional analyses and avoid their weaknesses, and it has become a preferred approach in recent studies.

The literature on the impact of climate change on crop production has shown that while moderate warming may benefit crop and pasture yields in temperate regions, further temperature increases can reduce crop yields in all regions (Carter et al. 1994; Lobell and Asner 2003; Tubiello and Rosenzweig 2008; Schlenker and Roberts 2009). In addition, some studies suggest that higher variance in climate conditions leads to lower average crop yields and greater yield variability (Semenov and Porter 1995; Ferris et al. 1998; McCarl, Villaviencio, and Wu 2008; among others). Weather extremes can also cause disease outbreaks and influence agricultural production (Yu and Babcock 1992; Anyamba et al. 2014). In livestock studies, evidence indicates that when an animal's thermal environment is altered due to climate change, the animal's health and reproduction can be affected. The feed conversion rate can also be affected (St-Pierre, Cobanov, and Schnitkey 2003; Morrison 1983; Fuquay 1981). Mukherjee, Bravo-Ureta, and Vries (2012) and Key and Sneeringer (2014) indicate that an increase in a temperature humidity index (THI) could help explain the technical inefficiency of dairy production based on stochastic frontier estimates. In an aggregate economy study, Dell, Jones, and Olken (2012) use historical cross-country data to identify the relationship between temperature shocks and economic growth. They find that climatic effects vary across countries with different economic development stages. They suggest that in the long run, countries may adapt to a particular temperature, mitigating the short-run economic impacts.

In light of recent developments in the literature, in this chapter we use state panel data to study the impact of climate change and extreme weather on US agricultural productivity empirically, for the entire farm sector (including both crop and livestock production). One major challenge in quantifying climatic effects on the aggregate sector is constructing appropriate climatic variables. While Dell, Jones, and Olken (2012) use historical fluctuations in temperature within countries to identify impacts on aggregate economic outcomes and find significant results, our climate variables are not limited to temperature and also include precipitation and humidity estimates, as precipitation is relevant to crop production. The scientific literature suggests that a heat stress that exceeds livestock's optimal thermoneutral zone (THI load) can reduce fertility, feed efficiency, weight gain, and so on (NRC 1983; Fuquay 1981; Hansen and Aréchiga 1999; West, Mullinix, and Bernard

2003). THI load has been shown to be an effective measure in evaluating the environmental effects on livestock. The Oury index, on the other hand, is an aridity index that combines temperature and precipitation in the measurement and is effective in connecting climatic effects to crop growth (Oury 1965; Zhang and Carter 1997). A lower Oury index indicates drier conditions that would be less favorable to crop production. Drawing upon the prior literature, we use historical temperature, humidity, and precipitation data to form a THI and an Oury index (an aridity index). The mean levels of THI and Oury indexes reflect changes in annual weather outcomes for individual states over the study period. Shocks of THI and Oury indexes, which measure the degree of unexpected deviations from their historical (1941 to 1970) means, are used to capture the unexpected extreme weather effects.

We use constructed weather variables and aggregate economic data within states to examine the relationships between climatic variables and regional agricultural productivity. Given that there may be spatial heterogeneity, we also include state characteristic variables—including irrigated area, state-level R&D, extension, and road infrastructure—in alternative model specifications in addition to using a fixed-effect approach. We further conduct scenario analyses to project how future temperature and precipitation changes, under climate-change expectations, affect agricultural productivity using 2000 to 2010 as the reference period.

In this study, we have four major findings. First, using the THI load and Oury indexes, we find that the patterns of climate change varied from region to region in the last half century (1960 to 2010), with some states becoming drier or warmer, while some states have little change on average but have become more volatile in more recent years. Second, using mean levels of THI and Oury indexes, we find that a higher THI load and lower Oury index (much drier condition) will lower a state's productivity. However, some estimated coefficients become insignificant when more state characteristic variables are incorporated into the estimation. Third, when using THI shock and Oury shock variables, the results are more robust across model specifications in both signs and coefficient estimates. Positive THI shocks and negative Oury shocks will lower state technical efficiency. This suggests that over the long run, each state has gradually adapted to state-specific climate conditions (the average level of temperature and precipitation and the degree of weather fluctuations). It is the unexpected weather shocks that are affecting regional productivity more profoundly. Fourth, using weather shock variables, we project potential impacts of increasing temperature and extreme weather (the expected climate-change phenomenon) on US regional productivity. Results show that the same degree changes in temperature or precipitation will have uneven impacts on regional productivities, with Delta, Northeast, and Southeast regions incurring much greater effects than the other regions, using 2000 to 2010 as the reference period.

This chapter is the first empirical study, we think, to estimate the climatic effect on regional agricultural productivity from the perspective of the entire farm sector, including both livestock and crop production. The study adds new insight into identifying the climatic effects on aggregate agricultural productivity. Our evidence suggests that weather shocks have more consistent and profound impacts on regional productivity when each state faces its particular weather condition. The diverse weather impacts on regional productivity from the same degree of changes in temperature or precipitation suggest the need for state-specific research programs to help producers manage their own climatic situations and future challenges.

We organize the remainder of the chapter as follows: Section 2.1 introduces the empirical approach. Section 2.2 describes the data and variables and provides descriptive statistics. Section 2.3 presents patterns of state productivity growth and climate changes. Section 2.4 the empirical results and discussion. Section 2.5 reports the projection of regional productivity based on climate change scenarios. Section 2.6 provides concluding remarks.

2.1 Empirical Framework

In the literature on climate and its economic impacts, some studies incorporate climate variables along with other input variables in one production function to test for climatic effects on crop yield, livestock production, economic performance, or productivity growth. There are also studies that model weather variables as factors that impact technical inefficiency but aren't in the production equation (see Key and Sneeringer 2014, for example). In a study of climatic effects on US dairy productivity, Key and Sneeringer (2014) assert that operators in a region under adverse weather conditions will operate further from the production frontier (i.e., be less technically efficient) even when they have technology similar to that of other operators in different regions. That study employed a stochastic frontier production approach in its estimates, where climate variables were incorporated as determinants of a one-sided error that drove farm production from its production frontier. In this study, we employ the same approach to evaluate the potential impacts of climate change and extreme weather on US regional agricultural productivity. To validate our choices of model specifications and weather variables, we also perform out-of-sample validation tests. We divide the data set into estimation sets (80 percent of observations, from 1961 to 1995) and validation sets (20 percent of observations, from 1996 to 2004) to evaluate forecasting performances among various model specifications and alternative weather variables (see table 2A.1 in the appendix to this chapter for examples). The likelihood-ratio (LR) test results at the bottom of table 2A.2 indicate that we reject the hypothesis of no inefficiency for all estimated stochastic frontier models. The results show that utilizing THI and Oury indexes as determinants of a one-sided inefficiency term along with other external control variables under the stochastic frontier model setup leads to better forecast performances. The mean standard errors of predictions of those models are the lowest among estimated models (see table 2A.2 for details).

2.1.1   Stochastic Frontier Production Function

The stochastic frontier approach was first developed by Aigner, Lovell, and Schmidt (1977) and Meeusen and van den Broeck (1977) and has been applied to numerous studies. In earlier applications, researchers tried to explain those inefficiency effects by conducting a two-step approach that requires predicting the inefficiency scores first and then running a regression model that relates the inefficiency scores and the explanatory variables in a second step. Using cross-section data, Kumbhakar, Ghosh, and McGuckin (1991), Reifschneider and Stevenson (1991), and Huang and Liu (1994) later proposed models that allow the estimation of technical inefficiency effects with parameters simultaneously estimated in the stochastic frontier function and inefficiency model. Battese and Coelli (1995) further proposed a model to estimate the technical inefficiency effects in a stochastic frontier production function for panel data. Since Wang and Schmidt (2002) have theoretically explained that two-step procedures are biased, in this study we follow Key and Sneeringer (2014) to employ a one-step procedure to test the climatic effects on regional productivity using a state panel data of 48 contiguous states for the period from 1960 to 2004. Each state is treated as an individual producer facing its particular climate patterns, state-specific characteristics, and resources.

Under the stochastic frontier production function framework, the model can be expressed as

$$(1) \qquad \ln(y_{it}) = f(x_{it}, \boldsymbol{\beta}) + v_{it} - u_{it},$$

where y_{it} is the observed aggregate output of state i at time t, and $f(x_{it}, \boldsymbol{\beta})$ is the maximum output that can be produced with a technology described by parameters $\boldsymbol{\beta}$ (to be estimated) and a vector of inputs x_i. The deviations (ε_{it}) from the frontier are composed of a two-sided random error (v_{it}) and a one-side error term ($u_{it} \geq 0$). v_{it} is a random error that can be positive or negative and is assumed to be normally and independently distributed, with a zero mean and constant variance of σ_v^2. u_{it} is assumed to be half-normally and independently distributed, $u_{it} \sim N^+(0, \sigma_u^2)$.

In a one-step approach, we assume the technical inefficiency component is heteroskedastic, that the variance σ_{ui}^2 depends on a vector of exogenous variables z_i and a set of parameters $\boldsymbol{\gamma}$ (to be estimated), such as climate variables and state-specific characteristics that can affect the individual state's ability to adopt the best technology given its input level:

$$(2) \qquad \sigma_{ui}^2 = \exp(z_i'\boldsymbol{\gamma}).$$

Therefore, z_i affects the mean and variance of the inefficiency term u_i. If $u_i = 0$, then state i is at the production frontier and is technically efficient. If $u_i > 0$, then state i is deviated from the frontier and is technically inefficient. The technical efficiency of state i (TE_i) is defined as the ratio of the ith state's observed output to its feasible output (the maximum output it can produce with given inputs). Once the technical inefficiency u_i is estimated, technical efficiency (TE_{it}) can be obtained by the following formula:

$$(3) \qquad TE_{it} = \frac{y_i}{\exp(f(x_{it}, \beta) + v_{it})} = \exp(-u_{it}).$$

TE_{it} ranges between 0 and 1, with 1 being on the frontier. In this study, the empirical stochastic frontier production function to be estimated is

$$(4) \qquad \ln y_{it} = \beta_0 + \sum_{k=1}^{K} \beta_k \ln x_{kit} + \beta_t t + \sum_{j=1}^{J} \beta_j D_j + \sum_{m=1}^{M} \beta_m D_m + v_{it} - u_{it},$$

where y_i is an implicit quantity of state i's total output; x_{ki}'s are implicit quantities of state i's k inputs, including labor, capital, land, and intermediate goods; t is a time trend to capture natural technical changes driven by research and development from both public and private sectors (public R&D and private R&D) over time; D_j's are state dummy variables ($j = 1 \ldots 47$), and D_m's are time dummy variables ($m = 1 \ldots 43$) to capture cross-state, time-invariant, unobserved heterogeneity. The time dummy can also help reflect part of the development of technical change effects driven by the aggregate knowledge stock that are not captured by the time trend but could have shifted the production frontier unevenly across years. Equation (4) can be viewed as a log-linearized form of the Cobb-Douglas (C-D) production function.[1] We estimate an inefficiency variance regression model simultaneously with equation (4)—that is,

$$(5) \qquad \ln \sigma_{uit}^2 = \gamma_0 + \sum_{n=1}^{N} \gamma_n z_{nit} + \omega_{it},$$

where ω_{it} is a disturbance term with standard normal distribution, z's include climate variables, irrigation-ready land density that may help mitigate the impacts of adverse weather, and other control variables that capture the heterogeneity of individual states.

We include various forms of climate variables in our estimation, including the THI load (for livestock) and the Oury index (an aridity index for crops), in their mean or "shock" (the unit of standard deviation from its historical

---

1. We choose the C-D functional form to approximate the underlying technology of the production frontier in this study because it is easy to interpret the estimated coefficients directly, and fewer parameters must be estimated.

norm) measures. We also include state-specific characteristic variables that may affect each state's technical efficiency, including R&D stock, extension capacity, and road density, as these variables are suggested to have impacts on state-level productivity in the literature (Alston et al. 2010; Wang et al. 2012; Jin and Huffman 2016, among others). We will explain how we construct those variables in the next section. The stochastic frontier is estimated by a maximum likelihood (ML) procedure.

2.2   Variables, Data Sources, and Descriptive Analysis

We employ a panel of state-level aggregate agricultural output, as well as inputs of labor, capital, land, and intermediate goods, to form the stochastic frontier production function. To identify the impacts of climate change on technical inefficiency changes, we construct climate variables that can capture the impacts on either crops or livestock production. We also construct measures of the share of irrigated land area and other local public good variables—R&D, extension, capacity, and road density—as control variables to test for the robustness of the climatic effects on state inefficiency.

2.2.1   Agricultural Output and Inputs

We draw state-specific aggregates of output and capital, labor, intermediate goods, and land input from the USDA state productivity accounts. Agricultural output and the four inputs are implicit quantity measurements based on the Törnqvist index approach over detailed output and input information. A full description of the underlying data sources and aggregation procedures can be found in Ball et al. (1999) and the USDA Economic Research Service (ERS) website (USDA-ERS 2017).

2.2.2   Weather Variables

Since our purpose is to estimate an overall impact of climate changes on the agricultural sector, we need to consider weather variables that have strong relationships with livestock or crops. However, there is no single measurement that can capture the weather impacts on both livestock and crops, as livestock production is more related to animals' year-round thermal environment, while crop production is affected by precipitation and temperature during the growing seasons. In addition, researchers have found nonlinear temperature effects for agriculture (Deschênes and Greenstone 2007; Schlenker and Roberts 2009). To meet our objective, we construct two different weather measures to capture their effects on either livestock or crops. One is the THI, a combined measure of temperature and relative humidity that has been shown to have significant impacts on livestock production, and another is the Oury index, an aridity index that combines temperature and precipitation information that can capture more impacts on crop production than a single measure of temperature or precipitation. We draw monthly temperature and precipitation data at the county level from a weather data set produced by Oregon State University's PRISM[2] Climate Group (Daly et al. 2008). Since PRISM interpolates between weather stations to generate climate estimates for each 4 km grid cell in the United States, we are able to link county-level weather information and agricultural production to construct climate variables that could explain climate variations across regions and over time.

Livestock scientists have found that livestock productivity is related to climate through a THI measure (Thom 1958; St-Pierre, Cobanov, and Schnitkey 2003; Zimbelman et al. 2009). THI can be measured using the following equation:

$$(6) \qquad THI = (\text{dry bulb temperature } °C)$$
$$+ (0.36 \times \text{dew point temperature } °C) + 41.2.$$

When animal stress is above a certain THI threshold, productivity declines. Following St-Pierre, Cobanov, and Schnitkey (2003) and Key and Sneeringer (2014), we generate a minimum and maximum THI for each month and location based on minimum and maximum dry-bulb temperatures and dew-point data from PRISM. To estimate the THI load—the number of hours that the location has a THI above the threshold—we employ a method proposed by St-Pierre, Cobanov, and Schnitkey (2003) to estimate a sine curve between the maximum and minimum THI over a 24-hour period. We then estimate the number of hours and degree to which the THI is above threshold[3] (See Key and Sneering 2014 appendix for more details). To construct a state-level THI load, we aggregate up the county-level[4] monthly calculations to the state-level using county animal units derived from the Census of Agriculture (USDA-NASS 2002) as the weight.

Weather is a critical factor influencing the production of crops. While precipitation and temperature are mostly considered in previous studies due to lack of information on other factors such as sunshine and wind velocity, Oury (1965) recommended the use of an aridity index in identifying the relationship between crop production and weather. Oury asserted that it is hard to define a meaningful relationship between crop production and

---

2. The PRISM Climate Group gathers climate observations from a wide range of monitoring networks, applies sophisticated quality-control measures, and develops spatial climate data sets to reveal short- and long-term climate patterns. The PRISM data can be accessed at http://www.prism.oregonstate.edu.

3. We employ a THI load threshold of 70 for dairy cows, as it is the lowest threshold among a broad category of livestock production (St-Pierre, Cobanov, and Schnitkey 2003).

4. Climate estimates were limited only to cropland areas as defined by the combination of the Cultivated Crops and the Pasture/Hay classes in the National Land Cover Dataset (NLCD 2006). Therefore, it eliminates the effect of urban heat islands, mountains, etc.

weather based only on one weather factor, since they are interrelated. The proposed aridity index, which is termed the Oury index, is defined (Oury 1965; Zhang and Carter 1997) as

$$(6) \qquad\qquad W_s = \frac{P_s}{1.07^{T_s}},$$

where W represents the aridity index (Oury index), s is the month ($s =$ 1 . . . 12), P_s is the total precipitation for month s in millimeters, and T_s is the mean temperature for month s in degrees Celsius. The Oury index can be viewed as rainfall normalized with respect to temperature. We draw county-level monthly temperature and precipitation data from PRISM to aggregate up to a state-level Oury index, using county cropland density drawn from the National Land Cover Database (NLCD 2006) as the weight. The NLCD cropland pixels are composed of the combination of NLCD classes 81 (pasture/hay) and 82 (cultivated crops), with the notion that pasture/hay is a potentially convertible land cover to cultivated crops. The cropland area in the weight data is therefore a representation of current and potential cultivated cropland.

While all months of the year were considered for the THI measures, only the primary growing season months, approximately April through August, were considered for the Oury aridity index. Both THI and Oury measures were generated for a 30-year span from 1941 to 1970 and for individual years from 1961 to 2004 (our study period).

To measure the impacts of unexpected weather shocks or potential weather extremes on regional productivity, we construct Oury shock and THI shock variables as

$$(7) \qquad \text{Oury shock}_{i,t} = (\text{Oury}_{i,t} - \text{Oury}_{i,LR})/\text{Stdv of Oury}_{i,LR}$$

$$(8) \qquad \text{THI shock}_{i,t} = (\text{THI}_{i,t} - \text{THI}_{i,LR})/\text{Stdv of THI}_{i,LR},$$

where $\text{Oury}_{i,t}$ is the Oury mean of year t for state i, $\text{Oury}_{i,LR}$ is the long-run Oury mean for state i calculated using historical Oury mean data between 1941 and 1970, $\text{THI}_{i,t}$ is the THI load of year t for state i, $\text{THI}_{i,LR}$ is the long-run THI mean calculated using historical THI mean data between 1941 and 1970, and $\text{Stdv}_{i,LR}$ is the standard deviation of historical Oury means or historical THI means. Since each state has its unique weather variation pattern, a same-level change in Oury mean or THI mean may result in different Oury shock or THI shock estimates given that the long-run values of Oury mean, THI mean, and long-run standard deviations of those indexes vary from state to state. We suspect that even with the same degree of deviations from historical Oury mean (Oury_{LR}) or TH mean (THI_{LR}), some states may perform better than others if they have expected and adapted to a larger weather variation climatic pattern in the past.

We compared Oury and THI indexes with other potential weather variables (see table 2A.1 for examples) using out-of-sample validation tests. We report the mean standard errors of prediction statistics for each model in table 2A.2. Since the good weather index (dd830) has a "wrong" sign (negative) in most of the estimates, coefficients of Palmer index are mostly insignificant, and the bad weather index (dd30) has a similar result to the maximum temperature variable (see table 2A.1 for weather variable descriptions), we only report out-of-sample test results of those using maximum temperature, precipitation, Oury mean, THI mean, Oury shock, and THI shock weather variables (see table 2A.2). The results show that stochastic frontier model estimates with Oury and THI weather variables have better forecast performances among estimated models.

2.2.3   Irrigation-Ready Land Density (Irrigation Density) Variable

Irrigation infrastructure can help mitigate the impact of adverse weather. We construct an irrigation-ready land density (share of irrigated land area, irrigation density thereafter) variable to capture the impact of irrigation-system availability in production. The variable is constructed as the ratio of irrigated land area to total cropland. The cropland and irrigated land area are available for the census of agriculture years (USDA-NASS, 2013) for each state. We employ a cubic spline technique to interpolate the information between census years. The expanded irrigated areas and cropland areas are used to construct a panel of irrigation density variables across states and over time.

2.2.4   R&D, Extension, and Roads

To capture specific state characteristics that could have also impacted the state's technical inefficiency, we included state-level variables on public agricultural R&D stock, extension, and roads. Annual data on public agricultural research expenditures and a research price index used to deflate expenditures are provided by Huffman (see Jin and Huffman 2016 for data construction details.) The extension variable is a measure of extension capacity calculated as the total full-time equivalent (FTE) extension staff divided by the total number of farms. Data on FTEs by state were drawn from the Salary Analysis of the Cooperative Extension Service from the Human Resource Division at the USDA (USDA-NIFA). Road infrastructure is a road-density index constructed by dividing total road miles excluding local (e.g., city street) miles by total land area.

2.3   Patterns of State Productivity Growth and Climate Changes

We summarize state-level TFP growth from 1960 to 2004[5] (USDA-ERS 2017) as well as the mean and standard deviation of the normal THI index

5. USDA's state productivity indexes only cover the period of 1960 to 2004.

and Oury index over the historical period from 1941 to 1970 in table 2A.3 to provide some background information on state-specific characteristics. In general, TFP growth varied across and within USDA's production regions. Given the variances in geoclimate conditions and natural resources, states tend to have notable differences in their composition of livestock and crop production. For example, states in the Northeast region tend to have a higher ratio of livestock production, while the Corn Belt and Pacific regions tend to produce more crops than livestock. Usually, a higher THI indicates more intensive heat stress and can hinder livestock productivity growth. On the other hand, a lower Oury index indicates a much drier condition that would lower crop production. If the Oury index is lower than 20, it indicates a very dry situation that could be seen as a drought condition, and if the Oury index is less than 10, it implies a "desert-like" state (Zhang and Carter 1997).

While the relative THI and Oury index levels could result in geospatial differences in technical inefficiency, an unexpected climate "shock," such as extreme weather, could cause more of an impact, as farmers will have expected climate patterns to be similar to the past. Farmers could have already invested in appropriate facilities, such as irrigation systems or cooling systems, in areas with a low Oury index or high THI loads. It is the unexpected weather changes that result in inefficient input use as yields decline (or a waste of inputs when crops cannot be harvested) as well as a decrease in livestock production due to unexpected heat stress. According to table 2A.3, some regions may have much higher variation in their Oury index than in their THI index, such as the mountain and Pacific regions. If farmers expect dramatic variation from year to year in advance, they may have already invested in an irrigation system to dampen the impacts of climate changes on farm production.

TFP growth estimates usually move closely with output growth. According to ERS's US agricultural productivity accounts (USDA-ERS 2017), in 1983 and 1995, the dramatic impacts from adverse weather events caused significant drops in both output and TFP (see Wang et al. 2015 for more discussion). In figure 2.1, we map the normal Oury index ($Oury_{i,LR}$) (based on 1941–1970 data) and Oury indexes in 1983 and 1995 at the state level. We find that the Oury index varied for many states in 1983 and 1995, while the shocks (figure 2.2) from its norm show a different picture regarding climate changes.

Figure 2.3 presents the normal THI load ($THI_{i,LR}$) (based on 1941–1970 data) as well as the THI indexes in 1983 and 1995 across states. When compared with the Oury index, however, THI load shows less variation over time. Nevertheless, if we look at the maps of shock indexes in different years (figure 2.4), we may find that there are noticeable differences over the years.

If bad weather is expected and farmers invest in facilities to reduce the potential damage from adverse weather conditions, then the impacts of extreme weather on farm production could decline. Figure 2.5 shows

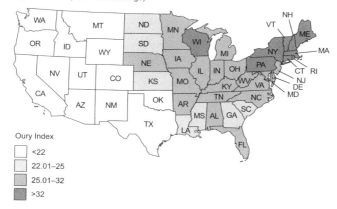

A   Oury Index Norm (1941–1970 Average)

Oury Index

- [ ] <22
- [ ] 22.01–25
- [ ] 25.01–32
- [ ] >32

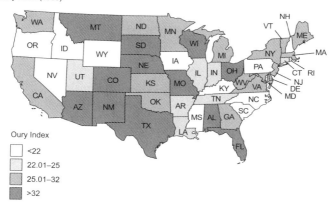

B   Oury Index (1983)

Oury Index

- [ ] <22
- [ ] 22.01–25
- [ ] 25.01–32
- [ ] >32

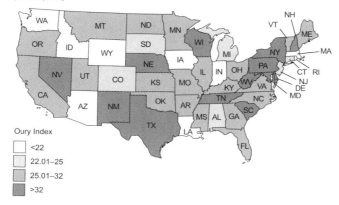

C   Oury Index (1995)

Oury Index

- [ ] <22
- [ ] 22.01–25
- [ ] 25.01–32
- [ ] >32

Fig. 2.1   Oury index comparison, the norm (1941 to 1970), 1983, and 1995
Source: Authors' calculation.

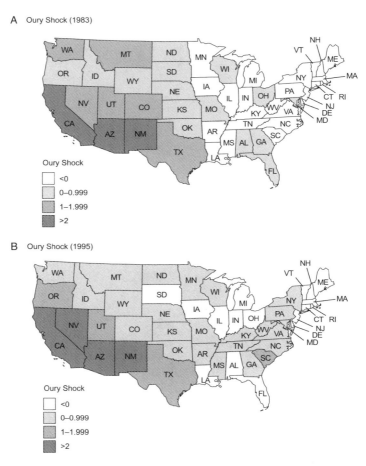

Fig. 2.2   The climate-shocks comparison using the Oury index: 1983 versus 1995
Source: Authors' calculation.

irrigation-density changes over time. In general, Pacific regions and moun-
tainous regions have more intensive irrigation systems than other regions.

2.4   Empirical Results

We first estimate equation (4) and test the hypothesis of no inefficiency effect
that $H_0: \sigma_u^2 = 0$, against the alternative hypothesis of $H_1: \sigma_u^2 > 0$. The L-R test
result shows that the null hypothesis is rejected at the 1 percent significance
level, indicating that the stochastic frontier approach is valid in our study. We
then estimate the stochastic frontier model (equation [4]) and the inefficiency
determinants regression model (equation [5]) simultaneously using alter-

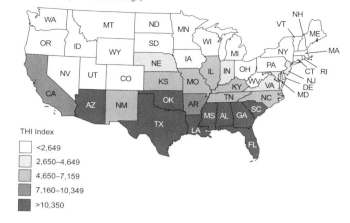

A THI Index Norm (1941–1970 Average)

THI Index
☐ <2,649
☐ 2,650–4,649
☐ 4,650–7,159
☐ 7,160–10,349
■ >10,350

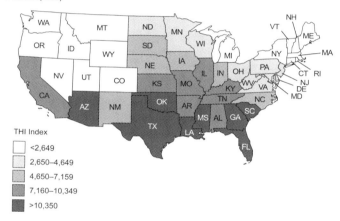

B THI Index (1983)

THI Index
☐ <2,649
☐ 2,650–4,649
☐ 4,650–7,159
☐ 7,160–10,349
■ >10,350

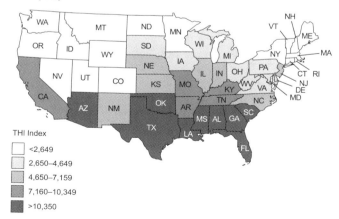

C THI Index (1995)

THI Index
☐ <2,649
☐ 2,650–4,649
☐ 4,650–7,159
☐ 7,160–10,349
■ >10,350

Fig. 2.3   THI load comparison, the norm, 1983, and 1995
Source: Authors' calculations.

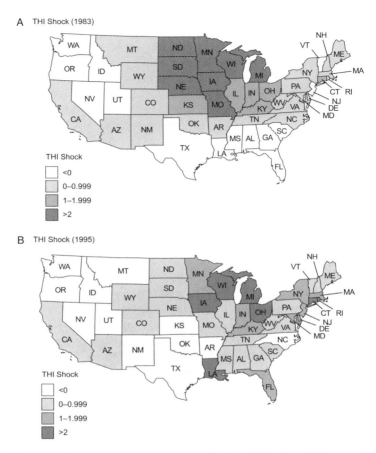

Fig. 2.4   The climate-shocks comparisons using the THI index: 1983 versus 1995
Source: Authors' calculation.

native weather variables and model specifications as a robustness check.[6] Empirical results of both production regression and inefficiency determinant regression are presented in table 2.1. Models 1 and 2 evaluate climatic effects on state inefficiency by including only weather and irrigation den-

6. There is a challenge estimating production functions given that inputs can be endogenous. While we have done some experiments using inputs from previous year (a common approach used in the literature) as an instrument in the estimation, we only report the results based on the output and input variables from the same year. There are two reasons behind this choice: first, the coefficients in the production function are similar given that input uses are rather stable from one year to another (not like output); second, we want to capture the concurrent effects so that the inefficiency component can capture both output changes and input changes (not endogeneity-adjusted) in the same year. Still, future studies can consider applying some other IV techniques (e.g., Levinsohn and Petrin 2003; Shee and Stefanou 2014; Amsler, Prokhorov, and Schmidt 2014) for comparison purpose.

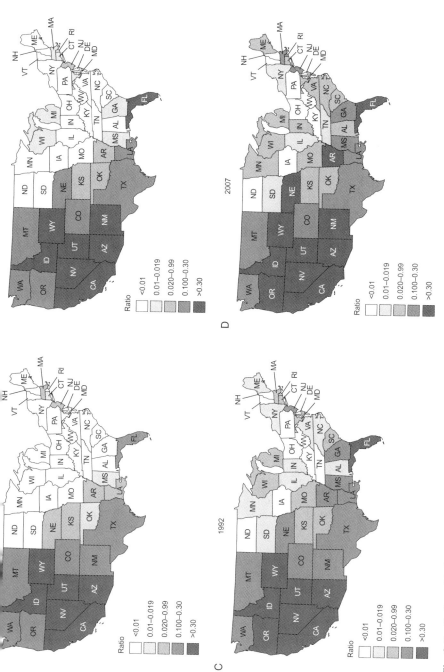

Fig. 2.5 Ratios of irrigation-ready land area to total cropland area (irrigation density) at census years

Note: "Ratio" indicates the share of irrigation-ready land area to total cropland area.

Source: Author's calculation using data from the agricultural census in various years.

sity variables as inefficiency determinants. Models 3 and 4 add state-specific variables—public R&D stock, extension capacity, and road density—as control variables to check the robustness of the estimated climatic impacts on state inefficiency. Models 1 and 3 use mean levels of THI and Oury indexes, while model 2 and 4 use THI shocks and Oury shocks as weather variables. Since outputs and inputs are all in natural logarithms, the input coefficients can be interpreted as output elasticities. According to the estimates of production function on the top section of table 2.1, the output elasticities for specific input across four models are consistent, with the output elasticity of intermediate goods at its highest, about 0.6, and capital's output elasticity at its lowest, about 0.07 to 0.08. Since the hypothesis of constant return to scale is rejected, we can infer a decreasing return to scale with input coefficients totaling less than one.

The signs of the coefficients of weather variables are as expected and consistent no matter the measures. Results of the inefficiency determinants regressions indicate that the combined effects of higher temperature and lower precipitation that result in a higher THI load or a lower Oury index measure can drive state production away from its best performance. However, without controlling for state-specific variables, the coefficient of the THI load becomes insignificant in model 1. According to the results, one unit increase in the THI load could result in a worse inefficiency, with the inefficiency term $(\ln \sigma_u^2)$ increasing by 0.00002 percent in model 1 and 0.00006 percent in model 3. On the other hand, one unit decrease in the Oury index (drier conditions) could cause further inefficiency, with the inefficiency term increasing by 0.026 percent in model 1 and 0.02 percent in model 3. Using "shock" measures (units of standard deviations relative to historical norms) of the THI load and Oury index as weather variables in model 2 and model 4, the estimates are all significant, and the magnitudes of those coefficients are consistent between the two models. According to both models, a single unit shock of the THI load will result in about a 0.3 percent deterioration in the inefficiency term, while a unit of negative shock (drier conditions) will result in about a 0.18 percent deterioration in the inefficiency term.

The results show that the "unexpected" deviation from the state's historical norm in weather variations have more consistent impacts on state production efficiency than the mean-level changes of weather variables. It implies that farmers in a region with more temperature or precipitation variations may have adapted more to the environment by adopting technologies or practices that can mitigate the damages from adverse weather. For example, drier regions, such as California and Nevada, usually have higher irrigation-ready land density than other regions, and that may partially offset the negative impacts of bad weather. The negative coefficients of irrigation density indicate that a state with a higher density in irrigation-system-ready land areas tends to be closer to its best production performance when holding other factors constant. After controlling for state-

Table 2.1 Stochastic frontier models estimates with alternative inefficiency determinants

Variables	Model 1 Coefficient	Model 1 t-ratio	Model 2 Coefficient	Model 2 t-ratio	Model 3 Coefficient	Model 3 t-ratio	Model 4 Coefficient	Model 4 t-ratio
$\ln y$								
Technology (time trend)	0.0009	6.86***	0.0010	7.49***	0.0010	7.23***	0.0010	7.73***
ln(capital)	0.0813	4.10***	0.0775	3.96***	0.0705	3.59***	0.0785	4.11***
ln(materials)	0.5959	44.35***	0.5952	45.24***	0.5920	45.49***	0.5879	45.42***
ln(labor)	0.0982	10.60***	0.0998	10.98***	0.1089	11.57***	0.1079	11.66***
ln(land)	0.1124	6.55***	0.1055	6.25***	0.1083	6.23***	0.0995	5.80***
$\ln \sigma_v^2$ (noise)								
Constant	−5.8828	−59.40***	−5.8048	−52.68***	−5.8232	−71.97***	−5.8362	−66.84***
$\ln \sigma_u^2$ (inefficiency)								
Constant	−4.5181	−26.02***	−5.2706	−25.05***	−2.4305	−1.14	−2.7825	−1.52
THI load	0.00002	1.31			0.00006	3.38***		
Oury index	−0.0257	−4.29***			−0.0201	−3.06***		
THI load shock			0.3087	5.40***			0.3073	5.25***
Oury index shock			−0.1831	−2.15***			−0.1831	−2.15***
Irrigation density	−1.6170	−2.89***	−1.4210	−1.93***	−2.8771	−3.45***	−2.2217	−3.01***
lnR&D					−0.3867	−2.86***	−0.3314	−2.67***
lnExtension					−0.6245	−3.71***	−0.4787	−2.69***
lnRoad					−0.8779	−3.68***	−0.7994	−3.78***
State fixed effects	Yes		Yes		Yes		Yes	
Time fixed effects	Yes		Yes		Yes		Yes	
Log-likelihood	2,679		2,698		2,713		2,726	
X^2(95)	16,400,000	prob > X^2 = 0	11,700,000	prob > X^2 = 0	15,900,000	prob > X^2 = 0	14,600,000	prob > X^2 = 0
Observations	2,112		2,112		2,112		2,112	

Source: Authors' calculation.

specific characteristics, the irrigation density's impacts on inefficiency are also larger in models 3 and 4.

The signs of the coefficient estimates of state-specific control variables— R&D stock, extension, road density—are consistent with the literature, wherein higher knowledge capital (R&D stock), extension capacity, and road density can enhance an individual state's productivity and push its production toward its best performance using given inputs and the best technology. Since R&D, extension, and road-density variables are all in natural log (Ln) form, a 1 percent increase in road density and extension capacity may have higher impacts on improving technical inefficiency than a 1 percent increase in local R&D stock. This implies that while public R&D stock can contribute to overall technical changes by pushing up the general production frontier for all states, its contribution in improving a local state's inefficiency may be less than that of other local public goods. The state extension activity and intensified road infrastructure can help disseminate knowledge, reduce transportation costs, and improve a state's technical efficiencies by catching up with others.

Based on the results from model 4, we estimate box and whisker plots of individual states' inefficiencies. The mean and distribution of states' inefficiency scores and rankings are presented in figure 2.6. We find that over the study period, California ranks first in productivity performance (least inefficiency), making it the most productive state among all 48 contiguous states. The top six most efficient states also include Arizona, Florida, New Jersey, Massachusetts, and New York. According to the predicted inefficiency scores, individual states' productivity is strongly affected by their state-specific characteristics such that even with similar weather patterns and natural resources, productivity can differ significantly.[7]

2.5   Potential Impacts of Future Climate Change on US Agricultural Production: Scenario Analysis

To estimate the heat-stress- and drought-related production losses attributable to climate change (mean level changes) and extreme weather (weather shock), we simulate the climate change projections in temperature and precipitation in the 2030s that result in various THI load and Oury index estimates. There are many global models projecting future climate changes, and while the magnitudes of future temperature or precipitation may be different from one projection to another, the direction of the projections consistently point toward more frequent heat waves, warmer temperatures,

---

7. The results could also imply that if the major federal/state water storage and allocation system that helped support the high-valued irrigated agricultural sector in California is not to be as resilient in future years under prolonged drought conditions due to an absence of significant new capital investment, California may not be as efficient as in the past.

Efficiency Scores

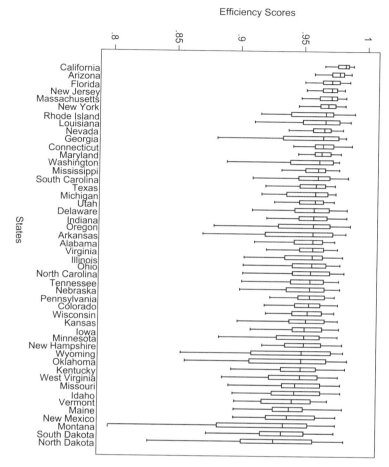

Fig. 2.6   Box and whiskers plots of state efficiency estimates and rankings based on model 4

and increasing incidences of extreme weather. Key and Sneeringer (2014) project the potential impacts of climate change on US dairy production in 2030 based on four climate-change scenarios drawn from the projections of four general circulation models—CNR, ECH, CSIRO, and MORPC (see Key and Sneeringer 2014 data appendix for details). Under their scenarios, temperature change during the period of 2010 to 2030 ranges from 0.65°C to 1.38°C. According to the Environmental Protection Agency,[8] earth's average temperature has risen by 0.83°C over the past century and is projected to rise another 0.3°C to 4.8°C over the next hundred years. According to the

8. See https://www3.epa.gov/climatechange/basics/ for more details.

US Global Change Research Program Report (USGCRP 2014),[9] the overall temperatures will continue to warm over the century in the United States, with a projected average increase by the end of the century of approximately 3.9°C to 6.1°C under the high-emission scenario and 2.2°C to 3.6°C under the low-emission scenario. We draw information from various projected trends in future temperature and precipitation changes to form three scenarios from mild to extreme. The scenarios are as follows:

Scenario 1: We assume a mild climate change during the growing season of the 2030s, with a 1°C increase relative to 1940–1970 temperature levels.
Scenario 2: We assume a more serious climate change scenario in the 2030s, with a 2°C increase relative to 1940–1970 temperature levels.
Scenario 3: We assume an extreme-weather scenario during the 2030s, with a 2°C temperature increase and one-inch decrease in monthly average precipitation relative to 1940–1970 levels.

We estimate the production response as if there are no changes in prices, input use, technology, or farm practices.[10] The projections are conducted using model 4 estimates, where the weather variables are shocks of the THI load and the Oury index with state-specific control variables kept constant as in the following equation:

$$(9) \quad \ln \sigma^2_{uit} = \gamma_0 + \gamma_1 z_{THI\_shock,it} + \gamma_2 z_{Oury\_shock,it} + r_3 z_{irrigation\_density,it} + r_4 \ln RD_{it}$$

$$+ r_5 \ln ET_{it} + r_6 \ln RO_{it} + \omega_{it}; \; \omega_{it} \sim N(0, \sigma^2_\omega).$$

Since each state has its own genuine pattern of historical climatic variations, each could have adjusted its farm production by adopting various production practices or technologies to adapt to the weather it is facing (Yang and Shumway 2015; Huang, Wang, and Wang 2015; Marshall et al. 2015; Heisey and Day-Rubenstein 2015). Therefore, the unexpected same-degree change in temperature and precipitation may have different impacts on an individual state's THI shock and Oury index shock estimates, resulting in varying effects on state production efficiency estimates. The impact of temperature changes on estimated state inefficiency can be derived by taking the first derivative of equation (9) with respect to temperature changes as follows:

9. Established under the Global Research Act of 1990, the US Global Change Research Program (USGCRP) has provided strategic planning and coordination to 13 participating federal agencies working to advance the science of global environmental change. The third National Climate Assessment, released by USGCRP in May 2014, is the most comprehensive and authoritative report on climate change and its impacts in the United States. See http://nca2014.globalchange.gov/ for more details.
10. This is the so-called dumb farmer (a naïve case) assumption (Mendelsohn, Nordhaus, and Shaw 1994; Key and Sneeringer 2014), where farm operators are assumed not to anticipate or respond to changing environmental conditions. The impacts may be reduced by allowing for some level of adaptation by the producer.

$$(10) \quad \frac{\partial \ln \sigma_{ui}^2}{\partial T} = \frac{\partial \ln \sigma_{ui}^2}{\partial Z_{THI\_shock,i}} \frac{\partial Z_{THI\_shock,i}}{\partial T} + \frac{\partial \ln \sigma_{ui}^2}{\partial Z_{Oury\_shock,i}} \frac{\partial Z_{Oury\_shock,i}}{\partial T}$$

$$= \gamma_1 \times \frac{\partial Z_{THI\_shock,i}}{\partial T} + \gamma_2 \times \frac{\partial Z_{Oury\_shock,i}}{\partial T}.$$

The impact of precipitation changes on state inefficiency can be derived by taking the first derivative of equation (9) with respect to precipitation changes as follows:

$$(11) \quad \frac{\partial \ln \sigma_{ui}^2}{\partial P} = \frac{\partial \ln \sigma_{ui}^2}{\partial Z_{Oury\_shock,i}} \frac{\partial Z_{Oury\_shock,i}}{\partial P} = \gamma_2 * \frac{\partial Z_{Oury\_shock,i}}{\partial P}.$$

The total impact of projected temperature changes and precipitation changes is the sum of equations (10) and (11):

$$(12) \quad \frac{\partial \ln \sigma_{ui}^2}{\partial T} + \frac{\partial \ln \sigma_{ui}^2}{\partial P} = \gamma_1 \times \frac{\partial Z_{THI\_shock,i}}{\partial T} + \gamma_2$$

$$\times \left(\frac{\partial Z_{Oury\_shock,i}}{\partial T} + \frac{\partial Z_{Oury\_shock,i}}{\partial P} \right).$$

We predict the potential impacts of three climate-change scenarios in the 2030s on state production inefficiency using the average weather conditions from 2000 to 2010 as the baseline. The results are reported in table 2.2 and are grouped by production region (see notes in table 2.2 for region details). All regions will move further away from the production frontier with increasing temperature and declining precipitation. On average, a 1°C increase in temperature will cause the production efficiency to decrease by 0.38 percent in the Pacific region and 1.31 percent in the Delta region relative to the 2000–2010 mean inefficiency level ($\ln \sigma_u^2$; see table 2.2). When temperature increases by 2°C, the production efficiency will decrease further, ranging from 0.73 percent in the Pacific region to 3.23 percent in the Delta region relative to the 2000–2010 mean inefficiency level ($\ln \sigma_u^2$).

The results imply that the impacts of temperature changes on production efficiencies are not linear and vary across regions. According to the coefficient of variation (CV) estimates, the weather impacts are more consistent within the Lake States region and the Northern Plains region than in other regions. While the temperature changes seem to cause a more serious impact on the Delta region, the variation is also the largest within that region. Several factors can cause these differences, including different historical climate patterns in those states and varying degrees of irrigation development. Under scenario 3 (extreme weather), the temperature increases by 2°C and precipitation decreases by 1 inch on average, and the impacts are more consistent for states within the same region, as the CV declines in almost

Table 2.2   **Potential impacts of climate changes and extreme weather on regional productivity in 2030–2040: Scenario analysis relative to 2000–2010 mean inefficiency level (ln σ_u^2)**

Regions	Temperature increases by 1°C			Temperature increases by 2°C			Temperature increases by 2°C; precipitation declines by 1 inch		
	Mean	Standard deviation	CV	Mean	Standard deviation	CV	Mean	Standard deviation	CV
Appalachian	0.45	0.15	0.33	1.19	0.39	0.33	1.26	0.38	0.36
Corn Belt	0.68	0.35	0.51	1.73	0.77	0.45	1.80	0.77	0.43
Delta	1.31	0.93	0.71	3.23	2.48	0.77	3.28	2.48	0.7
Lake States	0.61	0.04	0.06	1.70	0.05	0.03	1.79	0.04	0.0
Mountain	0.41	0.24	0.58	0.91	0.30	0.32	1.04	0.31	0.30
Northeast	0.42	0.19	0.45	1.78	0.97	0.55	1.85	0.97	0.5
Northern Plains	0.66	0.11	0.16	1.66	0.31	0.19	1.74	0.32	0.1
Pacific	0.38	0.08	0.20	0.73	0.13	0.18	0.84	0.12	0.1
Southeast	0.77	0.25	0.33	1.85	0.68	0.37	1.92	0.68	0.3
Southern Plains	0.69	0.22	0.32	1.51	0.63	0.42	1.57	0.62	0.4

Notes: States according to region: Appalachian: WV, TN, NC, VA, KY; Corn Belt: OH, IA, MO, IN, II Delta: LA, AR, MS; Lake States: MN, MI, WI; Mountain: CO, UT, AZ, NM, WY, NV, ID, MT; North east: NH, PA, ME, MD, RI, MA, DE, CT, VT, NY, NJ; Northern Plains: ND, SD, KS, NE; Pacific: OF CA, WA; Southeast: SC, AL, GA, FL; Southern Plains: TX, OK.

Sources: Authors' calculation.

all regions when compared to scenario 2 (medium weather impact). This indicates that extreme weather, which is beyond the expected climatic change pattern, can have more disastrous effects on all states.

Responses of agricultural productivity to climate change (mean level changes of Oury index and THI load) and extreme weather shocks (deviations from historical average variations of Oury index and THI load) can inform agricultural policy decisions. For example, while farmers are expected and sometimes observed to adapt to the shifting long-run climate pattern, Dell, Jones, and Olken (2014) argue that certain governmental agricultural support programs (such as subsidized crop insurance) could have reduced farmers' incentives to adapt. Therefore, there could be a tradeoff between reducing farmers' revenue risk and increasing agricultural productivity. The diverse weather impacts on regional productivity from a certain degree of temperature and precipitation changes suggest the need for state-specific research programs to help producers manage their state-specific climatic situations and future climate-change challenges. To help agriculture adapt to climate change, Heisey and Day-Rubenstein (2015) suggest the use of genetic resources to develop new crop varieties that are more tolerant to both abiotic and biotic stresses. However, they also indicate that given the public-goods characteristics of genetic resources, there can be obstacles for private research and development. Creating incentives for the private sector through intellectual property rules for genetic resources and international agreements governing genetic resource exchanges could promote greater use of genetic resources for climate-change adaptation.

2.6   Summary and Conclusions

This chapter employs state panel data from 1960 to 2004 to identify the role of climate change on US agricultural productivity using a stochastic frontier production function method. Climate/weather variables are measured using the THI load and Oury index at both their mean levels and the degree of deviation from the historical variation norms (from 1941 to 1970) at the state level. We also incorporate irrigated land area density and measures of local public goods—R&D, extension, and road infrastructure—to capture the effects of state characteristics and check for the robustness of the estimate of climate variable impact.

The state production data and climate information show noticeable variations across and within production regions. Some regions seem to have faster overall TFP growth—the Northeast, Corn Belt, and Delta regions—than others during the study period. Results indicate that a higher THI load can drive farm production away from its best performance. However, a higher Oury index, irrigated land area density, local R&D, Extension, and road density can enhance state farm production and move it closer to the production frontier. Although the relative levels of the THI and Oury index could result in geospatial differences in technical inefficiency, the unexpected extreme weather "shock" seems to have more robust impacts on estimated inefficiency, and this could be because farmers expect some degree of weather variation based on past experience and would have already made preparations. Therefore, it is the unexpected climatic shocks that result in either an increased use of inputs or a drop in production.

While most studies evaluating the climatic effect on agricultural productivity focus on specific crop or livestock commodities, it is also important to identify the climatic effect on regional agricultural productivity through its impacts on technical inefficiency. Responses of agricultural productivity to climate change at the state level can then inform state-specific agricultural policy decisions.

Appendix

Table 2A.1   **Summary statistics of potential weather variables**

Weather variables	Variable description	N	Mean	Std. dev.	Min.	Max.
dd830	Good-weather index: degree-days between 8°C and 30°C between March and August	2,112	1,804.25	512.06	920.45	3,098.31
dd30	Bad-weather index: degree-days when temperature is above 30°C between March and August	2,112	27.44	47.48	0.00	376.15
prec	Total precipitation in inches between March and August	2,112	8.01	3.65	0.48	18.6
max_5_8	Average max temperature between May and August	2,112	27.88	3.17	21.55	39.4
Palmer3_8	Palmer index between April and August	2,112	0.00	1.10	−4.11	5.9
THI_mean	Annual mean of THI load index	2,112	4,964.61	5,251.69	0.87	25,566.6
THI_mean_norm	Average THI mean between 1940 and 1970	2,112	5,044.42	5,165.42	195.48	20,328.1
THI_stdv_norm	Average THI dev between 1940 and 1970	2,112	1,306.33	1,099.55	223.34	6,012.6
THI_shock	(THI mean − THI norm) / THI_stdv_norm	2,112	−0.02	1.16	−6.12	8.7
Oury_mean	Annual mean of Oury index between March and August	2,112	25.34	10.93	0.51	58.9
Oury_mean_norm	Average Oury_mean between 1940 and 1970 between March and August	2,112	24.47	8.69	2.37	35.5
Oury_stdv_norm	Average Oury dev between 1940 and 1970 between March and August	2,112	16.32	3.78	4.08	24.0
Oury_shock	(Oury mean − Oury norm) / Oury_stdv_norm	2,112	0.25	1.34	−1.91	12.8

Source: Authors' calculation.

Table 2A.2 Out-of-sample model specifications comparison

Model specifications	Linear regression models											
	M1	M2	M3	M4	M5	M6	M7	M8	M9	M10	M11	M12
Weather variables												
Max temp. (5–8)	x									x		
Precipitation (3–8)	x			x								
Oury mean							x			x		
THI mean					x			x			x	
Oury shock			x			x			x			
THI shock			x			x			x			x
Other variables												
Time, state fixed effects	x	x	x	x	x	x	x	x	x	x	x	x
External control variables				x	x	x	x	x	x	x	x	x
Input variables					x	x	x	x	x	x	x	x
Models												
Linear model	x	x	x	x	x	x						
Stochastic frontier models												
A. No variable in the inefficiency term							x	x	x	x	x	x
B. Only weather variables in the inefficiency term												
C. Weather and other control variables are all in the inefficiency term												
Mean standard errors of predictions	0.9055	0.9427	0.9206	0.8117	0.838	0.8235	0.5273	0.5453	0.5353	0.5114	0.5277	0.5193
L-R test $H_0: \sigma_u = 0$ (no inefficiency term)	NA	NA	NA	NA	NA	NA	NA	NA	NA	NA	NA	NA

(continued)

Table 2A.2   (continued)

Model specifications	Stochastic frontier models (I)								
	M13	M14	M15	M16	M17	M18	M19	M20	M21
Weather variables									
Max temp. (5–8)	x						x		
Precipitation (3–8)	x						x		
Oury mean		x		x				x	
THI mean		x		x				x	
Oury shock			x		x	x			x
THI shock			x		x	x			x
Other variables									
Time, state fixed effects	x	x	x	x	x	x	x	x	x
External control variables	x	x	x	x	x	x	x	x	x
Input variables				x	x	x	x	x	x
Models									
Linear model									
Stochastic frontier models									
A. No variable in the inefficiency term	x	x	x	x	x	x	x	x	x
B. Only weather variables in the inefficiency term									
C. Weather and other control variables are all in the inefficiency term									
Mean standard errors of predictions	0.7514 ***	0.7542 ***	0.7336 ***	0.4985 ***	0.5153 ***	0.5055 ***	0.4854 ***	0.5004 ***	0.4917 ***
L-R test H_0: $\sigma_u = 0$ (no inefficiency term)	***	***	***	***	***	***	***	***	***

Stochastic frontier models (II)

Model specifications	M22	M23	M24	M25	M26	M27	M28	M29	M30
Weather variables									
Max temp. (5–8)	x								
Precipitation (3–8)	x								
Oury mean		x		x			x		
THI mean		x			x			x	
Oury shock			x		x			x	
THI shock			x			x			x
Other variables									
Time, state fixed effects	x	x	x	x	x	x	x	x	x
External control variables	x	x	x	x	x	x	x	x	x
Input variables				x	x	x	x	x	x
Models									
Linear model									
Stochastic frontier models									
A. No variable in the inefficiency term									
B. Only weather variables in the inefficiency term	x	x	x						
C. Weather and other control variables are all in the inefficiency term				x	x	x	x	x	x
Mean standard errors of predictions	0.0286	0.0282	0.0346	0.0242	0.0242	0.0240	0.0234	0.0219	0.0215
L–R test $H_0: \sigma_u = 0$ (no inefficiency term)	***	***	***	***	***	***	***	***	***

Notes: "NA" indicates "not applicable." "***" indicates that according to the L–R test results, we reject the hypothesis of $\sigma_u = 0$ (no inefficiency term) at 1 percent significance level.

Sources: Authors' calculation.

Table 2A.3   **State characteristics on productivity growth and climate indexes**

Production region	State	TFP annual growth (%)	Livestock/crop ratio (1960–2004)	THI_mean_norm	THI_stdv_norm	Oury_mean_norm	Oury_stdv_norm
Northeast	Connecticut	2.20	1.04	1,055.67	369.43	34.96	21.85
	Delaware	1.80	2.65	4,852.78	434.19	27.60	15.90
	Maine	1.90	0.67	334.10	288.76	35.54	21.02
	Maryland	1.83	1.68	3,854.23	1,219.64	27.85	16.52
	Massachusetts	2.29	1.28	837.76	507.73	34.82	22.52
	New Hampshire	2.00	1.09	400.82	400.96	34.91	20.69
	New Jersey	1.67	1.47	3,036.90	1,343.49	30.95	19.14
	New York	1.48	2.28	631.08	425.65	33.22	19.19
	Pennsylvania	1.81	1.55	2,132.22	1,176.03	34.03	20.20
	Rhode Island	2.48	0.57	1,082.13	223.34	33.45	24.66
	Vermont	1.62	1.22	460.23	431.81	34.84	18.42
Lake States	Michigan	2.41	0.68	1,337.86	565.03	29.15	18.46
	Minnesota	1.86	0.98	1,316.14	541.74	30.48	16.84
	Wisconsin	1.59	1.77	1,278.79	554.74	32.64	17.61
Corn Belt	Illinois	1.96	0.65	4,700.84	2,053.02	29.33	19.38
	Indiana	2.28	0.47	3,333.96	1,300.01	31.05	20.07
	Iowa	1.87	0.72	2,464.54	683.11	31.38	18.19
	Missouri	1.62	1.10	6,959.88	824.95	29.46	19.86
	Ohio	2.16	0.73	2,483.27	756.51	30.19	18.40
Northern Plains	Kansas	1.05	1.03	7,067.55	1,509.53	23.00	17.48
	Nebraska	1.60	0.93	4,244.28	920.75	25.68	17.53
	North Dakota	1.90	1.47	1,135.88	362.00	24.17	16.20
	South Dakota	1.51	0.96	2,385.50	887.56	24.89	16.98

Appalachian	Kentucky	1.61	0.88	6,493.57	1,190.49	27.85	15.95
	North Carolina	1.84	1.33	6,815.53	2,358.49	26.89	13.18
	Tennessee	1.13	0.88	7,085.80	1,830.86	26.26	15.92
	Virginia	1.53	3.29	3,616.45	1,769.74	26.63	13.68
	West Virginia	1.29	1.91	2,409.00	1,605.48	31.13	16.45
Southeast	Alabama	1.32	2.43	12,354.32	2,545.32	25.34	16.03
	Florida	1.44	0.33	20,328.13	1,819.72	26.73	13.90
	Georgia	1.91	1.56	12,544.53	2,573.72	23.97	13.49
	South Carolina	1.61	0.73	11,534.97	1,927.22	24.26	12.62
Delta	Arkansas	1.93	0.79	9,604.32	2,283.24	25.33	19.22
	Louisiana	1.93	0.68	16,369.98	656.32	24.58	16.22
	Mississippi	1.98	1.03	14,649.88	1,650.05	23.81	16.65
Southern Plains	Oklahoma	0.58	1.54	12,017.31	1,660.94	22.00	18.92
	Texas	1.14	1.31	14,224.99	3,888.87	15.41	14.57
Mountain	Arizona	1.53	1.14	15,465.14	3,681.95	2.37	4.08
	Colorado	1.10	1.58	1,537.62	785.93	17.21	13.61
	Idaho	2.01	1.03	927.67	726.82	12.23	13.29
	Montana	1.38	0.69	235.59	384.94	18.53	15.18
	Nevada	1.24	0.30	1,259.17	722.29	7.12	9.04
	New Mexico	1.44	0.46	5,982.29	2,428.52	10.05	10.54
	Utah	1.55	1.88	860.60	790.21	10.46	11.34
	Wyoming	0.66	1.75	195.48	409.08	17.70	16.09
Pacific	California	1.66	0.48	7,412.25	6,012.63	3.61	16.09
	Oregon	2.58	0.50	355.74	490.08	12.26	15.34
	Washington	1.73	0.43	465.32	731.14	9.47	12.08

Source: Authors' calculation.

References

Aigner, D., C. Lovell, and P. Schmidt. 1977. "Formulation and Estimation of Stochastic Frontier Production Function Models." *Journal of Econometrics* 6:21–37.

Alston, J., M. A. Anderson, J. James, and P. Pardey. 2010. *Persistence Pays: U.S. Agricultural Productivity Growth and the Benefits from Public R&D Spending*. New York: Springer.

Amsler, C., A. Prokhorov, and P. Schimidt. 2014. "Endogeneity in Stochastic Frontier Models." *Business Analytics Working Paper Series* BAWP-2015-01, February 2015.

Anyamba, A., J. L. Small, S. C. Britch, C. J. Tucker, E. W. Pak, C. A. Reynolds, J. Crutchfield, and K. J. Linthicum. "Recent Weather Extremes and Impacts on Agricultural Production and Vector-Borne Disease Outbreak Patterns." *PLoS One* 9 (3): e92538.

Ball, V. E., F. Gollop, A. Kelly-Hawke, and G. Swinand. 1999. "Patterns of Productivity Growth in the U.S. Farm Sector: Linking State and Aggregate Models." *American Journal of Agricultural Economics* 81:164–79.

Burke, M., and K. Emerick. 2016. "Adaptation to Climate Change: Evidence from US Agriculture." *American Economic Journal: Economic Policy* 8 (3): 106–40.

Battese, G., and T. Coelli. 1995. "A Model for Technical Inefficiency Effects in a Stochastic Frontier Production Function for Panel Data." *Empirical Economics* 20:325–32.

Carter, T. R., M. L. Parry, H. Harasawa, and S. Nishioka. 1994. "Intergovernmental Panel on Climate Change Technical Guidelines for Assessing Climate Change Impacts and Adaptations." Report, University College London and Centre for Global Environmental Research.

Daly, C., M. D. Halbleib, J. I. Smith, W. P. Gibson, M. K. Doggett, G. H. Taylor, J. Curtis, and P. Pasteris. 2008. "Physiographically-Sensitive Mapping of Temperature and Precipitation across the Conterminous United States." *International Journal of Climatology* 28:2031–64.

Dell, M., B. F. Jones, and B. A. Olken. 2009. "Temperature and Income: Reconciling New Cross-Sectional and Panel Estimates." *American Economic Review* 99 (2): 198–204.

Dell, M., B. F. Jones, and B. A. Olken. 2012. "Temperature Shocks and Economic Growth: Evidence from the Last Half Century." *American Economic Journal: Macroeconomics* 4 (3): 66–95.

Dell, M., B. F. Jones, and B. A. Olken. 2014. "What Do We Learn from the Weather? The New Climate–Economy Literature." *Journal of Economic Literature* 52 (3): 740–98.

Deschênes, O., and M. Greenstone. 2007. "The Economic Impacts of Climate Change: Evidence from Agricultural Output and Random Fluctuations in Weather." *American Economic Review* 97 (1): 354–85.

Di Falco, S., and M. Veronesi. 2014. "Managing Environmental Risk in Presence of Climate Change: The Role of Adaptation in the Nile Basin of Ethiopia." *Environmental and Resource Economics* 57:553–77.

EPA (Environmental Protection Agency). 2018. "Climate Change Research." https://www.epa.gov/climate-research.

Ferris, R., R. H. Ellis, T. R. Wheeler, and P. Hadley. 1998. "Effect of High Temperature Stress at Anthesis on Grain Yield and Biomass of Field-Grown Crops of Wheat." *Annals of Botany* 82:631–39.

Fuquay, J. W. 1981. "Heat Stress as It Affects Animal Production." *Journal of Animal Science* 52:164–74.

Hansen, P. J., and C. F. Aréchiga. 1999. "Strategies for Managing Reproduction in the Heat-Stressed Dairy Cow." *Journal of Animal Science* 77 (Suppl. 2): 36–50.

Hatfield, J., G. Takle, R. Grotjahn, P. Holden, R. C. Izaurralde, T. Mader, E. Marshall, and D. Liverman. 2014. "Agriculture. Climate Change Impacts in the United States: The Third National Climate Assessment." In *U.S. Global Change Research Program*, edited by J. M. Melillo, Terese (T. C.) Richmond, and G. W. Yohe, 150–74. DOI: 10.7930/J02Z13FR. http://nca2014.globalchange.gov/report/sectors/agriculture.

Heisey, P., and K. Day-Rubenstein. 2015. *Using Crop Genetic Resources to Help Agriculture Adapt to Climate Change: Economics and Policy*. Economic Information Bulletin Number 139, USDA Economic Research Service, April.

Huang, C. J., and J.-T. Liu. 1994. "Estimation of a Non-neutral Stochastic Frontier Production Function." *Journal of Productivity Analysis* 5:171–80.

Huang, J., Y. Wang, and J. Wang. 2015. "Farmers' Adaptation to Extreme Weather Events through Farm Management and Its Impacts on the Mean and Risk of Rice Yield+ in China." *American Journal of Agricultural Economics* 97 (2): 602–17.

IPCC (Intergovernmental Panel on Climate Change). 2007. *Climate Change 2007: The Physical Science Basis. Contribution of Working Group I to the Fourth Assessment Report of the IPCC*. Cambridge: Cambridge University Press.

Jin, Y., and W. Huffman. 2016. "Measuring Public Research and Extension and Estimating Their Impacts on Agricultural Productivity: New Insights from U.S. Evidence." *Agricultural Economics* 47 (1): 15–31.

Key, N., and S. Sneeringer. 2014. "Potential Effects of Climate Change on the Productivity of U.S. Dairies." *American Journal of Agricultural Economics* 96 (4): 1136–56.

Kim, K., and J. P. Chavas. 2003. "Technological Change and Risk Management: An Application to the Economics of Corn Production." *Agricultural Economics* 29:125–42.

Kumbhakar, S. C., S. Ghosh, and J. T. McGuckin. 1991. "A Generalized Production Frontier Approach for Estimating Determinants of Inefficiency in U.S. Dairy Farms." *Journal of Business and Economic Statistics* 9 (3): 279–86.

Levinsohn, J., and A. Petrin. 2003. "Estimating Production Functions Using Inputs to Control for Unobservables." *Review of Economic Studies* 70 (2): 317–41.

Liang, X., Y. Wu, R. G. Chambers, D. L. Schmoldt, W. Gao, C. Liu, Y. Liu, C. Sun, and J. A. Kennedy. 2017. "Determining Climate Effects on US Total Agricultural Productivity." *Proceedings of the National Academy of Sciences of the USA* 114(12):E2285–E2292

Lobell, D. B., and G. P. Asner. 2003. "Climate and Management Contributions to Recent Trends in U.S. Agricultural Yields." *Science* 299:1032.

Lobell, D. B., W. Schlenker, and J. Costa-Roberts. 2011. "Climate Tends and Global Crop Production since 1980." *Science* 333:616.

McCarl, B. A., X. Villavicencio, and X. Wu. 2008. "Climate Change and Future Analysis: Is Stationarity Dying?" *American Journal of Agricultural Economics* 90 (5): 1241–47.

Meeusen, W., and J. van den Broeck. 1977. "Efficiency Estimation from Cobb-Douglas Production Function with Composed Error." *International Economic Review* 18:435–44.

Mendelsohn, R., W. D. Nordhaus, and D. Shaw. 1994. "The Impact of Global

Warming on Agriculture: A Ricardian Analysis." *American Economic Review* 84 (4): 753–71.

Morrison, S. R. 1983. "Ruminant Heat Stress: Effect on Production and Means of Alleviation." *Journal of Animal Science* 57:1594–1600.

Mukherjee, D., B. E. Bravo-Ureta, and A. D. Vries. 2012. "Dairy Productivity and Climatic Conditions: Econometric Evidence from Southeastern United States." *Journal of Agricultural and Resource Economics* 57:123–40.

NASA (National Aeronautics and Space Administration). 2018. "Climate Change and Global Warming." https://climate.nasa.gov/.NLCD (National Land Cover Database). 2006. "Completion of the 2006 National Land Cover Database for the Conterminous United States." *Photogrammetric Engineering and Remote Sensing* 77 (9): 858–64.

NRC (National Research Council). 1983. *Changing Climate: Report of the Carbon Dioxide Assessment Committee*. Washington, DC: National Academies Press.

Oury, B. 1965. "Allowing for Weather in Crop Production Model Building." *American Journal of Agricultural Economics* 47 (2): 270–83.

Paltasingh, K. R., P. Goyari, and R. K. Mishra. 2012. "Measuring Weather Impact on Crop Yield Using Aridity Index: Evidence from Odisha." *Agricultural Economics Research Review* 25 (2): 205–16.

Parry, M. L., O. F. Canziani, J. Palutikof, P. van der Linden, and C. E. Hanson. 2007. *Climate Change 2007: Impacts, Adaptation and Vulnerability. Contribution of Working Group II to the Fourth Assessment Report of the Intergovernmental Panel on Climate Change*. Cambridge: Cambridge University Press.

PRISM Climate Group, Oregon State University. Created March 2014. http://prism .oregonstate.edu.

Reifschneider, D., and R. Stevenson. 1991. "Systematic Departures from the Frontier: A Framework for the Analysis of Firm Inefficiency." *International Economic Review* 32:715–23.

Sachs, J. D., and A. M. Warner. 1997. "Sources of Slow Growth in African Economies." *Journal of African Economies* 6 (3): 335–76.

Schimmelpfennig, D. 1996. "Uncertainty in Economic Models of Climate-Change Impacts." *Climatic Change* 33:213–34.

Schlenker, W., M. Hanemann, and A. C. Fisher. 2006. "The Impact of Global Warming on US Agriculture: An Econometric Analysis of Optimal Growing Conditions." *Review of Economics and Statistics* 88 (1): 113–25.

Schlenker, W., and M. J. Roberts. 2009. "Nonlinear Temperature Effects Indicate Severe Damages to US Crop Yield under Climate Change." *Proceedings of the National Academy of Sciences* 106 (37): 15594–98.

Semenov, M. A., and J. R. Porter. 1995. "Climatic Variability and the Modelling of Crop Yields." *Agricultural and Forest Meteorology* 73 (3/4): 265–83.

St-Pierre, N. R., B. Cobanov, and G. Schnitkey. 2003. "Economic Loss from Heat Stress by US Livestock Industries." *Journal of Dairy Science* 86 (E Suppl.): E52–E77.

Thom, E. C. 1958. "Cooling Degree Days." *Air Conditioning, Heating and Ventilation* 55:65–69.

Tubiello, F. N., and C. Rosenzweig. 2008. "Developing Climate Change Impact Metrics for Agriculture." *Integrated Assessment Journal* 8 (1): 165–84.

USDA-ERS (US Department of Agriculture Economic Research Service). 2017. "Agricultural Productivity in the US Statistics." https://www.ers.usda.gov/data -products/agricultural-productivity-in-the-us/.

USDA-NASS (US Department of Agriculture National Agricultural Statistics

Service). 2002. Census data from http://www.nass.usda.gov/Data_and_Statistics /index.asp.

USDA-NASS (US Department of Agriculture National Agricultural Statistics Service). 2017. "Data and Statistics." http://www.nass.usda.gov/Data_and_Statistics /index.asp.

USDA-NIFA (US Department of Agriculture National Institute of Food and Agriculture). "Salary Analyses of State Extension Service Positions," various years.

USGCRP (US Global Change Research Program). 2014. "Climate Change Impacts in the United States." http://s3.amazonaws.com/nca2014/low/NCA3_Climate _Change_Impacts_in_the_United%20States_LowRes.pdf?download=1.

Wang, H. J., and P. Schmidt. 2002. "One-Step and Two-Step Estimation of the Effects of
Exogenous Variables on Technical Efficiency Levels." *Journal of Productivity Analysis* 18:129–144.

Wang, S. L., V. E. Ball, L. E. Fulginiti, and A. Plastina. 2012. "Accounting for the Impacts of Public Research, R&D Spill-ins, Extension, and Roads in U.S. Regional Agricultural Productivity Growth, 1980–2004." In *Productivity Growth in Agriculture: An International Perspective*, edited by K. O. Fuglie, S. L. Wang, and V. E. Ball, 13–31. Oxfordshire: CAB International.

Wang, S. L., P. Heisey, D. Schimmelpfennig, and V. E. Ball. 2015. *Agricultural Productivity Growth in the United States: Measurement, Trends, and Drivers.* Economic Research Report Number 189, USDA Economic Research Service, July.

West, J. W., B. G. Mullinix, and J. K. Bernard. 2003. "Effects of Hot, Humid Weather on Milk Temperature, Dry Matter Intake, and Milk Yield of Lactating Dairy Cows." *Journal of Dairy Science* 86:232–42.

Yang, S., and C. R. Shumway. 2015. "Dynamic Adjustment in US Agriculture under Climate Change." *American Journal of Agricultural Economics* 98 (3): 910–24.

Yu, T., and B. A. Babcock. 1992. "Are U.S. Corn and Soybeans Becoming More Drought Tolerant?" *American Journal of Agricultural Economics* 92 (5): 1310–23.

Zhang, B., and C. A. Carter. 1997. "Reforms, the Weather, and Productivity Growth in China's Grain Sector." *American Journal of Agricultural Economics* 79 (4): 1266–77.

Zimbelman, R. B., R. P. Rhoads, M. L. Rhoads, G. C. Duff, L. H. Baumgard, and R. J. Collier. 2009. *A Re-evaluation of the Impact of Temperature Humidity Index (THI) and Black Globe Humidity Index (BGHI) on Milk Production in High Producing Dairy Cows.* Funded by NRI Grant # 2006-01724, Department of Animal Sciences, University of Arizona.

Farming under Weather Risk
Adaptation, Moral Hazard, and Selection on Moral Hazard

Hsing-Hsiang Huang and Michael R. Moore

3.1 Introduction

As the climate system continues to warm, episodes of drought and extreme precipitation are more likely to occur in North America (Christensen et al. 2013). Questions about changes in local temperature and precipitation events have been a practical concern to most of society (Brooks 2013). Agricultural productivity and profitability are of particular importance due to their direct connection to weather (e.g., Deschênes and Greenstone 2007; Fisher et al. 2012; Moore and Lobell 2014). Extreme weather events—including excessive heat, drought, and precipitation—are known to cause harmful impacts on crop yields (Schlenker and Roberts 2009; Lobell et al. 2014; Urban et al. 2015). According to the "smart farmer" hypothesis (Mendelsohn, Nordhaus, and Shaw 1994), however, farmers adapt to weather variation and can adapt to climate change to mitigate these impacts. Yet we know little about the mechanism(s) of adaptation: Is it through crop choice, deployment of farm labor, or timing of production activities? Another possibility is that farmers manage weather risk through crop insurance. As with all insurance markets, crop insurance raises the prospect of market failure through

Hsing-Hsiang Huang is a research associate at the University of Michigan.

Michael R. Moore is a professor of environmental economics at the University of Michigan.

We thank Joshua Woodward, who provided insightful comments as the discussant at the NBER Understanding Productivity Growth in Agriculture Conference. For valuable feedback, we thank two anonymous referees, Gloria Helfand, Ryan Kellogg, Mike McWilliams, Wolfram Schlenker, and participants at the NBER conference, the Association of Environmental and Resource Economists' 2016 Annual Summer Conference, and the 2016 Heartland Environmental and Resource Economics Workshop. We are grateful to Wolfram Schlenker for generously sharing weather data and to Peter Brody-Moore for outstanding research assistance. For acknowledgments, sources of research support, and disclosure of the authors' material financial relationships, if any, please see http://www.nber.org/chapters/c13941.ack.

adverse selection and moral hazard. The limited evidence on crop insurance suggests that, when treated with extreme heat, production areas with higher levels of insurance generate lower crop yields—that is, insurance may create a moral-hazard incentive for less adaptation (Annan and Schlenker 2015). Once again, the mechanisms underlying this outcome remain unstudied.

In this chapter, we study farmers' crop choice and crop insurance take-up in response to preplant precipitation from the perspectives of adaptation, moral hazard, and selection on moral hazard. Crop choices are analyzed as land use—hereafter labeled "cropping pattern," or how many acres of cropland are allocated to various crops. Cropping pattern is a possible adaptive strategy to preplant precipitation, as crops vary in their physiological requirements for water (Anderson, Wang, and Zhao 2012). At the same time, cropping pattern is potentially susceptible to the moral-hazard incentive of insurance. In addition to deciding on cropping pattern in early spring (Haigh et al. 2015), farmers in the US Midwest make crop insurance decisions by a March 15 deadline for corn and soybeans. Insurance is purchased by crop-specific acreage, and farmers decide on what percentage of yield to insure up to a maximum of 85 percent of the crop's historical average yield (where 85 percent coverage translates into a 15 percent deductible). Our variable for preplant precipitation includes precipitation from October 1 of the previous year through the March 15 insurance deadline. Our identification strategy relies on exogenous variation in this variable—that is, interannual variation in preplant precipitation is plausibly random within a given spatial unit, as with other weather variables (Dell et al. 2014).

In tandem with the weather experiment, we exploit a quasi experiment created by a federal agricultural policy from 2009 to 2011—the Supplemental Revenue Assistance Payments (SURE) program—to examine moral hazard in cropping pattern and selection on moral hazard in insurance take-up. The SURE program augmented private crop insurance (at no charge to the farmer) with what was termed a "shallow loss" provision (Glauber 2013)—that is, a provision to insure against relatively small reductions in crop yields that normally are part of the deductible. The provision substantially reduced deductibles on crop insurance, to 10 percent (Shields 2010; USDA-FSA 2009), thereby increasing the incentive for moral hazard in farmer decision-making (Smith and Watts 2010).[1] From the vantage point of an insurance agent, a farmer's hidden action was not merely planting a particular crop. Rather, it was planting a particular crop under conditions of extreme preplant precipitation. By interacting the SURE program and preplant precipitation, we estimate the treatment effect of SURE's reduced deductibles on cropping pattern to generate evidence on moral hazard.

Selection on moral hazard is the idea that an individual's selection of

1. Deductibles are a well-known feature of insurance policy design for reducing moral hazard—that is, reducing the incentive provided by insurance for risk-taking in relation to an uncertain outcome (Varian 1992).

insurance coverage is affected by the expected behavioral response to the coverage (Einav et al. 2013). Einav et al. show, for example, that individuals with a greater behavioral response to a health insurance contract purchase greater coverage. The issue in our study is whether farmers who increase (decrease) a crop's acreage under the SURE program purchase higher (lower) insurance coverage on the crop; this is moral hazard followed by selection on moral hazard. Higher coverage, notably, will generate a larger payout for a given crop yield. We investigate insurance take-up in a similar way to cropping pattern. By interacting the program and preplant precipitation, we estimate the treatment effect of SURE's reduced deductibles on insurance take-up to generate evidence on selection on moral hazard.

We investigate these topics using data from four large agricultural states in the US Midwest: Illinois, Iowa, Nebraska, and North Dakota. Illinois and Iowa are included in their entirety, while only the rain-fed, agricultural regions of North Dakota and Nebraska are included (i.e., irrigated agriculture is excluded as in Schlenker et al. 2005). We apply high-resolution spatial data on land use (crops) and weather.[2] We apply county-level data on insurance take-up and prepare county-level weather data to match the insurance data. Insurance take-up is measured using farmers' expenditures on insurance premiums, as in Deryugina and Kirwan (2018). The study spans 2001 to 2014. With SURE being a short-lived program (2009 to 2011), both the beginning and end of the program are subject to analysis. A key question is, After program termination, does cropping-pattern adaptation to preplant precipitation return to its preprogram status? To implement this, we interact preplant precipitation with both the policy change in 2009 and its termination after 2011.

We estimate piecewise linear regressions, by state and crop, to allow for heterogeneous effects of preplant precipitation across states. Illinois and Iowa are dominated by corn and soybean production, whereas several crops are planted in North Dakota and Nebraska, which suggests that farmers in the latter states may have more options for crop substitution. Previous research has found a strong nonlinearity in the relationship between precipitation during the growing season and crop yields (Schlenker and Roberts 2009; Annan and Schlenker 2015; Burke and Emerick 2016). The piecewise linear approach, following Schlenker and Roberts (2009) and Burke and Emerick (2016), allows us to identify the effects of both a risk of water deficit and a risk of excess water on farmers' cropping patterns and insurance take-up responses to preplant precipitation.[3] In this setting of exogenous variation in preplant precipitation, unobserved characteristics of farms and farmers

2. With Minnesota and South Dakota included, the study area would encompass a block of six contiguous states. They are not included, however, because their high-resolution cropland data do not begin until 2006.

3. Both drought and excess precipitation are frequent entries in the Causes of Loss database on crop insurance claims, which is maintained by the RMA (http://www.rma.usda.gov/data /cause.html).

may be correlated with both cropping pattern and preplant precipitation. For instance, in a semiarid area that typically experiences low precipitation as part of its climate, farmers may have adjusted in various ways (e.g., with farm machinery or tillage practices) to the higher probability of low precipitation. We control for this time-invariant unobserved heterogeneity with fixed effects. By using fine-scale spatial data, we pair a panel of crop-level land uses with preplant precipitation from 2001 to 2014 at a one-square-mile level, containing 640 acres. These one-square-mile blocks of farmland, called *sections*, tend to have only one or a few owners per section according to the Public Land Survey System (PLSS).[4] We employ section fixed effects in the land-use regressions, as in Holmes and Lee (2012).[5] We employ county fixed effects in the insurance take-up regressions.

Our results show heterogeneity across states in cropping-pattern adaptation to preplant precipitation from 2001 to 2007.[6] Farmers in North Dakota and Nebraska are much more responsive than those in Iowa and Illinois. When preplant precipitation is too little or too much, they plant fewer acres in corn, which is relatively water-sensitive, and more acres in soybeans, grassland, and/or wheat. In Illinois, although farmers are less responsive, the adaptation effects are nevertheless statistically significant for their three crops (corn, soybeans, and grassland). Iowa appears to combine the ideal climatic and soil conditions for growing corn and soybeans such that they are optimal choices under a wide range of preplant precipitation conditions.

During the SURE regime from 2009 to 2011, farmers in all four states changed cropping patterns in response to SURE's reduced deductibles. Farmers in North Dakota and Nebraska planted more acres in corn and fewer acres in wheat, soybeans, and grassland crops when facing extreme preplant precipitation. Although less responsive in magnitude, statistically significant effects were also found for corn and soybeans in Illinois and Iowa. Moral hazard under the SURE program provides a clear explanation for this risk-taking in cropping pattern. Farmers apparently were substituting crop insurance for adaptation as a means of managing risk.

Notably, after the program's termination from 2012 to 2014, farmers largely reversed course, returning cropping patterns close to the original, preprogram patterns of 2001 to 2007.

4. A section contains four quarter sections of 160 acres apiece. The quarter section is the land unit that was distributed for free under the 1862 Homestead Act to individuals who agreed to settle and farm the land. It is the original foundation of private ownership. We do not use a quarter section as the analytical unit because it does not cover all parts of North Dakota and Iowa.

5. In addition to accounting for unobserved heterogeneity at a fine scale, using the section as the spatial unit of analysis takes advantage of high-resolution weather data, thus avoiding the problem of generating aggregated precipitation variables with relatively small variation. We discuss this further in the "Data" subsection in section 3.3.

6. We omit data from 2008 in generating the main results, as there is some ambiguity about whether the SURE program was operating prior to the March 15 deadline for crop insurance decisions in 2008.

We find limited evidence of selection on moral hazard in expenditures on crop insurance premiums in response to preplant precipitation. In both Iowa and Illinois, the SURE treatment effects for both corn insurance premiums and corn acres have the same sign and (in seven of eight cases) are highly statistically significant. That is, farmers are increasing (decreasing) insurance expenditures on corn when they increase (decrease) corn acres. The results for expenditures on soybean insurance premiums in both Iowa and Illinois are somewhat weaker, as they follow soybeans acres in sign and significance on one side of the precipitation thresholds, but not both sides, in the piecewise linear regressions. Precipitation varies more spatially than does temperature such that the use of county-level data on preplant precipitation in the insurance regressions may explain these few differences across the acreage and insurance results. Insurance regressions are not estimated for Nebraska and North Dakota, as the crop insurance data are problematic for those states.[7]

Our chapter is related to three strands of literature: adaptation to weather variation and climate change, risk-taking behavior as a moral hazard of insurance, and selection on moral hazard in insurance coverage. A growing literature addresses adaptation to climate change by economic agents in various sectors—for example, agriculture, energy consumption, and human health.[8] As in our chapter, most of this research uses historical data to estimate the impact of extreme weather as a basis to understand prospective adaptation to future climate change. In the agricultural sector, negative effects on crop yields are caused by extreme heat during the growing season (Schlenker and Roberts 2009), drought (Lobell et al. 2014), and extremely wet planting conditions (Urban et al. 2015). Our study differs in three regards: (i) it examines cropping patterns as a mechanism of adaptation[9] instead of crop yield as an outcome of adaptation; (ii) it focuses on an intermediate-run production perspective by analyzing the cropping pattern decision, in contrast to the very-short-run (growing season) and short-run (planting-growing season) perspectives of the aforementioned studies; and (iii) it uses high-resolution spatial data on land use and weather instead of relying solely on county-level data.

Our chapter is also related to the extensive empirical literature on moral

---

7. Annan and Schlenker (2015) describe these problems with the crop insurance data. We discuss this in more detail in the "Data" subsection in section 3.3.

8. Related literature includes Deschênes and Greenstone (2007); Schlenker and Roberts (2009); Fisher et al. (2012); and Urban et al. (2015) on agriculture; Davis and Gertler (2015) and Mansur et al. (2008) on energy consumption; and Barreca et al. (2016) and Deschênes and Greenstone (2011) on human health.

9. Our research is similar to that of Kala (2017), Khanal et al. (2017), Miller (2014), and Rosenzweig and Udry (2014), all of whom study farmer adaptation to expected precipitation during the growing season in the context of developing economies. Our research also relates to recent studies that conduct randomized controlled trials to elicit the effect of rainfall insurance programs on farmers' response to weather risk (Cole et al. 2017; Karlan et al. 2014; Mobarak and Rosenzweig 2014). Our results are consistent with their findings that a risk-management program induces farmers to switch to production of riskier crops.

hazard in insurance markets (see, for example, Einav, Finkelstein, and Levin 2010; Finkelstein 2015). In the agricultural sector, Weber, Key, and O'Donoghue (2016) review research related to moral hazard in the crop insurance market. Two studies reach contrary conclusions on the topic. Weber, Key, and O'Donoghue (2016) find no evidence of moral hazard with respect to crop productivity, crop specialization, and input use, while Roberts, O'Donoghue, and Key (2014) find such evidence with respect to crop yield. Deryugina and Kirwan (2018) find that expectations of agricultural disaster aid affect the crop insurance decision, a type of moral hazard. Our study is most similar to that of Annan and Schlenker (2015), who are the first to connect the two topics of adaptation to weather and moral hazard in insurance. They find that crop insurance gives farmers a disincentive to reduce damage to crop yields from extreme heat. Insurance thus perversely makes farmers less responsive to the weather (moral hazard).

A key feature of our chapter is the study of moral hazard's hidden action—for instance, planting corn after experiencing extreme preplant precipitation—instead of the outcome of the hidden action. Other research, in contrast, commonly assesses an outcome of the action instead of the action itself. For example, Einav et al. (2013) study the response in health insurance utilization to increased insurance coverage as a form of moral hazard; they do not study individuals' efforts in maintaining their health.[10] Similarly, Annan and Schlenker (2015) examine the effect of crop insurance coverage on crop yield; they do not study farmers' reduction in input use as the mechanism for explaining lower yield.[11] In our case, data on preplant precipitation are not recorded in an insurance contract. Thus the choice of which crop to grow, conditional on preplant precipitation, is not observed by the insurance company. From the vantage point of the analyst, our unique data set translates this choice from unobservable to observable at a high degree of spatial resolution in the PLSS section.

Lastly, our chapter is related to research by Einav et al. (2013), who conduct the first study of selection on moral hazard. Moral hazard and adverse selection are conventionally analyzed as distinct phenomena of insurance markets, but Einav et al. connect the two by investigating an individual's

---

10. Einav et al. (2013) write of the "abuse of terminology" related to the notion of "moral hazard" used in the literature on health insurance. They note that "moral hazard" should refer to a hidden action that would affect an individual's health status. Beginning with Arrow (1963), however, "moral hazard" has instead referred to the responsiveness of health-care spending to insurance coverage. Only by assumption does health-care spending relate directly to health status and moral-hazard behavior. In this general context, Einav et al. (2013) follow convention by defining "moral hazard" as the price elasticity of demand for health care rather than as a hidden action that would affect health status.

11. Annan and Schlenker (2015) argue that an increase in insurance coverage caused a decrease in yield as a consequence of unobserved moral-hazard behavior. They rule out, albeit indirectly, that the lower yield is due to insuring lower-quality land through the crop insurance market.

selection of insurance coverage dependent on the expected behavioral response to the coverage. Here we complement our focus on moral hazard in cropping pattern by examining the effect of preplant precipitation on crop insurance take-up—that is, whether crop insurance coverage shifts in response to SURE's reduced deductibles in the same way as cropping pattern. This is a new perspective on adverse selection in the crop insurance market. Adverse selection is no longer considered to be a major concern in this market due to risk adjustment in contract pricing—that is, setting insurance premiums based on farm-level data on historical crop yields and insurance claims (Du, Feng, and Hennessy 2017).[12] Our research reconsiders the possibility of adverse selection in crop insurance based on asymmetric information about how preplant precipitation affects cropping pattern. In doing so, we follow Einav et al.'s (2013) recommendation for research into selection on moral hazard in a context other than health insurance.

The interdependent topics of adaptation, moral hazard, and selection on moral hazard relate to significant public policy issues. Understanding farmers' adaptation to weather risk is essential for designing government programs to efficiently deal with the risk (Mendelsohn 2000). The importance and cost of these programs might only increase given that episodes of extreme weather are likely to increase under a changing climate.

The rest of the chapter proceeds as follows: Section 3.2 describes the relevant background. Section 3.3 describes the empirical strategy and data. Section 3.4 reports preliminary material on the effect of preplant precipitation on crop yields—this sets the stage for the main results. Section 3.5 presents the main regression results on land use, including adaptation and moral hazard in response to preplant precipitation. Section 3.6 presents the main regression results on crop insurance take-up and how it relates to land use—that is, selection on moral hazard. Section 3.7 describes robustness checks on the land-use results. Section 3.8 offers concluding remarks.

3.2 Background

3.2.1 Precipitation and Crop Growth in the Midwest

Crops need water to grow. The amount of water available for crop growth in rain-fed agriculture depends on the interaction between precipitation and the water-holding capacity of soil. In the Midwest, the amount of rainfall is usually favorable, and the soil is deep with a high water-holding capacity such that cultivated crops can grow without irrigation. Compared to other crops, corn is sensitive to water stress (Steduto et al. 2012). Anderson, Wang, and

---

12. Risk adjustment—the standard approach to mitigating adverse selection—is executed by setting insurance premiums based on observable characteristics of the buyer that predict his or her insurance claims (Einav et al. 2013).

Zhao (2012) compare the sensitivity of crop growth to water input and report that corn's average sensitivity to water is greater than the sensitivity of other major crops in the region (soybeans, wheat, and alfalfa). Thus when farmers expect extreme precipitation, they may substitute other crops for corn.[13]

Precipitation both prior to the growing season and during the growing season is important for crop growth, as this total supply provides the water to crops. Relative to growing-season precipitation, preplant precipitation provides three distinct influences on farmers' cropping pattern decisions. First, preplant precipitation can affect root growth. Precipitation from October through April is important in this region for recharging soil moisture. By recharging soil, preplant precipitation is then available as water to enhance root growth during the growing season (Neild and Newman 1990).

Second, preplant precipitation can affect crop growth through indirect mechanisms. For example, Iowa experienced exceptionally warm winters in 2011 and 2012. The resulting lower preplant precipitation affected insect ecology and water quality, which contributed to poor crop production in those years (Al-Kaisi et al. 2013). At the other extreme, excess preplant precipitation can increase the risk of seedling diseases. Farmers may extend the planting period in response to excess preplant precipitation, but this increases the risk of foregoing yield in the late summer (Steduto et al. 2012; Urban et al. 2015).

Third, preplant precipitation can affect farmers' expectation of total water available for crop growth. In this region, positive (negative) snowfall anomalies in winter are associated with wetter (drier) than normal conditions during the summer (Quiring and Kluver 2009). Our precipitation data also support this relationship. Thus the realized lower (higher) precipitation prior to the growing season signals to farmers a higher likelihood of experiencing drier (wetter) conditions for crop growth.

3.2.2   Crop Insurance

Since the 1980s, the US government has relied on two policy tools, crop insurance and ad hoc crop disaster payments, to help farmers recover from financial losses due to natural disasters (Chite 2008). Two advantages of crop insurance, according to policymakers, are its ability to replace costly disaster payments and to assist more producers. Relative to disaster payments, insurance is also viewed as providing lower incentives for moral hazard and for planting crops on marginal lands (Glauber and Collins 2002).[14] To increase participation rates, subsidy provisions for crop insurance thus were included

---

13. In table 2 of Anderson, Wang, and Zhao (2012), the index of water-use efficiency (WUE) is compared across major US crops. The WUE index is a proxy for a crop's average sensitivity to water. The index for corn is set at 1.0 as a benchmark. The indexes of other major crops in our study region are as follows: 0.65 for soybeans, 0.71 for wheat, and 0.43 for alfalfa. The smaller values indicate that, relative to corn, growth of these crops is less sensitive to water input.

14. Deryugina and Kirwan (2018) examine the relationship between crop insurance and disaster payments. They find that expected disaster payments affect producers' crop-insurance decisions.

in major legislative programs in 1980, 1994, and 2000, with the expectation of reducing reliance on disaster payments (Shields and Chite 2010).

The crop insurance market blends private incentives and government intervention.[15] On the demand side, farmers purchase insurance by crop and pay premiums adjusted to their own historical crop yields and insurance claims. Farmers select either yield-based insurance or revenue-based insurance, where the latter includes both yield and crop price provisions. Farmers also select coverage levels. These range in five-unit intervals from 55 percent to 85 percent, and in some regions only to 75 percent, for yield coverage and the yield provision of revenue-based insurance. The percentages are relative to a benchmark of 100 percent of the farm's historical average yield of the crop. For the price provision, coverage levels range in five-unit intervals from 60 percent to 100 percent. These percentages are relative to a 100 percent benchmark set by the expected market price, as determined on futures markets. A larger coverage level naturally translates into a higher premium for insuring a given acreage of a crop. A larger coverage level also translates into a smaller deductible—that is, the deductible equals 100 percent minus the coverage percent.

Here we study the demand side of crop insurance using expenditures on premiums as the outcome variable. In 2014, farmers paid $3.79 billion in premiums to insure 294 million acres of crops (Shields 2015). Nationally, this covered the vast majority of planted acreage of corn (87 percent), soybeans (88 percent), and wheat (84 percent).

The supply side of the crop insurance market relies on private insurance companies operating with substantial government intervention. Nineteen companies sell crop insurance to farmers, yet they function under the purview of USDA's Risk Management Agency (RMA) and its Federal Crop Insurance Corporation (FCIC). The FCIC strictly limits the type of policies that can be sold, and it derives formulas for premium rates that are developed in the context of the federal government's subsidy provisions. In 2014, the crop-insurance subsidy totaled $6.27 billion. Thus the farmer-paid premiums of $3.79 billion (38 percent) plus the $6.27 billion in subsidy (62 percent) equaled the gross insurance premiums, $10.06 billion. Both private and public expenditures on crop insurance are substantial.

3.2.3   The Supplemental Revenue Assistance Payments Program

The crop insurance program, by the mid-2000s, had failed to replace disaster payments despite substantial growth in its participation rates.[16] To

---

15. Shields (2015) provides an excellent introduction to crop insurance, including its type of products, institutional setting, and historical experience in the United States. We rely on this for many of the details here.

16. The US Congress continued to establish ad hoc disaster assistance primarily through emergency supplemental appropriations. Thirty-nine acts established disaster payments to farmers between 1989 and 2007, and such payments were provided every year during this period (Chite 2010).

further promote crop insurance, the US Congress authorized a new program in the 2008 Farm Bill, the SURE program (Shields 2010). The SURE program supplemented crop insurance by compensating producers for so-called shallow losses—that is, losses that were part of a policy's deductible. To be eligible for a SURE payment, a farmer needed to purchase insurance on all planted crops. Then to qualify for a payment, the farm (i) had to be located in a federally declared disaster county or a county bordering a disaster county or (ii) had to suffer a crop loss that exceeded 50 percent of expected yield. In its formula, the SURE payment increased with the farmer's insured coverage level.

Previous research has argued that the SURE program was likely to encourage moral hazard in farmer decision-making by both reducing the deductible at which payments began and converting to a whole-farm revenue approach. First, SURE payments were initiated when a crop suffered a yield loss of 10 percent or more—that is, farmers could insure 90 percent of their expected yield when SURE payments were combined with insurance indemnities (Glauber 2013; Smith and Watts 2010). This contrasts with the typical maximum of 85 percent coverage of expected yield under crop insurance. This substantial reduction of deductibles under SURE created incentives for risk-taking in crop choice and production. Empirically, Bekkerman, Smith, and Watts (2012) find that the SURE program markedly increased insurance participation rates, measured by the ratio of net insured acres to total planted acres at the county level.

Second, SURE payments were based on a whole-farm revenue approach, whereas prior to 2008, payments were based on crop-specific losses. To take advantage of SURE payments, farmers might eliminate crops from their rotations, thereby reducing the diversity inherent in a portfolio of crops (Shields 2010). Growing a single crop might increase the chance that a farm would drop below its guaranteed revenue threshold at which program payments were triggered. Therefore, changes in crop-choice decisions could be evidence of response to the program's incentives.

Payments to farmers were substantial under the SURE program. Bekkerman, Smith, and Watts (2012) report that $2.11 billion in SURE payments were made for low production in 2008, which is about five times higher than the Congressional Budget Office's original estimated annual payments under the program, $425 million (CBO 2011). The US Government Accountability Office reports total SURE payments of $2.52 billion for fiscal years 2008 to 2012 (USGAO 2014).

The SURE program ran for only a short time, 2008 through 2011. The program's timeline suggests that farmers did not make 2008 planting decisions with information about the program. At the same time, farmers later received SURE payments for 2008 crop losses. We excluded 2008 from the main analysis because of this ambiguity about program timing relative to farmer decision-making.

3.3   Empirical Strategy

This section includes three parts: a simple conceptual motivation of land-use and insurance decision-making under weather risk; description of the econometric models for studying land use, insurance take-up, and crop yield; and description of the data.

3.3.1   Conceptual Motivation

We motivate the econometric analysis of land use and insurance take-up with a simple stylized example that considers farmer decision-making faced with growing-season weather risk. It begins with conditions prior to the SURE program and continues with an extension to the SURE program. For the sake of illustration, we consider a farmer's choice to plant wheat or corn on a North Dakota farm.

Pre-SURE program. March 15 is the deadline for purchasing crop insurance. The farmer will purchase insurance in any case in our example; but because the insurance is crop specific, the insurance decision is, in fact, the decision on which crop to grow—wheat or corn.

The farmer observes preplant precipitation on March 15. Preplant precipitation is the signal for soil moisture conditions in early May (the window for planting) and for precipitation during the growing season. Here we posit that preplant precipitation is relatively low on March 15, and this signal creates conditional probabilities of two precipitation outcomes for the planting and growing seasons. Only two outcomes are considered for ease of exposition.

State of nature 1: adequate precipitation for growing both wheat and corn (at probability p_1)

State of nature 2: adequate precipitation for growing wheat, but low precipitation for growing corn (at probability $(1 - p_1)$).

Profit is generated from allocating cropland to either wheat (W) or corn (C). Expected profit, by crop, encompasses profit (π) under the two states of nature. These are

$$E\pi^W = p_1\pi_1^W + (1 - p_1)\pi_2^W$$

and

$$E\pi^C = p_1\pi_1^C + (1 - p_1)\pi_2^C.$$

We posit that, given the relatively low preplant precipitation, the expected profit from growing wheat exceeds the expected profit from growing corn, or

$$E\pi^W > E\pi^C.$$

The farmer thus allocates cropland to wheat, not corn, given corn yield's sensitivity to water input. In extrapolating to our empirical analysis, we expect wheat acres to increase and corn acres to decrease as preplant precipitation decreases to a level of water deficit in North Dakota. The farmer also purchases crop insurance for wheat, not corn.

SURE program. In the hypothetical, the SURE program reduces the deductible on crop insurance; farms with yield losses in the 75 percent to 90 percent range of historical yields now qualify for SURE payments. We suppose, on the farm considered here, that corn yield is below 90 percent of historical yield in state of nature 2. Conventional profit from corn is now augmented with a SURE payment, with the new profit designated as $\pi_2^{C'}$. With $\pi_2^{C'} > \pi_2^C$, we posit that corn production now generates higher expected profit than wheat, or

$$E\pi^{C'} = p_1\pi_1^C + (1 - p_1)\pi_2^{C'} > E\pi^W.$$

The farmer changes crops, now allocating cropland to corn, not wheat. This illustrates the moral hazard created by the SURE program: the farmer is taking a risk on corn. The farmer also purchases crop insurance for corn, not wheat. Once again extrapolating to the empirical analysis, we expect the program to increase corn acres and decrease wheat acres—relative to preprogram levels—over the range of relatively low preplant precipitation levels. In addition, we expect insurance coverage to increase on corn, reflecting selection on moral hazard. These are the type of treatment effects expected from the SURE program.

3.3.2 Piecewise Linear Regression Models

Our study area includes four major agricultural states in the Midwest: the entire states of Iowa and Illinois and the regions east of the 100th meridian in North Dakota and Nebraska that rely on rain-fed farming. The study encompasses 2001 to 2014. By beginning in 2001, we avoid the period prior to the major change in crop insurance policy (substantially increasing premium subsidies) that was enacted in 2000 with the Agricultural Risk Protection Act. We span the SURE program years, 2009 to 2011, which enables analysis of the postprogram period as part of the research design. By ending in 2014, we avoid a new supplemental insurance program that was enacted in the Agricultural Act of 2014 and implemented in 2015.

In the analysis, we exploit random year-to-year variation in preplant precipitation as a natural experiment. Preplant precipitation operates as a continuous treatment variable, with the treatment intensity varying across the observed range of preplant precipitation. In tandem with the weather experiment, we utilize the SURE program's shock to insurance deductibles as a quasi experiment. The identifying assumption of the estimation strategy for SURE treatment effects is that local preplant precipitation shocks are exogenous to the policy changes in 2009 and 2012. We find no evidence that our preplant precipitation variable and the policy changes are correlated. More generally, it is unlikely that annual preplant precipitation caused a policy change such as the SURE program or that the SURE program caused a change in preplant precipitation.

Land-use regressions. Previous research has demonstrated a strong non-linearity in the relationship between precipitation during the growing season and crop-yield outcomes (Annan and Schlenker 2015; Burke and Emerick 2015; Schlenker and Roberts 2009). These findings—that both water shortage and water excess affect yield negatively—motivate our approach to investigating whether farmers adjust cropping pattern based on realized preplant precipitation. Many of the previous studies use higher-order terms of precipitation to capture the nonlinear effect. However, using these functional forms in a panel setting means that a unit-specific mean reenters the estimation, raising omitted variables concerns, as identification in the panel models is no longer limited to location-specific variations over time (McIntosh and Schlenker 2006). We instead use a piecewise linear approach, following Schlenker and Roberts (2009) and Burke and Emerick (2015). This allows us to identify the effects of both risks—water shortage and water excess—on farmers' cropping pattern response to preplant precipitation. Our use of high-resolution spatial data on land use and weather facilitates estimation of a flexible model that can detect nonlinearities and thresholds in the effect of preplant precipitation on land allocation to crops.

We model log planted acres of a crop in section i, state s, and year t ($cropacre_{ist}$) as a piecewise linear function of preplant precipitation with a threshold (or kink) at p_0. The effect of the new SURE program in 2009 on cropping pattern adaptation to precipitation risk is identified with the interaction term between our preplant precipitation variable $prec_{it}$ and a policy dummy $d09_t$ equal to 1 if the year is 2009 to 2011. Similarly, the effect of the termination of the SURE program on cropping pattern adaptation to precipitation risk is identified with the interaction term between $prec_{it}$ and a policy dummy $d12_t$ equal to 1 if the year is 2012 or later. We estimate the fixed effects model

$$(1) \quad cropacre_{ist} = \alpha + \beta_1 prec_{it;p<p_0} + \beta_2 prec_{it;p<p_0} d09_t + \beta_3 prec_{it;p<p_0} d12_t$$
$$+ \beta_4 prec_{it;p>p_0} + \beta_5 prec_{it;p>p_0} d09_t + \beta_6 prec_{it;p>p_0} d12_t$$
$$+ \gamma temp_{it} + X\theta + \mu_i + \delta_t + g_s(t) + \epsilon_{ist},$$

where the variable $prec_{it;p<p_0}$ is the difference between preplant precipitation and p_0 interacted with an indicator variable for preplant precipitation being below the threshold p_0. $prec_{it;p>p_0}$ is similarly defined for preplant precipitation above the threshold. We allow the data to determine p_0 by looping over all possible thresholds and selecting the model with the lowest sum of squared residuals. The variable $temp_{it}$ is the average preplant temperature from October 1 to March 15. X is a vector of control variables, including planting-season precipitation, temperature, and future crop price. The planting-season variables control for the fact that farmers may revise land-use decisions subsequent to March 15 based on updated weather conditions. The μ_i are section fixed effects that control for unobserved time-invariant characteristics that affect cropland use, such as climate and soil quality. Because the PLSS aligns with patterns of farm ownership and management, the section fixed effects can also control for unobserved farmer characteristics such as management skills and risk perception (Holmes and Lee 2012). Year fixed effects δ_t account for unobserved common year-specific effects across sections, such as crop prices, and statewide and national policies, such as crop insurance premiums and biofuel policies. Similar to Annan and Schlenker (2015), we include $g_s(t)$ as a quadratic time trend, by state, to control for trends in agricultural technologies (such as seed types or drainage capital) that might affect yields and related land-use decisions.

The parameters of interest are the set of $\boldsymbol{\beta}$. β_1 and β_4 provide estimates of how farmers' crop acreage decisions respond to preplant precipitation prior to the SURE program both below and above the threshold, respectively; these parameters estimate adaptation. β_2 and β_5 provide estimates of the SURE treatment effects, or how farmers *change* their response to preplant precipitation under the SURE program; these parameters estimate moral hazard. Hence $\beta_1 + \beta_2$ and $\beta_4 + \beta_5$ provide estimates of how farmers respond to preplant precipitation under the SURE program below and above the threshold, respectively. β_3 and β_6 provide estimates of how farmers *change* their response after the SURE program relative to during the program. $\beta_1 + \beta_2 + \beta_3$ and $\beta_4 + \beta_5 + \beta_6$ provide estimates of how farmers respond to preplant precipitation after the SURE program both below and above the threshold, respectively. These parameters once again estimate adaptation.

Equation (1) is estimated by crop and by state for Illinois, Iowa, Nebraska, and North Dakota.

An important note with respect to the SURE treatment effects (β_2 and β_5) is that we do not observe purchase of crop insurance at the section level. That is, when observing land use in a section, we do not know whether the crops are insured. Insurance participation rates are quite high in general, with almost 90 percent of US corn, soybean, and wheat acres covered by insurance. Nevertheless, the implication is that the estimated treatment effects are underestimates of the true effects.

Lastly, an ambiguity arises with observations from 2008. The SURE program was part of a policy enacted on May 22, 2008, so it is unlikely that farmers could have included information about the program in insurance and planting decisions by March 15 of 2008. Nevertheless, we exclude observations from 2008 from our main analysis and then include them in the preprogram period in a robustness check.

Insurance take-up regressions. We estimate crop insurance take-up using the same structure of a piecewise linear function. We model log insurance premiums per planted acre of a crop in county c, state s, and year t (*premiums$_{cst}$*) as a piecewise linear function of total preplant precipitation with a threshold at p_0. Here we apply the actual value of the threshold p_0 from the land-use regression as a way to gauge whether the SURE treatment effect on insurance take-up follows the SURE treatment effect on land use (selection on moral hazard). We estimate the fixed effects model

$$(2) \quad premiums_{cst} = \alpha + \beta_1 prec_{ct;p<p_0} + \beta_2 prec_{ct;p<p_0}d09_t + \beta_3 prec_{ct;p<p_0}d12_t$$
$$+ \beta_4 prec_{ct;p>p_0} + \beta_5 prec_{ct;p>p_0}d09_t + \beta_6 prec_{ct;p>p_0}d12_t$$
$$+ \gamma temp_{ct} + X\theta + \mu_c + \delta_t + g_s(t) + \epsilon_{cst},$$

where μ_c are county fixed effects that control for unobserved time-invariant characteristics that affect insurance take-up, such as expected disaster payments in the county or the historical probability of a county being declared a disaster county. Other variables are defined as in equation (1).

The outcome variable in each insurance regression is specified as a rate, premiums divided by total planted acres, and not simply premiums.[17] To demonstrate selection on moral hazard, farmers need to purchase better insurance coverage when, for example, they are increasing acreage in a crop after being treated with the SURE program. With the county-level data, this requires showing increases in insurance coverage per acre of a crop—that is, the rate of insurance must be increasing. Thus the parameters of interest are the SURE treatment effects, β_2 and β_5, and how they compare with the respective β_2 and β_5 for a particular crop from the land-use regressions.

Equation (2) is estimated for corn and soybean insurance premiums by state for Illinois and Iowa.

Crop yield regressions. We estimate crop yield regressions while once again using the same structure of a piecewise linear function. We model log crop yield in county c, state s, and year t (*cropyld$_{cst}$*) as a piecewise linear function of preplant precipitation with a threshold at p_0. We estimate the fixed effects model

$$(3) \quad cropyld_{cst} = \alpha + \beta_1 prec_{ct;p<p_0} + \beta_2 prec_{ct;p<p_0}d09_t + \beta_3 prec_{ct;p<p_0}d12_t$$
$$+ \beta_4 prec_{ct;p>p_0} + \beta_5 prec_{ct;p>p_0}d09_t + \beta_6 prec_{ct;p>p_0}d12_t$$
$$+ \gamma temp_{ct} + X\theta + \mu_c + \delta_t + g_s(t) + \epsilon_{cst},$$

where X is a vector of variables for weather during the planting and growing seasons that serve as controls. We allow the data to determine p_0 by looping

---

17. Deryugina and Kirwan (2018) use premiums as their outcome variable, arguing that it captures both the intensive margin (choice of a discrete coverage level) and extensive margin (insured acres) of crop insurance. Annan and Schlenker (2015) use the rate of insurance, insured acres divided by total planted acres.

over all possible thresholds and selecting the model with the lowest sum of squared residuals. Other variables are defined as in equations (1) and (2).

Equation (3) is estimated for corn and soybean yields using data pooled across Illinois, Iowa, and eastern North Dakota. Once again, the parameters of interest are the set of β, and they are interpreted in a similar way as the β in equation (1). These parameters show the estimated effects of preplant precipitation on crop yields.

3.3.3   Data

The unit of analysis for studying land use is the PLSS section, which is a 1 × 1 mile square piece of land. We use a geographic information system (GIS) data layer to define sections (ESRI 2015). By state, the number of sections is as follows: Illinois, 45,372; Iowa, 50,020; Nebraska, 14,426; and North Dakota, 27,151 (table 3.1). Sections in eastern North Dakota and eastern Nebraska with irrigated land are excluded.[18] Following Schlenker et al. (2005), the analysis focuses solely on rain-fed farming.

The unit of analysis for studying insurance take-up and crop yield is the county. By state, the number of counties is as follows: Illinois, 102; Iowa, 99; and North Dakota, 28. The county-level statistical analysis excludes eastern Nebraska because of its preponderance of irrigated agriculture; almost two-thirds of PLSS sections in eastern Nebraska rely on irrigation.

Land-use data. The land-use data are from the National Agricultural Statistics Service (NASS)'s Cropland Data Layer (CDL) program, which provides high-resolution geospatial data on crops planted and other types of land cover for the United States.[19] For the four states, we constructed a balanced panel of planted acres by crop within the 640 acre PLSS sections from 2001 to 2014 (2002 to 2014 for Nebraska). The section-level data are generated by summing over the CDL grids within each section.

Table 3.1 presents summary statistics for mean acreage by state for corn, soybeans, spring wheat, and grassland, averaged over the sections and study period. The most common crops in North Dakota are spring wheat and soybeans, which sum to 228 acres per section. Corn is the most common crop in Illinois and Iowa, with soybeans also grown at high levels. Grassland is a major type of land cover in all four states, especially in North Dakota and Nebraska. Grassland is a single land-cover category, not a crop. Since CDL data are less reliable for differentiating among several land-cover types— including alfalfa, fallow/idle cropland, unmanaged grassland, pasture, and hay—these land covers are combined into a single *grassland* category.

---

18. Data on the sections with irrigated agriculture are from the 250-meter scale irrigation map in 2007 from the Moderate Resolution Imaging Spectroradiometer (MODIS) Irrigated Agriculture Dataset for the United States (MIrAD-US). See Brown and Pervez (2014) for documentation.

19. Donaldson and Storeygard (2016) highlight the CDL as an example of high-resolution satellite data with promising potential for application in economics.

Table 3.1 **Summary statistics**

		North Dakota			Iowa		
	Unit	Mean	Median	Std. dev.	Mean	Median	Std. dev.
Panel (A): Section-level variables for land-use regressions							
Corn acreage[a]	acre	49.51	6.75	88.29	222.85	222.30	134.61
Soybean acreage[a]	acre	118.74	71.10	132.80	170.63	162.23	116.05
Spring wheat acreage[a]	acre	110.49	72.13	120.68	0.10	0	1.79
Grassland acreage[a]	acre	196.52	149.85	172.58	151.82	111.83	131.21
Preplant precipitation[b]	mm	127.99	122.04	47.49	226.37	218.53	67.36
Preplant temperature[b]	°C	−6.19	−6.55	2.24	−0.65	−0.68	2.13
Planting precipitation[b]	mm	152.07	148.41	47.01	251.71	240.75	70.17
Planting temperature[b]	°C	7.12	7.43	2.21	11.04	11.03	1.85
Sections		27,151			50,020		
Observations		352,963			650,260		

		Illinois			Nebraska		
Corn acreage[a]	acre	194.71	181.10	146.88	68.95	9.68	99.23
Soybean acreage[a]	acre	157.77	145.13	119.55	55.51	1.35	90.68
Spring wheat acreage[a]	acre	0	0	0.30	0.01	0	0.51
Grassland acreage[a]	acre	102.67	74.70	97.40	433.52	501.76	199.43
Preplant precipitation[b]	mm	380.52	360.06	108.55	156.29	145.84	52.11
Preplant temperature[b]	°C	2.74	2.77	2.28	0.70	0.77	1.68
Planting precipitation[b]	mm	264.72	248.42	93.95	203.47	198.75	73.84
Planting temperature[b]	°C	13.31	13.35	1.97	11.29	11.22	1.87
Sections		45,372			14,426		
Observations		589,836			173,112		

		Iowa			Illinois[f]		
Panel (B): County-level variables for insurance demand regressions							
Corn insurance premiums[d]	1,000 $	3,982	3,361	2,625	3,567	2,589	3,223
Soybean insurance premiums[d]	1,000 $	1,814	1,591	1,153	1,558	1,217	1,281
Corn premiums per acre[e]	$/acre	31.05	29.44	17.10	29.79	28.79	17.93
Soybean premiums per acre[e]	$/acre	18.94	16.94	10.31	17.16	15.67	11.15
Preplant precipitation[b]	mm	226.93	218.50	67.57	389.16	366.63	114.88
Preplant temperature[b]	°C	−0.36	−0.37	2.18	3.17	3.20	2.37
Planting precipitation[b]	mm	252.08	240.06	69.65	267.56	250.42	96.31
Planting temperature[b]	°C	11.67	11.64	1.89	14.04	14.10	2.03
Counties		99			102		
Observations		1,287			1,291		

[a] Authors' calculations with the Cropland Data Layer, 2001–2014.

[b] Authors' calculations with Schlenker and Roberts (2009) weather data, 2001–2014.

[c] Authors' calculations with the Soil Survey Geographic (SSURGO) database. Larger values indicate poorer soil quality. See the appendix for our calculation of weighted land capability at the section level.

[d] Authors' calculations with the Risk Management Agency's Summary of Business Reports and Data, 2001–2014.

[e] Premiums divided by planted acres by crop. Data on planted acres are from the National Agricultural Statistics Service.

[f] The number of observations for corn in Illinois is 1,285. Summary statistics of preplant and planting precipitation and temperature for the sample of corn in Illinois are very similar to the values reported here using the 1,291 observations from the soybean sample in Illinois.

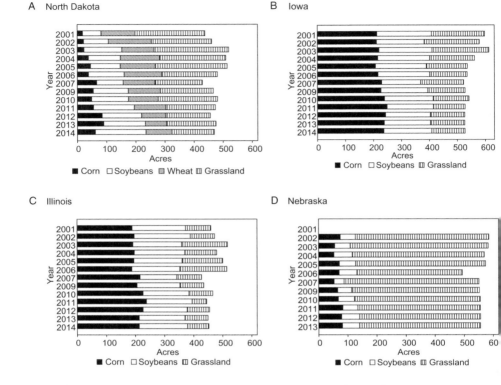

Fig. 3.1   Average cropland and grassland acres at the section level

Notes: The graphs display acreages of major types of cropland use across years. Data at the section level are extracted from the Cropland Data Layer. Panels (A)–(D) use nonirrigated PLSS sections.

Figure 3.1 displays acreages of major types of cropland use across years. On average, acreages of corn and soybeans in North Dakota are larger after 2012 than from 2009 to 2011, which are larger than those before 2008. The differences could be driven by the price effects of biofuel policy, which we control for with year fixed effects. Acreages of corn and soybeans are relatively stable across the three periods in other states. Grassland acreage decreases after 2008 in all states, especially in North Dakota, where it decreases over time for the entire study period.

Weather data (section level). The weather data are an updated version of those used in Schlenker and Roberts (2009), which consist of daily precipitation and maximum and minimum temperatures at 4 × 4 kilometer grid cells in the United States from 1950 to 2014. For each cell, preplant precipitation is the accumulated precipitation from October 1 in the previous year to March 15 in the current year—that is, precipitation from the end of the previous growing season through the deadline for purchasing crop insurance. Preplant temperature is computed by averaging daily average temperature over the same period. Planting-season precipitation is the accumulated precipitation from March 16 to May 31 for Iowa, Illinois, and Nebraska and from March 15 to June 15 for North Dakota. Planting-season temperature is the average of daily temperatures over these same periods. To match the spatial delineation of the land-use data, these four data series are converted to the section level by averaging each series over the intersected cells.

Using the section as the unit of analysis takes advantage of the high-resolution precipitation data. While temperature is a large-scale weather event, precipitation tends to be a microscale event—that is, precipitation intrinsically varies more spatially because local vegetation and geography can affect it. Use of aggregated weather data may result in small variation in precipitation variables.[20]

Mean preplant precipitations in North Dakota and Nebraska are 127.99 mm and 156.29 mm, respectively, which is substantially lower than the 226.37 mm of Iowa and 380.52 mm of Illinois (table 3.1). Illinois also has relatively larger variation in preplant precipitation. Using the raw data, figure 3.2 presents different forms of the nonlinear relationship between preplant precipitation and corn acreage for each state during the three periods: before 2008, 2009 to 2011, and 2012 to 2014. In North Dakota, for example, relatively low preplant precipitation occurred from 2001 to 2007 and after 2012, while relatively high preplant precipitation occurred from 2009 to 2011, as can be seen in panel (A). In Illinois and Iowa, figure 3.2 shows that the relationships between preplant precipitation and corn acreage are somewhat similar across the three periods. In North Dakota and Nebraska, in contrast, the relationships between preplant precipitation and corn acreage from 2009 to 2011 appear very different from those during the other two periods.

One concern with the land-use regressions is that the section and year fixed effects can absorb a significant amount of the variation in the preplant precipitation variables (Fisher et al. 2012). Following Fisher et al. (2012), we explore how much of the variation is absorbed by the fixed effects. The appendix reports results showing that substantial residual variation exists to implement our approach (table 3A.2). This conclusion is reinforced by the standard errors on the various estimated coefficients on the preplant precipitation variable in the (subsequent) land-use regressions.

Weather data (county level). We also use the same raw data to produce county-level weather data for the crop insurance regressions and the yield

---

20. Mearns et al. (2001) and Fezzi and Bateman (2015) show that climate impact studies that use aggregated precipitation data to analyze a large spatial scale (such as county level or country level) may fail to capture the high variation of precipitation and thus may underestimate its importance.

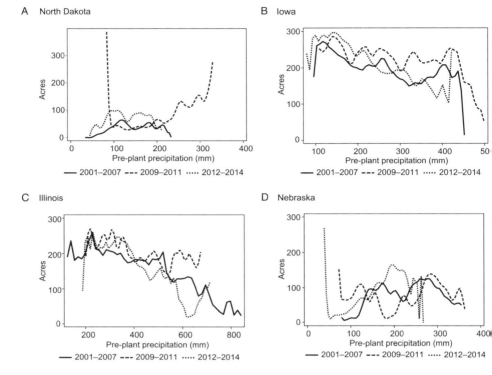

Fig. 3.2   Relationship between corn acres and preplant precipitation

Notes: These plots are generated by kernel-weighted local polynomial smoothing with the following settings: kernel = epan2, degree = 3, and bandwidth = 20. Data at the section level are extracted from the cropland data layer and Schlenker and Roberts (2009) weather data. Panels (A)–(D) use nonirrigated PLSS sections. Preplant precipitation is in millimeters.

regressions. For the crop insurance regressions, the four county-level weather variables are preplant precipitation, preplant temperature, planting-season precipitation, and planting-season temperature. Their summary statistics are reported for the states with insurance regressions, Illinois and Iowa (table 3.1).

County-level weather data are also produced for the yield regressions for the relevant states: Illinois, Iowa, and eastern North Dakota. Seven variables are developed: preplant precipitation, preplant temperature, planting-season precipitation, planting-season temperature, growing-season precipitation, growing-season temperature, and the daily maximum temperatures during July. Summary statistics for the three-state region are reported in the appendix (table 3A.3).

Insurance data. County-level administrative data on insurance premiums are from the RMA. We use the dollar value of premiums paid by farmers.[21] These data cover corn and soybeans in Illinois and Iowa. Our dependent variable in the insurance regressions is premiums divided by total planted acres of the respective crop, or dollars per acre. County-level data on total planted acres are from the NASS. Summary statistics are reported in table 3.1.

We exclude North Dakota from the state-based analysis of insurance premiums. With only 28 counties, eastern North Dakota presents challenges for obtaining accurate regression estimates. More important, the crop insurance data are of questionable quality in North Dakota. The data were first questioned by Annan and Schlenker (2015), who were concerned with data on total planted acres. To understand this further, we display data on insured acres from RMA versus planted acres from NASS (figure 3.3). Beginning in 2008 and continuing through 2014, the number of insured acres equaled and, in several years, greatly exceeded planted acres for corn and soybeans in the state. For this reason, we do not estimate insurance take-up regressions for the crops in North Dakota.[22]

Futures price data. National data on futures prices for corn, soybeans, and wheat are from the RMA. They represent monthly average prices for February of the current growing season. These are the prices used in the formulas for revenue-based insurance of these respective crops. Thus futures price variables may help explain both land-use and insurance decisions.

Yield data. County-level data on crop yields of corn and soybeans in bushels per acre are from the NASS. Summary statistics are reported in the appendix for the study region of Illinois, Iowa, and eastern North Dakota (table 3A.3). Wheat yield is not studied, as wheat is not one of our crops in Illinois and Iowa. Similarly, grassland is not studied; grassland is an amalgamation of land covers and so does not have related yield data.

3.4   Preliminary Considerations: Does Preplant Precipitation Affect Crop Yield?

We begin with preliminary analysis that examines the effect of preplant precipitation on crop yields. The intent is to establish that preplant precipitation affects crop yields—that is, that there is an empirical justification for farmers to include preplant precipitation in decision-making. We pool the county-level data from 2001 to 2014 across three states: Illinois, Iowa, and North Dakota (with North Dakota limited to counties in the eastern part

---

21. Premiums paid by farmers are relevant for decision-making, while the premium subsidy paid by the federal government is not.

22. The difference between planted acres and insured acres could be explained by "acres prevented from planting" before the planting deadline under the crop insurance program. Additional research on this topic is needed to understand the incentive that crop insurance provides not to plant acres and how that interacts with preplant weather.

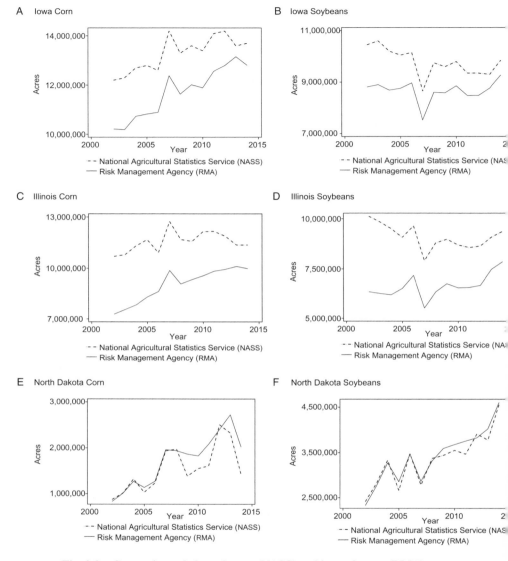

A   Iowa Corn

- - National Agricultural Statistics Service (NASS)
—— Risk Management Agency (RMA)

B   Iowa Soybeans

- - National Agricultural Statistics Service (NAS
—— Risk Management Agency (RMA)

C   Illinois Corn

- - National Agricultural Statistics Service (NASS)
—— Risk Management Agency (RMA)

D   Illinois Soybeans

- - National Agricultural Statistics Service (NA
—— Risk Management Agency (RMA)

E   North Dakota Corn

- - National Agricultural Statistics Service (NASS)
—— Risk Management Agency (RMA)

F   North Dakota Soybeans

- - National Agricultural Statistics Service (NAS
—— Risk Management Agency (RMA)

Fig. 3.3   Comparison of planted acres (NASS) and insured acres (RMA)

Notes: The graphs display planted acres and insured acres for corn and soybeans across years by state. Planted acres are data from the NASS. Insured acres are data from the RMA's Summary of Business Reports and Data. Data for North Dakota only include 28 counties east of the 100th meridian.

of the state).[23] Pooling the data across states is appropriate with yield regressions.[24] We apply equation (3) to estimate piecewise linear regressions for corn yield and soybean yield, using the common structure in our approach to assessing effects before, during, and after the SURE program. In addition to preplant precipitation and preplant temperature, other weather variables (just described) are included as controls. The appendix describes the variables and full results in more detail.

The results show that preplant precipitation affects crop yields with small but significant effects in most cases. Begin with corn yields (table 3A.4 and figure 3A.2). Below the precipitation threshold, the effect of preplant precipitation is positive and highly significant in the pre-SURE phase from 2001 to 2007 and positive but insignificant in the post-SURE phase from 2011 to 2014. Above the threshold, preplant precipitation exerts negative and highly significant effects in both the pre- and post-SURE phases.

Turn next to soybean yields. Below the precipitation threshold, the effect of preplant precipitation is negative and highly significant in the pre-SURE phase and negative but insignificant in the post-SURE phase. Above the threshold, preplant precipitation exerts negative and significant effects in both the pre- and post-SURE phases.

With the SURE program, the respective *changes* in corn yields and soybean yields are positive, with three of four estimated coefficients highly significant on variables that interact the SURE program with preplant precipitation (table 3A.4 and figure 3A.2). This is interesting per se, as it counters intuition that risk-taking during the SURE program will lead to productivity losses. In a separate study, we are investigating soil quality as a possible mechanism to explain this. Farmers might have grown corn and soybeans on land with higher-quality soil during the SURE program.

To summarize: the two yield regressions provide empirical support for the idea that farmers consider preplant precipitation in land-use and insurance take-up decision-making.

23. We exclude our study counties in Nebraska from the analysis of crop yields due to the high rate of irrigation in eastern Nebraska. In these counties, 63.4 percent of the sections are in irrigated agriculture and 36.6 percent are in rain-fed agriculture. This preponderance of irrigation skews the county-level data on crop yields.

24. Pooling the data across states is appropriate with yield regressions but not land-use regressions. With land use, individual farms typically grow more than one crop each season, and multiple crops are competing to be selected for planting in any given field. This competition can vary across states—for example, corn competes with wheat for land use in North Dakota but does not compete with wheat in Iowa. This implies a multioutput technology with tradeoffs that may differ from state to state such that state-specific regressions may be warranted. Yield, in contrast, implies a single-output technology that depends primarily on agronomic considerations in the short run such that pooling data across states is defensible. Empirically, several studies apply data pooled across states when examining the effect of extreme weather on crop yield (e.g., Schlenker and Roberts 2009; Lobell et al. 2014; Urban et al. 2015).

3.5   Results I: Adaptation and Moral Hazard in Land Use

Results from the land-use regressions (equation (1)) are reported in three subsections. The first discusses the main estimation results for a single crop, corn, which is recognized as a water-sensitive crop, and a major crop, in the Midwest. The second discusses results for a single state, North Dakota, which has a diversity of crops and land allocations. The third discusses results for the other three crops and states.

Prior to reporting results, we first explain why we do not pool the data and estimate a single regression for each crop that encompasses the four states. After all, the section fixed effects account for several time-invariant unobservables at the section level, such as soil quality, climate factors, and farm management skills. But our focus on cropping pattern—and the various crop substitutions that result in substantially different acres allocated to a particular crop across states—provides one rationale for the state-level analysis. We can observe this heterogeneity in the average cropland allocations in a section and how those allocations vary across states (figure 3.1).

A second factor favoring state-level regressions is the heterogeneity across states in preplant precipitation thresholds. In the piecewise linear approach, we allow the data for a state to determine each crop's threshold by looping over all possible thresholds based on equation (1) and then selecting the model with the lowest sum of squared residuals. As an example, the thresholds of preplant precipitation for corn vary widely across states: 100 mm in North Dakota, 370 mm in Iowa, 395 mm in Illinois, and 135 mm in Nebraska (table 3.2). With different thresholds, the piecewise linear functions vary substantially across states. Figure 3.4 illustrates this using the regression results for corn.

Overall, we estimate 13 land-use regressions for the four crops across the four states. The effects of preplant precipitation are captured in 77 estimated coefficients, with 51 of these reflecting the interaction with the SURE program and post-SURE program. Of the 77 estimates, 52 are statistically significant—that is, preplant precipitation exerts meaningful causal effects on agricultural land use.

3.5.1   The Effect of Preplant Precipitation on Corn Acres

The regression results for corn show economically and statistically significant responses to preplant precipitation in the study states (table 3.2). Farmers in states with relatively poorer natural capital in their climate and soil conditions[25] were more responsive—these are North Dakota and Nebraska. Farmers in Iowa and Illinois, in contrast, were less responsive to both pre-

---

25. The appendix describes data on soil quality at the section level across the four states. Illinois and Iowa have relatively high soil quality, while Nebraska has the poorest soil quality. Soil quality in North Dakota approaches that of Illinois and Iowa.

Table 3.2   **Land-use estimation results for corn**

	North Dakota (1)	Iowa (2)	Illinois (3)	Nebraska (4)
Preplant precipitation below threshold	−0.010**	−0.000	−0.000	−0.009***
	(0.004)	(0.000)	(0.000)	(0.003)
Preplant precipitation below threshold × after 2008	−0.015	−0.001**	0.001***	0.012***
	(0.041)	(0.000)	(0.000)	(0.003)
Preplant precipitation below threshold × after 2011	0.008	0.000	−0.001**	−0.006***
	(0.042)	(0.000)	(0.000)	(0.002)
Preplant precipitation above threshold	−0.006***	−0.001	−0.001***	−0.005***
	(0.002)	(0.003)	(0.000)	(0.001)
Preplant precipitation above threshold × after 2008	0.009***	0.006**	0.001	0.004***
	(0.002)	(0.003)	(0.000)	(0.001)
Preplant precipitation above threshold × after 2011	−0.010***	−0.010***	−0.001***	0.001
	(0.003)	(0.003)	(0.000)	(0.001)
Preplant temperature	−0.389**	−0.068***	0.013	−0.099*
	(0.151)	(0.023)	(0.049)	(0.056)
Preplant temperature squared	−0.019***	−0.004**	0.001	−0.015**
	(0.005)	(0.002)	(0.003)	(0.007)
Planting precipitation	−0.004	0.001	−0.000	−0.004***
	(0.003)	(0.000)	(0.001)	(0.001)
Planting precipitation squared	0.000	−0.000*	0.000	0.000***
	(0.000)	(0.000)	(0.000)	(0.000)
Planting temperature	−0.047	0.171***	−0.000	0.019
	(0.132)	(0.035)	(0.062)	(0.087)
Planting temperature squared	0.004	−0.006***	0.004**	0.002
	(0.007)	(0.001)	(0.002)	(0.003)
Corn futures price	0.628***	0.192***	0.038	0.157***
	(0.213)	(0.034)	(0.032)	(0.042)
Observations	352,963	650,260	589,836	173,112
R-squared	0.158	0.027	0.026	0.090
Number of PLSS sections	27,151	50,020	45,372	14,426
Threshold of preplant precipitation	100	370	395	135

Notes: Dependent variable in all regressions is the log of corn acres. Regressions estimated using piecewise linear functional form with the fixed effects estimator. Regressions include section fixed effects, year fixed effects, and a quadratic time trend by state. Regressions (1)–(4) use nonirrigated PLSS sections. Standard errors are clustered at the county level and shown in parentheses, and *, **, and *** denote statistical significance at the 10 percent, 5 percent, and 1 percent levels, respectively.

plant precipitation and the interaction of preplant precipitation with the SURE program.

North Dakota: farmers are quite responsive to both preplant precipitation and its interaction with the SURE program. Column (1) of table 3.2 reports the results for corn in North Dakota. Before the policy change in 2009, a 1 mm decrease in preplant precipitation below the threshold decreases corn acreage by 1.0 percent, while a 1 mm increase in preplant precipitation above the threshold decreases corn acreage by 0.6 percent. The results

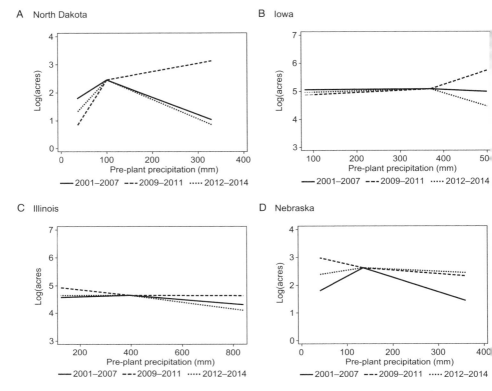

Fig. 3.4   Predicted effects of preplant precipitation on corn acres (by policy regime)
Notes: The graphs display the predicted means of log(corn acres) in the sections as a function of preplant precipitation. Panels (A)–(D) use nonirrigated PLSS sections. Preplant precipitation is in millimeters.

imply that farmers adapted to abnormal preplant precipitation by planting fewer acres in corn. This adaptation strategy was adopted even though the crop insurance program was in place. The program had created moral hazard problems even before 2009 (Roberts, O'Donoghue, and Key 2014).

Under the SURE program from 2009 to 2011, we do not obtain a statistically significant effect below the threshold, perhaps because there are relatively few observations below the threshold in North Dakota during this period. However, above the threshold, a 1 mm increase in preplant precipitation actually *increases* corn acreage by 0.3 percent, which is the sum of the coefficients −0.006 and 0.009. The result suggests that farmers chose to grow corn despite the risk of excess precipitation, implying that the program introduced moral hazard into land-use decisions in North Dakota.

Results from after the program's termination in 2012 only strengthen this perspective. Here a 1 mm increase in preplant precipitation *decreases* corn acreage by 0.7 percent, which is derived as the sum of −0.006, 0.009, and −0.010. Notice that the effect returns to a similar slope as before the SURE program was enacted—that is, the increase of the corn acreage function due to the new policy in 2009 was virtually offset by the decrease due to termination of the policy in 2012. This lends credibility to the interpretation of the SURE program exerting a causal effect.

Figure 3.4 illustrates the piecewise linear estimation results for North Dakota in panel (A). Before 2009, corn acreage increases linearly up to the endogenous threshold of preplant precipitation (100 mm) and then decreases linearly above that threshold; the solid line depicts this inverted-V-shaped effect. Under the SURE policy, the relationship changes substantially, as shown by the dashed line. However, after the program's termination, the relationship returns virtually to the original inverted-V-shaped effect of pre-2009; this is the dotted line in the figure.

Nebraska: farmers are responsive to preplant precipitation. Like North Dakota, farmers in Nebraska show responsiveness in corn acres as a function of preplant precipitation (column (4) of table 3.2 and panel (D) of figure 3.4). Before the policy change in 2009, a 1 mm decrease in preplant precipitation below the threshold decreases corn acreage by 0.9 percent. After the policy change in 2009, the estimated coefficient of 0.012 shows a substantial increase in corn acres such that a 1 mm decrease now increases acreage by 0.3 percent. Farmers thus are willing to risk corn production in the face of a water deficit, apparently due to the risk protection of the SURE program. Following the program's termination, farmers return to fewer corn acres when faced with preplant precipitation below the threshold.

Above the threshold in Nebraska, we find a similar pattern to North Dakota's result both before 2009 and during the SURE program. But the estimates are smaller, and we find no evidence about corn acreage change after termination of the SURE program. The results suggest that above the threshold, corn acreage in Nebraska is not as sensitive to the program changes as in North Dakota.

Iowa and Illinois: farmers are generally less responsive to preplant precipitation and its interaction with the SURE program. Relative to North Dakota and Nebraska, farmers are less responsive in corn acres in Iowa and Illinois, states in which both mean preplant precipitation and soil quality are much higher (table 3.2 and figure 3.4). Before 2009, the estimated coefficients on preplant precipitation are not statistically significant in Iowa. Iowa appears to combine the ideal climatic and soil conditions for growing corn such that it is the optimal choice under a range of preplant precipitation conditions. In Illinois, the coefficient is statistically significant and indicates a small 0.1 percent decrease in acres given a 1 mm increase in preplant precipitation above the threshold. Though small, some adaptation is occurring in Illinois.

Three of four treatment effects are statistically significant under the SURE program, and three of four treatment effects are also significant in the post-SURE period. The SURE effect above the threshold in Iowa is similar in magnitude to that in North Dakota; a 1 mm increase in preplant precipitation increases corn acreage by 0.6 percent. After program termination in 2012, the decrease in the corn acreage function offsets this effect. Farmers reverse course, once again supporting the idea that the SURE program generates a causal effect.

The pairing of high-quality soils and plentiful precipitation for corn growth characterizes much of the natural capital that underlies the production technology for agriculture in Illinois and Iowa. Consequently, corn is not a marginal crop as a function of preplant precipitation in these two states.

3.5.2   Cropping Pattern in North Dakota

We return to the perspective of cropping pattern in describing results for North Dakota's diverse mix of corn, grassland land cover, soybeans, and spring wheat.[26] Table 3.3 reports regression results, and figure 3.5 graphs the piecewise linear functions. We learned that North Dakota farmers are responsive in corn acres: in the pre-2009 period, corn acres decrease as preplant precipitation decreases (increases) below (above) the threshold. What substitutes for corn during this period? Below the threshold, soybean acres increase substantially as precipitation decreases. Wheat, however, responds like corn, and grassland acres show no effect. Above the threshold, all three crops respond positively to preplant precipitation in substituting for corn. In fact, 11 of 12 estimated coefficients above the threshold are statistically significant.

When treated with the SURE program, corn acres shift upward, while wheat, soybeans, and grassland acres generally shift downward as a function of preplant precipitation above the thresholds.

Termination of the SURE program generated several statistically significant responses both above and below the precipitation thresholds. Above the thresholds, the acreage relationships for corn, grassland, and wheat returned toward the preprogram relationship. This was also the case for wheat below the threshold.

Overall, in response to preplant precipitation, farmers in North Dakota show adaptation through cropping pattern followed by moral hazard in cropping pattern under the SURE program.

3.5.3   Other Crops and States

The other main results include grassland land covers and soybeans in states other than North Dakota. In general, grassland acres show statisti-

---

26. Note that the type of wheat grown in North Dakota is spring wheat, not winter wheat. Spring wheat is planted during the normal spring planting season, and thus its acreage may be influenced by preplant precipitation.

Table 3.3   **Land-use estimation results for North Dakota**

	Corn (1)	Soybeans (2)	Grassland (3)	Wheat (4)
Preplant precipitation below threshold	−0.010**	0.092***	0.001	−0.020***
	(0.004)	(0.031)	(0.002)	(0.004)
Preplant precipitation below threshold × after 2008	−0.015	—	−0.001	−0.911***
	(0.041)	—	(0.004)	(0.056)
Preplant precipitation below threshold × after 2011	0.008	−0.084**	0.006	0.954***
	(0.042)	(0.037)	(0.005)	(0.058)
Preplant precipitation above threshold	−0.006***	0.008***	0.013***	0.004**
	(0.002)	(0.001)	(0.002)	(0.002)
Preplant precipitation above threshold × after 2008	0.009***	−0.005***	−0.018***	−0.008***
	(0.002)	(0.002)	(0.003)	(0.002)
Preplant precipitation above threshold × after 2011	−0.010***	−0.003	0.007**	0.004**
	(0.003)	(0.002)	(0.003)	(0.002)
Preplant temperature	−0.389**	0.521**	−0.357***	0.542***
	(0.151)	(0.195)	(0.128)	(0.079)
Preplant temperature squared	−0.019***	0.025***	−0.003	0.017***
	(0.005)	(0.008)	(0.003)	(0.005)
Planting precipitation	−0.004	−0.001	0.005*	0.003
	(0.003)	(0.003)	(0.003)	(0.003)
Planting precipitation squared	0.000	0.000	−0.000*	−0.000
	(0.000)	(0.000)	(0.000)	(0.000)
Planting temperature	−0.047	0.014	−0.316***	−0.118
	(0.132)	(0.122)	(0.108)	(0.116)
Planting temperature squared	0.004	−0.019***	0.020***	0.006
	(0.007)	(0.005)	(0.003)	(0.005)
Crop-specific futures price	0.628***	−0.061	−0.219**	0.069
	(0.213)	(0.065)	(0.098)	(0.052)
Observations	352,963	352,963	352,963	352,963
R-squared	0.158	0.165	0.359	0.162
Number of PLSS sections	27,151	27,151	27,151	27,151
Threshold of preplant precipitation	100	65	125	85

Notes: Dependent variable in all regressions is the log of acres. Regressions estimated using piecewise linear functional form with the fixed effects estimator. Regressions include section fixed effects, year fixed effects, and a quadratic time trend by state. Standard errors are clustered at the county level and shown in parentheses, and *, **, and *** denote statistical significance at the 10 percent, 5 percent, and 1 percent levels, respectively.

cally significant but small responses to preplant precipitation as an adaptation strategy in Iowa, Illinois, and Nebraska (table 3.4). Nebraska and Illinois show similar patterns here of adapting to precipitation extremes by changing grassland acres. These effects are quite small, with estimated coefficients in the 0.001 to 0.003 range in absolute value.

Soybean acres show similarly small responses to preplant precipitation, with fewer estimated coefficients being statistically significant (table 3.5). Like corn, soybeans are not a marginal crop as a function of preplant pre-

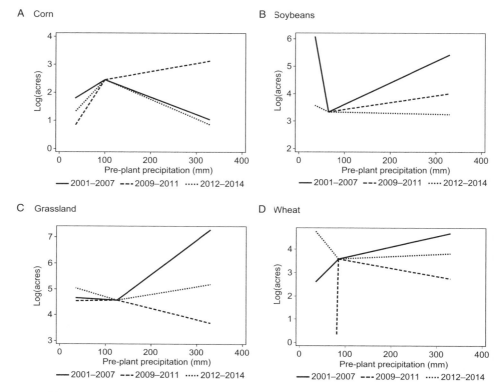

Fig. 3.5   Predicted effects of preplant precipitation on cropland acres in North Dakota (by policy regime)

Notes: The graphs display the predicted means of log(crop acres) in the sections as a function of preplant precipitation. Preplant precipitation is in millimeters.

cipitation in Iowa. However, soybeans are part of the cropping pattern response to the SURE program in both Iowa and Illinois. Farmers substitute away from soybeans below the thresholds in Iowa and Illinois and above the threshold in Iowa. Following the program's termination, farmers return to their preprogram response to precipitation above the thresholds in Iowa and Illinois. In Nebraska, there is substitution toward soybean acres, both below and above the threshold, in response to the SURE program.

3.6   Results II: Selection on Moral Hazard in Insurance Take-up

We use equation (2) to estimate insurance take-up regressions for two crops in two states: corn and soybeans in Illinois and Iowa.[27] In the piecewise linear

---

27. As mentioned earlier, insurance regressions are not estimated for crops in Nebraska and North Dakota due to issues in the county-level data that are not present in the section-level data.

Table 3.4   **Land-use estimation results for grassland**

	North Dakota (1)	Iowa (2)	Illinois (3)	Nebraska (4)
Preplant precipitation below threshold	0.001	−0.002*	0.002***	0.003*
	(0.002)	(0.001)	(0.000)	(0.001)
Preplant precipitation below threshold × after 2008	−0.001	0.005***	0.000	−0.004*
	(0.004)	(0.001)	(0.001)	(0.002)
Preplant precipitation below threshold × after 2011	0.006	0.002	−0.002**	0.004***
	(0.005)	(0.001)	(0.001)	(0.001)
Preplant precipitation above threshold	0.013***	−0.002***	0.001*	0.003***
	(0.002)	(0.000)	(0.000)	(0.000)
Preplant precipitation above threshold × after 2008	−0.018***	0.000	0.000	−0.002***
	(0.003)	(0.001)	(0.000)	(0.001)
Preplant precipitation above threshold × after 2011	0.007**	0.001***	−0.000	−0.001
	(0.003)	(0.000)	(0.001)	(0.001)
Preplant temperature	−0.357***	0.141***	−0.057	0.024
	(0.128)	(0.027)	(0.083)	(0.024)
Preplant temperature squared	−0.003	−0.005***	0.001	−0.000
	(0.003)	(0.001)	(0.003)	(0.004)
Planting precipitation	0.005*	0.000	−0.003***	−0.000
	(0.003)	(0.000)	(0.001)	(0.000)
Planting precipitation squared	−0.000*	0.000	0.000***	−0.000
	(0.000)	(0.000)	(0.000)	(0.000)
Planting temperature	−0.316***	−0.458***	0.096	−0.095**
	(0.108)	(0.051)	(0.075)	(0.043)
Planting temperature squared	0.020***	0.010***	−0.005**	−0.004***
	(0.003)	(0.001)	(0.002)	(0.001)
Corn futures price	−0.219**	0.048***	−0.549***	0.096***
	(0.098)	(0.015)	(0.099)	(0.027)
Observations	352,963	650,260	589,836	173,112
R-squared	0.359	0.295	0.344	0.183
Number of PLSS sections	27,151	50,020	45,372	14,426
Threshold of preplant precipitation	125	170	435	140

Notes: Dependent variable in all regressions is the log of grassland acres. Regressions estimated using piecewise linear functional form with the fixed effects estimator. Regressions include section fixed effects, year fixed effects, and a quadratic time trend by state. Regressions (1)–(4) use nonirrigated PLSS sections. Standard errors are clustered at the county level and shown in parentheses, and *, **, and *** denote statistical significance at the 10 percent, 5 percent, and 1 percent levels, respectively.

regressions, the threshold values for preplant precipitation are taken from the land-use regressions for the respective crops and states. For example, the threshold of 370 mm from the corn acres regression in Iowa is applied as the threshold in the comparable insurance regression. Table 3.6 reports the results, and figure 3.6 graphs the results as a function of preplant precipitation.[28]

28. The estimated coefficients on the variables for futures prices for corn and soybeans lend credibility to the overall results on insurance take-up. These prices serve directly as parameters of revenue-based crop insurance. When insurance pays out, indemnity increases in futures price. The four estimates are positive and highly significant.

Table 3.5   Land-use estimation results for soybeans

	North Dakota (1)	Iowa (2)	Illinois (3)	Nebraska (4)
Preplant precipitation below threshold	0.092***	0.001	0.000*	−0.006***
	(0.031)	(0.001)	(0.000)	(0.001)
Preplant precipitation below threshold × after 2008	–	−0.004***	−0.001*	0.005**
	–	(0.001)	(0.000)	(0.002)
Preplant precipitation below threshold × after 2011	−0.084**	−0.000	−0.000	0.000
	(0.037)	(0.001)	(0.000)	(0.002)
Preplant precipitation above threshold	0.008***	0.001	−0.001***	−0.001
	(0.001)	(0.000)	(0.000)	(0.001)
Preplant precipitation above threshold × after 2008	−0.005***	−0.002***	0.001**	0.002**
	(0.002)	(0.000)	(0.000)	(0.001)
Preplant precipitation above threshold × after 2011	−0.003	0.002***	−0.002***	0.001
	(0.002)	(0.001)	(0.000)	(0.001)
Preplant temperature	0.521**	−0.004	−0.091***	−0.179***
	(0.195)	(0.019)	(0.035)	(0.035)
Preplant temperature squared	0.025***	−0.006***	−0.005***	−0.017***
	(0.008)	(0.001)	(0.002)	(0.005)
Planting precipitation	−0.001	−0.000	0.000	−0.003***
	(0.003)	(0.001)	(0.001)	(0.001)
Planting precipitation squared	0.000	0.000	0.000	0.000**
	(0.000)	(0.000)	(0.000)	(0.000)
Planting temperature	0.014	0.088**	−0.127**	0.080
	(0.122)	(0.039)	(0.055)	(0.070)
Planting temperature squared	−0.019***	0.003***	0.009***	0.004*
	(0.005)	(0.001)	(0.002)	(0.002)
Soybeans futures price	−0.061	0.051**	0.070***	−0.014
	(0.065)	(0.025)	(0.016)	(0.015)
Observations	352,963	650,260	589,836	173,112
R-squared	0.165	0.073	0.083	0.079
Number of PLSS sections	27,151	50,020	45,372	14,426
Threshold of preplant precipitation	65	180	405	140

Notes: Dependent variable in all regressions is the log of soybean acres. Regressions estimated using piecewise linear functional form with the fixed effects estimator. Regressions include section fixed effects, year fixed effects, and a quadratic time trend by state. Regressions (1)–(4) use nonirrigated PLSS sections. Standard errors are clustered at the county level and shown in parentheses, and *, **, and *** denote statistical significance at the 10 percent, 5 percent, and 1 percent levels, respectively.

In studying selection on moral hazard, the question is whether SURE's treatment effect on crop insurance premiums per planted acre follows the sign and significance of the treatment effect on crop acres.[29] The results for corn provide reasonably strong supporting evidence. First, for corn acres in Iowa, the SURE treatment effect is negative and significant below the

29. We study land use and insurance take-up as concurrent decisions that reveal moral hazard and selection on moral hazard. In contrast, Einav et al. (2013) develop a two-period model with selection of insurance coverage in the first period and health-care utilization in the second period.

Table 3.6   Estimation results for crop insurance take-up

	Iowa		Illinois	
	Corn (1)	Soybeans (2)	Corn (3)	Soybeans (4)
Preplant precipitation below threshold	−0.000	0.000	−0.000	−0.000**
	(0.000)	(0.000)	(0.000)	(0.000)
Preplant precipitation below threshold × after 2008	−0.001**	−0.003***	0.001***	0.001***
	(0.000)	(0.001)	(0.000)	(0.000)
Preplant precipitation below threshold × after 2011	0.000	−0.001	−0.001*	−0.002***
	(0.000)	(0.001)	(0.000)	(0.000)
Preplant precipitation above threshold	−0.007***	0.000**	−0.001***	−0.000***
	(0.001)	(0.000)	(0.000)	(0.000)
Preplant precipitation above threshold × after 2008	0.006***	0.001***	0.001***	0.000
	(0.001)	(0.000)	(0.000)	(0.000)
Preplant precipitation above threshold × after 2011	−0.008***	−0.000	0.002***	0.001**
	(0.003)	(0.000)	(0.001)	(0.000)
Preplant temperature	−0.038**	−0.101***	0.014	−0.060*
	(0.015)	(0.018)	(0.035)	(0.032)
Preplant temperature squared	−0.004***	−0.005***	−0.005***	−0.006***
	(0.001)	(0.001)	(0.001)	(0.001)
Planting precipitation	0.001***	0.001***	0.001*	0.000
	(0.000)	(0.000)	(0.000)	(0.000)
Planting precipitation squared	−0.000**	−0.000***	0.000	0.000
	(0.000)	(0.000)	(0.000)	(0.000)
Planting temperature	−0.008	0.032	0.150***	0.161***
	(0.026)	(0.024)	(0.038)	(0.054)
Planting temperature squared	0.001	−0.001	−0.004***	−0.003**
	(0.001)	(0.001)	(0.001)	(0.002)
Corn/soybeans futures price	0.334***	0.201***	0.129***	0.115***
	(0.030)	(0.015)	(0.026)	(0.012)
Observations	1,287	1,287	1,285	1,291
R-squared	0.956	0.966	0.915	0.936
Number of counties	99	99	102	102
Threshold of preplant precipitation	370	180	395	405

Notes: Dependent variable in all regressions is the log of crop insurance premiums per planted acre. Regressions estimated using piecewise linear functional form with the fixed effects estimator. Regressions include county fixed effects, year fixed effects, and a quadratic time trend by state. Standard errors are clustered at the county level and shown in parentheses, and *, **, and *** denote statistical significance at the 10%, 5%, and 1% levels, respectively.

threshold; and positive and significant above the threshold (table 3.2). Corn insurance premiums follow the same pattern of treatment effects: negative and significant below; and positive and significant above (table 3.6). In addition, the magnitudes of the estimated coefficients are quite similar across the two regressions. Second, for corn acres in Illinois, the treatment effect is positive and significant below the threshold; and positive but insignificant above the threshold (table 3.2). Corn insurance premiums show roughly the same pattern: the treatment effects are positive and statistically significant

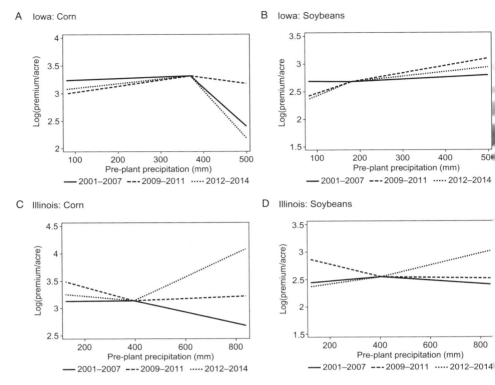

Fig. 3.6   Predicted effects of preplant precipitation on crop insurance premiums (by policy regime)

Notes: The graphs display the predicted means of log(premium/acre) in the counties as a function of preplant precipitation. Preplant precipitation is in millimeters.

both below and above the threshold. Moreover, the magnitudes of the estimated coefficients are quite similar across these two regressions.

The results for soybeans provide mixed evidence, with supporting evidence in each state on one side, but not both sides, of the respective thresholds. First, for soybeans acres in Iowa, the SURE treatment effect is negative and significant both below and above the threshold (table 3.5). Soybean insurance premiums follow the same pattern below the threshold, but they are positive and significant above the threshold (table 3.6). Second, for soybeans acres in Illinois, the treatment effect is negative and significant below the threshold; and positive and significant above the threshold. The treatment effects for soybean insurance premiums, in contrast, are positive and significant below the threshold and insignificant above the threshold.

We conclude, overall, that the results show limited evidence of selection on moral hazard. The county-level data on insurance premiums and weather may be a limiting factor in producing results that accord more closely to the soybean acreage results generated with section-level data.

Table 3.7   **Robustness checks for corn across states**

	North Dakota			Iowa		
	(1a)	(1b)	(1c)	(2a)	(2b)	(2c)
Preplant precipitation below threshold	−0.010**	−0.009**	−0.010**	−0.000	0.000*	−0.000
	(0.004)	(0.003)	(0.004)	(0.000)	(0.000)	(0.000)
Preplant precipitation below threshold × after 2008	−0.015	−0.016	−0.011	−0.001**	−0.001***	−0.001**
	(0.041)	(0.040)	(0.039)	(0.000)	(0.000)	(0.000)
Preplant precipitation below threshold × after 2011	0.008	0.008	0.004	0.000	0.000	0.000
	(0.042)	(0.042)	(0.040)	(0.000)	(0.000)	(0.000)
Preplant precipitation above threshold	−0.006***	−0.006***	−0.005	−0.001	0.000	−0.001
	(0.002)	(0.002)	(0.004)	(0.003)	(0.001)	(0.003)
Preplant precipitation above threshold × after 2008	0.009***	0.009***	0.008***	0.006**	0.004***	0.006*
	(0.002)	(0.002)	(0.002)	(0.003)	(0.001)	(0.003)
Preplant precipitation above threshold × after 2011	−0.010***	−0.010***	−0.010***	−0.010***	−0.009***	−0.010***
	(0.003)	(0.003)	(0.003)	(0.003)	(0.003)	(0.003)
Preplant temperature	−0.388**	−0.415***	−0.414***	−0.068***	−0.058**	−0.103***
	(0.152)	(0.139)	(0.140)	(0.023)	(0.023)	(0.030)
Preplant temperature squared	−0.019***	−0.020***	−0.015**	−0.004**	−0.002	−0.004**
	(0.005)	(0.005)	(0.006)	(0.002)	(0.002)	(0.002)
Planting precipitation	−0.004	−0.003	−0.006*	0.001	0.000	0.000
	(0.003)	(0.002)	(0.003)	(0.000)	(0.000)	(0.000)
Planting precipitation squared	0.000	0.000	0.000	−0.000*	−0.000	−0.000
	(0.000)	(0.000)	(0.000)	(0.000)	(0.000)	(0.000)
Planting temperature	−0.049	−0.048	−0.011	0.171***	0.125***	0.194***
	(0.133)	(0.126)	(0.131)	(0.035)	(0.030)	(0.036)
Planting temperature squared	0.004	0.004	0.003	−0.006***	−0.004***	−0.006***
	(0.007)	(0.007)	(0.007)	(0.001)	(0.001)	(0.001)
Corn futures price	0.628***	−0.236	0.330	0.192***	0.018	0.104***
	(0.213)	(0.172)	(0.209)	(0.034)	(0.026)	(0.035)
Observations	352,235	380,114	352,963	650,104	700,280	650,260
R-squared	0.158	0.147	0.159	0.027	0.027	0.027
Number of PLSS sections	27,095	27,151	27,151	50,008	50,020	50,020
Threshold of preplant precipitation	100	100	100	370	370	370

(continued)

3.7   Robustness Checks

In this section, we explore the sensitivity of our land-use regression results to three different modeling choices.

Removing sections that have zero acres of a crop during the study period. The first robustness check examines whether the results change if observations are removed from the small number of sections that have zero acres of a crop during the entire study period. As shown in columns with (a) in table 3.7, the estimated effects of preplant precipitation on corn acreage under the different policy regimes are almost the same as our main results reported in table 3.2. This is not surprising because the shares of the sections

Table 3.7 (continued)

	Illinois			Nebraska		
	(3a)	(3b)	(3c)	(4a)	(4b)	(4c)
Preplant precipitation below threshold	−0.000	−0.000	−0.000	−0.009***	−0.007**	−0.009**
	(0.000)	(0.000)	(0.000)	(0.003)	(0.003)	(0.003)
Preplant precipitation below threshold × after 2008	0.001***	0.001**	0.001	0.012***	0.010***	0.012**
	(0.000)	(0.000)	(0.000)	(0.003)	(0.003)	(0.003)
Preplant precipitation below threshold × after 2011	−0.001**	−0.001*	−0.000	−0.006***	−0.005***	−0.006**
	(0.000)	(0.000)	(0.000)	(0.002)	(0.002)	(0.002)
Preplant precipitation above threshold	−0.001***	−0.001**	−0.000	−0.005***	−0.004***	−0.005**
	(0.000)	(0.000)	(0.000)	(0.001)	(0.001)	(0.001)
Preplant precipitation above threshold × after 2008	0.001	0.001*	0.001	0.004***	0.002***	0.004**
	(0.000)	(0.000)	(0.001)	(0.001)	(0.001)	(0.001)
Preplant precipitation above threshold × after 2011	−0.001***	−0.001***	−0.001***	0.000	0.001	0.000
	(0.000)	(0.000)	(0.001)	(0.001)	(0.001)	(0.001)
Preplant temperature	0.014	0.014	0.051	−0.102*	−0.114**	−0.046
	(0.049)	(0.049)	(0.046)	(0.056)	(0.055)	(0.084)
Preplant temperature squared	0.001	0.001	0.004	−0.016**	−0.013*	−0.017**
	(0.003)	(0.003)	(0.003)	(0.007)	(0.007)	(0.007)
Planting precipitation	−0.000	0.000	−0.000	−0.004***	−0.004***	−0.004**
	(0.001)	(0.001)	(0.001)	(0.001)	(0.001)	(0.001)
Planting precipitation squared	0.000	−0.000	0.000	0.000***	0.000***	0.000**
	(0.000)	(0.000)	(0.000)	(0.000)	(0.000)	(0.000)
Planting temperature	−0.001	0.031	0.009	0.017	0.098	−0.054
	(0.062)	(0.064)	(0.062)	(0.087)	(0.075)	(0.123)
Planting temperature squared	0.004**	0.003*	0.004**	0.002	−0.001	0.003
	(0.002)	(0.002)	(0.002)	(0.003)	(0.002)	(0.004)
Corn futures price	0.038	0.009	0.088***	0.157***	0.164**	0.232**
	(0.032)	(0.039)	(0.031)	(0.043)	(0.070)	(0.031)
Observations	588,068	635,208	589,836	172,056	187,538	173,112
R-squared	0.026	0.033	0.030	0.091	0.086	0.094
Number of PLSS sections	45,236	45,372	45,372	14,338	14,426	14,426
Threshold of preplant precipitation	395	395	395	135	135	135

Notes: Dependent variable in all regressions is the log of acres. Regressions estimated using piecewise linear functional form with the fixed effects estimator. Regressions include section fixed effects, year fixed effect, and a quadratic time trend by state. Columns with (a) drop the sections having zero acres of the crops planted over our sample period. Columns with (b) include observations in 2008 as a control year. Columns with (c) include potential endogenous variables, including aggregated precipitation and average temperature in the prior growing season from April to September and the interaction term between preplant precipitation and temperature. Standard errors are clustered at the county level and shown in parentheses, and *, **, and *** denote statistical significance at the 10 percent, 5 percent, and 1 percent levels, respectively.

with zero corn acres during the study period are very small in each of the four states. The same conclusion applies to the other crops in the four states.

Treating 2008 as a control year. The second robustness check examines whether the results are sensitive to inclusion of observations from 2008 as part of the preprogram period—that is, expanding the period from 2001 to

2008 rather than 2001 to 2007.[30] In columns with (b) in table 3.7, we observe that the estimated effects of preplant precipitation on corn acreage under the different policy regimes are similar to our main results reported in table 3.2. The same conclusion applies to the other crops in the four states.

Including potentially endogenous variables. The third robustness check examines potential endogenous variables that may be correlated with both preplant precipitation and cropping pattern decisions. These variables include an interaction term between preplant precipitation and preplant temperature, aggregated precipitation from April through September of the previous growing season, and average temperature during the same previous growing season. As reported in columns with (c) in table 3.7 for corn, the coefficients of our preplant precipitation variables under different policy regimes retain the same sign with similar magnitudes and statistical significance when compared to our main estimation results, as reported in table 3.2. One minor exception is Illinois, where three estimated coefficients change from significant to insignificant, although they remain quite small in magnitude. For the other crops in the four states, the sign, magnitude, and significance are similar to the main results.

3.8 Conclusion

This chapter develops a cohesive analysis of adaptation, moral hazard, and selection on moral hazard in farmer decision-making in response to preplant precipitation. The focus on preplant precipitation as a natural experiment created an opportunity to study both cropping pattern and crop insurance as part of an intermediate-run production frame. Prior to the SURE program, we find considerable heterogeneity in adaptation in cropping pattern, with farmers in Nebraska and North Dakota much more responsive than farmers in Illinois and Iowa. Adaptation is a form of self-insurance in the lexicon of Ehrlich and Becker (1972), whereby the choice of cropping pattern reduces the size of a prospective loss without changing the probability of extreme precipitation outcomes (as an artifact of the natural experiment).

The SURE program's shock to insurance deductibles created an opportunity to study moral hazard in cropping pattern and selection on moral hazard in crop insurance coverage. With cropping pattern, the finding continues that farmers in Nebraska and North Dakota are more responsive than in Illinois and Iowa. Following the program's termination, farmers largely reverted to the preprogram cropping pattern, lending credibility to a causal

---

30. Alternatively, we could have included observations from 2008 as part of the treatment period (2009–2011), since the SURE program was enacted on May 22, 2008. We did not do this for two reasons. First, that date is appreciably after the normal planting time in this region. Second, the program was the most complex that USDA's Farm Service Agency had ever undertaken such that it took some time to educate farmers about the program (Shields 2010).

interpretation of the program's impact. With insurance expenditures, the analysis covers Illinois and Iowa, where farmers increase (decrease) the rate of expenditure on corn when they increase (decrease) corn acres. They do so to a lesser degree with soybeans. This demonstrates a complementarity between risk-taking in land use and insuring the risk in the crop insurance market. This complementarity constitutes a specific form of adverse selection in an insurance market. To our knowledge, ours is the first study of selection on moral hazard in an insurance market other than health insurance.

The use of high-resolution spatial data on land use and weather—with the PLSS section as the unit of analysis for land use—created new insight into the mechanisms of adaptation and moral hazard. Cropping pattern and agricultural land use have long been conjectured as an important mechanism of adaptation to weather risk and climate change, and here we provide strong empirical support for the conjecture. Further insight comes with the link to moral hazard as a hidden action: the relationship between cropping pattern and preplant precipitation is neither observed by the insurance agent nor recorded in the insurance contract. The spatial data translated this relationship from an unobservable to an observable one for the econometric analysis. Lastly, the hidden action on cropping pattern under the SURE program translates into hidden information in the crop insurance market. Insurance companies, unwittingly, may be insuring different risks than those represented by farms' historical crop yields.

Evidence about farmers' adaptation to weather risk is essential for understanding the impact of climate change—after all, climate change is a change in weather risk. Agriculture is of particular importance due to its related impacts on economic growth, migration, and human conflict.[31] Looking to the future, the major climate vulnerability for the Midwestern agricultural sector is the risk of excess precipitation (Andresen, Hilberg, and Kunkel 2012). Widespread flooding events already occur over much of the region, and excessive rainfall events occur during the summer. While regional climate projections for the end of the century come with substantial uncertainty, the projections include increased precipitation, increased extreme precipitation, and little change or even a small decrease in summer precipitation (Winkler, Arritt, and Pryor 2012). Research is needed to investigate the effect of both existing and future climate change on land-use change in the globally significant Midwest agricultural sector as well as in other major agricultural regions of the world.

A challenge for public policymakers is to design efficient risk-management policies in a setting of climate change. When designing policies to encourage efficient adaptation, it is important to account for perverse incentives

---

31. Related literature includes, for example, Dell et al. (2012) and Burke et al. (2015) on economic growth; Feng et al. (2010) and Hornbeck (2012) on migration; and Miguel et al. (2004) and Hsiang et al. (2013) on human conflict.

for risk-taking provided by government insurance programs. Although the SURE program ended in 2011, the Agricultural Act of 2014 reconstituted a similar program to cover shallow losses that are typically part of the insurance deductible. Again designed to supplement crop insurance, this program—the Agriculture Risk Coverage program—created incentives for risk-taking in crop choice and production. Research is needed on this new program following the approach developed here, as program payments in 2015 were quite large, $5.9 billion (USDA-FSA 2017). More generally, research is needed to understand the interrelationship among adaptation, moral hazard, and selection on moral hazard across the range of sectors linked directly to weather and climate change.

Appendix

In the appendix, we (i) provide additional detail on the data and variables in the analysis, (ii) analyze the residual variation in the section-level preplant precipitation variables after controlling for fixed effects, and (iii) report on the variables and output from the yield regressions for corn and soybeans.

Data

Section 3 of the main text provides the primary description of the data and variables. We provide supplemental details here.

PLSS sections. The PLSS imposed a grid of squares on the acquired lands of the early United States. The Fifth Principal Meridian was planned in 1815 to govern the grid for Illinois, Iowa, Nebraska, and North Dakota. We use a GIS data layer for the PLSS (ESRI 2015). The 1×1 mile section grid scale facilitates comparison of grids across years when the grid spacing of the cropland data changed from 56 m to 30 m in 2006. The grid scale also makes tractable the analysis of local precipitation impacts.

Land use. The CDL program provides raster-formatted geospatial data on crops planted and other nonagricultural types of land cover for the United States. Each grid corresponds to a specific crop or type of land cover. The CDL's land cover classifications include more than 50 crops and come with a spatial resolution of 30 m or 56 m. Our study area covers the four states that have a relatively long panel of annual CDL data in the Midwest. We intersect CDL data with the PLSS sections using the Python language for ArcGIS and calculate acres for each crop planted within a section as an aggregation of the CDL grids within the section. Since CDL data before 2006 are less reliable (with the spatial resolution of 56 m), we focus on crops with high classification accuracy, ranging from 85 percent to 95 percent, including corn, soybeans, and spring wheat. In addition, since CDL data are less reliable for differentiating among several land cover types—including alfalfa, fallow/idle cropland, unmanaged grassland, pasture, and hay—these land covers are combined into a single *grassland* land cover category.

Weather. The weather data are an updated version of those used in Schlenker and Roberts (2009), which consists of daily precipitation and maximum and minimum temperatures at 4-by-4 kilometer grid cells for the entire United States from 1950 to 2014. We compute weather variables by starting at the cell level and then aggregating to either the section level or the county level. These weather data cells are intersected with the PLSS sections using the Python language for ArcGIS.

Soil quality. The soil-quality data provide a useful perspective on the intrinsic quality of cropland across the states of Illinois, Iowa, Nebraska, and North Dakota. We do not describe these data in the main text, as they are not used in the regressions (instead relying on section fixed effects to control for soil quality). Nevertheless, they help explain the greater diversity of cropping pattern in Nebraska and North Dakota relative to Illinois and Iowa.

The soil-quality data are from USDA's Soil Survey Geographic (SSURGO) database. This spatially high-resolution database provides 10 × 10 meter grid cells for the entire United States. We extract data on land capability classification and calculate area-weighted average land capability for each section. Land capability classification shows the suitability of soils for most kinds of field crops. The criteria used in grouping the soils involve the landscape location, slope of the field, depth, texture, reactivity of the soil, erosion hazard, wetness, rooting-zone limitations, and climate, which are associated with both soil water-holding capacity and farmers' cropping pattern decisions. Class 1 and class 2 are defined as *good quality soils* for cropping. Class 3 and class 4 are *moderate quality soils* that have severe limitations for cropping and/or require careful conservation practices. *Poor quality soils* in class 6, class 7, and class 8 have very severe limitations that make them generally unsuitable for cultivation.

Figure 3A.1 in the appendix to this chapter displays the distribution of weighted land capability for our sample in the four states. Overall, Illinois and Iowa have a large share of good quality and moderate quality soils and only a small amount of poor quality soils. North Dakota has a large share of moderate quality soils but no good quality soils with weighted land capability less than 2. Nebraska similarly does not have any good quality soils with weighted land capability less than 2, and it has a substantial amount of poor quality soils.

The summary statistics for weighted land capability at the section level are shown in table 3A.1.

These numbers reinforce the more detailed data in figure 3A.1. Illinois and Iowa have the highest quality soil for their cropland, followed closely by North Dakota. Nebraska's cropland has the poorest quality soil of these four states by a substantial margin.

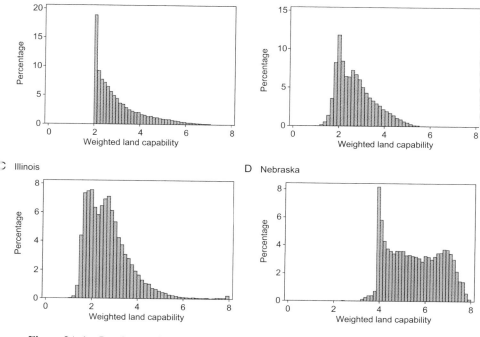

Figure 3A.1   Land capability class

Notes: The histograms display the percentage of sections belonging to a class of weighted land capability. Weighted land capability is calculated by the authors with the Soil Survey Geographic (SSURGO) database. Larger values indicate poorer soil quality. Panels (A)–(D) use rain-fed (nonirrigated) PLSS sections.

Table 3A.1   Summary statistics for weighted land capability by state

	Mean	Median	Std. dev.
Illinois	2.77	2.61	1.01
Iowa	2.74	2.59	0.83
Nebraska	5.52	5.45	1.15
North Dakota	3.03	2.68	1.05

Source: Authors' calculation.

Variation in Preplant Precipitation: Do Fixed Effects Absorb a Significant Amount of the Variation in the Section-Level Variables?

Our empirical approach relies on interannual variation in preplant precipitation after controlling for section and year fixed effects. A concern with this approach is that the fixed effects can absorb a significant amount of the variation in the precipitation variables. Following Fisher et al. (2012), we

Table 3A.2   **Variation of preplant precipitation under various sets of fixed effects**

		R^2 (1)	σ_e (2)	$\|e\| > 10$ mm (3)
North Dakota	No FE	—	47.5 mm	83.8%
	Section FE	0.116	44.7 mm	86.4%
	Section FE + year FE	0.802	21.1 mm	57.8%
Iowa	No FE	—	67.4 mm	91.7%
	Section FE	0.270	57.5 mm	87.0%
	Section FE + year FE	0.832	27.6 mm	73.4%
Illinois	No FE	—	108.6 mm	93.2%
	Section FE	0.419	82.8 mm	89.7%
	Section FE + year FE	0.784	50.4 mm	83.6%
Nebraska	No FE	—	52.1 mm	85.9%
	Section FE	0.177	47.3 mm	83.1%
	Section FE + year FE	0.779	24.5 mm	67.2%

Notes: This table summarizes regressions of section-level preplant precipitation on various sets of fixed effects (FE) to assess how much variation is absorbed by the FE. Column (1) reports the R^2s of the regressions. Column (2) reports the standard deviation of the residuals (remaining preplant precipitation variation) in millimeters. Column (3) reports the fraction of the observations having a residual larger than 10 mm.

explore how much of the variation is absorbed by the fixed effects. Table 3A.2 summarizes regressions of preplant precipitation against three sets of fixed effects: an intercept, section fixed effects, and section and year fixed effects. The table reports three items: R^2, the standard deviation of the residual preplant precipitation variation not absorbed by the fixed effects in millimeter equivalent, and the fraction of residuals with an absolute value larger than 10 mm.

In North Dakota, for example, the standard deviation of preplant precipitation is 47.5 mm without fixed effects. After including section and year fixed effects, the remaining variation of 21.1 mm provides enough residual variation to implement our semiparametric approach. Of note, the same conclusion applies in the other three states—that is, the variation in the preplant precipitation variables remains substantial after accounting for fixed effects.

Yield Regressions: Summary Statistics and Output

Section 4 of the main text reports on the yield regressions for corn and soybeans. The purpose of the yield regressions is to establish that preplant precipitation affects crop yield, thus making preplant precipitation a valid factor in farmer decision-making. As reported in the main text, the regressions accomplish this purpose.

Since the yield regressions are only preliminary to the land-use and insurance take-up regressions, we report in the appendix on the summary statistics of the variables for the yield regressions (table 3A.3) and the regression results (table 3A.4). The data are county-level panel data from 2001 to

Table 3A.3   **Summary statistics of variables for yield regressions**

		Corn		Soybeans	
	Unit	Mean	Std. dev.	Mean	Std. dev.
Yield	bushels/acre	151.57	32.75	44.55	9.27
Preplant precipitation, accumulated	mm	287.36	131.73	286.38	131.64
Preplant temperature, daily average	°C	0.59	3.60	0.53	3.68
Planting-season precipitation, daily average	mm	3.57	1.35	3.85	1.38
Planting-season temperature, daily average	°C	13.70	2.03	17.41	2.35
June–August precipitation, monthly average	mm	102.38	36.30	102.11	36.30
June–August temperature, monthly average	°C	24.79	1.84	24.77	1.87
Maximum temperature in July, daily average	°C	29.52	2.31	29.50	2.34
Counties		229		229	
Observations		2,903		2,931	

Notes: Data represent three states: Illinois, Iowa, and the counties east of the 100th meridian in North Dakota. Yield variables are authors' calculations using data from National Agricultural Statistics Service. Weather variables are authors' calculations using data from Schlenker and Roberts (2009).

Table 3A.4   **Regression estimates of crop yield**

	Corn		Soybeans	
Preplant precipitation below threshold	0.0003***	(0.0001)	–0.0004***	(0.0001)
Preplant precipitation below threshold × after 2008	0.0001	(0.0002)	0.0008***	(0.0001)
Preplant precipitation below threshold × after 2011	–0.0004*	(0.0002)	–0.0004***	(0.0001)
Preplant precipitation above threshold	–0.0005***	(0.0001)	–0.0004***	(0.0001)
Preplant precipitation above threshold × after 2008	0.0006***	(0.0001)	0.0013***	(0.0002)
Preplant precipitation above threshold × after 2011	–0.0018***	(0.0003)	–0.0013***	(0.0002)
Preplant temperature	0.0858***	(0.0101)	0.0188***	(0.0067)
Planting-season precipitation	–0.0067**	(0.0028)	0.0004	(0.0024)
Planting-season temperature	–0.0011	(0.0084)	0.0082	(0.0075)
June–August precipitation	0.0049***	(0.0004)	0.0046***	(0.0003)
June–August precipitation, squared	–0.0000***	(0.0000)	–0.0000***	(0.0000)
June–August temperature	0.6237***	(0.0708)	0.5150***	(0.0512)
June–August temperature, squared	–0.0130***	(0.0014)	–0.0113***	(0.0010)
Maximum temperature in July	–0.1007***	(0.0084)	–0.0058	(0.0073)
Observations	2,903		2,931	
R-squared	0.741		0.712	
Number of counties	229		229	
Threshold of preplant precipitation	320		430	

Notes: Dependent variable in all regressions is the log of crop yield. Regressions estimated using piecewise linear functional form with the fixed effects estimator. Regressions include state-by-year fixed effects, county fixed effects, year fixed effects, and a quadratic time trend by state. Standard errors are clustered at the county level and shown in parentheses, and *, **, and *** denote statistical significance at the 10 percent, 5 percent, and 1 percent levels, respectively.

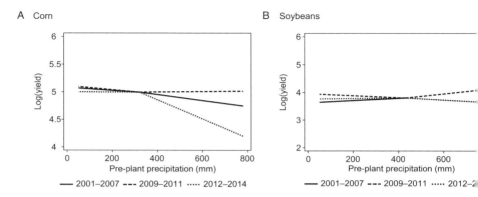

Figure 3A.2   Predicted effects of preplant precipitation on crop yield (by policy regime)

Notes: The graphs display the predicted means of log(yield) in the counties in the states of Illinois, Iowa, and North Dakota (east of the 100th meridian) as a function of preplant precipitation. Preplant precipitation is in millimeters.

2014 that are pooled for Illinois, Iowa, and eastern North Dakota. Corn yield has 2,903 observations, and soybean yield has 2,931 observations, both over 229 counties. The regressors are primarily weather variables. Precipitation and temperature variables are developed for each of the three phases of the crop production cycle: preplanting season, planting season, and growing season. In addition, a variable is developed for the daily average maximum temperature in July. These variables are guided, in part, by prior research on crop yield; Schlenker and Roberts (2009) study the effect of growing-season temperature on crop yield, and Urban et al. (2015) study the effect of extremely wet planting conditions on crop yield.

The main text reports on the results, which show small but (in most cases) statistically significant effects of preplant precipitation. The SURE treatment effects, in particular, are positive and significant in three of four cases (table 3A.4). These are contrary to expectations; in a separate work, we are investigating whether farmers planted corn and soybeans on land with higher-quality soils during the SURE program as a possible mechanism to explain these results. Figure 3A.2 graphs the piecewise linear functions for these two regressions.

The other weather variables, in large part, exert the expected effects on yield, as informed by the prior research (Schlenker and Roberts 2009; Urban et al. 2015). Planting-season precipitation has a significant, negative effect on corn yield. Both precipitation and temperature during the growing season (June–August) have positive, significant effects on corn yields and soybean yields. All four response functions are quadratic, with negative, small in absolute value, and significant estimated coefficients on the squared terms of the growing-season weather variables in both the corn and soybean regressions. High maximum temperatures in July have a negative effect on corn yield.

References

Al-Kaisi, M. M., R. W. Elmore, J. G. Guzman, H. M. Hanna, C. E. Hart, M. J. Helmers, E. W. Hodgson, A. W. Lenssen, A. P. Mallarino, A. E. Robertson, and J. E. Sawyer. 2013. "Drought Impact on Crop Production and the Soil Environment: 2012 Experiences from Iowa." *Journal of Soil and Water Conservation* 68:19–24.

Anderson, S., C. Wang, and J. Zhao. 2012. "Let Them Eat Switchgrass? Modeling the Displacement of Existing Food Crops by New Bioenergy Feedstocks." Working Paper, Michigan State University, Department of Economics.

Andresen, J., S. Hilberg, K. Kunkel. 2012. "Historical Climate and Climate Trends in the Midwestern USA." In *U.S. National Climate Assessment Midwest Technical Input Report*, coordinated by J. Winkler, J. Andresen, J. Hatfield, D. Bidwell, and D. Brown. http://glisa.msu.edu/docs/NCA/MTIT_Historical.pdf.

Annan, F., and W. Schlenker. 2015. "Federal Crop Insurance and the Disincentive to Adapt to Extreme Heat." *American Economic Review* 105 (5): 262–66.

Arrow, K. 1963. "Uncertainty and the Welfare Economics of Health Care." *American Economic Review* 53 (5): 941–73.

Barreca, A., K. Clay, O. Deschênes, M. Greenstone, and J. S. Shapiro. 2016. "Adapting to Climate Change: The Remarkable Decline in the US Temperature-Mortality Relationship over the Twentieth Century." *Journal of Political Economy* 124 (1): 105–59.

Bekkerman, A., V. H. Smith, and M. J. Watts. 2012. "The SURE Program and Incentives for Crop Insurance Participation: A Theoretical and Empirical Analysis." *Agricultural Finance Review* 72 (3): 381–401.

Brooks, H. E. 2013. "Severe Thunderstorms and Climate Change." *Atmospheric Research* 123 (1): 129–38.

Brown, J. F., and M. S. Pervez. 2014. "Merging Remote Sensing Data and National Agricultural Statistics to Model Change in Irrigation Agriculture." *Agricultural Systems* 127:28–40.

Burke, M., and K. Emerick. 2016. "Adaptation to Climate Change: Evidence from US Agriculture." *American Economic Journal: Economic Policy* 8 (3): 106–40.

Burke, M., S. M. Hsiang, and E. Miguel. 2015. "Global Non-linear Effect of Temperature on Economic Production." *Nature* 527:235–39.

CBO (Congressional Budget Office). 2011. "CBO March 2011 Baseline for CCC and FCIC." March 18, unpublished.

Chite, R. M. 2008. "Crop Insurance and Disaster Assistance in the 2008 Farm Bill." Congressional Research Service, CRS Report RL34207.

Chite, R. M. 2010. "Emergency Funding for Agriculture: A Brief History of Supplemental Appropriations, FY1989-FY2009." Congressional Research Service, CRS Report RS31095.

Christensen, J. H., K. Krishna Kumar, E. Aldrian, S.-I. An, I. F. A. Cavalcanti, M. de Castro, W. Dong, P. Goswami, A. Hall, J. K. Kanyanga, A. Kitoh, J. Kossin, N.-C. Lau, J. Renwick, D. B. Stephenson, S.-P. Xie and T. Zhou. 2013. "Climate Phenomena and Their Relevance for Future Regional Climate Change." In *Climate Change 2013: The Physical Science Basis. Contribution of Working Group I to the*

Fifth Assessment Report of the Intergovernmental Panel on Climate Change, edited by T. F. Stocker, D. Qin, G.-K. Plattner, M. Tignor, S. K. Allen, J. Boschung, A. Nauels, Y. Xia, V. Bex, and P. M. Midgley. Cambridge: Cambridge University Press.

Cole, S., X. Giné, and J. Vickery. 2017. "How Does Risk Management Influence Production Decisions? Evidence from a Field Experiment." *Review of Financial Studies* 30 (6): 1935–70.

Davis, L. W., and P. J. Gertler. 2015. "Contribution of Air Conditioning Adoption to Future Energy Use under Global Warming." *Proceedings of the National Academy of Sciences* 112 (19): 5962–67.

Dell, M., B. F. Jones, and B. A. Olken. 2012. "Temperature Shocks and Economic Growth: Evidence from the Last Half Century." *American Economic Journal: Macroeconomics* 4 (3): 66–95.

Dell, M., B. F. Jones, and B. A. Olken. 2014. "What Do We Learn from the Weather? The New Climate–Economy Literature." *Journal of Economic Literature* 52 (3): 740–98.

Deryugina, T., and B. Kirwan. 2018. "Does the Samaritan's Dilemma Matter? Evidence from U.S. Agriculture." *Economic Inquiry* 56 (2): 983–1006.

Deschênes, O., and M. Greenstone. 2007. "The Economic Impacts of Climate Change: Evidence from Agricultural Output and Random Fluctuations in Weather." *American Economic Review* 97 (1): 354–85.

Deschênes, O., and M. Greenstone. 2011. "Climate Change, Mortality, and Adaptation: Evidence from Annual Fluctuations in Weather in the US." *American Economic Journal: Applied Economics* 3:152–85.

Donaldson, D., and A. Storeygard. 2016. "The View from Above: Applications of Satellite Data in Economics." *Journal of Economic Perspectives* 30 (4): 171–98.

Du, X., H. Feng, and D. A. Hennessy. 2017. "Rationality of Choices in Subsidized Crop Insurance Markets." Forthcoming in the *American Journal of Agricultural Economics*.

Ehrlich, I., and G. S. Becker. 1972. "Market Insurance, Self-Insurance, and Self-Protection." *Journal of Political Economy* 80 (4): 623–48.

Einav, L., A. Finkelstein, and J. Levin. 2010. "Beyond Testing: Empirical Models of Insurance Markets." *Annual Review of Economics* 2 (1): 311–36.

Einav, L., A. Finkelstein, S. P. Ryan, P. Schrimpf, and M. R. Cullen. 2013. "Selection on Moral Hazard in Health Insurance." *American Economic Review* 103 (1): 178–219.

ESRI (Environmental Systems Research Institute). 2015. ArcGIS, version 10.1. Redlands, CA.

Feng, S., A. B. Krueger, and M. Oppenheimer. 2010. "Linkages among Climate Change, Crop Yields and Mexico-US Cross-Border Migration." *Proceedings of the National Academy of Sciences of the United States* 107 (32): 14257–62.

Fezzi, C., and I. Bateman. 2015. "The Impact of Climate Change on Agriculture: Nonlinear Effects and Aggregation Bias in Ricardian Models of Farmland Values." *Journal of the Association of Environmental and Resource Economics* 2 (1): 57–92.

Finkelstein, A. 2015. *Moral Hazard in Health Insurance*. New York: Columbia University Press.

Fisher, A. C., W. M. Hanemann, M. J. Roberts, and W. Schlenker. 2012. "The Economic Impacts of Climate Change: Evidence from Agricultural Output and Random Fluctuations in Weather: Comment." *American Economic Review* 102 (7): 3749–60.

Glauber, J. W. 2013. "The Growth of the Federal Crop Insurance Program." *American Journal of Agricultural Economics* 95 (2): 482–88.

Glauber, J. W., and K. J. Collins. 2002. "Crop Insurance, Disaster Assistance, and the Role of the Federal Government in Providing Catastrophic Risk Protection." *Agricultural Finance Review* 62 (2): 81–101.

Haigh, T., E. Takle, J. Andresen, M. Widhalm, J. S. Carlton, and J. Angel. 2015. "Mapping the Decision Points and Climate Information Use of Agricultural Producers across the U.S. Corn Belt." *Climate Risk Management* 7:20–30.

Holmes, T. J., and S. Lee. 2012. "Economies of Density versus Natural Advantage: Crop Choice on the Back Forty." *Review of Economics and Statistics* 94 (1): 1–19.

Hornbeck, R. 2012. "The Enduring Impact of the American Dust Bowl: Short- and Long-Run Adjustments to Environmental Catastrophe." *American Economic Review* 102 (4): 1477–1507.

Hsiang, S. M., M. Burke, and E. Miguel. 2013. "Quantifying the Influence of Climate on Human Conflict." *Science* 341:1235367.

Kala, N. 2017. "Learning, Adaptation, and Climate Uncertainty: Evidence from Indian Agriculture." Working Paper, MIT Sloan School of Management.

Karlan, D., R. Osei, I. Osei-Akoto, and C. Udry. 2014. "Agricultural Decisions after Relaxing Credit and Risk Constraints." *Quarterly Journal of Economics* 129 (2): 597–652.

Khanal, A. R., A. K. Mishra, and M. Bhattarai. 2017. "Assessing the Impact of Weather Risk on Land Use Intensity: A Nonstationary and Dynamic Panel Modeling Approach." *Land Economics* 93 (1): 40–58.

Lobell, D. B., M. J. Roberts, W. Schlenker, N. Braun, B. B. Little, R. M. Rejesus, and G. L. Hammer. 2014. "Greater Sensitivity to Drought Accompanies Maize Yield Increase in the U.S. Midwest." *Science* 344 (6183): 516–19.

Mansur, E. T., R. Mendelsohn, and W. Morrison. 2008. "Climate Change Adaptation: A Study of Fuel Choice and Consumption in the US Energy Sector." *Journal of Environmental Economics and Management* 55:175–93.

McIntosh, C. T., and W. Schlenker. 2006. "Identifying Non-linearities in Fixed Effects Models." Working Paper, University of California, San Diego, School of Global Policy and Strategy.

Mearns, L. O., W. Easterling, C. Hays, and D. Marx. 2001. "Comparison of Agricultural Impacts of Climate Change Calculated from High and Low Resolution Climate Change Scenarios: Part I. The Uncertainty Due to Spatial Scale." *Climatic Change* 51:131–72.

Mendelsohn, R. 2000. "Efficient Adaptation to Climate Change." *Climatic Change* 45:583–600.

Mendelsohn, R., W. D. Nordhaus, and D. Shaw. 1994. "The Impact of Global Warming on Agriculture: A Ricardian Analysis." *American Economic Review* 84 (4): 753–71.

Miguel, E., S. Satyanath, and E. Sergenti. 2004. "Economic Shocks and Civil Conflict: An Instrumental Variables Approach." *Journal of Political Economy* 112 (4): 725–53.

Miller, B. M. 2014. "Does Validity Fall from the Sky? Observant Farmers and the Endogeneity of Rainfall." Working Paper, University of California, San Diego, Department of Economics.

Mobarak, A. M., and M. R. Rosenzweig. 2014. "Risk, Insurance and Wages in General Equilibrium." NBER Working Paper no. 19811, Cambridge, MA, National Bureau of Economic Research.

Moore, F. C., and D. B. Lobell. 2014. "Adaptation Potential of European Agriculture in Response to Climate Change." *Nature Climate Change* 4:610–14.

Neild, R. E., and J. E. Newman. 1990. "Growing Season Characteristics and Requirements in the Corn Belt." Purdue University, Cooperative Extension Service. National Corn Handbook-40.

Quiring, S. M., and D. B. Kluver. 2009. "Relationship between Winter/Spring Snowfall and Summer Precipitation in the Northern Great Plains of North America." *Journal of Hydrometeorology* 10:1203–17.

Roberts, M. J., E. O'Donoghue, and N. Key. 2014. "Separating Moral Hazard from Adverse Selection: Evidence from the U.S. Federal Crop Insurance Program." Working Paper 201410, University of Hawaii at Manoa, Department of Economics.

Rosenzweig, M. R., and C. Udry. 2014. "Rainfall Forecasts, Weather, and Wages over the Agricultural Production Cycle." *American Economic Review: Papers and Proceedings* 104 (5): 278–83.

Schlenker, W., W. M. Hanemann, and A. C. Fisher. 2005. "Will U.S. Agriculture Really Benefit from Global Warming? Accounting for Irrigation in the Hedonic Approach." *American Economic Review* 95 (1): 395–406.

Schlenker, W., and M. J. Roberts. 2009. "Nonlinear Temperature Effects Indicate Severe Damages to U.S. Crop Yields under Climate Change." *Proceedings of the National Academy of Sciences of the United States* 106 (37): 15594–98.

Shields, D. A. 2010. "A Whole-Farm Crop Disaster Program: Supplemental Revenue Assistance Payments (SURE)." Congressional Research Service, CRS Report RS40452.

Shields, D. A. 2015. "Federal Crop Insurance: Background." Congressional Research Service, CRS Report R40532.

Shields, D. A., and R. M. Chite. 2010. "Agricultural Disaster Assistance." Congressional Research Service, CRS Report RS21212.

Smith, V. H., and M. J. Watts. 2010. "The New Standing Disaster Program: A SURE Invitation to Moral Hazard Behavior." *Applied Economic Perspectives and Policy* 32 (1): 154–69.

Steduto, P., T. C. Hsiao, E. Fereres, and D. Raes. 2012. *Crop Yield Response to Water.* Rome: Food and Agriculture Organization of the United Nations.

Urban, D. W., M. J. Roberts, W. Schlenker, and D. B. Lobell. 2015. "The Effect of Extremely Wet Planting Conditions on Maize and Soybean Yields." *Climatic Change* 130:247–60.

USDA-FSA (US Department of Agriculture Farm Service Agency). 2009. Supplemental Revenue Assistance Payments (SURE) Program: Backgrounder. Accessed April 14, 2017. https://www.fsa.usda.gov/Internet/FSA_File/sure_bkgder_122309.pdf.

USDA-FSA (US Department of Agriculture Farm Service Agency). 2017. 2015 ARC/PLC Payments. Accessed April 16, 2017. https://www.fsa.usda.gov/Assets/USDA-FSA-Public/usdafiles/arc-plc/pdf/2015%20arc%20plc%20payments%20feb%202017.pdf.

USGAO (US Government Accountability Office). 2014. "USDA Farm Programs: Farmers Have Been Eligible for Multiple Programs and Further Efforts Could Help Prevent Duplicative Payments." GAO-14-428, July.

Varian, H. R. 1992. *Microeconomic Analysis.* 3rd ed. New York: W. W. Norton and Company.

Weber, J., N. Key, and E. O'Donoghue. 2016. "Does Federal Crop Insurance Make Environmental Externalities from Agriculture Worse?" *Journal of the Association of Environmental and Resource Economists* 3 (3): 707–42.

Winkler, J. A., R. W. Arritt, and S. C. Pryor. 2012. Climate Projections for the Midwest: Availability, Interpretation and Synthesis. In *U.S. National Climate Assessment Midwest Technical Input Report,* coordinated by J. Winkler, J. Andresen, J. Hatfield, D. Bidwell, and D. Brown. http://glisa.msu.edu/docs/NCA/MTIT_Future.pdf.

4

Intranational Trade Costs, Reallocation, and Technical Change
Evidence from a Canadian Agricultural Trade Policy Reform

Mark Brown, Shon M. Ferguson,
and Crina Viju-Miljusevic

4.1 Introduction

The impact of trade liberalization and competitive pressure on the real-location of resources and aggregate technical progress continues to be an important area of study. At the same time, many countries maintain subsidies and trade barriers aimed at preserving small farms that are identified by many commentators as impediments in trade agreement negotiations. It is thus crucial to understand the distributional impacts of trade reform and subsidy removal across the farm population and their combined implications for aggregate outcomes such as technology adoption and land-use adaption.

In this chapter, we exploit the removal of a railway transportation subsidy on the Canadian Prairies in 1995 to study the relative contribution of reallocation versus within-farm changes due to the reform on aggregate

Mark Brown is the chief of regional and urban economic analysis in the Economic Analysis Division at Statistics Canada.

Shon M. Ferguson is a research fellow at the Research Institute of Industrial Economics (IFN) in Stockholm, Sweden.

Crina Viju-Miljusevic is an associate professor at the Institute of European, Russian and Eurasian Studies at Carleton University.

We thank Paul Rhode, Martin Beaulieu, Danny Leung, and seminar participants at the NBER Understanding Productivity Growth in Agriculture Conference, Statistics Canada, and Agriculture and Agri-Food Canada for comments and suggestions. We thank the Canadian Centre for Data Development and Economic Research (CDER) at Statistics Canada for providing access to the data and, in particular, Afshan Dar-Brodeur for her assistance throughout the process. We thank Jason Skotheim and Gary Warkentine for assistance with the freight-rate data. Financial assistance from the Jan Wallander and Tom Hedelius Foundation and the Marianne and Marcus Wallenberg Foundation is gratefully acknowledged. For acknowledgments, sources of research support, and disclosure of the author's or authors' material financial relationships, if any, please see https://www.nber.org/chapters/c13945.ack.

technology adoption and land use. The subsidy, worth C$700 million per year (Klein et al. 1994) was applied to the region's main export crops. As locations farthest from seaport experienced the greatest increase in transportation costs when the export subsidy was removed, the impact of the reform was location-dependent. Furthermore, the export-dependent nature of grain production on the prairies, combined with the unique institutional features of the grain marketing and transportation system at the time, imply that the increase in freight rates translated directly into a decrease in the price of grains at the farm gate.[1] Ferguson and Olfert (2016) exploited this large regional variation in this historic reform in order to identify the causal effects of the subsidy loss on the aggregate adoption of new technologies for sowing grain crops and several other aspects of land use. Their study used data aggregated at the Census Consolidated Subdivision (CCS) level, which allowed for a comparison in average technology adoption across regions, but due to data limitations, they could not investigate the distributional impact of the reform within each spatial unit over time.

Using a detailed farm-level panel, we decompose the aggregate technology adoption and land use in each region into several components, which capture adaption through within-farm change and the reallocation of cropland between incumbent and entering and exiting farms. We find that the shift from producing low-value to high-value crops for export, the adoption of new seeding technologies, and reduction in summer fallow observed at the aggregate level between 1991 and 2001 were driven mainly by the within-farm effect. While the reallocation of cropland played a minor role in the shorter time horizon, it plays a larger role over the 1991 to 2011 period, accounting for more than half of aggregate technology adoption and land-use changes. Although technology adoption and land-use changes occurred across the prairies, the pace of change was much faster in those areas where transportation costs rose through the within-farm and reallocation effects— both are economically, and statistically, significant channels by which the farm population adapts to economic shocks.

This study contributes to a growing literature on the impact of trade liberalization and reallocation on aggregate technical change. Melitz (2003)

---

1. Two main institutional features allow us to infer farm gate prices for wheat (the main export crop at the time) directly from the freight-rate data. First, the Canadian Wheat Board (CWB) marketed wheat and barley on behalf of prairie farmers and "pooled" prices for a given quality of grain delivered during each "crop year" (August 1–July 31). Price pooling meant that the wheat price per tonne at the farm gate equaled the pooled price minus the cost per tonne of railway transportation to seaport. Pooling prices regardless of whether wheat was exported to the east or west also meant that any divergences in world wheat prices between east- and west-coast seaports did not affect the spatial variation in prices across the prairies. Second, freight rates were regulated, publicly available, and constant during each crop year, which meant that freight rate changes translated directly into changes in the price of wheat at the farm gate. The combination of CWB price pooling and a constant export basis within each crop year implies that all farmers delivering their grain at a given location received the same price, net of railway freight costs, regardless of which day during the crop year they delivered.

showed theoretically that trade liberalization raises aggregate productivity by reallocating production from low-productivity firms to high-productivity firms, with strong empirical support by many studies that exploited historical trade reforms, including Chile (Pavcnik 2002) and Canada (Trefler 2004). Our results also contribute to a related empirical literature positing that trade liberalization or competitive pressure induces technology adoption and efficiency improvements within farms (Paul, Johnston, and Frengley 2000) or firms in other industries (Galdon-Sanchez and Schmitz 2002; Schmitz 2005; Lileeva and Trefler 2010; Bustos 2011; Bloom, Draca, and Van Reenen 2015).

The idea that reallocation of land from contracting farms to growing farms leads to aggregate technical change is motivated by several studies. A survey of the literature by Sumner (2014) suggests a positive relationship between farm size and productivity in developed countries such as the United States. Adamopolous and Restuccia (2014) find that differences in farm size across countries can explain a great deal of the cross-country differences in agricultural productivity. Empirical studies using Canadian farm data suggest that larger farms are more likely to adopt conservation (or what is also termed "minimum") tillage (Davey and Furtan 2008) and, in particular, zero tillage (Awada 2012).

Our work contributes to a broader literature that focuses on the impact of technology diffusion on farm size, including Olmstead and Rhode (2001).[2] Our work is also complementary to recent research by Collard-Wexler and De Loecker (2015) that emphasizes the role of technology adoption in driving the reallocation process and within-firm efficiency improvements that together raised aggregate productivity in the US steel industry.

Our methodology builds on Foster, Haltiwanger, and Krizan (2001) and Foster, Haltiwanger, and Syverson (2008), who decompose aggregate total factor productivity (TFP) growth into separate components, but we depart from the literature by performing the decomposition within each finely detailed spatial unit and then using these components as separate outcome variables in regressions where the variable of interest is the change in railway freight rates. Our regression approach allows us to determine the impact of the reform on each component of aggregate technology adoption and land-use change, which, to the best of our knowledge, is a unique contribution to the literature.

4.2 Background

We begin with a brief overview of the grain transportation subsidy and its reform as well as a description of the grain market in western Canada. Finally, we discuss the advent of zero tillage technology in the region.

---

2. See Sunding and Zilberman (2001) for a comprehensive literature review of technology adoption in agriculture, and see Olmstead and Rhodes (2008) for a historical background of innovation in the US context.

4.2.1   The Western Grain Transportation Act and Structural Change

In 1995, the Canadian government eliminated a transportation subsidy on railway shipments of grain from the Canadian Prairies to seaport, known as the Western Grain Transportation Act (WGTA).[3] The decision ended one of the longest-running agricultural subsidies in the world, first known as the Crow's Nest Pass Agreement of 1897.[4] These subsidized freight rates were commonly referred to as the "Crow Rate." The removal of the transportation subsidy increased the cost of exporting grain from the Canadian Prairies by $17 to $34/tonne, equivalent to 8 percent to 17 percent of its value.[5] These increased transportation costs translated directly into lower grain prices at the farm gate, since grain was exported almost exclusively by rail.[6]

The subsidization of railway freight rates to move Western Canadian grains to export position was a vital part of the national policy of the late 19th century to settle the prairie provinces and develop the so-called wheat economy. While the subsidized grain producers benefitted from the subsidy, livestock producers and processors were disadvantaged by the resulting higher local prices of grains, and the Crow Rate was seen as contributing to dependence on a very narrow range of crops whose export was subsidized (Klein and Kerr 1996). Removal of the transportation subsidy was expected to have large impacts on the grains and livestock industries in the region (Kulshreshtha and Devine 1978).

While the repeal of the WGTA affected farmers in all locations across the prairies to some extent, there was substantial geographical heterogeneity in the size of this impact. Prior to the reform, railway freight rates for shipping wheat from the prairies to export position (Vancouver, BC, or Thunder Bay, ON) ranged from $8 to $14/tonne, depending on location. After the reform, the freight rates more than tripled to $25 to 46/tonne, with the highest freight rates in locations that were farthest from the seaports. It is this spatial heterogeneity that Ferguson and Olfert (2016) used to untangle the impact of the WGTA repeal from other concurrent changes in the production and marketing of grain that affected all locations equally or did not share the same geographical pattern as the shock to railway freight rates.[7]

---

3. After the October 1993 federal election, the new government moved quickly to eliminate the WGTA. The reform was passed in Parliament in February 1995, and the elimination of the WGTA was effective August 1, 1995 (Doan, Paddock, and Dyer 2003).

4. See Vercammen (1996) for a detailed overview of reforms to the Western Canadian grain transportation system.

5. This assumes an average grain price of $200/tonne.

6. In the case of export of CWB grains at the time, farmers deliver their grain to the grain companies' "elevator," a short-term storage facility usually located along a rail line. The grain is then loaded onto rail cars for transport to ports on Canada's west coast (Vancouver or Prince Rupert), the Lakehead (Thunder Bay), or Hudson's Bay (Churchill) and then loaded on ships for export; grain destined for the eastern US market enters via rail to Minneapolis.

7. For example, grain handling and transportation innovations such as high-throughput elevators and unit trains were gradually being adopted across the prairies, possibly resulting in adaptations by farmers, but these were generally the same in all locations and not differentiated by distance to the nearest seaport.

The timing of the WGTA removal is attributable to two external factors that were beyond the control of the grain industry in western Canada. First, a recession in the early 1990s forced the Canadian federal government to cut spending. Second, the General Agreement on Tariffs and Trade deemed the WGTA to be a trade-distorting export subsidy, and the Canadian government faced international pressure to reduce export subsidies during the Uruguay Round.[8]

Farmers were partially compensated for the higher freight rates resulting from the repeal of the WGTA, with a one-time payment of $1.6 billion, with an additional $300 million allocated to assist producers who were most severely affected and to invest in rural roads. Payments were based on a formula that considered each farm's acreage of eligible land, productivity, and distance to seaport. This compensation was equivalent to approximately two years of the annual subsidy amount and may have helped farmers finance the purchase of new zero tillage equipment.[9] Nevertheless, despite its large size, Schmitz, Highmoor, and Schmitz (2002) calculated that the payment was not large enough to fully compensate farmers for the loss of the subsidy.

Two other domestic reforms occurred around the same time as the WGTA repeal. First, the federal government began to speed up the process permitting railways to abandon prairie branch rail lines that were too inefficient to maintain. Second, the federal government also amended the Canada Wheat Board (CWB) Act in order to change the point of price equivalence to St. Lawrence/Vancouver, rather than Thunder Bay/Vancouver. The new pricing regime accounted for the cost to ship grain on lake freighters from Thunder Bay to the mouth of the St. Lawrence Seaway.[10] In addition, Canada and the United States gradually eliminated import tariffs for wheat, canola, and other grains over a nine-year period that ended January 1, 1998, as part of the 1988 Canada-United States Free Trade Agreement (CUSFTA) and the 1994 North American Free Trade Agreement (NAFTA; USDA-NASS 2002).

It is important to note that the WGTA subsidized exports of grain to non-US locations, and thus the repeal of the WGTA made it relatively more attractive to export to the United States. In the case of grains exported by

---

8. In particular, the Uruguay Round's Agriculture Agreement stipulated that export subsidies were to be reduced by 36 percent of what was spent in 1991 and 1992 by the year 2000. Moreover, this reduction was to apply to at least 21 percent of the volume shipped in 1991 and 1992 (Kraft and Doiron 2000).

9. Vercammen (2007) shows, for example, that the risk of farm bankruptcy may induce farmers to invest the proceeds of direct payments into productivity-enhancing investments.

10. The relocation of the eastern export basis point for CWB grains discouraged the export of wheat and barley to ports in eastern Canada. However, west-coast capacity constraints led to an additional measure, the "freight rate adjustment factor" (FAF), which had the effect of reestablishing freight rates consistent with a Thunder Bay export basis point, for eastward movement of wheat and barley. Financed by all producers across the prairies, the FAF largely averted the additional impact of moving the eastern basis point to St. Lawrence (Fulton et al. 1998). Freight rates for wheat, adjusted for west-coast capacity constraints, can thus be interpreted as an "export basis."

the CWB (wheat and barley for human consumption), the CWB's catchment area for exports to the United States was located in southern Manitoba. The WGTA repeal would have increased the US catchment area, resulting in more wheat exports to the United States via Manitoba. The increase in exports to the United States moderated the freight increase after 1995 observed in southern Manitoba locations and is captured by our freight-rate data.

Overall, it was expected that some farmers would adapt to the new environment by shifting away from low-value (wheat) exports and toward high-value export crops such as canola (Doan, Paddock and Dyer 2003, 2006). It was also expected that farmers would produce more feed grain for the local livestock industry. Finally, the lower farmgate prices were expected to encourage farmers to pursue economies of size in grain production.

It is important to note, however, that the 1990s were a dynamic time for grain production on the Canadian Prairies for several reasons, not just because of the repeal of the WGTA. Improvements in farm equipment encouraged larger and more efficient farms, and the development of herbicide-resistant canola varieties led to their increasing popularity (Beckie et al. 2011). World prices for agricultural commodities also varied widely during this period, which likely affected farmers' production and technology adoption decisions. It is thus a challenging empirical question to determine how much of the aggregate changes in land use and technology adoption stemming from within-farm changes and reallocation were caused by the reform. To the best of our knowledge, such an empirical investigation has not been undertaken to date.

4.2.2   The Advent of Zero Tillage in Western Canada

The 1990s marked the beginning of large-scale adoption of a new seeding technology called zero tillage in Western Canada. The technology was a seeding method that could prepare the seedbed and deposit the seed all in one operation while disturbing the soil as little as possible. The conventional seeding method involved tilling the soil several times, which dried the soil and removed the previous year's crop residue from the surface, hence leading to erosion problems under windy conditions. The benefits of zero tillage were to reduce fuel use, conserve soil moisture, decrease soil erosion, and reduce labor requirements. Zero tillage technology was an extension of existing "minimum tillage" technology, which involved less tillage than conventional methods (often seeding in one operation) but disturbed the soil more than zero tillage technology.

The moisture conservation benefits of zero tillage allowed many farms to sow a crop every year in their fields instead of leaving them to lay idle every 2nd or 3rd year, a practice commonly referred to as "summer-fallowing." This practice allowed for moisture to accumulate for the next year and allowed for the control of weeds using tillage. Planting a crop every year, however, also meant that more fertilizer needed to be applied, since leaving the soil idle increased plant-available nitrogen levels through the natural soil process of mineralization. Furthermore, zero tillage depends on the use of herbicides to control weeds that conventional tillage helps control.[11]

Zero tillage became the dominant seeding technology on the prairies, increasing from 8 percent to 59 percent of cultivated acres between 1991 and 2011. At the same time, the use of "minimum tillage" technology was relatively stable between 1991 and 2011 at 25 percent of cultivated acres. Zero tillage has been adopted in many countries (Derpsch et al. 2010).

4.3 Data

We combine freight rate data with a unique new farm-level data set derived from the Census of Agriculture. This section explains the data sources and how they were combined.

4.3.1 Census of Agriculture Microdata

The analysis is based on the longitudinal Census of Agriculture File (L-CEAG), which is constructed from the quinquennial Census of Agriculture (CEAG). Stretching from 1986 to 2011, the L-CEAG traces the evolution of the farm population over five-year intervals, permitting the longitudinal analysis of continuing farms and their operators as well as the identification of entering and exiting farms.

The census data also indicates the location of each farm at the CCS level. A CCS is equivalent to a rural municipality in the case of Saskatchewan and Manitoba and a county in the case of Alberta. We use data for several years before and after the 1995 reform in order to identify the effect of the WGTA repeal on farm outcomes. We therefore use data from 1991 and 2001 census years in the baseline estimations.

The data includes a rich set of information, such as farm size and the number of acres devoted to different crops and summer fallow. We also use census data on the use of different tillage technologies. Constant 2011 CCS boundaries were used to control for changes in boundaries between years and amalgamations of CCSs over time. The CCS boundaries are illustrated in figure 4.1.

The definition of agricultural operation used by the Census of Agriculture includes many operations where farming is not the main occupation of the operator and gross farm revenues are very small. Small acreages, for

---

11. Awada (2012) posits that four factors hastened the adoption of zero tillage in western Canada during the 1990s in general. First, the zero tillage seeding equipment improved substantially during this time. Second, the price of "Roundup" herbicide decreased to a point where it became economical to use it as a primary weed control method. Third, interest rates decreased, making it easier for farmers to finance the cost of the new technology. Finally, the price of fuel increased during this time.

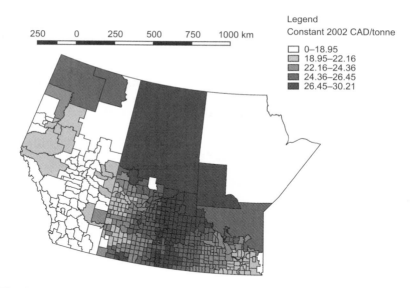

Fig. 4.1   Freight rate changes between 1991 and 2001 and 2011 CCS boundaries for Alberta, Saskatchewan, and Manitoba
Notes: Areas with no fill indicate CCSs without census data or CCSs where data was amalgamated with neighboring CCSs for confidentiality reasons.
Source: Statistics Canada and *Freight Rate Manager*.

example, are included in the definition of a "census farm." Since we want to focus on the behavior of grain farms of sufficient size to avoid including hobby or lifestyle farms, we restrict our sample to farms with a gross farm income of C\$30,000 (constant 2002 dollars) in 1991, which is the average income for Canadian low-income grain and oilseed farms during the study period (Statistics Canada 2016). We also restrict the sample to only "grain and oilseed farms" (longitudinal NAICS 17 to 22) that are defined by Statistics Canada using the derived market value of commodities reported.

4.3.2   Freight Rate Data

We combine data on farm outcomes from the Census of Agriculture with railway freight rate data supplied by *Freight Rate Manager*, a service provided by a consortium of government, academic, and farmer organizations.[12] The freight rate data encompass the freight rate (price per tonne) for wheat from almost 1,000 delivery locations spread across Alberta, Saskatchewan, and Manitoba.[13] Since we do not know where each farm in the

12. This service provides farmers with information on the cost of shipping various crops by rail, depending on their location. See http://freightratemanager.usask.ca/index.html for more details on the source of the freight-rate data.
13. Using shipment volume data from the Canadian Grain Commission (2014) for each station, we exclude stations that report total train deliveries per year of 1000 mt or less.

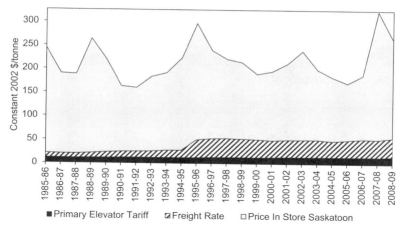

Fig. 4.2   Primary elevator tariff, freight rate, and price in store, Saskatoon, SK, #1 Canada Western Red Spring Wheat, 12.5 percent protein
Source: Saskatchewan Agriculture and Food.

census delivers its grain, we measure average railway freight rates for each CCS in the data using the nearest delivery point available each census year. We measure freight rates from several grid points within each CCS, using a 0.1 degree grid of the earth's surface, and then take the average freight rate for all grid points within a given CCS as our measure of each CCS's average freight rate.[14]

We measure average local trucking costs from the farm to the delivery location using the average distance measure from each grid point to the nearest delivery location. The change in distances over time reflects the effect of the branch line abandonment and the consolidation of delivery points that occurred at the same time as the subsidy repeal.

The pattern of freight rate changes between 1991 and 2001 by CCS is illustrated in figure 4.1. Note that while freight rates increased for all locations between 1991 and 2001, there was a large variation in the size of this increase, even within individual provinces. The largest freight increases were in northeastern Saskatchewan, which is the most remote location in terms of distance to both the West Coast and Thunder Bay.

Figure 4.2 illustrates the abrupt increase in freight rates in the 1995 to 1996 crop year, using data for Saskatoon, Saskatchewan, a location in the middle of the Canadian Prairies. On a constant dollar basis, rates were effectively invariant across the other years. Hence we are confident that the changes in observed freight rates are due to the policy change rather than

---

14. We restrict the grid points only to those where crops are actually grown, using satellite data from Ramankutty et al. (2008). Grid points are excluded if less than 10 percent of the surrounding land is devoted to crops or pasture. The average number of grid points in a CCS is 17, and the median number of grid points in a CCS is 12. See Ferguson and Olfert (2016) for an example of how grid points are matched to delivery locations.

any endogenous relationship between farm production and freight rates.[15] The figure also illustrates that primary elevator tariffs for wheat, which is the fee charged by grain companies to store and load grain onto railway cars, were generally constant over the 1986 to 2009 period[16] and that wheat prices fluctuated greatly during this period.

4.3.3   Soil and Weather Data

The weather data include lagged August precipitation and average July temperature in each CCS. We posit that the previous year's weather will influence planting decisions in the subsequent year. The weather data are taken from the University of East Anglia's high-resolution (10′) data set of surface climate over global land areas (New et al. 2002). We match the weather data from the centroid of each grid area to its nearest CCS using geographic information system techniques.

The soil data describes the percentage of each CCS that is brown, dark brown, black, dark gray, or gray soil. The color of the soil is determined by the level of organic matter it contains, which is itself related to the vegetation and hence by long-run weather. Brown soil is found in the most arid parts of the prairies that were previously a grassland ecosystem. Black soil is found in moister areas of the prairies that were previously covered by long grass and deciduous trees. Gray soil is found in areas with coniferous forests. The soil data originates from the Soil Landscapes of Canada database (AAFC 2010).

4.4   Defining Entering, Exiting, and Continuing Farms

As with any longitudinal firm population, a full understanding of their dynamics depends on the rules that are imposed to identify continuing, entering, and exiting farms. The L-CEAG identified agriculture operations[17] (hereafter farms) using a longitudinally consistent code that is maintained across census years[18] and is largely based on the headquarters location of

---

15. Freight rates and production are inherently endogenous because freight rates influence the equilibrium level of production, while production through transportation density and fronthaul and backhaul effects can influence freight rates (see Behrens and Brown 2018).

16. Handling charges and freight rates for canola and other grains evolved similarly to those for wheat (SAFRR 2003, tables 2–43 and 2–44).

17. An agriculture operation is a "farm, ranch or other agriculture operation producing agriculture products" (http://www.statcan.gc.ca/eng/ca2011/gloss). See http://www.statcan.gc.ca/pub/95-629-x/2007000/4123857-eng.htm for a more detailed discussion.

18. One of the concerns with working with a longitudinal file is the quality of the longitudinal identifier. In construction of the cross-sectional Census of Agriculture file, considerable effort is put into identifying farms that may be false births, with the most effort put into identifying large-farm false births and deaths. This means that these errors may be more likely for smaller farms, inflating their entry and exit rates. False births and deaths were one of the concerns when constructing the longitudinal file, but tests of the data (e.g., identifying entering farms in the same geographic unit matching exiting farms with the same size and operator age five years on) suggested that this was at most a minor problem.

the farm. Of course, decisions have to be made when farms change hands or are merged into larger operations whether they are continuers, exiters, or entrants.[19] These are based on a set of basic rules that allow the farm population to be classified into these three groups.

4.4.1   Continuing Farms

Mechanically, farms are considered to be continuers if their response to the subsequent census is under the same identifier. The identifier is maintained if the farm is an ongoing operation[20] and has the same headquarters location. This is the case even if the farm is sold, as long as it continues to be associated with the original headquarters location and the new operator's information is available (i.e., name and age). The rule holds regardless of whether the sale is an intergenerational transfer or the farm is sold to someone outside of the family.

4.4.2   Exiting Farms

If the respondent indicates that the farm is no longer operating (i.e., selling agriculture products for sale or the intent for sale), the farm has exited, and its identifier is terminated. Furthermore, if the farm is purchased by an ongoing operation farm, under most circumstances it will be treated as an exit, and all its land and assets will be combined with the purchasing farm operations. The purchasing farm identifier is maintained, and the purchased farm identifier is terminated.

4.4.3   Entering Farms

If a new farm is identified on the Farm Register and qualifies as an operating farm based on the census response, then it is a new farm and given a unique farm identifier. The farm is also considered to be an entrant if the farm is sold to a new operation and the headquarters location cannot be associated with the farm under the previous owner.[21] The farm is given a new identifier, and the old identifier is terminated.

It is, in the end, likely impossible to codify every possible scenario to discern whether a farm is continuing or is an exit or an entrant. Nevertheless, farms are generally treated as continuers if they are taken over and maintained as ongoing and independent operations but are exits if they cease operation or are taken over by another farm that continues to operate. They are entrants if they are new to the Farm Register or it is not clear that the farm that has been sold is identifiable as a continuing farm.

---

19. See also Nagelschmitz et al. (2016) for a similar but more in-depth discussion of the identification of continuing, exiting, and entering farms.

20. An ongoing operation is one that produces agricultural products for sale or with the intent to sale.

21. In the case of a dissolved partnership, where the farm is split and begins operations as separate entities, the old farm identifier is terminated, and new operations are treated as entrants.

4.5   Farm Dynamics and Technological Change

We decompose the change in the composition of farmland, either in its land use (focusing on *wheat, canola,* and *summer fallow*[22]) or in the application of the type of tillage (*conventional, minimum,* and *zero till*), resulting from the contributions of the *continuing, entering,* and *exiting* farms. In so doing, the decomposition provides a means to measure how the competitive process influences these outcomes. There are several ways that these outcomes can be decomposed into the contributions of entering, exiting, and continuing farms.[23] We adopt the Foster, Haltiwanger, and Krizan (2001) approach but do so with an eye to its limitations.

Defining L_{gt}^o as the percentage share of land accounted for by outcome o (i.e., land use or tillage type) in region g ($\in$ prairies, CCS) at time t, we can decompose the percentage point change in share of farmland (ΔL_{gt}^o) between year $t - \tau$ and t into the contributions of continuing (C), entering (E), and exiting (X) farms (f):

$$(1) \quad \Delta L_{gt} = \sum_{f \in C} s_{f,t-\tau} \Delta L_{ft} + \sum_{f \in C} (L_{f,t-\tau} - L_{g,t-\tau}) \Delta s_{ft} + \sum_{f \in C} \Delta L_{ft} \Delta s_{ft}$$
$$+ \sum_{f \in E} s_{ft}(L_{ft} - L_{g,t-\tau}) - \sum_{f \in X} s_{f,t-\tau}(L_{f,t-\tau} - L_{g,t-\tau}).$$

To simplify the notation, the outcome index o is dropped. The first three terms in the decomposition capture the effect of the continuing farm population (C). The first term is the *within* farm effect and measures the contribution of change in the share of acres in land use to which a tillage technology is applied while holding the share of land accounted for by the farm to its level at the start of the period. The second term captures the *between* farm effect, where the farm makes a positive contribution if it is growing and its land-use/till-technology share is above average at the start of the period. The third term is the *cross* effect and is positive if growing farms are also more intensively using a land use/till technology.

While the first three terms tell us the extent to which change is driven by incumbent farms, it is only the *within* term that measures the extent to which incumbent farms drive change independent of shifts in farmland. The *between* and *cross* terms capture the effect of shifts in acreage between growing and declining farms on outcomes and, therefore, measure an aspect of how the reallocation of resources across farms drive overall change. Their contributions are positive if farms that have higher than average intensity in

---

22. We focus on wheat and canola because both crops are sold primarily to export markets and have different value-to-weight ratios. The effect of changing freight rates might also be applied to barley, for instance, but it is both exported and used for domestic consumption, reducing the expected effect of rising freight rates, as farmers are less dependent on foreign markets. Wheat and canola are also used because they are two of the most important crops that, along with summer fallow, account for about two-thirds of land use by 2011.

23. For a review of various decomposition methods as applied to productivity, see Baldwin and Gu (2006).

year $t - \tau$ increase their share (*between*) or because there was concomitant growth in both intensity and shares (*cross*) over τ years.

The fourth and fifth terms capture the effects of *entry* (E) and *exit* (X). Entry has a positive effect if entrants use the technology more intensively than the farm population at the start of the period, while exit has a positive effect if they use technology less intensively at the start of the period compared to the overall farm population.

The Foster, Haltiwanger, and Krizan (2001) decomposition is not without limitations, but it likely provides a reasonable representation of the effect of changes in the farm population on outcomes. One concern is the potential bias in the continuing farm components resulting from regression to the mean (Baldwin and Gu 2006). That is, farms with initially large sizes (e.g., because of an expansion of rented land to produce more of a particular crop) are more likely to see a subsequent decline in both size and share of acreage in a particular land use/technology in the subsequent period. Hence the use of initial farm shares and outcome variable shares in the three incumbent farm components may be correlated because of these transitory effects rather than some underlying economic process. However, in this instance, we are less concerned about this effect because we have chosen to focus the analysis on longer-term trends that are less sensitive to transitory shocks associated with regression to the mean (Baldwin and Gu 2006).

A second concern[24] surrounds the implicit assumption of who is replacing whom in the farm population. The Foster, Haltiwanger, and Krizan (2001) decomposition assumes that entering farms are replacing the average farm at the start of the period, while the average farm at the start of the period is replacing exiting farms. In other sectors of the economy that are imperfectly competitive, this assumption may not hold. For instance, in many manufacturing industries, entry and exits tend to replace each other as the churn involves small firms that are often less productive than larger firms and compete for the same small market segments (Baldwin 1995; Baldwin and Gu 2006). Here it isn't apparent a priori that entering farms are taking land from exits or declining incumbents. We believe it is reasonable, at least as a starting point, to assume that entering farms are replacing the average farm and the average farm is replacing exiting farms.

4.6   Decomposing the Sources of Aggregate Changes in Technology Adoption

We begin the analysis by decomposing aggregate changes in technology-adoption and land-use patterns into the contributions by exiting, entering,

---

24. A third concern is that the Foster et al. (2001) decomposition is sensitive to bias stemming from measurement error. We don't believe that this particular form of error, which is more likely to occur when measuring output and employment in productivity decompositions, is a major concern here.

Table 4.1   Decomposition of the change in land-use/tillage-type adoption rates between 1991 and 2001 for farms with above- and below-median changes in railway freight rates

Type	Transport cost	Adoption rate 1991	Adoption rate 2001	Total change	Within	Between	Cross	Exit	Entry
Canola	Above median	0.10	0.14	0.04	0.02	0.00	0.01	0.00	0.01
	Below median	0.12	0.13	0.01	0.00	0.00	0.01	0.00	0.00
Total wheat	Above median	0.49	0.36	−0.13	−0.11	0.01	−0.01	0.00	−0.02
	Below median	0.43	0.37	−0.06	−0.06	0.01	0.00	0.00	−0.01
Summer	Above median	0.26	0.13	−0.13	−0.09	−0.01	−0.01	0.00	−0.02
fallow	Below median	0.21	0.15	−0.06	−0.05	−0.01	0.00	0.00	−0.01
Zero till	Above median	0.09	0.38	0.29	0.16	0.01	0.08	0.00	0.04
	Below median	0.08	0.31	0.24	0.14	0.00	0.06	0.00	0.04
Minimum till	Above median	0.26	0.30	0.04	0.03	0.00	0.00	0.00	0.00
	Below median	0.28	0.34	0.06	0.04	0.00	0.01	0.00	0.00
Conventional	Above median	0.66	0.32	−0.33	−0.20	−0.01	−0.08	0.00	−0.05
till	Below median	0.64	0.35	−0.29	−0.18	−0.01	−0.06	0.00	−0.04

Notes: Acres of crops—summer fallow and by tillage type—are measured as a proportion of total farmland in 1991 and 2001 (the adoption rate) for farms classified to longitudinal NAICS 17 to 22. Totals may not add due to rounding. Entrants and exits and incumbent farms are identified using the longitudinal farm identifier derived from each farm's longitudinal identifier. The restricted sample excludes farms with revenues of $30,000 or less. The decomposition is adapted from Foster, Haltiwanger, and Krizan (2001). The *within* component measures the contribution of incumbent farms to the aggregated change based on their initial share in acres. The *between* component captures the effect of growth in the measured adoption rate of crops/tillage relative to the average weighted by the change in the farm's share of crop land. The *cross-product* (cross) term measures whether farms with changes in their share of land in crops also experience change in their adoption rate. The last two terms measure the effect of *entrants* and *exits* on the adoption rate. The effect of *exits* will be positive if they have lower than average adoption rates, while the effect of *entrants* will be positive if they have above average adoption rates.

Source: Statistics Canada, authors' calculations.

and continuing farms between 1991 and 2001 (table 4.1) based on the Foster, Haltiwanger, and Krizan (2001) decomposition expressed in (1). For the change in the adoption rate (outcome) and its decomposition, the prairie farm population is divided into two groups: farms experiencing changes in railway freight rates above and below that of the median farm. Splitting the sample this way allows us to test initially on an informal basis, and subsequently on a formal basis, the relationship between transport costs and shifts in the farm population. However, before reviewing the decomposition results, we first set the scene by describing the basic pattern in the farm-level data.

4.6.1   Aggregate Changes in Land Use and Technology Adoption

In terms of land use, there is an overall shift in the share of land devoted to wheat and summer fallow toward canola between 1991 and 2001 (see "Total change" column of table 4.1). This is the case irrespective of whether the farm incurs below or above median changes in railway freight rates. For instance, the share of land devoted to the production of wheat fell by 13 percentage points (49 percent to 36 percent) for farms with above-median freight rate increases and 6 percentage points (43 percent to 37 percent) for farms with below-median freight rate increases. The share of land devoted to the production of canola increased by 4 percentage points and 1 percentage point for farms subject to above-median and below-median freight rate increases, respectively. This shift toward production from low-value to high-value export crops due to the reform is akin to the Alchian and Allan (1964) conjecture from the producer's perspective, since the increase in per-unit trade costs increased the relative price of canola compared to wheat.

The share of land in summer fallow declined by 13 percentage points and 6 percentage points for farms subject to above-median and below-median freight rate increases, respectively. In contrast, the share of land where zero till was used rose by 29 percentage points (9 percent to 38 percent) for farms with above-median freight rate increases and 24 percentage points (8 percent to 31 percent) for farms with below-median freight rate increases. Conventional till saw a similar and opposite shift, while minimum till saw little change. Again, there appears to be a stronger effect across all three technologies for farms with above-median changes to freight rates. Ferguson and Olfert (2016) suggest that the declining importance of summer fallow is related to the shift away from conventional till toward minimum till and especially zero till technology, since the moisture conservation benefits of new tillage technologies reduced the need for summer fallow.

The 1991 to 2001 period allows only six years of the farm population to adapt to the 1995 change in transportation costs, whose effect is partially cushioned by a one-time payout to farms in partial compensation for the change. Moreover, while individual farms may have the capacity to shift their crops and technology relatively quickly, it may take longer for this change to play out in terms of farm dynamics, as those farms that are better able to adapt will enter/expand, and those less able will exit/contract. Therefore, it is also necessary to look over a longer time frame.

As a result, we extend the analysis by a further 10 years, from 1991 to 2011 (table 4.2). Over this longer period, the total change in land use and related technological change is even more apparent. In particular, the shift toward the production of canola and away from wheat is more pronounced and so too is the adoption of zero till technology instead of conventional till.[25] Minimum till is the one exception— it becomes less popular by the end of the period, as it is apparently eclipsed by zero till technology that was only in its infancy in 1991. Still, the essential pattern of greater change for those farms with above-median freight rate shocks remains, essentially

---

25. The 1991 adoption rates reported in tables 1 and 2 are not identical, which is due to small differences in the median freight rate for the two time horizons.

Table 4.2   Decomposition of the change in land-use/tillage-type adoption rates between 1991 and 2011 for farms with above- and below-median changes in railway freight rates

Type	Transport cost	Adoption rate 1991	2011	Total change	Total change decomposition Within	Between	Cross	Exit	Entry
Canola	Above median	0.07	0.27	0.20	0.07	0.00	0.06	0.00	0.06
	Below median	0.15	0.31	0.16	0.06	0.01	0.04	0.00	0.05
Total wheat	Above median	0.49	0.32	−0.17	−0.09	0.01	−0.04	0.00	−0.05
	Below median	0.42	0.34	−0.08	−0.05	0.00	0.00	0.00	−0.03
Summer fallow	Above median	0.30	0.09	−0.21	−0.09	−0.01	−0.05	0.00	−0.06
	Below median	0.17	0.05	−0.12	−0.05	−0.01	−0.02	0.00	−0.04
Zero till	Above median	0.11	0.69	0.58	0.22	0.00	0.20	0.00	0.15
	Below median	0.06	0.60	0.54	0.22	0.00	0.15	0.00	0.17
Minimum till	Above median	0.26	0.22	−0.05	−0.01	0.00	−0.03	0.00	−0.01
	Below median	0.28	0.25	−0.03	0.00	0.00	−0.02	0.00	−0.02
Conventional till	Above median	0.63	0.10	−0.53	−0.21	0.00	−0.18	0.00	−0.14
	Below median	0.67	0.15	−0.51	−0.22	−0.01	−0.14	0.00	−0.13

Notes: Acres of crops—summer fallow and by tillage type—are measured as a proportion of total farm land in 1991 and 2011 (the adoption rate) for farms classified to longitudinal NAICS 17 to 22. Totals may not add due to rounding. Entrants and exits and incumbent farms are identified using the longitudinal farm identifier derived from each farm's longitudinal identifier. The restricted sample excludes farms with revenues of $30,000 or less. The decomposition is adapted from Foster, Haltiwanger, and Krizan (2011). The *within* component measures the contribution of incumbent farms to the aggregated change based on their initial share in acres. The *between* component captures the effect of growth in the measured adoption rate of crops/tillage relative to the average weighted by the change in the farm's share of crop land. The *cross-product* (cross) term measures whether farms with changes in their share of land in crop also experience change in their adoption rate. The last two terms measure the effect of *entrants* and *exits* on the adoption rate. The effect of *exits* will be positive if they have lower than average adoption rate while the effect of *entrants* will be positive if they have above average adoption rates.

Source: Statistics Canada, authors' calculations.

confirming Ferguson and Olfert's (2016) descriptive findings, but with micro data instead of aggregate data. Left open to question, of course, is whether these outcomes are the result of the incumbent farm adapting to the price shock and/or the reallocation of land from declining incumbent and exiting farms to growing incumbent and entering farms—and following from this, whether the apparent association between transportation costs and these changes stands up to more rigorous statistical testing. We address these questions in turn.

4.6.2   Decomposition of Farm Outcomes

Across tables 4.1 and 4.2, we find that the within-farm effect, which isolates the incumbent farm adoption of technology holding farm size constant, is the largest contributor to aggregate changes in technology and land use for the time period from 1991 to 2001. As per table 4.1, the within-farm effect for zero till adoption explains about 16 percentage points of the total 29 percentage points of aggregate change for farms with above-median transport costs and 14 percentage points out of the total 24 percentage point change for farms with below-median transport costs. A strong within-farm effect can be observed in the decline of conventional till technology, accounting for 20 percentage points out of the total change of 33 percentage points for farms with above-median transport costs and 18 percentage points of the total of 29 percentage point change for farms with below-median transport costs. The within-farm effect is also strong when looking at land use, explaining around 11 percentage points of the total of 13 percentage point decline in land used for wheat production for farms with above-median transport costs and 6 percentage points out of a total of 6 percentage points for farms with below-median transport costs.

The decomposition was performed again for the period 1991 to 2011 to examine whether the same components are important over a long period of time (table 4.2). Over this longer period, the within-farm effect is losing importance and the cross and entry terms combined become the most important component. For example, table 4.2 shows that from the total 58 percentage point change in zero till adoption, the within-farm effect explains 22 percentage points, while the cross and entry effects together explain 35 percentage points for farms with above-median transport costs. In contrast, for the farms with below-median transport costs, of the total of 54 percentage point change, the within term explains 22 percentage points and cross and entry terms sum to 32 percentage points. The same trend can be observed for the other technology and land-use variables. Thus the reallocation of land through the expansion of incumbent farms and the entry of new farms gain importance in the long run. Competitive reallocation matters for understanding aggregate technology adoption.

Casual inspection of tables 4.1 and 4.2 suggests that the effect of transportation costs varies substantially across the components. By focusing, for example, on zero till technology, its adoption is stronger for farms with above-median transport costs. For the period from 1991 to 2001, the entry term does not play an important role, thus the adoption of zero till technology in higher-transport-cost areas is associated with farms that have adopted the technology and are expanding and not with new entrants. The situation changes for the period from 1991 to 2011, when the entry gains importance and thus, in the long run, the adoption of zero till technology in higher-cost areas is explained by farms that have adopted the technology and expand and new entrants. Hence entry would have occurred only after incentives had changed. These dynamics hold true for all variables considered.

4.7   Regression Analysis

Overall, the preliminary results in tables 4.1 and 4.2 suggest that the increase in transportation costs has a within-farm effect in the short run, while reallocation becomes more important in the long run. In order to test this hypothesis more formally, we now perform the decomposition analysis separately for each CCS and apply a regression analysis. The following first-differenced model is used to estimate the effect of transport costs on the five decomposition effects: within, between, cross, entry, and exit. The regressions are run separately for the 1991 to 2001 and 1991 to 2011 time periods at the CCS level.

The model for the periods from 1991 to 2001 and 1991 to 2011 is specified as follows:

$$(2) \qquad \Delta L_{gt}^c = \alpha + \beta \Delta freight_{gt} + \delta \Delta dist_{gt} + \gamma controls_g + \varepsilon_{gt},$$

where ΔL_{gt}^c is the change in the outcome variable of interest for the components c ($c \in$ Total change, within, between, cross, entry, and exit) for CCS g between the prereform year 1991 and postreform years 2001 and 2011. The independent variables $\Delta freight_{gt}$ and $\Delta dist_{gt}$ represent the change in average freight cost per ton of grain shipped from CCS g to port between 1991 and two different years, 2001 and 2011, and the change in average distance from each CCS to its nearest delivery point over the same two periods of time, respectively. The various control variables include January and July temperatures, annual precipitation, dummy variables for the provinces of Alberta and Manitoba, and shares of soil types (black, gray, dark gray, brown, and dark brown). We run the model with just $\Delta freight_{gt}$ and $\Delta dist_{gt}$ (model 1) and with the controls added (model 2). First-differencing subsumes CCS fixed effects, yet allows us to control for long-run weather as an explanatory variable for changes in the decomposition components. The constant term captures any effects that are constant across all CCSs, such as world grain prices, the advent of new technologies, or the effect of tariffs negotiated at the WTO or regionally via the CUSFTA or NAFTA. The constant in the first-differenced specification is analogous to the posttreatment period dummy in a difference-in-differences specification.

The model is run on a balanced panel of 464 CCSs. A CCS is included in the estimation if we are able to measure the total change in all the outcome variables and the independent variables over both the 1991 to 2001 and 1991 to 2011 periods. This means there will be a different set of farms represented in the sample compared to the one used to produce tables 4.1 and 4.2. Nevertheless, as table 4.3 demonstrates, there is no qualitative difference between the change in the outcome variables for the 1991 and 2001 periods and 1991 and 2011 periods and those reported in tables 4.1 and 4.2 (after taking the mean of the above- and below-median transport costs).

4.7.1   Land-Use Regressions

The main results are summarized in figures 3 and 4, where we report the point estimates and the 90 percent confidence intervals for the railway freight

Table 4.3   Average change in share of acreage in crops and till technology across consolidated census subdivisions, 1991 to 2001 and 1991 to 2011 (percentage points)

Period	Land use/technology	Average	Standard deviation
1991–2001	Canola	2.6	7.2
	Wheat	−20.3	14.5
	Summer fallow	−8.9	8.4
	Zero till	23.1	17.5
	Minimum till	4.5	13.9
	Conventional till	−27.6	16.9
1991–2011	Canola	17.7	10.3
	Wheat	−27.8	16.9
	Summer fallow	−15.5	11.3
	Zero till	50.4	25.0
	Minimum till	−1.6	17.8
	Conventional till	−48.8	19.0

Notes: Reported in the average total change, and its standard deviation, in the share of acreage in the crop or where the till technology is applied across 464 Consolidated Census Subdivisions (CCSs). These form a balanced panel for both the 1991 to 2001 and 1991 to 2011 periods and match the sample used in the regression estimates.

Source: Statistics Canada, authors' calculations.

rate coefficient (β) for the 1991 to 2001 and 1991 to 2011 periods.[26] The effect of increased freight rate on crop production is presented in figure 4.3. We find evidence that an increase in the freight rate resulted in positive changes for most components (within, cross, and entry) explaining changes in canola production and a decrease of these same components related to wheat production and summer fallow. The within-farm effect reacted the most to the change in transportation costs, meaning that the policy change created a strong incentive for incumbent farms in areas with high transport costs to reallocate land from wheat production and summer fallow to canola production or to other high-value crops. The point estimates for the within-farm term over the 1991 to 2001 period with controls suggest that every one dollar per tonne increase in transportation costs increased the absolute value of the within-farm component by 0.52 percentage points for canola, 0.69 for wheat, and 0.56 for summer fallow.

The impacts of changes in railway freight rates on reallocation are sustained and even larger in some cases over the longer period of time, as the results for the period from 1991 to 2011 show. The effect of changes in railway freight rates on the cross component is (in relative terms) becoming

26. We report the regression tables for models 1 and 2, where the dependent variable is the total change in adoption, in the appendix. These tables include extra columns, where we add the precipitation and province indicators separately.

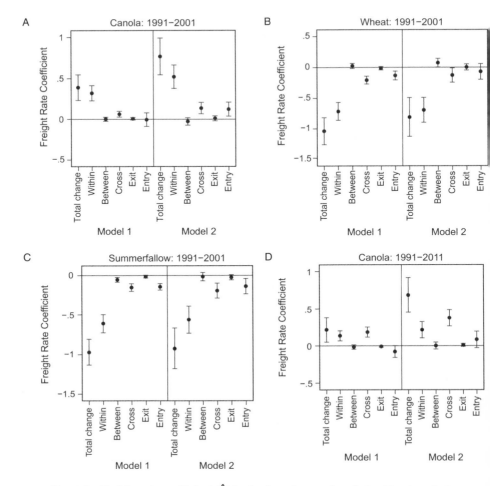

Fig. 4.3 **Freight rate coefficient (β̂) by land-use type and period, without controls (model 1) and with controls (model 2).**

Notes: All models are estimated using a balanced panel of 464 CCSs. The dependent variables are the change in acres in percentage points and its components (within, between, cross, exit, and entry) derived from the Foster, Haltiwanger, and Krizan (2001) decomposition. Presented are the coefficients on *freight* and their 90-percent confidence interval based on robust standard errors. The coefficients represent the total change (or its components) of the share of land in percentage points with respect to a $1 change in transportation costs incurred per tonne shipped.

Source: Statistics Canada, authors' calculations.

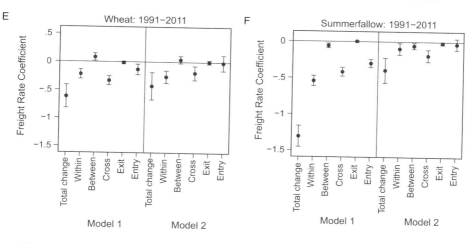

Fig. 4.3   (cont.)

larger during the period from 1991 to 2011, showing that reallocation of land from slow-adapting farms to fast-adapting farms becomes more important in the long run. The change in the entry and exit components are not statistically significant except for wheat, and this does not hold when controls are added. Hence in the longer run, the effect of transportation costs on land use runs through the incumbent farm population rather than being associated with the exit of farms that may not have adapted their land use or the entry of farms that on average use less land for wheat and summer fallow and more land for canola. The inclusion of controls does not qualitatively change the results, although the point estimates do change, which suggests that excluding the controls leads to a problem of omitted variable bias.

4.7.2   Tillage Technology Regressions

The increase of freight rate on tillage technology adoption is presented in figure 4.4. We find evidence that an increase in railway freight rates resulted in a positive change in the within, cross, and exit components explaining zero tillage adoption, and a negative change in the within, cross, and exit components related to conventional tillage. The results on minimum tillage are mixed, and the point estimates for the within and cross terms only become statistically significant once controls are added. The zero tillage results show that the within-farm effect is responsive to the increase in railway freight rates, thus incumbent farms from high-transport-cost areas are the ones that implement this technology. However, the change in the cross component is as large as the change in the within term, and the cross term is the largest in the 2011 horizon. Thus in places hardest hit by the loss of the transportation subsidy, farms that adopted the zero tillage technology

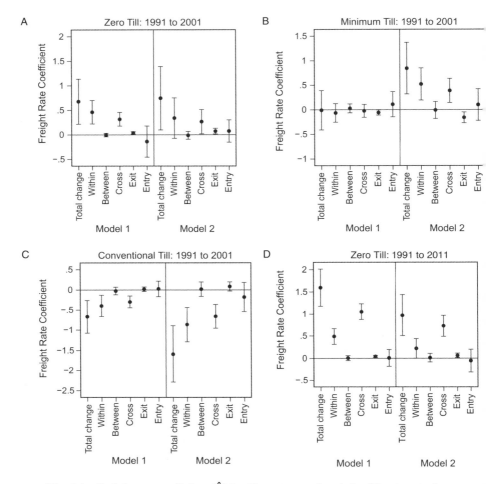

Fig. 4.4 **Freight rate coefficient ($\hat{\beta}$) by tillage type and period, without controls (model 1) and with controls (model 2).**

Notes: All models are estimated using a balanced panel of 464 CCSs. The dependent variables are the change in acres in percentage points and its components (within, between, cross, exit, and entry) derived from the Foster, Haltiwanger, and Krizan (2001) decomposition. Presented are the coefficients on *freight* and their 90-percent confidence interval based on robust standard errors. The coefficients represent the total change (or its components) in the share of land in percentage points with respect to a $1 change in transportation costs incurred per tonne shipped.

Source: Statistics Canada, authors' calculations.

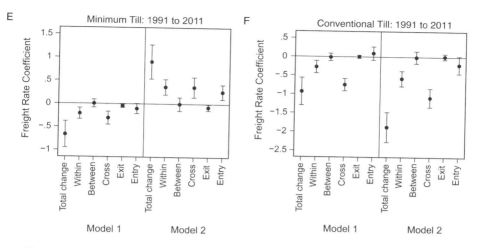

Fig. 4.4   (cont.)

tended to simultaneously increase their size, while farms slower to adopt zero tillage tended to downsize over the 20-year horizon. The same picture can be drawn based on the conventional tillage results, with farms that are moving away from this technology being the ones that expand in size. The results for minimum tillage in the 20-year horizon again only become robust once controls are added.[27]

4.8   Conclusion

The sudden and spatially differentiated increases in freight rates experienced in western Canada after 1995 serves as a useful natural experiment that allows us to evaluate the relative contribution of reallocation versus within-farm adaptation to understand reform-induced aggregate changes in technology adoption and land use. The results suggest that the reform induced a within-farm effect in the short run, while reallocation occurred in the longer term. Hence the competitive process plays an important role in aggregate technological change and in land-use change, albeit one that

---

27. The results for minimum tillage are volatile across the specifications of tables 4A.2 and 4A.4 in the appendix. In the 10-year horizon (table 4A.2), the point estimate for $\Delta\text{freight}_{gt}$ becomes statistically significant only once the province indicators are added. In the 20-year horizon (table 4A.4), the point estimate for $\Delta\text{freight}_{gt}$ is negative and statistically significant, then becomes positive and statistically significant when adding the precipitation control, then loses statistical significance when adding the province indicators, and finally becomes positive and statistically significant once all controls are added. We conclude that these results are not consistent enough to make any assertion about the impact of higher railway freight rates on minimum tillage. Our lack of conclusive evidence for an effect on minimum tillage corroborates with Ferguson and Olfert (2016), who find no effect on minimum tillage in the aggregated CCS-level data.

focuses on the reallocation of land among growing and declining incumbent farms rather than through the entry and exit process. These results, therefore, are consistent with the literature that finds that competitive pressure induces technology adoptions within the farms sector (Paul, Johnston, and Frengley 2000) and a broader set of industries (see Collard-Wexler and De Loecker 2015). To the extent that this competitive reallocation leads to productivity growth either through the adoption of technology or through the shift to larger farm sizes, these results are also in line with Melitz's (2003) theoretical findings.

Methodologically, these findings suggest that moving from the aggregate to the micro level through the development of farm-level panel data sets has the potential to provide insight. This chapter has focused on developing a better understanding of a transportation cost shock on both within-farm changes and competitive reallocation, with both being important. Further exploration of the farm-level data may help uncover the underlying economic mechanisms that induced farmers to change their land use and tillage technology in response to the reform. A natural next step is to focus on the incumbent farm population at the micro level to examine how farms have adapted to change and whether this is conditioned on farm size, as these results point to the effect of shifts in farmland toward growing and likely large farms.

Appendix
Additional Regression Results

Presented below are the regression results for the total change term for the land-use and technology decompositions across periods (tables 4A.1–4A.4). Model 1 only includes the change in the freight rate and the distance shipped to the nearest delivery point between 1991 and 2001 and between 1991 and 2011, while model 2 augments model 1 with a full set of controls as laid out in equation 2. The coefficients on the change in freight rates correspond to those reported in figures 4.3 and 4.4. Also included is a set of intermediate models that include precipitation (model 1a) and provincial binary variables (model 1b). While the inclusion of controls, especially in the intermediate models, at times weaken the effect of freight rates, in the fully specified model (model 2), the estimated effect remains statistically significant.

	Canola				Wheat				Summer fallow			
	Model 1	Model 1a	Model 1b	Model 2	Model 1	Model 1a	Model 1b	Model 2	Model 1	Model 1a	Model 1b	Model 2
Δfreight$_{g,2001-1991}$	0.390[a]	0.439[a]	0.408[a]	0.768[a]	-1.039[a]	-1.073[a]	-0.554[a]	-0.809[a]	-0.971[a]	-0.617[a]	-0.295[b]	-0.925[a]
	(0.095)	(0.094)	(0.131)	(0.135)	(0.136)	(0.134)	(0.182)	(0.194)	(0.099)	(0.091)	(0.149)	(0.155)
Δdist$_{g,2001-1991}$	-0.195[a]	-0.192[a]	-0.174[a]	-0.0880[c]	0.137[b]	0.136[b]	0.0751	-0.00248	-0.0472	-0.0274	-0.0139	-0.011
	(0.052)	(0.052)	(0.054)	(0.049)	(0.054)	(0.055)	(0.053)	(0.057)	(0.044)	(0.042)	(0.042)	(0.041)
jan_temp$_g$				0.234				-0.360				-0.534[b]
				(0.205)				(0.277)				(0.213)
july_temp$_g$				-0.0624				-2.034[a]				0.286
				(0.678)				(0.622)				(0.374)
precip$_g$		0.0115[b]		0.0418[a]		-0.00804		-0.0491[a]		0.0837[a]		0.00524
		(0.005)		(0.014)		(0.006)		(0.016)		(0.006)		(0.010)
Alberta			-0.363	2.175			6.818[a]	3.170[c]			6.356[a]	0.988
			(1.148)	(1.478)			(1.532)	(1.743)			(1.282)	(1.462)
Manitoba			2.450[a]	2.061[c]			-1.177	2.836[c]			11.27[a]	4.088[a]
			(0.746)	(1.156)			(0.857)	(1.661)			(0.728)	(1.098)
Black soil				8.905[a]				-5.660[b]				-1.505
				(2.350)				(2.500)				(1.434)
Dark gray soil				-0.438				0.819				-0.495
				(2.659)				(3.034)				(2.074)
Dark brown soil				12.41[a]				-6.250[c]				-11.63[a]
				(3.069)				(3.192)				(1.892)
Brown soil				8.757[b]				-4.808				-5.603[b]
				(3.651)				(3.823)				(2.411)
Constant	-5.487[b]	-11.16[a]	-6.567[c]	-34.99[a]	14.33[a]	18.30[a]	2.085	62.70[a]	15.19[a]	-26.13[a]	-5.189	0.663
	-2.375	-3.106	-3.389	-10.28	-3.365	-4.125	-4.633	-11.22	-2.482	-3.738	-3.909	-9.573
Observations	464	464	464	464	464	464	464	464	464	464	464	464
R-squared	0.109	0.119	0.138	0.414	0.179	0.182	0.230	0.387	0.132	0.442	0.396	0.624

Notes: Freight rates and average distance to the nearest delivery location are measured in terms of change between 1991 and 2001, while soil and weather data are fixed over time. Soil types are measured as shares, with gray soil excluded. Alberta and Manitoba are province binary variables with the excluded category being Saskatchewan. Robust standard errors in parentheses, with [a], [b], and [c] denoting significance at the 1 percent, 5 percent, and 10 percent levels, respectively.

Sources: Authors' calculations, Statistics Canada.

Table 4A.2   **Effect of higher freight rates on technology adoption, 1991 to 2001**

	Zero till				Minimum till				Conventional till			
	Model 1	Model 1a	Model 1b	Model 2	Model 1	Model 1a	Model 1b	Model 2	Model 1	Model 1a	Model 1b	Model 2
$\Delta freight_{g,2001-1991}$	0.677[b]	0.211	0.187	0.744[c]	−0.0099	0.238	1.661[a]	0.845[a]	−0.667[a]	−0.448[c]	−1.848[a]	−1.589[a]
	(0.279)	(0.267)	(0.332)	(0.393)	(0.244)	(0.236)	(0.293)	(0.319)	(0.248)	(0.246)	(0.330)	(0.423)
$\Delta dist_{g,2001-1991}$	−0.0041	−0.0302	−0.143	−0.0729	0.083	0.0969	−0.0219	0.0176	−0.0789	−0.0667	0.165	0.0552
	(0.101)	(0.0941)	(0.0879)	(0.106)	(0.0983)	(0.0890)	(0.0948)	(0.114)	(0.107)	(0.111)	(0.101)	(0.115)
jan_temp_g				1.679[a]				−0.215				−1.465[a]
				(0.618)				(0.492)				(0.560)
$july\_temp_g$				−0.670				−0.730				1.399
				(1.873)				(1.802)				(1.204)
$precip_g$		−0.110[a]		−0.0458		0.0584[a]		−0.0637[c]		0.0516[a]		0.109[a]
		(0.0158)		(0.0418)		(0.0129)		(0.0362)		(0.0156)		(0.0295)
Alberta			−1.592	−2.751			20.58[a]	12.74[a]			−18.99[a]	−9.985[a]
			(2.975)	(4.080)			(2.381)	(3.525)			(3.146)	(3.763)
Manitoba			−20.53[a]	−14.30[a]			7.716[a]	5.910[b]			12.81[a]	8.389[b]
			(1.792)	(3.638)			(1.760)	(2.958)			(2.068)	(3.485)
Black soil				1.719				−3.487				1.768
				(4.399)				(5.646)				(6.411)
Dark gray soil				−1.072				4.535				−3.463
				(4.842)				(7.238)				(7.688)
Dark brown soil				−0.624				−10.91				11.54
				(6.672)				(6.988)				(7.205)
Brown soil				−9.772				−16.93[b]				26.70[a]
				(8.236)				(8.173)				(8.335)
Constant	6.516	60.85[a]	24.46[a]	67.87[b]	4.262	−24.58[a]	−40.87[a]	20.72	−10.78	−36.27[a]	16.41[c]	−88.59[a]
	(7.164)	(8.743)	(8.662)	(33.56)	(6.259)	(7.242)	(7.740)	(26.14)	(6.557)	(9.256)	(8.732)	(24.32)
Observations	464	464	464	464	464	464	464	464	464	464	464	464
R-squared	0.015	0.139	0.249	0.278	0.002	0.058	0.114	0.277	0.016	0.045	0.263	0.346

Notes: Freight rates and average distance to the nearest delivery location are measured in terms of change between 1991 and 2001, while soil and weather data are fixed over time. Soil types are measured as shares, with gray soil excluded. Alberta and Manitoba are province binary variables with the excluded category being Saskatchewan. Robust standard errors in parentheses, with [a], [b], and [c] denoting significance at the 1 percent, 5 percent, and 10 percent levels, respectively.

Table. ... g ... on canola production and summer fallow, 1991 to 2011

	Canola				Wheat				Summer fallow			
	Model 1	Model 1a	Model 1b	Model 2	Model 1	Model 1a	Model 1b	Model 2	Model 1	Model 1a	Model 1b	Model 2
Δfreight$_{g,2001-1991}$	0.214[b]	0.465[a]	0.335[b]	0.687[a]	-0.614[a]	-1.069[a]	-0.529[a]	-0.429[a]	-1.308[a]	-0.514[a]	-0.708[a]	-0.394[a]
	(0.101)	(0.110)	(0.151)	(0.140)	(0.124)	(0.126)	(0.139)	(0.147)	(0.0890)	(0.0858)	(0.125)	(0.105)
Δdist$_{g,2001-1991}$	-0.212[a]	-0.194[a]	-0.203[a]	-0.101[a]	0.216[a]	0.183[a]	0.163[a]	0.0777[a]	-0.0308	0.0265	0.00145	0.0245
	(0.0388)	(0.0365)	(0.0376)	(0.0308)	(0.0253)	(0.0270)	(0.0236)	(0.0272)	(0.0282)	(0.0216)	(0.0220)	(0.0233)
jan_temp$_g$				-0.955[a]				0.672[c]				-0.462[c]
				(0.308)				(0.358)				(0.264)
july_temp$_g$				0.432				-3.786[a]				0.167
				(0.655)				(1.124)				(0.396)
precip$_g$		0.0385[a]		0.0107		-0.0699[a]		-0.0904[a]		0.122[a]		0.0400[a]
		(0.00976)		(0.0152)		(0.00883)		(0.0237)		(0.00876)		(0.0128)
Alberta			0.65	7.356[a]			7.972[a]	2.943			4.721[a]	4.104[b]
			(1.669)	(2.321)			(1.723)	(2.502)			(1.499)	(1.690)
Manitoba			2.849[b]	0.637			-6.958[a]	5.189[a]			12.46[a]	4.031[a]
			(1.398)	(1.740)			(1.242)	(1.876)			(1.011)	(1.295)
Black soil				10.22[a]				-6.946[b]				1.369
				(3.391)				(3.175)				(1.935)
Dark gray soil				-2.783				-0.883				1.021
				(3.651)				(3.717)				(2.078)
Dark brown soil				9.259[b]				-7.868[c]				-10.86[a]
				(4.118)				(4.232)				(2.648)
Brown soil				-4.357				-4.783				-5.833[c]
				(4.889)				(5.099)				(3.153)
Constant	13.41[a]	-11.31	7.943	-40.45[a]	5.278	50.17[a]	3.47	119.1[a]	34.46[a]	-44.00[a]	7.569	-26.27[b]
	(3.936)	(6.895)	(6.207)	(12.79)	(4.971)	(6.682)	(5.658)	(18.13)	(3.382)	(5.987)	(5.057)	(12.15)
Observations	464	464	464	464	464	464	464	464	464	464	464	464
R-squared	0.130	0.165	0.141	0.459	0.159	0.247	0.307	0.438	0.292	0.565	0.440	0.679

Notes: Freight rates and average distance to the nearest delivery location are measured in terms of change between 1991 and 2001, while soil and weather data are fixed over time. Soil types are measured as shares, with gray soil excluded. Alberta and Manitoba are province binary variables with the excluded category being Saskatchewan. Robust standard errors in parentheses, with [a], [b], and [c] denoting significance at the 1 percent, 5 percent, and 10 percent levels, respectively.

Sources: Authors' calculations, Statistics Canada.

Table 4A.4   **Effect of higher freight rates on technology adoption, 1991 to 2011**

	Zero till				Minimum till				Conventional till			
	Model 1	Model 1a	Model 1b	Model 2	Model 1	Model 1a	Model 1b	Model 2	Model 1	Model 1a	Model 1b	Model 2
$\Delta freight_{g,2001-1991}$	1.597^a	-0.0532	0.587^b	0.972^a	-0.663^a	0.529^a	0.312	0.905^a	-0.933^a	-0.476^b	-0.900^a	-1.876^a
	(0.254)	(0.235)	(0.246)	(0.284)	(0.171)	(0.182)	(0.230)	(0.224)	(0.223)	(0.211)	(0.251)	(0.243)
$\Delta dist_{g,2001-1991}$	0.117	-0.00177	-0.0401	0.00656	-0.0155	0.0706	0.0251	0.0145	-0.102^b	-0.0688	0.015	-0.0211
	(0.0757)	(0.0592)	(0.0515)	(0.0527)	(0.0660)	(0.0484)	(0.0537)	(0.0457)	(0.0474)	(0.0500)	(0.0517)	(0.0409)
jan_temp_g				2.863^a				-1.559^a				-1.304^b
				(0.702)				(0.559)				(0.536)
$july\_temp_g$				-0.286				-2.912^b				3.198^b
				(1.451)				(1.191)				(1.557)
$precip_g$		-0.254^a		-0.230^a		0.184^a		0.0742^b		0.0704^a		0.155^a
		(0.0208)		(0.0379)		(0.0155)		(0.0314)		(0.0177)		(0.0347)
Alberta			5.209^c	6.780^c			9.173^a	6.607^b			-14.38^a	-13.39^a
			(3.046)	(3.943)			(2.821)	(2.981)			(3.154)	(3.722)
Manitoba			-36.64^a	-18.44^a			18.45^a	11.45^a			18.19^a	6.993^b
			(2.685)	(4.599)			(2.262)	(3.733)			(2.530)	(3.278)
Black soil zone				4.797				-4.324				-0.473
				(5.141)				(4.835)				(4.200)
Dark gray soil zone				9.535				-4.073				-5.462
				(5.826)				(5.639)				(5.205)
Dark brown soil zone				-9.610				-7.905				17.51^a
				(6.904)				(6.146)				(5.767)
Brown soil zone				-25.96^a				-8.286				34.25^a
				(9.129)				(7.717)				(7.324)
Constant	-11.95	151.1^a	36.86^a	161.7^a	23.76^a	94.07^a	-19.53^b	-36.32	-11.81	-57.03^a	-17.33^c	-125.4^a
	(10.37)	(14.76)	(9.961)	(33.44)	(6.826)	(11.37)	(9.285)	(24.53)	(9.116)	(12.04)	(10.34)	(27.86)
Observations	464	464	464	464	464	464	464	464	464	464	464	464
R-squared	0.094	0.335	0.466	0.539	0.030	0.279	0.156	0.385	0.059	0.091	0.334	0.497

Notes: Freight rates and average distance to the nearest delivery location are measured in terms of change between 1991 and 2001, while soil and weather data are fixed over time. Soil types are measured as shares, with gray soil excluded. Alberta and Manitoba are province binary variables with the excluded category being Saskatchewan. Robust standard errors in parentheses, with [a], [b], and [c] denoting significance at the 1 percent, 5 percent, and 10 percent levels, respectively.

References

AAFC (Agriculture and Agri-Food Canada). 2010. "Soil Landscapes of Canada Version 3.2." Soil Landscapes of Canada Working Group.

Adamopoulos, T., and D. Restuccia. 2014. "The Size Distribution of Farms and International Productivity Differences." *American Economic Review* 104 (6): 1667–97.

Alchian, A. A., and W. R. Allen. 1964. *University Economics.* Wadsworth, CA: Belmont.

Awada, L. 2012. "The Adoption of Conservation Tillage Innovation on the Canadian Prairies." PhD thesis, University of Saskatchewan.

Baldwin, J. R. 1995. *The Dynamics of Industrial Competition.* New York: Cambridge University Press.

Baldwin, J. R., and W. Gu. 2006. "Plant Turnover and Productivity Growth in Canadian Manufacturing." *Industrial and Corporate Change* 15 (3): 417–65.

Beckie, H. J., K. N. Harker, A. Légère, M. J. Morrison, G. Séguin-Swartz, and K. C. Falk. 2011. "GM Canola: The Canadian Experience." *Farm Policy Journal* 8 (1): 43–49.

Behrens, K., and W. M. Brown. 2018. "Transport Costs, Trade, and Geographic Concentration: Evidence from Canada." In *Handbook of International Trade and Transportation,* edited by B. Blonigen and W. Wilson. Cheltenham, UK: Edward Elgar.

Bloom, N., M. Draca, and J. Van Reenen. 2015. "Trade Induced Technical Change: The Impact of Chinese Imports on Innovation, Diffusion and Productivity." *Review of Economic Studies* 83 (1): 87–117.

Bustos, P. 2012. "Trade Liberalization, Exports and Technology Upgrading: Evidence on the Impact of MERCOSUR on Argentinian Firms." *American Economic Review* 101 (1): 304–40. Canadian Grain Commission. 2014. "Grain Deliveries at Prairie Points." 1985–86, 1990–91, 1995–96, 2000–2001, and 2005–2006 Crop Years. Accessed August 8, 2014. http://www.grainscanada.gc.ca/statistics -statistiques/gdpp-lgpcp/gdppm-mlgpcp-eng.htm.

Collard-Wexler, A., and J. De Loecker. 2015. "Reallocation and Technology: Evidence from the US Steel Industry." *American Economic Review* 105 (1): 131–71.

Davey, K., and W. H. Furtan. 2008. "Factors That Affect the Adoption Decision of Conservation Tillage in the Prairie Region of Canada." *Canadian Journal of Agricultural Economics* 56 (3): 257–75.

Derpsch, R., T. Friedrich, A. Kassam, and H. Li. 2010. "Current Status of Adoption of No-till Farming in the World and Some of Its Main Benefits." *International Journal of Agricultural and Biological Engineering* 3 (1): 1–26.

Doan, D., B. Paddock, and J. Dyer. 2003. "Grain Transportation Policy and Transformation in Western Canadian Agriculture." *Proceedings of International Agricultural Policy Reform and Adjustment Project (IAPRAP)* Workshop, Paper #15748, October 23–25. Imperial College London: Wye Campus.

Doan, D., B. Paddock, and J. Dyer. 2006. "The Reform of Grain Transportation Policy and Transformation in Western Canadian Agriculture." In *Policy Reform and Adjustment in the Agricultural Sectors of Developed Countries,* edited by D. Blanford and B. Hill, 163–74. Oxfordshire, UK: CABI.

Ferguson, S. M., and M. R. Olfert. 2016. "Competitive Pressure and Technology Adoption: Evidence from a Policy Reform in Western Canada." *American Journal of Agricultural Economics* 98 (2): 422–46.

Foster, L., J. C. Haltiwanger, and C. J. Krizan. 2001. "Aggregate Productivity Growth: Lessons from Microeconomic Evidence." In *New Developments in Pro-*

ductivity Analysis, edited by C. R. Hulten, E. R. Dean, and M. J. Harper, 303–63. Chicago: University of Chicago Press.

Foster, L., J. Haltiwanger, and C. Syverson. 2008. "Reallocation, Firm Turnover, and Efficiency: Selection on Productivity or Profitability?" *American Economic Review* 98 (1): 394–425.

Fulton, M., K. Baylis, H. Brooks, and R. Gray. 1998. "The Impact of Deregulation on the Export Basis in the Canadian Grain Handling and Transportation System." Working Paper, Department of Agricultural Economics, University of Saskatchewan.

Galdon-Sanchez, J. E., and J. A. Schmitz Jr. 2002. "Competitive Pressure and Labor Productivity: World Iron-Ore Markets in the 1980s." *American Economic Review* 92 (4): 1222–35.

Klein, K. K., and W. A. Kerr. 1996. "The Crow Rate Issue: A Retrospective on the Contribution of the Agricultural Economics Profession in Canada." *Canadian Journal of Agricultural Economics* 44 (1): 1–18.

Klein, K. K., S. N. Kulshreshtha, G. Stennes, G. Fox, W. A. Kerr, and J. Corman. 1994. "Transportation Issues in Canadian Agriculture II: Analysis of the Western Grain Transportation and Feed Freight Assistance Acts." *Canadian Journal of Regional Science* 17 (1): 45–70.

Kraft, D. F., and J. Doiron. 2000. "Post Crow Influence on Prairie Feed Grain Prices." Paper presented September 29, 2000, at Western Nutrition Conference, Winnipeg.

Kulshreshtha, S. N., and D. G. Devine. 1978. "Historical Perspective and Propositions on the Crowsnest Pass Freight Rate Agreement." *Canadian Journal of Agricultural Economics* 26 (2): 72–83.

Lileeva, A., and D. Trefle. 2010. "Improved Access to Foreign Markets Raises Plant-Level Productivity . . . for Some Plants." *Quarterly Journal of Economics* 125 (3): 1051–99.

Melitz, M. J. 2003. "The Impact of Trade on Intra-industry Reallocations and Aggregate Industry Productivity." *Econometrica* 71 (6): 1695–1725.

Nagelschmitz, K., J.-F. Frenette, M. Brown, and S. Prasil. 2016. "The Canadian Longitudinal Census of Agriculture File—a Tool to Better Understand Structural Change of Canadian Farms." Paper presented at the Seventh International Conference on Agricultural Statistics in Rome, Italy, October 26 to 28.

New, M., D. Lister, M. Hulme, and I. Makin. 2002. "A High-Resolution Data Set of Surface Climate over Global Land Areas." *Climate Research* 21 (1): 1–25.

Olmstead, A. L., and P. W. Rhode. 2001. "Reshaping the Landscape: The Impact and Diffusion of the Tractor in American Agriculture, 1910–1960." *Journal of Economic History* 61 (3): 663–98.

Olmstead, A. L., and P. W. Rhode. 2008. *Creating Abundance*. New York: Cambridge University Press.

Paul, C. J. M., W. E. Johnston, and G. A. G. Frengley. 2000. "Efficiency in New Zealand Sheep and Beef Farming: The Impacts of Regulatory Reform." *Review of Economics and Statistics* 82 (2): 325–37.

Pavcnik, N. 2002. "Trade Liberalization, Exit, and Productivity Improvements: Evidence from Chilean Plants." *Review of Economic Studies* 69 (1): 245–76.

Ramankutty, N., A. T. Evan, C. Monfreda, and J. A. Foley. 2008. "Farming the Planet: 1. Geographic Distribution of Global Agricultural Lands in the Year 2000." *Global Biogeochemical Cycles* 22, DOI: 10.1029/2007GB002952.

SAFRR (Saskatchewan Agriculture, Food and Rural Revitalization). 2003. "Agricultural Statistics 2002." Regina, SK: SAFRR, Policy Branch.

Schmitz, J. A., Jr. 2005. "What Determines Productivity? Lessons from the Dramatic

Recovery of the U.S. and Canadian Iron Ore Industries Following Their Early 1980s Crisis." *Journal of Political Economy* 113 (3): 582–625.

Schmitz, T. G., T. Highmoor, and A. Schmitz. 2002. "Termination of the WGTA: An Examination of Factor Market Distortions, Input Subsidies and Compensation." *Canadian Journal of Agricultural Economics* 50 (3): 333–47.

Statistics Canada. 2016. "Distribution of Farm Families and Average Total Income by Typology Group and Farm Type, Unincorporated Sector, Annual." CANSIM Table 002-0030.

Sumner, D. A. 2014. "American Farms Keep Growing: Size, Productivity, and Policy." *Journal of Economic Perspectives* 28 (1): 147–66.

Sunding, D., and D. Zilberman. 2001. "The Agricultural Innovation Process: Research and Technology Adoption in a Changing Agricultural Sector." In *Handbook of Agricultural Economics*, vol. 1, edited by L. Gardner and G. C. Rausser, 207–61. Amsterdam: North Holland.

Trefler, D. 2004. "The Long and Short of the Canada-U. S. Free Trade Agreement." *American Economic Review* 94 (4): 870–95.

USDA (US Department of Agriculture). 2002. "Effects of North American Free Trade Agreement on Agriculture and the Rural Economy." Electronic Outlook Report, Economic Research Service WRS-02-1.

Vercammen, J. 1996. "An Overview of Changes in Western Grain Transportation Policy." *Canadian Journal of Agricultural Economics* 44 (4): 397–402.

Vercammen, J. 2007. "Farm Bankruptcy Risk as a Link between Direct Payments and Agricultural Investment." *European Review of Agricultural Economics* 34 (4): 479–500.

5

Electricity Prices, Groundwater, and Agriculture
The Environmental and Agricultural Impacts of Electricity Subsidies in India

Reena Badiani-Magnusson and Katrina Jessoe

5.1 Introduction

In developing countries, energy subsidies are significant, totaling over $220 billion (in 2005) for the largest 20 non-OECD countries (UNEP 2008). Nearly half of these subsidies are directed at rural households, primarily as electricity subsidies. The rationale is that agricultural electricity subsidies stimulate agricultural production through enhanced groundwater irrigation, benefiting poor rural households and stabilizing food prices. Yet little is known about the causal impact of agricultural electricity subsidies on groundwater usage and agricultural output despite their ubiquity as an agricultural policy tool and the magnitude of resources devoted to them (Birner et al. 2007; Fan, Gulati, and Sukhadeo 2008; Gandhi and

Reena Badiani-Magnusson is a senior economist at the World Bank.

Katrina Jessoe is an associate professor in the Department of Agricultural and Resource Economics at the University of California, Davis.

Thanks to Soren Anderson, Jim Bushnell, Richard Carson, Colin Carter, Larry Karp, Pierre Merel, Kevin Novan, David Rapson, Leo Simon, Wolfram Schlenker, Nick Ryan, and Jon Strand. This chapter also benefited from seminar participants at NEUDC, PACDEV, UC Berkeley, TREE, the NBER Understanding Productivity Growth in Agriculture Conference, and UCSD. Suzanne Plant provided excellent research assistance. Research support for this project was provided by the Giannini Foundation. The authors, alone, are responsible for any errors. The findings, interpretations, and conclusions expressed in this chapter are entirely those of the authors. They do not necessarily represent the views of the International Bank for Reconstruction and Development/World Bank and its affiliated organizations or those of the executive directors of the World Bank or the governments they represent. For acknowledgments, sources of research support, and disclosure of the authors' material financial relationships, if any, please see https://www.nber.org/chapters/c13948.ack.

Namboodiri 2009; Kumar 2005; Mukherji and Shah 2005; Scott and Shah 2004).[1,2]

We investigate these questions within the context of India, where approximately US$10 billion was spent in 2005 alone on agricultural electricity subsidies. These subsidies comprise the largest expenditure item in many state budgets, leading many to wonder about their impacts on agricultural production and the opportunity cost of not allocating these funds elsewhere (Tongia 2003). Anecdotal evidence has linked India's growth in groundwater irrigation, largely fueled by electricity subsidies, to increased agricultural yields, lower food prices, and increased demand for agricultural labor (Briscoe and Malik 2006; Modi 2005; Murgai 2001; Rosegrant, Ringler, and Zhu 2009). Others suggest that these subsidies have substantial environmental costs, including groundwater overexploitation (Kumar 2005; Shah et al. 2003; Shah 2009). However, largely driven by data limitations, few studies have isolated the impact of these subsidies on groundwater extraction and overextraction or their potential to raise agricultural output (Banerji, Meenakshi, and Khanna 2012; Banerji et al. 2013; Ray and Williams 1999; Somanathan and Ravindranath 2006).[3]

In this chapter, we seek to isolate the extent to which agricultural electricity subsidies impacted groundwater extraction and agricultural production between 1995 and 2004. A unique feature of agricultural electricity prices during our period of study is that almost all agricultural users exclusively pay a flat monthly fee for electricity. In other words, they do not face a volumetric charge for electricity. These flat monthly tariffs are primarily determined by state electricity boards, entities that are run and controlled by the state government. Guided by these features of our setting, we measure agricultural electricity prices as a fixed monthly rate that is set annually by each state and exploit variation in electricity prices across states over time.

1. There is, however, (in India) a long literature discussing the linkages between electricity subsidies, groundwater extraction, and agricultural output (Badiani-Magnusson, Jessoe, and Plant 2012; Gandhi and Namboodiri 2009; Mukherji and Shah 2005; Scott and Shah 2004). Some of these studies rely on interviews or survey data to show a strong positive correlation between subsidies, extraction, and agricultural output (Birner et al. 2007; Fan et al. 2008; Kumar 2005; Scott and Shah 2004).

2. See Schoengold and Zilberman (2005) for an overview of irrigation, including a discussion on the role of electricity subsidies, in developing countries.

3. Exceptions include simulation-based and empirical studies that seek to understand the impact of moving from a fixed rate to a volumetric pricing structure for agricultural electricity. One study simulates the impact of removing electricity subsidies on groundwater extraction and agricultural yields in North India and suggests that marginal cost pricing would increase yields and farm profits (Banerji et al. 2012). Another exploits a natural experiment to isolate the effect of a shift from fixed rates to volumetric rates on groundwater extraction and agricultural output (Banerji et al. 2013). A third study estimates the elasticity of demand for agricultural water and then simulates the effect of marginal cost electricity pricing on water demand (Somanathan and Ravi 2006). Finally, recent work evaluates the water and electricity impacts of a pilot program in which farmers voluntarily installed meters and were compensated on a volumetric basis for water savings (Fishman et al. 2014).

We focus on changes in fixed rates as opposed to changes in volumetric rates, since this tariff structure is the status quo agricultural pricing regime, making it the relevant setting in which to evaluate the effect of price changes on groundwater extraction and agricultural production. Given the tariff structure and the nature of our data, we posit that reductions in fixed fees influence groundwater extraction through the adoption and expansion of tubewell irrigation.

Using novel panel data from 344 districts, our empirical approach uses year-to-year variation in state electricity prices to compare a given district's groundwater demand under various prices, controlling for aggregate time shocks. The main identifying assumption behind this strategy is that electricity prices are orthogonal to other time-varying state and district determinants of groundwater demand. However, there are many reasons electricity prices might be systematically correlated with time-varying state unobservables that influence groundwater demand and agricultural production. First, politicians have used electricity pricing as a political tool, and state electoral cycles may be related to other state policies that influence agricultural production and groundwater extraction (Min 2010; Dubash and Rajan 2001). Price may also be systematically correlated with demand for other agricultural inputs such as fertilizer or supply-side electricity constraints in generation and transmission. Motivated by these observations, we gauge the plausibility of our identifying assumption by testing the robustness of our results to the inclusion of time-varying state and district observables.

Our results indicate that an increase in the monthly fixed rate of electricity decreases groundwater extraction along the extensive margin and the probability of groundwater overexploitation. Our estimates imply an extensive margin price elasticity of -0.18 and fit within the range of elasticities reported in meta-analysis (Scheierling, Loomis, and Young 2006). The relatively inelastic response to changes in fixed costs may be explained by features unique to the electricity sector in India. First, volumetric prices are zero, so changes in electricity tariffs should only affect the decision to adopt and expand tubewell irrigation. Second, though we observe and exploit sizable variation in electricity prices, this observed variation is small relative to the size of the subsidy. The relatively small price signal may dampen the groundwater response to price changes. Third, shortages and rationing of electricity imply that a limited supply may be the binding constraint for electricity and hence groundwater demand. Even with these caveats, we find that electricity subsidies meaningfully increase the probability of groundwater extraction and overexploitation, suggesting that there are likely long-run environmental costs from this policy.

These results add a critical data point to the growing literature on the price elasticity of demand for irrigated water in developing countries and bring an empirical perspective to bear on the theoretical literature surrounding the optimal management of groundwater (Huang et al. 2010; Sun, Sesmero, and Schoengold 2006). Obtaining credible elasticity estimates is a critical and necessary step to the design of groundwater management plans and more generally climate-change policies that account for increased variability in precipitation and increased frequency of drought. This is of particular importance in India, where groundwater irrigates 70 percent of irrigated agricultural land. Our results provide insights on the potential for price to encourage groundwater extraction on the extensive margin and suggest that even under a fixed-fee pricing regime, agricultural customers are sensitive to prices. We also provide an empirical counterpart to the rich theoretical and simulation-based literature on the economics of groundwater management (Gisser 1983; Ostrom 2011; Ostrom 1990; Provencher and Burt 1993; Strand 2010). Importantly, we test a fundamental assumption underpinning the theoretical literature—namely, that groundwater extraction and exploitation respond to price changes.

A second set of results demonstrates that subsidy-induced increases in groundwater extraction increase the value of agricultural output, particularly for water-intensive crops. The implied price elasticity of −0.29 for water-intensive agricultural output is consistent with the few existing estimates on the input price elasticity of agricultural output in India, though both our choice of agricultural input and our panel data approach differ from the previous literature (Lahiri and Roy 1985). We also find that for water-intensive crops, farmers are responding along the extensive margin, increasing the area on which crops are grown. The implied elasticity of acreage to groundwater demand is 0.12 and fits within the range of irrigation elasticities (for area) reported by others (Kanwar 2006). These results provide some of the first empirical confirmation that agricultural electricity subsidies achieved the intended objective of increasing agricultural production through the channel of irrigation and build on an emerging literature that considers the long- and short-run agricultural impacts of access to groundwater (Hornbeck and Keskin 2014; Sekhri 2011).

Finally, we explore one efficiency cost of this policy by calculating the efficiency gains from reducing this subsidy by 50 percent.[4] Conditional on certain assumptions, our back-of-the-envelope calculation reveals that the efficiency losses from this subsidy are small, amounting to 9 percent of every rupee spent. While electricity subsidies may create distortions in agricultural production and groundwater consumption, a coarse estimate suggests that the deadweight loss from them is low (Gisser 1993; Rosine and Helmberger 1974). These low efficiency costs are likely driven by three unique features of our setting: the absence of volumetric prices, the magnitude of subsidies for electricity, and constraints on the available electricity supply. Incorporating

---

4. The ideal exercise would also simulate the efficiency gains in shifting from flat-rate to volumetric pricing for electricity.

these considerations into demand estimates would likely increase the price elasticity for electricity and magnify the efficiency costs of these subsidies.

5.2 Electricity Prices and Tubewell Adoption

With the passage of the Electricity Supply Act of 1948, generation, transmission, and distribution of electricity in India were transferred from private ownership to state control. As part of this act, each state formed a vertically integrated State Electricity Board (SEB) responsible for the transmission, distribution, and generation of electricity as well as the setting and collection of tariffs (Tongia 2003). Until the early 1970s, the SEBs charged a volumetric rate for electricity based on metered consumption.

In an effort to increase agricultural production, the government of India in the 1960s began to subsidize a number of key agricultural inputs. This included an agricultural electricity subsidy that was implemented to encourage groundwater irrigation. Evidence suggests that this subsidy indeed increased agricultural energy use, which jumped from just 3 percent of total energy use to 14 percent by 1978 (Pachauri 1982). During the 1970s and 1980s, the number of tubewells also substantially increased. Due to the transaction costs involved with the metering of these newly installed tubewells, the SEBs introduced flat tariffs for agricultural electricity.

As agricultural profits increased and recognition of the importance of agricultural input subsidies grew, farmers began to organize themselves into political coalitions. Around the same time, political competition among state political parties was growing. To attract the agricultural vote, politicians took to using electricity pricing as a campaign tool. We see the first evidence of this in 1977, when one political party in Andhra Pradesh promised free power for agricultural electricity users if elected (Dubash and Rajan 2001). This practice only intensified over time, and by the 1980s, cheap agricultural electricity was a common campaign strategy, especially in agricultural states (Dubash 2007). Throughout our period of study, electricity pricing remains a powerful political tool. Indian politics is often said to come down to bijli, sadak, pani (electricity, roads, water), an observation that has been corroborated in household data (Min 2010; Besley et al. 2004).

The electricity pricing strategies of SEBs have been linked to a number of negative features of the electricity sector (Cropper et al. 2011 ; World Bank 2010). First, it has been argued that they are partly responsible for the financial insolvency of the sector. Though SEBs are required to generate a 3 percent annual return on capital, they operate at huge annual losses, totaling US\$6 billion or −39.5 percent of revenues in 2001 (Lamb 2006). Second, the financial instability of the electricity sector combined with low retail prices likely contributes to the intermittent, unpredictable, and low-quality electricity service that characterizes electricity provision in India (World

Bank 2010; Lamb 2006; Tongia 2003). Third, these subsidies may impose a drag on industrial growth. To partly recover costs, the SEBs charge commercial and industrial users rates that often exceed the marginal cost of supply.

Perhaps most concerning is the magnitude of these subsidies. The revenue losses from the electricity sector were the single largest drain on state spending and were estimated to amount to roughly 25 percent of India's fiscal deficit in 2002 (Mullen, Orden, and Gulati 2005; Tongia 2003; Monari 2002). As context, the amount spent on agricultural electricity subsidies was more than double expenditure on health or rural development (Mullen, Orden, and Gulati 2005; Monari 2002). Expenditures on agricultural electricity subsidies are likely to come at the cost of other social programs. Given the resources dedicated to these subsidies, it is important to quantify if and to what extent they encouraged groundwater extraction.

One unique feature of agricultural electricity prices in our setting is that during our period of study, almost all agricultural customers pay only a flat monthly fee, measured in rupees per horsepower, for electricity. That is, the volumetric rate per kilowatt hour (kWh) is zero. This rate structure is motivated in part from the fact that electricity usage for agricultural users is determined largely by pump size. Knowing this, the regulator can set monthly fixed fees that vary across pump capacity to achieve (in theory) a uniform implied price per kWh. In most states, customers face a uniform rate per horsepower (and hence kWh) across pump capacities.[5] For example, assume that one household has a 4 horsepower pump that utilizes 400 kWh in a month, while another has an 8 horsepower pump that uses 800 kWh per month. If the fixed fee for the farmer with the larger pump is double that of the farmer with the smaller pump, then the two users would face the same price per horsepower and implicit price per kWh. Regardless of whether a flat implicit volumetric price is achieved, this tariff structure only influences a customer's decisions on whether to install or operate and pump and what size pump to install. Conditional on these choices, a change in the fixed cost should have no impact on groundwater usage.

Given the ownership structure, financing options, and costs incurred with constructing and maintaining tubewells, it is likely that the decision to install, adopt, or maintain a shallow or deep tubewell will be sensitive to electricity prices. Most wells in India are privately owned and financed. Data from the Minor Irrigation Census of India indicate that during our study period, approximately 95 percent of shallow and 62 percent of deep tubewells were owned by individuals. Over 60 percent of these wells were self-financed, implying that farmers did not rely on private loans, bank loans, or government funding. The upfront costs to construct a deep and shallow tubewell are substantial, totaling at approximately $1,500 (or 1 lakh Rs) and $750, respectively, in the fourth wave of the Minor Irrigation Cen-

5. In a few states with tiered rates, the monthly fixed cost per horsepower varies by pump size.

sus. Further, roughly 45 percent of farmers spend between $15 and $150 dollars annually to maintain these tubewells. For comparison, the average annual cost to operate a 4 horsepower pump in our sample is roughly $60, or 8 percent of the cost of a shallow tubewell.

The strong link between electricity and groundwater use is guided by mechanical features of groundwater irrigation infrastructure and the regulatory landscape governing groundwater use in India. Most deep and shallow tubewells rely on electricity to pump water to the surface. These farmers face a marginal price for electricity consumption of zero, and landowners face no limitations on groundwater extraction (Gandhi and Namboodiri 2009). This creates a setting where the only constraints on groundwater pumping are pump capacity and the availability of the power supply.

5.3 Empirical Approach

This section describes the empirical strategy employed to test if groundwater demand is responsive to changes in agricultural electricity tariffs and then poses an approach to investigate how subsidy-induced changes in groundwater extraction impact agricultural production.

5.3.1 Demand for Groundwater

To begin our examination of the effect of a change in electricity prices in year t and state j on groundwater extraction in district i, we estimate an OLS model with district and year fixed effects and standard errors clustered at the state:

$$(1) \qquad W_{it} = \alpha_0 + \alpha_1 FC_{jt} + \lambda_t + \gamma_i + u_{it}.$$

W_{it} denotes groundwater consumption in million cubic meters (mcm), and FC_{jt}, our regressor of interest, is a measure of the fixed cost of electricity in year t and state j. The inclusion of year and district fixed effects allows us to flexibly control for aggregate time shocks such as national agricultural policies and fixed district unobservables such as soil type and hydrogeology.

Our empirical approach uses year-to-year variation in state electricity prices to compare a given district's groundwater demand under various prices controlling for aggregate annual shocks. The identification assumption upon which this approach hinges is that electricity prices are orthogonal to unobserved state-year and district-year determinants of groundwater extraction. However, for a number of reasons discussed later, electricity prices might be systematically correlated with unobservables that also impact groundwater use.

First, electricity pricing in India is a potential political tool and as such may reflect election cycles or the importance of the state's agricultural economy or may be systematically correlated with other state agricultural policies. During our period of study, electricity pricing was often at the discretion of state governments and politicians. It emerged as a political lever in the late 1970s and has remained a valuable campaign tool through the duration of our sample.[6] Election cycles may also influence other agricultural and energy policies that impact groundwater demand, either directly or indirectly. In fact, a growing literature has empirically tested if elections are systematically related to agricultural lending by publicly owned banks, expenditure on road construction, and tax collection and finds that the provision of many of these goods increased during election years (Cole 2009; Chaudhuri and Dasgupta 2005; Ghosh 2006; Khemani 2004). To account for the possibility that state-year election cycles may be systematically correlated with electricity prices and impact groundwater demand, we include an indicator variable set equal to one if a state-election occurs in a given year.[7]

Generation and transmission and distribution (T&D) losses may also be correlated with electricity prices and impact groundwater extraction through two channels. First, electricity is often rationed in India so that, at any given price, the quantity of electricity supplied may fall below the quantity demanded. Because of this, the available supply rather than the price may be driving groundwater extraction. Prices may also be correlated with generation since, with low electricity prices, generation constraints may be more likely to bind. Second, in addition to manipulating electricity prices, state governments may also alter electricity provision through other channels, such as turning a blind eye to electricity theft in certain areas. For these reasons, a failure to control for these variables may confound our estimation of the effect of electricity prices on groundwater demand.

To explicitly control for potential state-year and district-year observables that may confound the estimation of α_1, we augment equation (1) and estimate

$$(2) \qquad W_{it} = \alpha_0 + \alpha_1 FC_{jt} + \alpha_2 X_{it} + \alpha_3 X_{jt} + \lambda_t + \gamma_i + u_{it}.$$

In the regression, X_{it} denotes district-year rainfall, and X_{jt} is a vector of time-varying state observables, including whether a state election is held in a given year, annual generation, and transmission and distribution losses. Our identifying assumption in equation (2) is that the inclusion of time-varying

6. The trend between elections and electricity pricing began in Andhra Pradesh in 1977, when the Congress Party was the first in India to campaign on the basis of free power. The use of electricity as a campaign tool continued into 2004, the most recent year in our sample, when the Congress Party in Andhra Pradesh campaigned on the ticket of free power (Dubash 2007).

7. In India, state legislative assembly elections are scheduled every five years. However, if the lower parliament finds the state government unfit to rule, the government can issue an election, referred to as a midterm election, prior to the end of the five-year term. Recently, state midterm elections have become more common, though the frequency of midterm elections varies by state (NIC 2009). If a midterm election occurs, a constitutionally scheduled election will occur five years later. Due to midterm elections, there is substantial variation in electoral cycles across states.

state and district observables removes any of the bias present in our simple fixed effects model. More formally, conditional on X_{it}, X_{jt}, λ_t, and γ_i, we now assume that electricity prices are independent of potential outcomes. While we cannot directly test this assumption, we later conduct indirect tests that examine its plausibility.

5.3.2 Agricultural Output

Recall that the intent behind the provision of agricultural electricity subsidies was to increase agricultural output. To test the hypothesis that these subsidies increased agricultural production through the channel of groundwater extraction, we use an instrumental variables approach with standard errors clustered at the state:

$$(3) \qquad Y_{it} = \beta_0 + \beta_1 W_{it} + \beta_2 X_{it} + \beta_3 X_{jt} + \sigma_t + \eta_i + \varepsilon_{it}$$

$$W_{it} = \alpha_0 + \alpha_1 FC_{jt} + \alpha_2 X_{it} + \alpha_3 X_{jt} + \lambda_t + \gamma_i + u_{it}.$$

Our outcome variables V_{it} include log values of agricultural output and log area for total, water-intensive, and water-nonintensive crops in a district-year. Time-varying district and state observables are defined as in equation (2), and σ_t and η_i denote year and district fixed effects, respectively.

The key parameter of interest β measures the output and the area on which crops are grown with of agricultural output and the area on which crops are grown with respect to groundwater demand. Our instrumental variables approach restricts the variation in groundwater extraction to that induced by presumably exogenous variation in state-year electricity prices. Our choice to focus on price-induced changes in groundwater extraction is primarily policy driven. It remains largely unresolved whether agricultural electricity subsidies had the intended effect of increasing agricultural production through the channel of irrigation despite this objective serving as the impetus for electricity subsidies. Our empirical approach provides a setting to credibly test the policy question of interest.

5.4   Data and Descriptive Results

Our empirical examination of the relationship between electricity subsidies, groundwater extraction, and agricultural production relies on three main sources of data: district groundwater data collected by the Central Groundwater Board, annual state electricity data collected by the Council of Power Utilities, and annual district agricultural data compiled by the Directorate of Economics and Statistics within the Indian Ministry of Agriculture. We briefly describe these data and their limitations and begin to examine the plausibility of our main identifying assumption that—conditional on fixed district unobservables, year fixed effects, and select observables—state-year electricity prices are independent of unobservables.

5.4.1   Groundwater

District groundwater data obtained from the "Dynamic Ground Water Resources of India" reports are available for 280 districts in (a subset of) years 1995, 1998, 2002, and 2004, forming an unbalanced panel of groundwater data for 587 district-years in 13 states. The measurement and definition of annual groundwater extraction in these reports is unique, influencing the interpretation of our results and providing insight into the channel through which electricity prices may alter water usage. Specifically, these reports do not provide physical measures of annual groundwater extraction in a given year. Instead, they report a coarse estimate of annual demand based on the "number of abstraction structures multiplied by the unit seasonal draft." Thus groundwater extraction in our study captures the number of wells in a given district-year, accounting for specific crop demands, and leads us to interpret changes in groundwater demand as changes along the extensive margin in tubewell installation, adoption, and expansion.

Summary statistics on groundwater extraction and recharge are provided in table 5.1, where columns 1 through 3 report these statistics for the entire sample. On average, groundwater extraction amounts to 60 percent of recharge. However, this statistic masks the variation in extraction both across districts and over time. Restricting the sample to districts that record groundwater data in 1995 and 2004 reveals that groundwater extraction increased between 1995 and 2004 by 125 mcm, or 18.5 percent, though recharge increased as well. Two commonly deployed measures of groundwater overdevelopment—critical and overexploited—suggest that groundwater exploitation is also increasing over time. Critical status indicates that annual groundwater usage is greater than 75 percent of annual recharge and provides a signal that groundwater extraction may be approaching unsustainable levels. Within the period examined, 25 percent of districts move from normal to critical status, and 14 percent move to overexploited status, defined as a year in which extraction exceeds recharge.

The remaining columns of table 5.1 divide the sample based on the median electricity price and examine whether observables including groundwater demand differ across district-years with high and low electricity prices. A comparison of raw means highlights that annual groundwater extraction is significantly higher in areas with below-average electricity prices, providing the first piece of descriptive evidence that electricity rates and groundwater extraction may be inversely related. These differences are no longer significant once we condition on year and district fixed effects, though we cannot discern the extent to which this is driven by the coarse delineation of high and low electricity prices. Later, results using our baseline empirical specification address this possibility by measuring electricity prices continuously.

Table 5.1   Summary statistics: Groundwater and agricultural output

| | Mean (1) | Std. dev. (2) | Obs. (3) | Mean by elec. price | | Difference in means | |
				<65 Rs (4)	>65 Rs (5)	Unconditional (6)	District, year FE (7)
District-year variables							
GW extraction (mcm)	582	509	587	616	546	70*	52
GW recharge (mcm)	952	579	587	959	945	15	41
Value agriculture (million 1995 Rs)	2,441	2,729	583	2,244	2,644	401*	554**
Value H_2O intense	1,079	1,515	577	1,070	1,090	20	96
Value non-H_2O intense	144	290	575	112	178	66***	48
Area crops grown (1,000 hectares)	290	187	451	302	282	20	6
H_2O intense area	124	118	451	137	115	23**	2
Non-H_2O intense area	57	109	451	50	63	13	5
Fertilizer applied (tons)	36,534	30,077	382	35,189	37,827	2,638	3,007
State Variables							
FC electricity (Rs per hp-mth)	83.5	117	60	39	159	120**	73*
Generation (million kWh)	19,263	10,621	56	23,122	19,176	3,946***	3,352**
T & D losses (million kWh)	29	9	60	27	34	8***	2.4
Election year	0.18	0.39	50	0.52	0.07	0.4***	0.32

Notes: The table reports means, standard deviations, and counts for district-year and state-year variables. Columns (4)–(5) report means for district years in which electricity prices are less than and greater than the median. Column (6) reports the absolute value of the unconditional difference in means, and column (7) reports the absolute value of the difference conditional on year and district fixed effects with standard errors clustered at the state. Asterisks indicate significant differences in means: *** $p < 0.01$, ** $p < 0.05$, * $p < 0.1$.

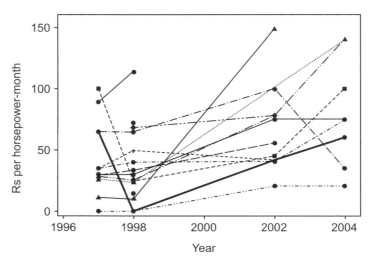

Fig. 5.1   State electricity prices by year, excluding prices > 300 Rs

5.4.2   Electricity Prices

Data on states' agricultural electricity prices, measured in 1995 Rs per horsepower-month (Rs/hp-mth), were collected for select years between 1995 and 2004.[8] During these years, all states in our sample offered an agricultural electricity rate that consisted exclusively of a monthly charge, where this charge primarily took the form of a fixed monthly fee per horsepower. On average, states charged a fixed fee of 83.5 rupees per hp-month for electricity, though some states such as Tamil Nadu provided agricultural electricity free of charge, and others charged rates that exceeded 500 rupees per hp-month. Figure 5.1 illustrates this cross-sectional variation as well as the temporal variation in electricity prices that our empirical strategy seeks to exploit. In it, we plot the fixed cost of electricity for all state-years except Madhya Pradesh, in which prices exceed 300 Rs per hp-month in some years.

Two complicating features of agricultural electricity tariffs in India are that a handful of states also offered some customers a volumetric rate and/or structured fixed fees such that the per-horsepower cost varied depending on pump size. In approximately 30 percent of the state-years in our sample, some agricultural users were at least offered a volumetric charge, though we are unable to discern how many users actually opted into these rates. Two observations lead us to believe that few if any users incurred a volumetric rate. First, between 1995 and 2004, meters for agricultural water use in

8. Electricity data were gathered from "Tariff Schedules of Electric Power Utilities," which were published in 1997, 1998, 2002, and 2005. In addition to reporting tariffs, these reports record the date that tariffs changed.

India were rare due to the high transaction costs involved with installation (Birner et al. 2007).[9] Second, qualitative evidence suggests that few if any agricultural users face a volumetric price for electricity (Banerji et al. 2013).

The presence of tiered rate structures may also complicate our analysis. In approximately 7 percent of the state-years in our sample, states impose tiered electricity rates, whereby the fixed monthly rate per horsepower varies depending on the size of the pump. Interestingly, we see evidence of both declining and increasing block rates. For customers in states with a tiered rate structure, a change in rates may differentially affect agricultural customers depending on pump size if, for example, a rate change is only introduced for one pump size. We address this issue by later testing whether our empirical results are robust to the exclusion of states with a tiered rate structure.

5.4.3   Agricultural Production Data

Annual district data between 2000 and 2004 on the value of crop output and crop acreage were provided by the District Agricultural Statistics Portal from the Ministry of Agriculture; summary statistics for the years 2002 and 2004 are reported in table 5.1.[10] Total agricultural production is measured as the sum of revenues from wheat, rice, cotton, sugar, maize, sorghum, and pearl millet, weighted by the 1995 price for each crop. These crops were chosen because they are prevalent in India and vary substantially in their water intensity and data were available during the period of study. We hold prices fixed at 1995 levels to decouple the effect of price changes from output changes. Water-intensive output is measured as the weighted sum of the value of production in rice and cotton, and water-nonintensive output is comprised of sorghum and millet. A crop was labeled as more or less water intensive based on its relative level of water inputs, as defined by Hoekstra and Chapagain (2007). As reported in table 5.1, water-intensive crops account for a large share of agricultural production, generating 44 percent of annual output and accounting for 43 percent of the area cultivated.

A comparison of raw means reveals that the acreage dedicated to water-intensive crops is significantly higher in districts with lower electricity prices and that the value of nonwater-intensive crops is higher in areas with high electricity prices. After controlling for fixed district unobservables and aggregate shocks, we find that with the exception of the value of agricultural output, production is balanced across district-years with high and low electricity prices. The value of agricultural output is inversely related to electricity prices and provides a reduced-form preview of the variation that we later

9. After 2004, some states such as West Bengal introduced metering (Mukherji et al. 2009).

10. In our analysis, we restrict our sample of agricultural production data to post-2000, since the pre- and post-2000 data come from two different sources, and the pre-2000 data may suffer from measurement issues. During interviews, the head of data collection at the Indian Ministry of Agriculture raised multiple concerns with agricultural statistics collected in the mid- to late-1990s.

exploit to investigate the effect of subsidy-induced changes in groundwater demand on agricultural production.

5.4.4   Confounding Observables

Isolating the causal effect of a change in the fixed cost of electricity on groundwater extraction could be achieved by simply comparing groundwater extraction across states and years with different electricity prices, if electricity prices were orthogonal to all determinants of groundwater extraction. However, electricity prices may be systematically correlated with district unobservables, aggregate shocks to the economy, and state-year unobservables. We also anticipate that demand for groundwater will depend on these factors. Our empirical approach controls for the first two possibilities by conditioning on district and year fixed effects; however, it assumes that electricity prices are independent of time-varying unobserved determinants of groundwater extraction. To examine the plausibility of this assumption, we evaluate whether state-year elections, generation, and transmission and distribution losses differ systematically across district-years with high and low electricity prices, using comparisons of unconditional and conditional means, where the latter comparison controls for district and year unobservables.

The differences reported in column 6 of table 5.1 make clear the flaws in an empirical approach that relies on a simple comparison of means across states and years with relatively high and low electricity prices. Potentially confounding observables including state-year elections, gross generation, and transmission and distribution losses differ systematically across high and low electricity prices. And while our preferred empirical approach will control explicitly for these observables, one indication that electricity prices may be systematically correlated with unobservables is if they are systematically correlated with observables. To explore the extent to which fixed district unobservables and aggregate shocks explain these systematic differences, in column 7 of table 5.1 we present differences in means conditional on district and year fixed effects. With the exception of generation (measured as gross generation in million kWh), the aforementioned observables as well as annual district fertilizer use do not significantly differ across district-years with high and low electricity prices. And while this does not imply that unobservables are balanced across electricity prices, it provides evidence to support the plausibility of our main identifying assumption.

5.5   Estimation Results

We begin by reporting results from a simple OLS model of demand for groundwater on annual state electricity prices, controlling for fixed district and year unobservables. As shown in column 1 of table 5.2, an increase in the fixed cost of agricultural electricity decreases annual district groundwater extraction, where we hypothesize that this reduction in demand occurs along the extensive margin of tubewell adoption and expansion. We find that district demand for groundwater decreases by 0.417 million cubic meters on average with a one-rupee increase in the price of electricity. This implies that a one-standard-deviation increase in the fixed cost of electricity would decrease demand for groundwater by 47 mcm or 8.5 percent.[11] The short-run elasticity of demand for groundwater is approximately −0.07 and fits within the wide range of elasticities, −0.002 to −1.97, reported in a meta-analysis of irrigation water demand elasticities (Scheierling, Loomis, and Young 2006).

As discussed in the estimation strategy, electricity prices may be systematically correlated with time-varying district and state unobservables that impact groundwater demand. And while we cannot rule out this possibility, we examine the robustness of the qualitative relationship between electricity prices and groundwater demand to a number of plausible confounding factors. Results from the augmented OLS are presented in columns 2 through 6 of table 5.2, where column 2 includes conditions on annual district rainfall and whether rainfall is reported in a district-year, column 3 includes an indicator variable denoting whether a state-year election occurred, column 4 controls for generation, column 5 includes annual transmission and distribution losses as a covariate, and column 6 includes all the aforementioned time-varying observables as covariates.

Our central finding that electricity subsidies led to an increase in groundwater demand remains after controlling for potential time-varying confounders. The magnitude of the treatment effect is stable across columns 2 through 5, in which we selectively control for surface water considerations, electoral cycles, and potential changes to the electricity supply. Interestingly, conditional on district and year fixed effects, these observables do not meaningfully impact groundwater extraction, perhaps suggesting that district and year fixed effects account for much of the explanatory power that these observables have on groundwater demand.[12]

Results from our preferred specification that conditions on all the time-varying state and district observables suggest an economically stronger though still relatively inelastic effect of electricity prices on groundwater extraction. A one-rupee increase in the monthly fixed rate per horsepower of electricity leads to a 1.05 million cubic meter decrease in groundwater extraction. This translates to a short-run price elasticity of −0.18 and is remarkably close to the median elasticity reported in a meta-analysis of irrigation water demand elasticities and recent panel data price elasticity estimates in the

---

11. The unit of observation for the electricity statistics in the preceding calculation is the district year, where the reported mean and standard deviation are 97 and 113 respectively. In contrast, the unit of observation for electricity statistics in columns 1–3 of table 1 is the state-year.

12. Simple OLS regressions analogous to those implemented in columns 2–5, except for the exclusion of district and year fixed effects, report a statistically significant effect of each covariate on groundwater extraction.

Table 5.2 OLS models of demand for groundwater

Demand groundwater	(1)	(2)	(3)	(4)	(5)	(6)	(7)	(8)
Fixed-cost electricity	-0.417**	-0.499	-0.402**	-0.513*	-0.578*	-1.054*	-3.214	69.78*
	(0.201)	(0.528)	(0.188)	(0.279)	(0.337)	(0.582)	(4.805)	(40.07)
Rainfall		-152.5				-202.6**	-204.3**	331.8
		(113.0)				(81.35)	(98.28)	(221.3)
Rainfall reported		-1,583				-2,054**	-2,103**	5,691*
		(1,202)				(815.5)	(1,007)	(3,163)
State-year election			-32.37			-39.44	-30.61	
			(62.71)			(64.28)	(75.29)	
Generation				-0.00429		-0.00724	0.00209	
				(0.00642)		(0.00915)	(0.0112)	
T & D losses					5.17	13.49	11.84	
					(6.177)	(8.992)	(8.362)	
Fixed effects	District year	District year	District year	District year	District year	District year	District year	District year
Observations	587	587	587	587	587	587	533	149
R-squared	0.913	0.917	0.913	0.913	0.914	0.921		

Notes: The dependent variable is the quantity in million cubic meters of groundwater extracted in a district year. Columns (1)–(8) report results from an OLS model with standard errors clustered at the state in parentheses. Columns (7) and (8) exclude state years in which prices decreased and increased, respectively. Asterisks denote significance: ***$p < 0.01$, **$p < 0.05$, *$p < 0.1$

High Plains Aquifer (Hendricks and Peterson 2012; Scheierling, Loomis, and Young 2006). And while our estimates align with those reported in other studies, we posit that three features unique to the electricity sector in India may explain the low price elasticity. First, the marginal price of agricultural electricity is zero. A change in the fixed fee for agricultural electricity may affect demand along the extensive margin, inducing farmers to install, expand, or operate a tubewell, but conditional on operating a tubewell, it should not impact electricity demand. Second, electricity shortages may limit customer sensitivity to price changes. Third, a substantial disconnect exists between the magnitude of the subsidies and our observed variation in electricity prices. Our elasticity estimates are based on sizable variation in electricity prices, but this variation is only a fraction of the subsidy amount provided to agricultural users. The limited variation in observed prices relative to the size of the subsidy may dampen the demand response to price changes. While agricultural users are likely to be more responsive to price changes under a regime in which volumetric pricing was introduced, supply-side constraints were removed, and electricity was priced at marginal costs, our estimates provide guidance on changes in groundwater demand through the channel of tubewell connections under the status-quo pricing regime.

We provide suggestive quantitative and qualitative evidence that changes in the fixed cost of electricity impact groundwater extraction through the channel of tubewell expansion and installation. First, we empirically disentangle the effects of positive and negative changes in electricity tariffs on groundwater use. Our hypothesis is that price changes should primarily operate in one direction, with price decreases leading to a sizable and meaningful increase in groundwater extraction. Indian farmers incur large costs to acquire access to groundwater, and it seems unlikely that relatively modest increases in electricity tariffs would induce farmers to discontinue pumping. In contrast, it seems quite plausible that a farmer would choose to install a new well or pump in response to a decline in the flat rate. To examine this possibility, we exclude state-years with price increases in column 7 and price decreases in column 8 of table 5.2. Price decreases induce a sizable increase in groundwater extraction, whereas price increases lead to a nonsignificant and comparably modest reduction in groundwater usage. These results suggest that one mechanism through which electricity subsidies impact groundwater extraction is the expansion of tubewells. This hypothesis is more plausible when one considers that the Central Ground Water Board estimates annual groundwater extraction based on the number of abstraction units in a given district-year.

A separate but related question examines the extent to which these subsidies impact the probability of groundwater overexploitation, a potential environmental cost attributable to them. Our outcome variables of interest are now indicator variables denoting whether annual district extraction crossed two exploitation thresholds: critical, where annual groundwater

Table 5.3   Linear probability model of groundwater exploitation

GW development	Critical (75%) (1)	Exploited (100%) (2)	Critical (75%) (3)	Exploited (100%) (4)
Fixed-cost electricity	−0.000708***	−0.000405	−0.000855***	−0.000495
	(0.000216)	(0.000547)	(0.000259)	(0.000497)
Rainfall			0.100	0.161
			(0.0899)	(0.108)
Rainfall reported			1.099	1.827
			(0.925)	(1.138)
State-year election			−0.0986***	−0.00484
			(0.0177)	(0.0654)
Generation			−1.65e-05**	−8.23e-06
			(7.45e-06)	(1.03e-05)
T & D losses			−0.00283	0.00298
			(0.00256)	(0.00884)
Fixed effects	District year	District year	District year	District year
Observation	593	593	593	593
R-squared	0.805	0.804	0.813	0.821

Notes: The dependent variable is an indicator variable set equal to one if groundwater extraction is 75 percent or 100 percent of annual groundwater recharge. Columns (1)–(4) report results from an OLS model with standard errors clustered at the state in parentheses. Asterisks denote significance: *** $p <$ 0.01, ** $p < 0.05$, * $p < 0.1$

usage is 75 percent of annual recharge, and overexploited, where usage is greater than supply. Results from the estimation of a linear probability model with district and year fixed effects are reported in table 5.3. Our results imply that a one-rupee increase in the fixed cost of electricity leads to between a 0.071 and 0.086 percentage point decrease in the probability that a district-year is listed as critical, and a one-standard-deviation increase in prices induces up to a 9.8 percentage point decrease. We also find a negative but not statistically significant relationship between electricity prices and overexploitation status, where the absence of explanatory power may be driven by the relatively small number of district-years designated as overexploited. These results suggest that one unintended cost of these subsidies is the overextraction of groundwater resources.

5.5.1   Agricultural Production

We estimate the effect of groundwater demand on agricultural production using an IV model and report results in table 5.4. In columns 1 through 3, the dependent variable is the value of total water-intensive and -nonintensive agricultural output, and in columns 4 through 6, the outcome variables are the area on which all water-intensive and -nonintensive crops are grown.

Our first-stage and reduced-form results indicate that electricity prices impact groundwater demand and agricultural output in the expected direction, with lower prices increasing both groundwater demand and agricul-

Table 5.4   **IV model of agricultural production**

	Value agricultural output			Area cultivated			Output total (7)
	Total (1)	H_2O intensive (2)	Less intensive (3)	Total (4)	H_2O intensive (5)	Less intensive (6)	
Groundwater demand (mcm)	3.110*** (0.460)	3.261*** (0.426)	−0.0736** (0.0301)	60.58*** (18.68)	24.79** (10.94)	5.823* (3.068)	
Fixed-cost electricity							−3.158 (2.156)
Ag-water elasticity	0.602	1.42	−0.198	0.119	0.117	0.0551	
Fixed effects	District year	District year	District year	District year	District year	District year	District year
Observations	202	200	202	202	202	202	202
F-stat	11.7	11.3	11.7	11.7	13.8	11.7	

Notes: The dependent variable is agricultural output (measured in millions of Rs) in columns (1)–(3) and hectares cultivated in columns (4)–(6). Columns (1)–(6) report results from an IV model in which electricity prices serve as an instrument for groundwater extraction. Column (7) reports results from the reduced form regression of agricultural output on electricity prices. Additional controls include generation, transmission and distribution losses, annual rainfall, rainfall reported, and the presence of a state election. Standard errors clustered at the state are in parentheses. Asterisks denote significance: *** $p < 0.01$, ** $p < 0.05$, * $p < 0.1$

tural output. Estimates from the first- stage mirror those reported in column 6 of table 5.2, except that the sample is restricted to the 202 district-years for which agricultural data are available.[13] The corrected F-statistic, reported in table 5.4, is 11.7, indicating that the instrument is sufficiently strong in predicting groundwater extraction. Results from the reduced-form relationship between electricity prices and agricultural output are reported in column 7 and show that higher electricity prices lead to an increase in agricultural output.

Electricity-price induced changes in groundwater extraction meaningfully impact both the value of agricultural output and the area on which crops are cultivated. This central result suggests that agricultural electricity subsidies operated through the intended channel of groundwater irrigation to increase agricultural production. The implied elasticity of the value of agricultural output to groundwater usage is 0.60, indicating that output is quite responsive to changes in groundwater use. However, recall that a 5.5 percentage point increase in the fixed cost of electricity is needed to induce a 1 percentage point increase in groundwater demand, so the implied price elasticity of the value of agricultural output is −0.12.

A second central finding to emerge is that the strong and positive effect

13. Recall that due to data quality concerns, we chose to focus exclusively on post-2000 data.

of groundwater demand on agricultural output occurs exclusively for water-intensive crops. The short-run electricity price elasticity for water-intensive agricultural output is −0.29 and the implied usage elasticity of water-intensive agricultural output is approximately 1.4, indicating that the value of agricultural output is highly sensitive to changes in the quantity of groundwater irrigation. In contrast, the value of nonintensive crops actually decreases in response to an increase in groundwater extraction. The juxtaposition of the response of water-intensive and -nonintensive crops to changes in groundwater extraction suggests that in addition to impacting the value of overall agricultural production, electricity subsidies are also influencing the mix of crops grown.

Turning to columns 4 through 6, we find that one margin along which farmers are responding to fluctuations in groundwater demand is the area cultivated. An increase in annual groundwater extraction, presumably for irrigation, leads to an increase in the total area dedicated to crop cultivation, where the elasticity of acreage to irrigation is 0.11. This imputed elasticity is consistent with studies in India on the acreage elasticities of agriculture with respect to irrigation (Kanwar 2006). Once we decompose the cultivated area into water-intensive and -nonintensive crops, we find that this response is primarily driven by water-intensive crops. An increase in irrigation causes an expansion in the area on which both water-intensive and -nonintensive crops are grown, but water-intensive acreage is twice as elastic. This finding provides a second piece of evidence that electricity subsidies are not only increasing agricultural production but also inducing farmers to shift production to water-intensive crops.

5.5.2   Robustness

The robustness of our results hinges on three assumptions: time-varying unobservables that impact groundwater demand are unrelated to electricity prices, electricity prices only impact agricultural production through the channel of groundwater, and a change in the fixed cost of electricity has a uniform effect on the cost per horsepower across all pump sizes. We examined the plausibility of the first assumption in tables 5.1 and 5.2. While we cannot rule out the possibility that time-varying unobservables bias our coefficient estimate on electricity prices, we provide evidence that some potentially confounding observables are balanced across high and low electricity prices. We now propose one check to examine the validity of our instrument and test the robustness of our results to the exclusion of states with tiered electricity prices.

Our measure of agricultural output captures changes in production gross of other inputs, such as fertilizer. Electricity subsidies may also affect demand for these inputs, which in turn may affect agricultural output. Knowing the impact of electricity prices on other agricultural inputs will provide insight into the extent to which electricity subsidies affect the value of agricultural

Table 5.5   **OLS model of demand for fertilizer**

Fertilizer use (tons)	All (1)	Nitrogen (2)	Phosphate (3)	Potassium (4)
Fixed-cost electricity	−11.12	3.044	−4.232	−9.934
	(44.52)	(21.18)	(15.04)	(17.36)
Rainfall	−331.7	−519.0	652.4	−465.1
	(4,933)	(3,252)	(1,438)	(906.7)
Rainfall reported	−3,881	−6,282	6,494	−4,094
	(50,983)	(33,901)	(14,690)	(9,292)
State-year election	5,089	2,012	1,396	1,682*
	(4,212)	(2,358)	(1,274)	(880.2)
Generation	−0.401	0.0516	−0.232	−0.221
	(1.401)	(0.715)	(0.462)	(0.487)
T & D losses	218.1	166.8	55.58	−4.298
	(580.9)	(304.3)	(183.7)	(185.9)
Fixed effects	District year	District year	District year	District year
Observation	382	382	382	381
R-squared	0.975	0.974	0.968	0.977

Notes: The dependent variable is the quantity of fertilizer applied in a district-year. Columns (1)–(4) report results from an OLS model with standard errors clustered at the state in parentheses. Asterisks denote significance: ***$p < 0.01$, **$p < 0.05$, *$p < 0.1$

production through channels aside from irrigation. We thus examine the extent to which electricity subsidies influence demand for fertilizer. Table 5.5 presents results from the estimation of equation (2), except now the dependent variable is annual tons of fertilizer use in a district. Regardless of our measure of fertilizer—all, nitrogen, phosphate, or potassium—electricity subsidies do not appear to influence the quantity of fertilizer used, suggesting that the previously reported changes in agricultural production are not capturing a change in fertilizer use. These results do not imply that electricity prices are a valid instrument; instead, they provide one piece of evidence that electricity subsidies are not impacting another critical input used in agricultural production.

The robustness of these results also hinges on our measure of electricity prices. One concern is that in states with tiered rates, a change in rates may only impact certain categories of users or may differentially impact customers depending on pump size. To address this possibility, we restrict our sample to state-years in which there is a uniform fixed cost per horsepower regardless of pump size. Table 5.6 reports results using the restricted sample, where column 1 presents results from an ordinary least squares model on groundwater extraction, column 2 presents results from a linear probability model of the probability that groundwater levels are at a critical level, and columns 3 through 4 report results from an instrumental variables model in which the dependent variables are total agricultural production and the cultivated area, respectively. The qualitative relationship between the

Table 5.6   Robustness test: Exclusion of states with tiered rate structure

	Groundwater demand (1)	Critical (75%) (2)	Agricultural output (3)	Cultivated area (4)
Fixed-cost electricity	−1.656** (0.745)	−0.000940 (0.000806)		
Groundwater demand			14.82** (6.958)	283.5** (133.9)
Rainfall	−201.3*** (54.47)	0.0973 (0.0887)	1.108 (0.930)	0.350 (0.311)
Rainfall reported	−2,097*** (549.8)	1.076 (0.918)	9.559 (8.922)	3.029 (2.996)
State-year election	−46.53 (45.60)	−0.100*** (0.0234)	−0.468*** (0.172)	−0.172*** (0.0619)
Generation	−0.000704 (0.00721)	−1.63e-05 (1.50e-05)	0.000143 (0.000151)	4.05e-05 (5.32e-05)
T & D losses	11.81** (5.665)	−0.00279 (0.00406)	0.523** (0.239)	0.179** (0.853)
Fixed effects	District year	District year	District year	District year
Observation	546	551	162	162
F-stat			4.05	4.05

Notes: The dependent variable is reported in each column heading. The sample is comprised exclusively of state years where the price per hp-mth of electricity is uniform across pump size. Columns (1)–(2) report results from an OLS model, and columns (3)–(4) report results from an IV model. Standard errors clustered at the state are in parentheses. Additional controls include generation, transmission and distribution losses, annual rainfall, rainfall reported, and the presence of a state election. Asterisks denote significance: *** $p < 0.01$, ** $p < 0.05$, * $p < 0.1$

groundwater extraction and electricity prices remains unchanged, though inference on the probability that a resource is overextracted becomes limited likely due to the small sample size and the relatively infrequent occurrence of critical district-years. We also continue to find that increases in groundwater demand result in economically and statistically significant increases in agricultural production and the area allocated to crop cultivation. These results suggest that the relationship between electricity prices, groundwater extraction, and agricultural production is not driven by states with tiered rate structures.

5.6   Welfare Costs

We now provide a partial approximation of the welfare costs of this policy. The ideal exercise would speak to two costs associated with the existing pricing regime: the absence of volumetric rates for electricity usage and the subsidies provided to agricultural electricity consumption. Given the difficulty in projecting customer behavior in transitioning from a fixed-cost rate structure to a two-part rate structure, we focus our attention on the latter cost. In what follows, we use derived demand for groundwater as laid out in equation (2), specify a long-run marginal cost curve, and then estimate the reduced deadweight loss from a 50 percent reduction in agricultural electricity subsidies. Our partial estimates of the efficiency costs are coarse and provide a back-of-the-envelope measure; nonetheless, they serve as a starting point to think about the policy's welfare costs.

We specify a long-run marginal cost curve for groundwater, assuming that it can be approximated using the average unit cost to supply electricity. We combine data collected by the Central Electricity Authority on the average per-kWh cost to supply electricity in a state-year with the statistic that a one-horsepower irrigation pump uses approximately 200 kWh per month. This provides an average cost of electricity per horsepower-month. We further assume that the long-run marginal cost of electricity is equal to the average cost of electricity in a state-year and that the electricity supply is infinitely elastic. This latter assumption implies that there is no change in producer surplus from the subsidy.

Driven by concerns about out-of-sample predictions, we choose to simulate a policy in which we reduce the subsidy by 50 percent. In the sample for which data on both unit costs and electricity prices are available, the average unit cost per horsepower is 190 Rs per month, though farmers on average pay only 55 Rs per month. A comparison of retail prices and unit costs also reveals that there is only one state-year in which the retail price overlaps with the observed unit cost for all state-years in our sample. In contrast, if we model a pricing policy in which we reduce the subsidy by 50 percent, there is substantial overlap across observed and simulated retail prices.

We now calculate the efficiency gain from a 50 percent reduction in the state level subsidy as

$$(4) \qquad p^o(GW(p^e) - GW(p^o)) - \int_{GW(p^o)}^{GW(p^e)} p(GW)dGW.$$

Prices denoted by p^e and p^o reflect the current price of electricity and the price associated with a 50 percent reduction in the electricity subsidy and are measured as the fixed monthly per horsepower price in a state-year. Groundwater extraction, $GW(\ )$, is the estimated quantity of groundwater extraction in a given district-year at price p and is estimated using equation (2).

Given the price inelasticity of demand in the short run and the assumption that the electricity supply is infinitely elastic, the partial efficiency loss associated with a reduction in the subsidy on fixed fees for electricity is small. It amounts to 9 paise for every rupee spent on electricity subsidies. The efficiency losses would almost certainly be larger if our welfare analysis also incorporated existing distortions in the sector, including the absence of marginal pricing for electricity, rationed electricity supplies, and the magnitude of the subsidy. For these reasons, we view our results as a first step in understanding the welfare costs of these subsidies.

5.7   Conclusion

Despite the magnitude of agricultural electricity subsidies in India, in both absolute and relative terms, and the controversy surrounding them, little is known about their causal impact on groundwater resources and agriculture. This study aims to inform this discussion by isolating their impact on groundwater extraction and overexploitation and agricultural output. Using detailed district panel data, we find that this policy increased groundwater extraction through the channel of tubewell adoption and expansion and had meaningful agricultural implications in terms of the value of both agricultural output and crop composition. Our results reveal an extensive margin price elasticity for groundwater demand of −0.18. They also show that subsidy-induced increases in groundwater extraction led to an increase in the value of water-intensive agricultural production and the area on which these crops are grown.

These findings provide some of the first empirical evidence that agricultural electricity subsidies indeed achieved the intended objective of increasing agricultural production through the channel of irrigation. Under certain assumptions and holding constant other existing distortions in the electricity sector, they also suggest that this policy was relatively efficient at transferring government expenditure. The efficiency losses from this subsidy amount to 9 percent, though our analysis remains silent on the costs incurred from imposing a rate structure comprised exclusively of fixed monthly fees for electricity. This consideration is of relevance given the passage of the Electricity Supply Act of 2003, which mandates metering for all categories of electricity users.

While these subsidies encouraged groundwater irrigation and increased agricultural production, they may come at a real and long-term environmental cost. There is substantial concern in India over the overexploitation of groundwater resources and the sustainability of India's current extraction patterns. Our results suggest that electricity subsidies have contributed to groundwater overexploitation, where we predict that a one-standard-deviation decrease in electricity prices will lead to a 10 percent increase in the probability that groundwater resources are listed as critical. They point to a potentially longer-run cost of electricity subsidies if current patterns of groundwater extraction compromise the quantity and perhaps quality of groundwater resources available for future use.

References

Badiani-Magnusson, R., K. Jessoe, and S. Plant. 2012. "Development and the Environment: The Implications of Agricultural Electricity Subsidies in India." *Journal of Environment and Development* 21 (2): 244–62.

Banerji, J., V. Meenakshi, and G. Khanna. 2012. "Social Contracts, Markets and Efficiency: Groundwater Irrigation in North India." *Journal of Development Economics* 98 (2): 228–37.

Banerji, J., V. Meenakshi, A. Mukherji, and A. Gupta. 2013. "Does Marginal Cost Pricing of Electricity Affect Groundwater Pumping Behavior of Farmers? Evidence from India." Impact Evaluation Report 4.

Besley, T., L. Rahman, R. Pande, and V. Rao. 2004. "The Politics of Public Good Provision: Evidence from Indian Local Governments." *Journal of the European Economic Association* 2 (2–3): 416–26.

Birner, R., S. Gupta, N. Sharma, and N. Palaniswamy. 2007. "The Political Economy of Agricultural Policy Reform in India: The Case of Fertilizer Supply and Electricity Supply for Groundwater Irrigation." New Delhi: IFPRI.

Briscoe, J., and R. P. S. Malik. 2006. *India's Water Economy: Bracing for a Turbulent Future.* New Delhi: Oxford University Press.

Chaudhuri, K., and S. Dasgupta. 2005. "The Political Determinants of Central Governments' Economic Policies in India: An Empirical Investigation." *Journal of International Development* 17:957–78.

Cole, S. 2009. "Fixing Market Failures or Fixing Elections? Agricultural Credit in India." *American Economic Journal: Applied Economics* 1 (1): 219–50.

Dubash, N. K. 2007. "The Electricity-Groundwater Conundrum: Case for a Political Solution to a Political Problem." *Economic and Political Weekly* 42 (52): 45–55.

Dubash, N. K., and S. C. Rajan. 2001. "Power Politics: Process of Power Sector Reform in India." *Economic and Political Weekly* 36 (35): 3367–87.

Fan, S., A. Gulati, and T. Sukhadeo. 2008. "Investment, Subsidies and Pro-poor Growth in Rural India." *Agricultural Economics* 39:163–70.

Fishman, R., U. Lall, V. Modi, and N. Parekh. 2014. "Can Electricity Pricing Save India's Groundwater? Evidence from Gujarat." Working Paper.

Gandhi, V. P., and N. V. Namboodiri. 2009. "Groundwater Irrigation in India: Gains, Costs and Risks." Indian Institute of Management Working Paper no. 2009-03-08.

Ghosh, A. 2006. "Electoral Cycles in Crime in a Developing Country: Evidence from the Indian States." Working Paper.

Gisser, M. 1983. "Groundwater: Focusing on the Real Issue." *Journal of Political Economy* 91:1001–27.

Gisser, M. 1993. "Price Support, Acreage Controls and Efficient Redistribution." *Journal of Political Economy* 101 (4): 584–611.

Gulati, A., and A. Sharma. 1995. "Subsidy Syndrome in Indian Agriculture." *Economic and Political Weekly* 30 (39): 93–102.

Hendricks, N., and J. Peterson. 2012. "Fixed Effects Estimation of the Intensive and Extensive Margins of Irrigation Water Demand." *Journal of Agricultural and Resource Economics* 37 (1): 1–19.

Hoekstra, A. Y., and A. K. Chapagain. 2007. "Water Footprints of Nations: Water Use by People as a Function of Their Consumption Patterns." *Water Resource Management* 21:35–48.

Hornbeck, R., and P. Keskin. 2014. "The Historically Evolving Impact of the Ogallala Aquifer: Agricultural Adaptation to Groundwater and Climate." *American Economic Journal: Applied Economics* 6 (1): 190–219.

Huang, Q., S. Rozelle, R. Howitt, J. Wang, and J. Huang. 2010. "Irrigation Water

Demand and Implications for Water Pricing Policy in Rural China." *Environment and Development Economics* 15 (3): 293–319.

Kanwar, S. 2006. "Relative Profitability, Supply Shifters and Dynamic Output Response, in a Developing Economy." *Journal of Policy Modeling* 28:67–88.

Khemani, S. 2004. "Political Cycles in a Developing Economy: Effect of Elections in the Indian States." *Journal of Development Economics* 73:125–54.

Kumar, D. M. 2005. "Impact of Electricity Prices and Volumetric Water Allocation on Energy and Groundwater Demand Management: Analysis from Western India." *Energy Policy* 33:39–51.

Lahiri, A. K., and P. Roy. 1985. "Rainfall and Supply-Response." *Journal of Development Economics* 18:314–34.

Lamb, P. M. 2006. "The Indian Electricity Market: Country Study and Investment Context." PSED Working Paper no. 48, Stanford, CA.

Min, B. 2010. "Distributing Power: Public Service Provision to the Poor in India." Paper presented at the American Political Science Association Conference, Toronto.

Modi, V. 2005. "Improving Electricity Services in Rural India." Working Paper no. 30, Center on Globalization and Sustainable Development.

Monari, L. 2002. *Power Subsidies: A Reality Check on Subsidizing Power for Irrigation in India*, Viewpoint 244. Washington, DC: World Bank, Private Sector and Infrastructure Network.

Mukherji, A., B. Das, N. Majumdar, N. C. Nayak, R. R. Sethi, and B. R. Sharma. 2009. "Metering of Agricultural Power Supply in West Bengal, India: Who Gains and Who Loses." *Energy Policy* 37:5530–39.

Mukherji, A., and T. Shah. 2005. "Groundwater Socio-ecology and Governance: A Review of Institutions and Policies in Selected Countries." *Hydrogeology Journal* 13 (1): 328–45.

Mullen, K., D. Orden, and A. Gulati. 2005. "Agricultural Policies in India. Producer Support Estimates 1985–2002." MTID Discussion Paper 82. Washington, DC: International Food Policy Research Institute.

Murgai, R. 2001. "The Green Revolution and the Productivity Paradox: Evidence from the Indian Punjab." *Agricultural Economics* 25:199–209.

Ostrom, E. 1990. *Governing the Commons: The Evolution of Institutions for Collective Action*. London: University of Cambridge Press.

Ostrom, E. 2011. "Reflections on 'Some Unsettled Problems of Irrigation.'" *American Economic Review* 101 (1): 49–63.

Pachauri. R. 1982. "Electric Power and Economic Development." *Energy Policy* 10 (3): 189–202.

Provencher, B., and O. Burt. 1993. "The Externalities Associated with the Common Property Exploitation of Groundwater." *Journal of Environmental Economics and Management* 24:139–58.

Ray, I., and J. Williams. 1999. "Evaluation of Price Policy in the Presence of Water Theft." *American Journal of Agricultural Economics* 81:928–41.

Rosegrant, M., C. Ringler, and T. Zhu. 2009. "Water for Agriculture: Maintaining Food Security under Growing Scarcity." *Annual Review of Environment and Resources* 34:205–22.

Rosine, J., and P. Helmberger. 1974. "A Neoclassical Analysis of the U.S. Farm Sector, 1948–1970." *American Journal of Agricultural Economics* 56:717–29.

Rud, J. P. 2011. "Electricity Provision and Industrial Development: Evidence from India." *Journal of Development Economics* 97 (2): 352–67.

Scheierling, S., J. Loomis, and R. Young. 2006. "Irrigation Water Demand: A Meta-analysis of Price Elasticities." *Water Resources Research* 42: W01411.

Schoengold, K., and D. Zilberman. 2007. "The Economics of Water, Irrigation, and Development." In *Handbook of Agricultural Economics*, vol. 3, edited by R. Evenson, P. Pingali, and T. P. Schultz, 2933–77. Amsterdam: North Holland.

Scott, C. A., and T. Shah. 2004. "Groundwater Overdraft Reduction through Agricultural Energy Policy: Insights from India and Mexico." *International Journal of Water Resources Development* 20 (4): 149–64.

Sekhri, S. 2011. "Missing Water: Agricultural Stress and Adaptation Strategies." University of Virginia Working Paper.

Shah, T. 2009. "Climate Change and Groundwater: India's Opportunities for Mitigation and Adaptation." *Environmental Research Letters* 4 (3): 1–13.

Shah, T., C. Scott, A. Kishore, and A. Sharma. 2003. "Energy-Irrigation Nexus in South Asia: Approaches to Agrarian Prosperity with Viable Power Industry." Research Report no. 70, Colombo, Sri Lanka, International Water Management Institute.

Somanathan, E., and R. Ravindranath. 2006. "Measuring the Marginal Value of Water and Elasticity of Demand for Water in Agriculture." *Economic and Political Weekly* 41 (26): 2712–15.

Strand, J. 2010. "The Full Economic Cost of Groundwater Extraction." Policy Research Working Paper 5494.

Sun, S., J. P. Sesmero, and K. Schoengold. 2016. "The Role of Common Pool Problems in Irrigation Efficiency: A Case Study in Groundwater Pumping Mexico." *Agricultural Economics* 47 (1): 117–27.

Tongia, R. 2003. "The Political Economy of Indian Power Sector Reforms." PSED Working Paper no. 4, Stanford, CA.

UNEP (United Nations Environment Program). 2008. "Reforming Energy Subsidies: Opportunities to Contribute to the Climate Change Agenda." Division of Technology, Industry, and Economics, https://unep.ch/etb/publications/Energy%20subsidies/EnergySubsidiesFinalReport.pdf.

World Bank. 2010. *World Development Indicators*. Washington, DC: World Bank.

6

Estimating the Impact of Crop Diversity on Agricultural Productivity in South Africa

Cecilia Bellora, Élodie Blanc, Jean-Marc Bourgeon, and Eric Strobl

6.1 Introduction

Diversity plays a key role in the resilience to external stresses of farm plants and animals. In particular, crop species diversity increases productivity and production stability (Tilman, Polasky, and Lehman 2005; Tilman and Downing 1994; Tilman, Wedin, and Knops 1996) in the sense that the probability to find at least one individual that resists to an adverse meteorological phenomenon (for example, a drought or a heatwave), or pests and diseases, increases with the diversity within a population. Furthermore, the larger a homogeneous population, the larger the number of parasites that use this population as a host and therefore the larger the probability of a lethal infection (Pianka 1999). Diversity also allows for species complementarities and, as a consequence, a more efficient use of natural resources (Loreau and Hector 2001). In short, crop biodiversity has the potential to

Cecilia Bellora is an economist at the Centre d'Études Prospectives et d'Informations Internationales (CEPII).

Élodie Blanc is a research scientist at the MIT Joint Program on the Science and Policy of Global Change.

Jean-Marc Bourgeon is a senior researcher at the French National Institute for Agricultural Research (INRA) and a professor of economics at École Polytechnique.

Eric Strobl is a professor of environmental and climate economics at the University of Bern.

This work was supported by the MIT Joint Program on the Science and Policy of Global Change. For a complete list of sponsors and US government funding sources, see http://globalchange.mit.edu/sponsors/. We would like to thank Eyal Frank and the participants of the NBER Understanding Productivity Growth in Agriculture Conference for their valuable comments. For acknowledgments, sources of research support, and disclosure of the authors' material financial relationships, if any, please see https://www.nber.org/chapters/c13942.ack.

enhance resistance to strains due to biotic and abiotic factors and to improve crop production and, possibly, farm revenues.[1]

For these reasons, after the large development of monocultures in the last decades, crop biodiversity is making a comeback. During the last century, farming activities specialized on the most productive crops, in particular in developed countries and in large areas of emerging economies. The decrease in crop biodiversity resulted in increased pest attacks (Landis et al. 2008) and has been compensated by the heavy use of agrochemicals. Nevertheless, chemicals generate negative externalities, irreversible in many cases, on water and soil quality, on wildlife, and on human health (Pimentel 2005; Foley et al. 2011; Jiguet et al. 2012; Beketov et al. 2013), which engender large economic costs (Gallai et al. 2009; Sutton et al. 2011). One of the main challenges for the future is to drastically reduce externalities while satisfying an increasing and changing food demand (Gouel and Guimbard 2018). In this context, crop biodiversity is seen more and more as a promising way to raise, or at least maintain, agricultural yields while decreasing the use of chemicals (McDaniel, Tiemann, and Grandy 2014). However, more estimations of the actual impacts of crop biodiversity on agricultural yields are needed to build solutions for farmers and to adopt relevant public policies. To this end, we empirically investigate the role of crop biodiversity on crop productivity.[2] We build a probabilistic model based on ecological mechanisms to describe crop survival and productivities according to diversity. From this analytic model, we derive reduced forms that are estimated using data on South African agriculture.

Our results contribute to the existing literature in three main ways. First, we confirm that diversity has a positive and significant impact on produced quantities. An increase in biodiversity is equivalent to a third of the benefits of a comparable increase in irrigation, where irrigation is known to be an important impediment to crop productivity in South Africa, due to unreliable precipitation. Previous empirical investigations on the role of biodiversity on production has produced sometimes contrasted results. Positive impact of biodiversity is found by Di Falco and Chavas (2006) and Carew, Smith, and Grant (2009) in wheat production in Italy and Canada, respectively. Smale et al. (1998) also focus on wheat yield and find a positive impact of biodiversity in rain-fed regions of Pakistan, while in irrigated areas, higher concentration on few varieties is associated with higher yields. Second, we adopt an approach based on ecology literature, while previous contribu-

---

1. The variation of farm revenues depends on the trade-off between the increase in biomass production and the opportunity cost of a larger crop diversity.

2. Crop biodiversity can be implemented in different ways and at various scales. Mixing several species in the same plot increases interspecific biodiversity, while the association of different varieties of the same crop increases intraspecific biodiversity. Agronomists and ecologists also explore the impact of a diversified landscape, where cultivate fields and uncultivated areas alternate. Our investigation is about interspecific crop diversity at the landscape level, as detailed in the following chapter.

tions used pure econometric methods, mainly moment-based approaches (Di Falco and Chavas 2006, 2009) stressing the crucial role played by skewness in addition to mean and variance. In these cases, the functional forms are disconnected from the ecology literature and therefore do not allow us to go into deep details on the way biodiversity impacts productivity. In the economic literature, models of endogenous interaction between biodiversity and crop production have been developed in theoretical papers that analyze the role and value of biodiversity against specialization on the most productive crops (Weitzman 2000; Brock and Xepapadeas 2003; Bellora and Bourgeon 2016) but have never been coupled with empirical investigations. In contrast, we build a probabilistic model that makes explicit the relationship between biodiversity and biotic and abiotic factors that affect agricultural production Stochastic shocks affecting agricultural production are endogenous, in accordance with ecology findings. This model can easily be linked to data and grounds our analysis on findings of ecology studies. This approach can also be extended to account for noncrop biodiversity (pastures, fallow land, noncultivated areas), which appears to also play a key role (Tscharntke et al. 2005), and to characterize the impacts on production variability. Third, we draw from the increasingly available satellite data (Donaldson and Storeygard 2016) to build a rich data set allowing us to estimate the impact of biodiversity on crop productivity based on our probabilistic model. A Normalized Difference Vegetation Index (NDVI) derived from the SPOT 5 satellite images, coupled with land-use classification, allow us to quantify the crop biomass produced on nearly 65,000 fields covering around 6.5 million hectares in South Africa. We quantify biodiversity using an index taken from the ecological literature, based on species richness (i.e., the total number of species) and their relative abundance, the Shannon index (Shannon 1948). This index captures the fact that biodiversity is high when the total number of species is large and the distribution of their relative abundances is homogeneous. We are then able to quantify the impacts of interspecific diversity on the productivity of various crops, while previous studies mainly looked at genetic diversity (i.e., intraspecific diversity of a single crop). We confirm that biodiversity has mainly a local impact: biodiversity is a significant predictor of crop productivity on perimeters having a radius smaller than 2 km.

   In the remainder of the chapter, the theoretical model that motivates our empirical investigations is developed in section 6.2, and section 6.3 details its empirical implementation. Then the database on South African agriculture is presented in section 6.4. In section 6.5, we empirically investigate the impact of crop biodiversity on crop production.

6.2   The Model

   A very robust stylized fact in ecology describes the impact of biotic factors on agricultural production: the more area dedicated to the same crop, the higher the number of pests specializing on this crop and the higher the frequency of their attacks (Pianka 1999). Relying on this stylized fact, we build a general probabilistic model of crop production where crops are affected by both abiotic (i.e., weather, water availability, soil properties) and biotic (i.e., pests) factors causing preharvest losses.[3] More precisely, we consider that the total agricultural production depends on the survival probability of each crop, which is directly linked to the probability of a pest attack. The frequency at which pest attacks occur is linked to the way crops are produced: the more diverse the crops, the lower the probability of a pest attack, the higher the survival probability, and therefore the higher the expected agricultural production. To describe the diffusion of pests, or equivalently the survival probabilities, we follow the literature in ecology and plant physiology and adopt a beta-binomial distribution, which is usual to depict spatial distributions that are not random but clustered, patchy, or heterogeneous (Hughes and Madden 1993; Shiyomi, Takahashi, and Yoshimura 2000; Chen et al. 2008; Bastin et al. 2012; Irvine and Rodhouse 2010).

We assume that a region (or a country) produces Z different crops on I fields of the same size, each field being sowed with one crop only.[4] Characteristics of field i are gathered in vector $X_i = (x_{i1}, \ldots, x_{iK})$ and are related to both abiotic factors and biotic factors. In particular, $\mathbf{X}_i$ contains information on the way crops are cultivated (irrigation but also soil quality and field location) and on biodiversity conditions. Depending on the crop cultivated, each field is divided in $n(z)$ patches that are subject to potential lethal strains due, for example, to adverse meteorological conditions or pathogens. We suppose that a patch on field i is destroyed with probability $1 - \lambda_i$ from one (or several) adverse condition and that otherwise it produces the potential yield $a(z)$ independently of the fate of the other patches on field i or elsewhere.[5] With $n(z)$ patches, the probability of t patches within field i remaining unaffected (and thus $n(z) - t$ destroyed) follows a binomial distribution

$$\Pr\{\tilde{T}_i = t \mid z, \lambda_i\} = \binom{n(z)}{t} \lambda_i^t (1 - \lambda_i)^{n(z)-t},$$

where $\tilde{T}_i$ is the random variable that corresponds to the number of patches that are indeed harvested among the $n(z)$ patches of field i sowed with crop

3. Losses due to biotic factors can be significant. Oerke (2006) finds that, from 2001 to 2003, without crop protection, losses in major crops due to pests comprised between 50 percent and 80 percent, at the world level. Thanks to crop protection, they fall between 29 percent and 37 percent. Similar results are found for the United States by Fernandez-Cornejo et al. (1998).

4. The model can be thought at different scales. It could represent a mixed intercropping system (Malézieux et al. 2009) or a diversified agricultural landscape, for instance. In the following empirical exercise, we apply it at a large geographic scale.

5. Obviously, this is a strong assumption. Pests and/or weather do not necessarily totally destroy a patch but rather affect the quantity of biomass produced. But in order to maintain tractability, we consider that a patch is either unaffected or totally destroyed, rather than partially affected, by adverse conditions. Thus our random variable is the number of harvested patches rather than the share of biomass that is lost on each patch.

z. We consider that the survival probability of the patches of a field, λ_i, is identically and independently distributed across patches. However, this probability may vary across fields of the same crop (we generally have $\lambda_i \neq \lambda_j$ for any couple of fields (i, j) sowed with the same crop): it depends on natural conditions but also on the characteristics $\mathbf{X}_i$ of the field. More precisely, the survival probability of patches on a given field is a draw from a beta distribution given by

$$\Pr(\lambda_i = \lambda \,|\, \mathbf{X}_i, z) = \frac{\Gamma[S_{ui}(z) + S_{di}(z)]}{\Gamma[S_{ui}(z)]\Gamma[S_{di}(z)]} \lambda^{S_{ui}(z)-1}(1 - \lambda)^{S_{di}(z)-1},$$

where $\Gamma(\cdot)$ is the gamma function, $S_{ui}(z) \equiv e^{\gamma(z)+\theta_u(z)X_i}$ and $S_{di}(z) \equiv e^{\beta(z)+\theta_d(z)X_i}$, $\gamma(z)$ and $\beta(z)$ are positive parameters that determine the randomness of the survival probability of a patch of crop z absent any field-specific effect, and the vectors $\boldsymbol{\theta}_u(z) = \{\theta_{uk}(z)\}_{k=1,\ldots,K}$ and $\boldsymbol{\theta}_d(z) = \{\theta_{dk}(z)\}_{k=1,\ldots,K}$ capture the influence of each field-specific effect X_i on the survival probability of crop z. The expected number of patches among $n(z)$ that are harvested on field i is given by $E[\tilde{T}_i \,|\, X_i, z] = n(z)\psi(z, X_i)$, where

(1)
$$\psi(z, X_i) = E[\lambda_i \,|\, X_i, z] = \frac{S_{ui}(z)}{S_{ui}(z) + S_{di}(z)}$$

is the expected probability that a particular patch of field i of crop z is harvested given its characteristics X_i. Absent field-specific effects ($\boldsymbol{\theta}_u(z) = \boldsymbol{\theta}_d(z) = 0$), the expected resilience of a particular stand of crop is given by $\exp\gamma(z)/(\exp\gamma(z) + \exp\beta(z))$. An increase in coefficient $\theta_{uk}(z)$ increases this resilience, while an increase in $\theta_{dk}(z)$ diminishes it, the extent of these effects depending on the corresponding field characteristics x_{ik}. The variance of the number of harvested patches on field i is given by $\sigma_i^2 = n(z)V(z, X_i)$, where

(2) $$V(z, X_i) = \psi(z, X_i)[1 - \psi(z, X_i)]\{1 + [n(z) - 1]\rho(z, X_i)\}$$

with

$$\rho(z, X_i) = [1 + S_{ui}(z) + S_{di}(z)]^{-1}.$$

Equation (2) corresponds to the variance of the survival probability of one patch on a field with characteristics X_i. Compared to the Bernoulli distribution, (2) contains an additional term that accounts for the correlation between patches induced by the common distribution of the survival probability, the correlation coefficient being given by $\rho(z, X_i)$.

The production on field $\tilde{Y}_i = a(z)\tilde{T}_i$ is given by $\tilde{Y}_i = a(z)\tilde{T}_i$. It can be equivalently written as

(3) $$\tilde{Y}_i = E[\tilde{Y}_i](1 + \tilde{\varepsilon}_i),$$

where $E[\tilde{Y}_i] = a(z)n(z)\psi(z, X_i)$ and $\tilde{\varepsilon}_i = (\tilde{T}_i - E[\tilde{T}_i])/E[\tilde{T}_i]$ has a mean equal to 0 and a variance given by

$$(4) \quad \sigma_{\varepsilon_i}^2 = \frac{1 - \psi(z, X_i)}{\psi(z, X_i)} \left(\frac{1}{n(z)} + \frac{n(z) - 1}{n(z)} \rho(z, X_i) \right) \approx \frac{1 - \psi(z, X_i)}{\psi(z, X_i)} \rho(z, X_i)$$

when $n(z)$ is large. This variance is mainly due to the correlation between patches on a field that share the same survival probability, captured by $\rho(z, X_i)$. Indeed, λ_i follows a beta distribution, but the parameters of the distribution depend on the field characteristics X_i and are thus different across fields. In other words, with a sufficiently large number of patches on each field, the difference in the quantities produced is mainly driven by field characteristics.

This simple ecological model of crop production can thus be summarized as follows: the number of patches that are harvested on field i, $\tilde{T}_i$, follows a beta-binomial distribution determined by the parameters $\gamma(z)$, $\beta(z)$, θ_{uk}, and θ_{dk}. Parameters θ_{uk} and θ_{dk} determine the impact of the kth field characteristic x_{ik} on $\tilde{T}_i$, in addition to the parameters $\lambda(z)$ and $\beta(z)$ that are shared by all fields that grow crop z. Depending on the values of θ_{uk} and θ_{dk}, each characteristic x_{ik} can increase or decrease the expected number of harvested patches on field i and skew the distribution of $\tilde{T}_i$ to the right or to the left, modifying the probability of extreme events like the loss of all the patches in a field.

In the following section, we build an empirical strategy to estimate the impact of the characteristics of a field on the distribution of $\tilde{T}_i$. In particular, we are interested in the impact on crop production of the crop biodiversity surrounding the field considered and expect this impact to be positive, according to findings and mechanisms described in the ecology literature.

6.3   Empirical Strategy

Starting from the probabilistic model, our aim is to estimate the parameters $\theta_u(z)$, $\theta_d(z)$, $\gamma(z)$, and $\beta(z)$ of the distribution of the survival probability $\tilde{T}$. We first have to derive from each field production the corresponding survival probability λ_i. They are obtained by dividing the production level by the potential maximum production $a(z)n(z)$ level. This potential production is not observed in practice; it is derived in the following from the maximum observed production level $Y_M(z) \equiv \max Y_i(z)$ using $a(z)n(z) = (1 + \alpha) Y_M(z)$, where $\alpha \geq 0$.[6] With a linear regression of the equation

$$(5) \quad \ln\left(\frac{\hat{\lambda}_i}{1 - \hat{\lambda}_i}\right) = \delta + \Delta X_i$$

for each type of crop, we obtain the estimate $\hat{\delta}(z)$ of $\gamma(z) - \beta(z)$ and $\hat{\Delta}(z)$ of $\theta_u(z) - \theta_d(z)$. This first regression estimates the contribution of biodiversity (and other field characteristics) to the ratio of survival and death probabilities. Coefficients Δ show the variation of the growth rate of the odds

---

6. In the following, we consider $\alpha = 0.5$. Robustness checks for $\alpha = 0.1$ are available in the appendix.

associated with a marginal increase in each explanatory variable. These first results are interesting per se but also allow us to derive an expected patch survival rate for each field i using

$$\hat{\psi}_i = 1/(1 + e^{-\hat{\delta}(z)-\hat{\Delta}(z)X_i})$$

and a series of dispersion values

$$\hat{\varepsilon}_i = (\hat{\lambda}_i - \hat{\psi}_i)/\hat{\psi}_i.$$

From (4), which can be written as

$$\sigma_{\varepsilon_i}^2 = \frac{1 - \psi(z, X_i)}{\psi(z, X_i) + S_{ui}},$$

we get, solving for S_{ui},

$$S_{ui} = \frac{1 - \psi(z, X_i)(1 + \sigma_{\varepsilon_i}^2)}{\sigma_{\varepsilon_i}^2}.$$

As $S_{ui} = \exp(\gamma + \boldsymbol{\theta}_u(z)X_i)$, we construct the variable

$$\hat{Z}_i = \frac{1 - \hat{\psi}_i(1 + \hat{\varepsilon}_i^2)}{\hat{\varepsilon}_i^2},$$

and we perform an OLS estimation of the equation

(6) $$\ln(\hat{Z}_i) = \gamma(z) + \boldsymbol{\theta}_u(z)X_i$$

to obtain $\hat{\gamma}(z)$ and $\hat{\boldsymbol{\theta}}_u(z)$. We then get $\hat{\beta}(z) = \hat{\gamma}(z) - \hat{\delta}(z)$ and $\hat{\boldsymbol{\theta}}_d(z) = \hat{\boldsymbol{\theta}}_u(z) - \hat{\boldsymbol{\Delta}}(z)$.

6.4   Data

Combining different data sources, we construct a very detailed original database on South African agriculture that quantifies the production and describes the characteristics of a very large number of fields using satellite data. First, field boundaries are identified, then agricultural production is characterized on each field by identifying the crops that are grown and measuring the biomass produced. Field characteristics are then collected, addressing particular water balance, length of the growing season, and crop interspecific biodiversity.

6.4.1   Crop Fields

Field boundaries, available for South African provinces of Free State, Gauteng, North West, and Mpumalanga, are determined using the Producer Independent Crop Estimate System (PICES), which combines satellite imagery, a geographic information system (GIS), point frame statistical platforms, and aerial observations (Ferreira, Newby, and du Preez 2006). Satellite imagery of cultivated fields is obtained from the SPOT 5 satellite at

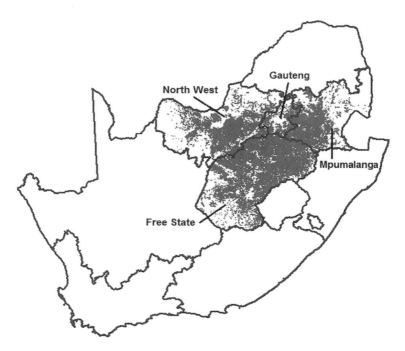

Fig. 6.1   Localization of the considered fields in South Africa

a 2.5 m resolution. Plot boundaries are then digitized using GIS, and field cloud covered polygons are removed before processing. Over the four regions of interest, PICES distinguishes circa 280,000 fields covering an area of around 6.5 million hectares. To approximately match the resolution of the crop production indicator we use (see section 6.4.2), which is only available at the 250 m resolution, the analysis is limited to fields larger than 6.25 ha. Additionally, we exclude pasture and fallow land. This restricts the sample to 64,682 fields. Figure 6.1 presents the location of the considered crop fields in South Africa. While the summary statistics in table 6.1 show that fields are on average about 28.4 ha, the large standard deviation (24.8) indicates that they vary substantially in size (the largest field is 720 ha large).

Using the digitized satellite images previously described, the Agricultural Geo-referenced Information System (AGIS) developed by the South African Department of Agriculture provides information on the crop cultivated on each field. To do so, sample points were selected randomly and surveyed by trained observers from a very light aircraft in order to determine crop type (Ferreira, Newby, and du Preez 2006). Crop information collected during the aerial surveys on the sample points was subsequently used as a training set for crop-type classification for each field and for accuracy assessment. These estimated crop classifications were then checked against a producer-

Table 6.1   **Plot summary statistics**

Variable	Mean	Standard deviation	Variable	Mean	Standard deviation
All crops			Maize		
NDVI	0.61	0.13	NDVI	0.61	0.13
Water balance	−41.07	11.73	Water balance	−42.60	11.89
Season length (days)	129.64	35.48	Season length (days)	126.98	35.33
Plot area (ha)	28.36	23.47	Plot area (ha)	22.72	2.04
Farm area (ha)	315.2	500.00	Farm area (ha)	193.63	3.53
Irrigation (%)	5.05	–	Irrigation (%)	4.94	21.67
Cotton			Sorghum		
NDVI	0.73	0.05	NDVI	0.69	0.10
Water balance	−28.61	14.54	Water balance	−33.54	7.70
Season length (days)	130.94	52.00	Season length (days)	125.20	26.17
Plot area (ha)	15.63	1.66	Plot area (ha)	19.27	1.91
Farm area (ha)	184.41	2.32	Farm area (ha)	45.63	2.79
Irrigation (%)	56.60	49.80	Irrigation (%)	1.96	13.87
Dry bean			Soybean		
NDVI	0.62	0.14	NDVI	0.71	0.09
Water balance	−38.96	12.39	Water balance	−32.18	7.59
Season length (days)	145.58	38.66	Season length (days)	129.19	30.14
Plot area (ha)	21.43	2.03	Plot area (ha)	19.09	1.91
Farm area (ha)	68.50	3.10	Farm area (ha)	95.98	2.95
Irrigation (%)	3.75	19.00	Irrigation (%)	5.89	23.55
Groundnuts			Sunflower		
NDVI	0.52	0.11	NDVI	0.59	0.13
Water balance	−55.56	6.34	Water balance	−44.20	12.10
Season length (days)	115.40	34.67	Season length (days)	131.27	38.01
Plot area (ha)	28.61	2.03	Plot area (ha)	20.54	2.01
Farm area (ha)	73.91	2.96	Farm area (ha)	80.59	3.14
Irrigation (%)	4.10	19.84	Irrigation (%)	7.80	26.81

based survey for the Gauteng region. The Gauteng census survey showed that less than 1.8 percent of crop types had been misclassified. All in all, seven summer crops were distinguished for the provinces of Free State, Gauteng, North West, and Mpumalanga for the summer season 2006/2007: cotton, dry beans, groundnuts, maize, sorghum, soybeans, and sunflowers. An example of the distribution of crop types is provided in figure 6.2. The summary statistics for the entire sample in table 6.2 show that maize was the dominant crop cultivated in the three provinces: maize fields represent nearly 70 percent of the total number of fields we consider. Other important crops were sunflowers and soybeans, standing at 15 and 11 percent, respectively. In contrast, all other crop types constituted less than 2 percent individually. One should note that even if one were to adjust the crop-type shares by their areas, a similar ranking remains, with a slight redistribution of shares toward the smaller crop types. For instance, the share of maize dropped to 62 percent of the total crop area.

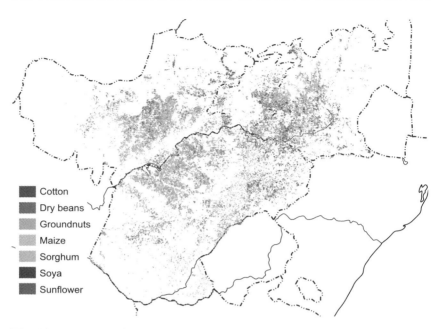

Fig. 6.2   Distribution of the studied crops in South Africa

Table 6.2   Distribution of the considered crops

Crop	Number of fields	Share of total fields (%)	Share of total area (%)
Dry beans	1,227	1.88	1.88
Groundnuts	1,292	2.5	2.50
Maize	45,256	69.77	72.27
Sorghum	715	1.10	0.93
Soybeans	6,825	10.52	8.80
Sunflowers	9,441	14.56	13.51
Cotton	106	0.16	0.10
Total	64,862	100.00	100.00

The AGIS crop-boundaries data set also provides information regarding irrigation, from which only 5 percent of the fields considered benefit (table 6.1).

Finally, all fields can be linked to their respective farms with a unique farm identifier. In total, the fields were owned by 12,462 different farms, where on average each farm was proprietor of five fields. However, ownership differed substantially, with the largest ownership gathering 193 fields and 3,704 single field farms.

6.4.2   Crop Production Measure

We estimate crop biomass production using the satellite-derived Normalized Difference Vegetation Index (NDVI). Vegetation indexes provide consistent spatial and temporal representations of vegetation conditions when locally derived information is not available. As a matter of fact, numerous studies have demonstrated that NDVI values are significantly correlated with biomass production, and therefore yields, of various crops, including wheat (Das, Mishra, and Kalra 1993; Gupta et al. 1993; Doraiswamy and Cook 1995; Hochheim and Barber 1998; Labus et al. 2002), sorghum (Potdar 1993), maize (Hayes and Decker 1996; Prasad et al. 2006), rice (Nuarsa et al. 2011; Quarmby et al. 1993), soybeans (Prasad et al. 2006), barley (Weissteiner and Kuhbauch 2005), millet (Groten 1993), and tomatoes (Koller and Upadhaya 2005). Moreover, NDVI has also been shown to provide a very good indicator of crop phenological development (Benedetti and Rossini 1993).

The NDVI index is calculated using ratios of vegetation spectral reflectance over incoming radiation in each spectral band. The NDVI data are extracted from the MOD13Q1 data set,[7] which gathers reflectance information collected by the MODerate-resolution Imaging Spectroradiometer (MODIS) instrument operating on NASA's Terra satellite (Huete et al. 2002). From these data, NDVI can be formulated as

$$NDVI = \frac{NIR - VIS}{NIR + VIS},$$

where the difference between near-infrared reflectance (NIR) and visible reflectance (VIS) values is normalized by the total reflectance and varies between -1 and 1 (Eidenshink 1992). The more biomass is produced, the more the NDVI is close to 1. Negative and very low values corresponding to water and barren areas were excluded from the analysis by design. Nevertheless, NDVI has some limitations. In particular, it enters an asymptotic regime for high values of biomass. It reaches its maximum when leaves totally cover the soil and does not allow us to distinguish between dense or very dense vegetation, contrary to other vegetation indexes that do not saturate over densely vegetated regions (Huete et al. 1997). In that sense, NDVI is less reliable in estimating the biomass production of dense vegetation, like forests. However, it is very sensible to photosynthetic activity and therefore remains highly indicative of the biomass produced in cultivated fields. Carlson and Ripley (1997) precisely describe the asymptotic regime of NDVI and Ma et al. (2001) confirm this analysis and relate biomass produced to NDVI using the following relationship, extrapolated for soybeans,

---

7. Available online at https://lpdaac.usgs.gov/lpdaac/content/view/full/6652.

(7) $Y = d + b\text{NDVI}^c$,

where Y represents the quantities produced (or the yield) and d, b, and c are three parameters. The only parameter needed in the following is c, taken equal to 4.54, following Ma et al. (2001).[8] Denoting

(8) $N_i = \text{NDVI}_i - \text{NDVI}_0$

with $\text{NDVI}_0 = |d/b|^{1/c}$, bN_i^c gives an estimation of the quantities produced on field i, $Y(i)$.[9]

Crop-growing seasons are characterized by the planting date and the phenology cycle, which determines the length of the season. In South Africa, planting generally occurs between October and December in order to reduce the vulnerability to erratic precipitation (Ferreira, Newby, and du Preez 2006). However, phenology cycles, and hence growing seasons, can differ substantially among crop types and even for fields of the same crop type. In order to take account of this, we used the TIMESAT program[10] (Jönsson and Eklundh 2002, 2004) to determine crop- and field-specific growing seasons. We are then able to approximate the start and end of growing seasons based on distribution properties of the NDVI. Summary statistics in table 6.1 show that growing seasons are on average 130 days, with a standard deviation of 35 days.

Finally, as is standard in the literature of satellite-derived plant-growth measures, we use the maximum NDVI over the growing season as an indicator of crop production (Zhang, Friedl, and Schaaf 2006). It takes on an average value of 0.61 with a standard deviation of 0.13 (see table 6.1).

6.4.3   Crop–Water Balance

An important determinant of crop growth is water availability. A common simple proxy for it is the difference between rainfall and the evaporative demand of the air,—that is, evapotranspiration. To calculate this, we use gridded daily precipitation and reference evapotranspiration data taken from the USGS Early Warning Famine climatic database.[11] More specifically, daily rainfall data, given at the 0.1-degree resolution (approximately 11 km), are generated with the rainfall estimation algorithm RFE (version 2.0) data set implemented by the National Oceanic and Atmospheric Administration (NOAA)-Climate Prediction Center (CPC) using a combination of rain gauges and satellite observations. Daily reference evapotranspiration data, available at a 1-degree resolution (approximately 111 km), were calculated

8. We take the estimate coming from the regression showing the best fit on data used by Ma et al. (2001).
9. For values smaller than NDVI_0, the produced quantities are equal to 0, the NDVI capturing the light reflected by the bare soil.
10. The algorithm within the TIMESAT software is commonly used to extract seasonality information from satellite time-series data.
11. http://earlywarning.usgs.gov/fews.

using a six-hour assimilation of conventional and satellite observational data of air temperature, atmospheric pressure, wind speed, relative humidity and solar radiation extracted from the NOAA Global Data Assimilation System. Using these gridded data, each field was then assigned a daily precipitation and potential evapotranspiration value over its growing season to then calculate out its average daily water balance. The mean and standard deviation of this measure are given in table 6.1.

6.4.4   Biodiversity Index

Among field characteristics, we are particularly interested in crop biodiversity. Diversity measures, extensively used in biology and ecology literature, take into account species richness (i.e., the number of species present) and evenness (i.e., the distribution of species). In the following, we quantify biodiversity at the field level, adopting one of the most widely used indicators, the Shannon index (Shannon 1948),

$$(9) \qquad H_\ell = -\sum_z B_\ell(z) \ln B_\ell(z),$$

where ℓ defines the size of the perimeter considered as relevant and $B_\ell(z)$ is the proportion of area within perimeter ℓ that is of crop z type. H_ℓ is then calculated for a given perimeter ℓ, defined by its radius, applied to the centroid of the field considered. The more diverse the crops are and the more equal their abundances, the larger the Shannon index. When all crops are equally common, all $B(z)$ values will equal $1/Z$ (Z being the total number of crops), and H will be equal to $\ln Z$. On the contrary, the more unequal the abundances of the crops, the smaller the index, approaching 0 (and being equal to 0 if $Z = 1$). With respect to other common indicators, like the Simpson's index,[12] the Shannon index is known to put less weight on the more abundant species and to be more sensitive to differences in total species richness and in changes in populations showing small relative abundances (Baumgärtner 2006). In our specification, the distance threshold for the radius ℓ is 0.75 km; the distance is then increased 250 m by 250 m to reach 3 km, the maximum distance considered. We provide summary statistics for the Shannon index in table 6.3. Widening the perimeter under consideration increases the value of the Shannon index substantially. For example, the 3 km index is nearly five times larger than the 0.75 km index. This suggests that crop types are strongly spatially agglomerated and thus locally less diverse.

6.5   Empirical Analysis

Our first empirical task is to investigate whether biodiversity affects crop field production. To this end, we rely on the strategy defined in section 6.3.

---

12. With our notations, the Simpson's index is given by $1 - \sum_z B_\ell^2(z)$.

Table 6.3   **Summary statistics for the Shannon index**

ℓ	All crops $\bar{H}$	σ_H	Dry bean $\bar{H}$	σ_H	Groundnuts $\bar{H}$	σ_H	Maize $\bar{H}$	σ_H	Sorghum $\bar{H}$	σ_H	Soybeans $\bar{H}$	σ_H	Sunflowers $\bar{H}$	σ_H
0.75 km	0.03	0.14	0.17	0.31	0.21	0.31	0.08	0.21	0.11	0.25	0.17	0.29	0.14	0.26
1.00 km	0.06	0.18	0.27	0.37	0.35	0.35	0.14	0.26	0.20	0.31	0.28	0.33	0.23	0.31
1.25 km	0.07	0.21	0.36	0.39	0.43	0.35	0.19	0.29	0.28	0.35	0.37	0.35	0.30	0.33
1.50 km	0.09	0.23	0.45	0.41	0.48	0.34	0.23	0.30	0.35	0.36	0.44	0.36	0.35	0.34
1.75 km	0.10	0.24	0.50	0.42	0.51	0.34	0.27	0.31	0.40	0.37	0.49	0.35	0.40	0.34
2.00 km	0.12	0.25	0.55	0.43	0.53	0.32	0.31	0.32	0.45	0.37	0.54	0.35	0.43	0.33
2.25 km	0.13	0.26	0.60	0.43	0.55	0.31	0.33	0.32	0.49	0.37	0.58	0.34	0.46	0.33
2.50 km	0.13	0.27	0.63	0.43	0.56	0.30	0.36	0.32	0.52	0.37	0.61	0.33	0.48	0.32
2.75 km	0.14	0.28	0.66	0.43	0.57	0.30	0.38	0.31	0.56	0.36	0.63	0.32	0.50	0.32
3.00 km	0.15	0.28	0.68	0.43	0.58	0.29	0.40	0.31	0.59	0.36	0.65	0.32	0.52	0.31

Note: The table reports the mean ($\bar{H}$) and the standard deviation (σ_H) of the distribution of the Shannon index, measured for the different crops considered, on different perimeters, characterized by their radius, ℓ.

In short, we build data on crop production using (7) and (8). We use them to calculate the survival probability in each field, $\hat{\lambda}_i$. Then with a linear regression on specification (5), we estimate the impact of biodiversity on the odds—that is the ratio of the probability for a given field to survive to the probability of death.

Crop productivity depends not only on crop biodiversity but also on more general natural conditions (weather, season length), field attributes (irrigation, area), and farm management attributes (pesticides, mechanization, economies of scale). Therefore, the vector of control variables **X** includes crop fixed effects, crop–water balance (WB) and its squared value (WB^2), an irrigation dummy indicator (IR), the season length ($SEAS\_LENGTH$), the logarithm of the field area in hectares (ln ($AREA$)), the latitude (LAT) and longitude (LON) of the centroid of the field, the percentage of cropland within a defined perimeter that is irrigated (PC_AREA_IR), and the percentage of land devoted to the same crop that belongs to the same farm, within a defined perimeter (PC_AREA_FARM). We also include farm fixed effects to capture crop management techniques that are common within farms as well as farmwide economies of scale. Crop-specific dummies allow us to control for the fact that different crops will have different vegetation growth intensity as captured by satellite reflectance data. Our identifying assumption is that after controlling for climatic factors and within-farm fixed effects, there are no other within-farm time-varying omitted factors that determine plant productivity and are correlated with biodiversity.

The results of the regression on equation (5) for all crops pooled are presented in table 6.4. In the first column, we simply include our field-specific control variables (vector X). The first column shows results for a perimeter defined by a radius ℓ equal to 0.75 km. As can be seen, crop–water balance

Table 6.4   Regression results, all crops pooled

Variables	ℓ = 0.75 km	ℓ = 1.00 km	ℓ = 1.25 km	ℓ = 1.50 km	ℓ = 1.75 km	ℓ = 2.00 km	ℓ = 2.25 km	ℓ = 2.50 km	ℓ = 2.75 km	ℓ = 3.00 km
H	3.6***	2.67**	3.73***	1.88**	1.68**	1.4*	0.16	0.29	-0.4	-1.02
	(1.16)	(1.04)	(1.05)	(0.72)	(0.82)	(0.8)	(0.91)	(0.83)	(1.00)	(0.93)
WB	0.59***	0.59***	0.58***	0.58***	0.59***	0.59***	0.61***	0.61***	0.61***	0.61***
	(0.14)	(0.14)	(0.14)	(0.13)	(0.14)	(0.14)	(0.14)	(0.14)	(0.14)	(0.14)
WB^2	0.01***	0.01***	0.01***	0.01***	0.01***	0.01***	0.01***	0.01***	0.01***	0.01***
	(0.00)	(0.00)	(0.00)	(0.00)	(0.00)	(0.00)	(0.00)	(0.00)	(0.00)	(0.00)
WB × IR	-0.93***	-0.96***	-0.96***	-0.97***	-0.96***	-0.95***	-0.95***	-0.95***	-0.96***	-0.96***
	(0.29)	(0.29)	(0.28)	(0.28)	(0.28)	(0.28)	(0.28)	(0.28)	(0.28)	(0.28)
WB^2 × IR	0.00	0.00	0.00	0.00	0.00	0.00	0.00	0.00	0.00	0.00
	(0.00)	(0.00)	(0.00)	(0.00)	(0.00)	(0.00)	(0.00)	(0.00)	(0.00)	(0.00)
SEAS_LEN	-0.27***	-0.27***	-0.27***	-0.27***	-0.27***	-0.27***	-0.27***	-0.27***	-0.27***	-0.27***
	(0.02)	(0.02)	(0.02)	(0.02)	(0.02)	(0.02)	(0.02)	(0.02)	(0.02)	(0.02)
ln(AREA)	-2.85***	-2.98***	-3.01***	-3.08***	-3.08***	-3.13***	-3.12***	-3.14***	-3.16***	-3.17***
	(0.4)	(0.4)	(0.4)	(0.39)	(0.39)	(0.39)	(0.4)	(0.4)	(0.4)	(0.4)
IR	31.63***	30.99***	30.51***	30.96***	31.73***	32.35***	32.73***	32.83***	32.83***	32.99***
	(5.05)	(5.09)	(5.11)	(5.12)	(5.12)	(5.12)	(5.1)	(5.06)	(5.09)	(5.09)
LON	72.94***	73.24***	74.39***	74.06***	73.87***	73.0***	72.34***	72.59***	72.54***	72.24***
	(14.53)	(14.49)	(14.45)	(14.53)	(14.55)	(14.53)	(14.52)	(14.43)	(14.41)	(14.47)
LAT	-22.44	-22.82	-23.01	-22.7	-22.56	-22.64	-22.74	-22.26	-21.84	-22.01
	(26.28)	(26.39)	(26.55)	(27.79)	(28.07)	(28.58)	(28.62)	(29.33)	(29.7)	(29.65)
PC_AREA_IR	12.22***	14.44***	17.93***	19.14***	18.27***	17.73***	14.86***	14.76***	14.73***	11.91***
	(1.64)	(1.77)	(1.54)	(1.83)	(2.13)	(2.02)	(2.36)	(2.19)	(2.69)	(2.61)
PC_AREA_FARM	1.39**	0.93	0.48	-0.42	-0.19	-0.74	-0.43	-1.36	-1.9	-2.16
	(0.63)	(0.63)	(0.78)	(0.9)	(0.84)	(0.93)	(1.12)	(1.3)	(1.43)	(1.65)

Note: ***, **, and * indicate 1 percent, 5 percent, and 10 percent significance levels, respectively. Robust standard errors are in parentheses, clustered at field level. Farm and crop fixed effects are included but not reported. Sample: 64,862 fields, 12,462 farms. Results for individual crops are reported in the appendix. For ease of reporting, all coefficients are scaled by a factor of 10^2.

has a significant positive and exponentially increasing impact on the survival rate of crops. However, having an irrigation system acts more to increase the survival rate of crops and therefore fields' productivity. It also makes crops less reliant on water balance (in a linear fashion) as would be expected. The coefficient on season length suggests that the longer the season lasts, the lower the crop survival rate. In other words, the longer the season, the higher the probability that an adverse event affects crops. Larger fields have lower survival rates than smaller ones. Finally, being located further east results in crop survival probability, possibly because of more favorable climatic or soil conditions, while being further south or north is inconsequential for field productivity within our sample.

If we consider now the degree of crop diversity, as measured by the Shannon index, we observe that an increase in surrounding biodiversity improves the survival ratio in a given field, and consequently its productivity. Arguably, however, our diversity index may just be capturing the fact that neighboring areas are different in ways that are correlated with the diversity of crops. To take account of these factors, we thus control for the percentage of the surrounding area that is irrigated and the percentage of the surrounding area of fields of the same crop type that belongs to the same farm.

When increasing the defined perimeter to calculate the Shannon index to 1 km, adjusting the variables *PC_AREA_IR* and *PC_AREA_FARM* in an analogous fashion, the impact of crop biodiversity on survival rate remains statistically significant but decreases by 26 percent. As far as control variables are concerned, the share of area irrigated unequivocally increases the biomass production, while the share of area belonging to the same farm within the perimeter we consider seems to have no significant impact on the biomass production. Further increasing the perimeter similarly continues to produce a significant positive impact of biodiversity, the coefficient increasing by 40 percent. However, when further expanding the threshold of our definition of the relevant neighborhood, biodiversity still acts as a significant predictor of survival probability, but its contribution decreases and finally disappears for a perimeter's radius greater than 2 km.[13] This suggests that biodiversity is relatively locally defined—that is, within less than 2 km but likely close to 1.25 km.

To better appreciate the contribution of the theoretical model specification, we compare the results to a reduced-form model specified as

(10) $$NDVI_i = \beta_1 H_i + \beta_2 Rain_i + \beta_3 ET_i + \theta_{Farm} + \varepsilon_i.$$

This simple correlation model only considers the effect of the Shannon index and simple weather variables (rain and evapotranspiration, which are used to calculate water balance) and the farm fixed effect. The results of the reduced-

---

13. We also experimented with increasing the perimeter up to 10 km, but the coefficient on *H* remains insignificant in all cases.

Table 6.5   Impact of biodiversity on the odds of survival probabilities

ℓ	Pooled crops	Dry beans	Groundnuts	Maize	Soya	Sunflowers
0.75	3.6***	−1.68	5.84	4.93***	−0.67	2.91
	(1.16)	(6.85)	(9.02)	(1.69)	(2.1)	(3.32)
1.00	2.67**	−0.23	−4.54	3.01**	0.52	4.59*
	(1.04)	(5.91)	(9.3)	(1.17)	(2.15)	(2.72)
1.25	3.73***	4.04	−5.38	3.15***	4.77**	2.57
	(1.05)	(5.57)	(10.51)	(1.16)	(2.22)	(2.41)
1.50	1.88**	7.68	−20.42*	0.8	5.74**	−1.05
	(0.72)	(6.73)	(11.02)	(0.94)	(2.22)	(3.14)
1.75	1.68**	4.98	−9.1	1.11	8.48***	−0.91
	(0.82)	(7.17)	(11.6)	(1.01)	(2.17)	(3.3)
2.00	1.4*	−4.28	4.96	0.84	9.6***	−3.08
	(0.8)	(7.14)	(11.42)	(0.91)	(2.6)	(3.62)
2.25	0.16	0.06	−1.59	−0.04	6.83**	−6.2**
	(0.91)	(6.95)	(13.47)	(1.05)	(2.59)	(3.11)
2.50	0.29	3.12	−2.44	0.71	6.47***	−9.12***
	(0.83)	(7.35)	(17.65)	(0.84)	(2.3)	(3.13)
2.75	−0.4	2.45	−1.96	0.69	5.73**	−11.9***
	(1.00)	(7.98)	(18.36)	(1.05)	(2.53)	(4.44)
3.00	−1.02	−3.28	−3.48	0.41	5.47*	−15.58***
	(0.93)	(7.44)	(18.64)	(1.21)	(2.8)	(4.59)
Fields	64,682	1,227	1,292	45,256	6,825	9,441

Note: ***, **, and * indicate 1 percent, 5 percent, and 10 percent significance levels, respectively. Robust standard errors are in parentheses, clustered at field level. Farm and crop fixed effects are included but not reported. Sample: 64,862 fields, 12,462 farms. The table shows the coefficients for the variable H_ℓ for each of the six crops considered. Complete regression results are reported in the annex. For ease of reporting, all coefficients are scaled by a factor 10^2.

form regression presented in table 6.6 show a strong and positive effect of biodiversity on NDVI for all perimeter radii up until 2000 m. These results are consistent with those obtained using the probabilistic model based on ecological mechanisms.

We then look at the heterogeneity of impacts across crops, considering sequentially each of the six crops for which data are available (cotton is not considered in the regressions by crop, since the available sample—106 fields, 0.16 percent of the total available fields and 0.1 of the total cropland considered—is too small). The results show that, on the one hand, biodiversity has a significant impact on survival probability of maize, soybeans, and sunflowers, and that the relevant perimeter size of the biodiversity index depends on the crop. Table 6.5 also reveals that biodiversity has no significant impact on dry beans, groundnuts, and sorghum. This can be explained by the fact that each of the latter crops represents less than 2 percent of the total number of fields. In other words, the area dedicated to these crops is small, and the fields are probably sufficiently scattered and don't suffer from the proliferation of their pests. Therefore, the biodiversity variation on the

Table 6.6   Regression results for the reduced form model, all crops pooled

Variables	$\ell = 0.75$ km	$\ell = 1.00$ km	$\ell = 1.25$ km	$\ell = 1.50$ km	$\ell = 1.75$ km	$\ell = 2.00$ km	$\ell = 2.25$ km	$\ell = 2.50$ km	$\ell = 2.75$ km	$\ell = 3.00$ km
H	79.59***	61.83***	62.71***	38.74***	31.09***	23.21***	7.029	5.255	−5.287	−13.54
	(12.13)	(11.69)	(11.83)	(8.873)	(9.115)	(8.439)	(9.227)	(8.097)	(10.13)	(10.00)
Rain	0.0684	0.0677	0.0678	0.0674	0.0669	0.0668	0.0669	0.0668	0.0668	0.0667
	(0.0499)	(0.0499)	(0.0501)	(0.0501)	(0.0502)	(0.0502)	(0.0502)	(0.0502)	(0.0502)	(0.0502)
ET	379.9***	380.2***	379.8***	379.7***	379.5***	379.4***	379.3***	379.3***	379.3***	379.2***
	(41.32)	(41.27)	(41.39)	(41.43)	(41.49)	(41.47)	(41.46)	(41.44)	(41.44)	(41.43)

Note: ***, **, and * indicate 1 percent, 5 percent, and 10 percent significance levels, respectively. Robust standard errors are in parentheses, clustered at field level. Farm fixed effects are included but not reported. Sample: 64,862 fields, 12,462 farms.

perimeter that we consider has a negligible marginal effect on the biomass production. When looking at how crop biomass production is affected by crop biodiversity, we see that the relevant perimeter for biodiversity varies: biodiversity has a positive and significant impact on the production of maize only for perimeters equal to or smaller than 1.25 km, whereas the relevant perimeter for soybeans is equal to or greater than 1.25 km. Surprisingly, biodiversity has a negative and significant impact on sunflower biomass production on perimeters with a radius larger than 2.25 km; a positive significant impact is found only for ℓ equal to 1.00 km. This heterogeneity is probably linked to the fact that pests responsible for biomass losses differ among the three crops we consider. Generally, the main potential crop losses are caused by weeds, but thanks to the improvement in weed control techniques, the main actual losses come from animals (mainly insects) and pathogens (Oerke 2007). More precisely, in South Africa, maize is mainly attacked by insects (DAFF 2014a), while sunflowers and soybeans are mainly attacked by diseases caused by fungi and viruses (DAFF 2009, 2014b).

The impact of irrigation also varies and depends on crop characteristics, as shown in tables 6A.1, 6A.2, and 6A.3 in the appendix to this chapter. Maize is one of the most efficient cultivated plants in South Africa as far as water use is concerned (DAFF 2014a), hence a positive and significant impact of irrigation. On the contrary, sunflowers are highly inefficient in water use and, as well as soybeans, are mostly rain-fed grown.[14] This could explain the absence of a significant impact of irrigation on biomass production for these crops. Finally, soybean biomass production is positively affected by the size of the field, while sunflower survival rates are inversely related to field size, and maize is unaffected. These effects could be related to plant physiology or to higher mechanization allowed by larger fields and having a positive impact on the final yield of soybean.

These results confirm the positive impact of crop biodiversity on agricultural production and underline its heterogeneity across crops, with sunflowers being an exception. Additional regressions considering land-use types surrounding the crop plots did not provide significant results. Furthermore, it is important to note that we estimate biodiversity effects in the presence of pesticides, for which we do not totally control. Indeed, farm fixed effects capture practices that are common to all the fields within the same farm, and crop fixed effects capture practices common to all crops, but the level of pesticides actually applied remains unknown. Then the effects we observe can be considered residual. The positive impact of biodiversity on crop survival, only second to the one of irrigation and more generally water management, is all the more important in that respect. Even when

---

14. Soybeans are mostly rain-fed grown because of low profitability and difficult water management. Indeed, water shortage is critical during the pod set stage, while excessive water supply prior to or after the flowering may jeopardize the final yield.

pesticides are possibly applied, biodiversity still has the capacity to improve crop survival rate.

The results presented detail the impact of crop biodiversity on crop survival rates. Our approach through a probabilistic model can be used to add a step to disentangle more precisely the mechanisms at stake. In particular, the parameters of the beta-binomial distribution of the survival probability of fields can be estimated, following the approach detailed in section 6.3. We perform an OLS regression on equation (6) to directly estimate the value of θ_d; θ_u is given by the difference between the coefficients found in the linear regressions on equations (5) and (6).

Results are presented in table 6.7, which reports the values of parameters θ_u and θ_d for all the explanatory variables for selected values of ℓ, and table 6.8, which shows the values of the parameters for the Shannon index, computed on all the possible perimeters. As is visible from table 6.7, in practice, significant individual values for the parameters of the beta-binomial distribution can be found in a limited number of cases. In particular, it is interesting to note that biodiversity has a positive impact on the survival rate of maize by increasing S_u more than S_d (see equation (1)), while the positive impact found for sunflowers comes from a larger decrease in S_d than in S_u. This difference in mechanisms at stake confirms the important role played by crop specificities (plant physiology as well as predominant pests) on the possible impacts of crop biodiversity on agricultural production.

6.6   Conclusion

Using a new large database built from satellite imagery, we confirm that crop biodiversity has a positive impact on agricultural production, which is heterogeneous across crops, sunflower being an exception. Maintaining a large diversity of crops in the landscape increases agricultural production level. These impacts, which were previously described at regional scales, are robust when we consider a larger area. We show the consistency of these results with the underlying ecologic and agricultural mechanisms. For this purpose, we build a probabilistic model in which stochastic factors linked to biodiversity—namely, pests—are endogenous, as is shown in the ecology literature, while previous results were derived using functional forms arbitrarily chosen.

In the absence of data on pesticide use, their effects are not precisely measured in this model, which only evaluates the residual effects of biodiversity. However, our approach can be easily extended to pesticides. This would have the advantage of measuring their effects not on an isolated field but rather within a varied set of agricultural productions. Nevertheless, our analysis shows that residual effects are important and that a better spatial distribution of crops could lead to a significant improvement in crop yields. This could be achieved if farmers distribute their crops on their farms to not only

Exp. variable	Pooled crops (ℓ = 1.25 km)		Maize (ℓ = 1.25 km)		Soya (ℓ = 2.00 km)		Sunflower (ℓ = 1.00 km)	
	θ_u	θ_d	θ_u	θ_d	θ_u	θ_d	θ_u	θ_d
H	14.09***	10.36***	14.55***	11.4***	4.78	4.82	−23.77**	−28.36***
WB	−0.42	−1.00	−0.45	−0.68	−3.70*	−4.19**	−0.65	−1.73
WB²	−0.01	−0.02**	0.00	−0.01	−0.05	−0.06	0.00	−0.01
WB × IR	0.21	1.17	0.23	0.67	2.11	2.40	−3.59*	−1.16
WB² × IR	0.00	0.00	0.01	0.01	0.05	0.04	−0.06**	−0.03
SEAS_LEN	0.05	0.32***	0.11*	0.42***	−0.37***	−0.05	0.10	0.22**
ln(AREA)	−1.99	1.02	−7.58***	−4.86**	1.81	−1.3	−6.64	2.39
IR	10.14	−20.38	−29.75	−81.89**	40.04	25.03	−5.21	−31.58
LON	9.13	−65.26	112.78	52.28	283.91*	116.49	−542.78***	−741.69***
LAT	−55.79	−32.78	−49.67	−55.66	−182.43	−94.14	−132.6	94.82
PC_AREA_IR	−4.72	−22.65***	−0.23	−23.70***	−11.01	−21.60	17.85	22.75
PC_AREA_FARM	3.26	2.78	4.75*	4.24	20.89**	19.91**	−10.17	−11.26

Note: ***, **, and * indicate 1 percent, 5 percent, and 10 percent significance levels, respectively. Standard t–tests are used for θ_u, estimated with equation (5), and a Z-test is used for θ_d, calculated using the coefficients produced by equations (5) and (6), as detailed in section 3. The values of ℓ presented correspond to the largest and most significant impact of crop biodiversity on the survival rate. For ease of reporting, all coefficients are scaled by a factor 10^2.

Table 6.8   Estimated values of the parameters of the distribution of the survival probabilities: Biodiversity parameters

Parameter	$\ell = 0.75$	$\ell = 1.00$	$\ell = 1.25$	$\ell = 1.50$	$\ell = 1.75$	$\ell = 2.00$	$\ell = 2.25$	$\ell = 2.50$	$\ell = 2.75$	$\ell = 3.00$
Maize										
γ	-13.53**	-14.59**	-18.33***	-16.49**	-18.12***	-16.69**	-15.15**	-15.45**	-15.28**	-17.26***
β	21.86***	20.72***	16.85**	18.84***	17.22***	18.71***	20.35***	20.04***	20.2***	18.24***
θ_u	8.25	15.55***	14.55***	13.73***	15.5***	10.87**	9.36**	8.72**	6.94	2.65
θ_d	3.32	12.55***	11.4***	12.93***	14.4***	10.03**	9.4**	8.01*	6.24	2.24
Soybeans										
γ	0.01	-1.97	-4.2	-3.58	-5.84	-4.11	-4.17	-4.55	-5.07	-6.66
β	11.88	9.77	7.51	8.21	5.96	7.73	7.74	7.36	6.82	5.25
θ_u	30.28***	24.05***	7.02	-1.9	12.77	4.78	-0.86	4.65	-0.92	8.73
θ_d	30.95***	23.53***	2.25	-7.64	4.29	-4.82	-7.69	-1.81	-6.65	3.25
Sunflower										
γ	-11.37	-11.37	-15.29**	-13.29*	-14.83*	-12.94	-12.2	-12.22	-11.75	-13.14
β	-3.56	-3.65	-7.66	-5.5	-7.07	-5.17	-4.33	-4.37	-3.9	-5.26
θ_u	-21.72	-23.77**	-14.21	-12.29	-15.01	-6.72	-19.69*	-28.42**	-27.24	-35.53**
θ_d	-24.63*	-28.36***	-16.77	-11.24	-14.1	-3.64	-13.48	-19.29	-15.34	-19.95

Note: ***, **, and * indicate 1 percent, 5 percent, and 10 percent significance levels, respectively. Standard t-tests are used for θ_d, estimated with equation (5), and a Z-test is used for θ_u, calculated using the coefficients produced by equations (5) and (6), as detailed in section 3. θ_u and θ_d presented here are those related to the Shannon index. For ease of reporting, all coefficients are scaled by a factor 10^2.

take account of these effects on their own yields but also take into account their surroundings, which supposes that they coordinate.

Describing the mechanisms governing the impact of biodiversity on crop survival, our model can also be extended to consider wild biodiversity. Indeed, maintaining uncultivated small areas in agricultural landscapes is considered to diminish pests attacks. Adding data on uncultivated areas to our data set, the contribution of these initiatives could be easily evaluated.

Furthermore, enriching the data set, in particular with data on pesticide use, could help precisely estimate the parameters of the beta-binomial distribution of survival probabilities. Characterizing the distribution could bring elements of the impacts of crop biodiversity on the variance and the skewness of the distribution—that is, on the probability of extreme events, in particular, the complete loss of the harvest. These results are rarely analyzed in the literature (Di Falco and Chavas 2009), while they are particularly relevant for farmers.

Notwithstanding these limitations, our results confirm that crop diversification can be seen as a possible strategy to increase agricultural productivity or maintain its level while decreasing the use of pesticides.

Appendix

Table 6.A1   Regression results, maize

Variables	ℓ = 0.75 km	ℓ = 1.00 km	ℓ = 1.25 km	ℓ = 1.50 km	ℓ = 1.75 km	ℓ = 2.00 km	ℓ = 2.25 km	ℓ = 2.50 km	ℓ = 2.75 km	ℓ = 3.00 km
H	4.93***	3.01**	3.15***	0.8	1.11	0.84	−0.04	0.71	0.69	0.41
	(1.69)	(1.17)	(1.16)	(0.94)	(1.01)	(0.91)	(1.05)	(0.84)	(1.05)	(1.21)
WB	0.26	0.23	0.23	0.23	0.26	0.27	0.27	0.27	0.27	0.28
	(0.2)	(0.21)	(0.21)	(0.21)	(0.21)	(0.21)	(0.21)	(0.21)	(0.21)	(0.21)
WB^2	0.01**	0.01**	0.01*	0.01*	0.01*	0.01**	0.01**	0.01**	0.01**	0.01**
	(0.00)	(0.00)	(0.00)	(0.00)	(0.00)	(0.00)	(0.00)	(0.00)	(0.00)	(0.00)
WB × IR	−0.4	−0.4	−0.43	−0.45	−0.45	−0.44	−0.43	−0.43	−0.43	−0.44
	(0.38)	(0.38)	(0.38)	(0.38)	(0.38)	(0.38)	(0.38)	(0.38)	(0.38)	(0.38)
WB^2 × IR	0.00	0.00	0.00	0.00	0.00	0.00	0.00	0.00	0.00	0.00
	(0.01)	(0.01)	(0.01)	(0.01)	(0.01)	(0.01)	(0.01)	(0.01)	(0.01)	(0.01)
SEAS_LEN	−0.31***	−0.31***	−0.31***	−0.31***	−0.31***	−0.31***	−0.31***	−0.31***	−0.31***	−0.31***
	(0.02)	(0.02)	(0.02)	(0.02)	(0.02)	(0.02)	(0.02)	(0.02)	(0.02)	(0.02)
ln(AREA)	−2.51***	−2.66***	−2.72***	−2.78***	−2.8***	−2.86***	−2.85***	−2.88***	−2.91***	−2.93***
	(0.5)	(0.5)	(0.5)	(0.5)	(0.5)	(0.49)	(0.5)	(0.5)	(0.5)	(0.51)
IR	52.59***	52.61***	52.14***	52.36***	53.26***	53.82***	54.09***	54.23***	54.24***	54.27***
	(6.78)	(6.82)	(6.89)	(6.81)	(6.77)	(6.74)	(6.77)	(6.8)	(6.79)	(6.79)
LON	59.25***	59.89***	60.5***	60.51***	59.83***	59.09***	58.65***	59.06***	58.95***	58.85***
	(16.43)	(16.44)	(16.56)	(16.69)	(16.73)	(16.72)	(16.65)	(16.6)	(16.55)	(16.52)
LAT	6.01	5.64	5.98	6.14	6.32	6.32	6.33	6.75	6.35	6.58
	(29.09)	(29.11)	(29.47)	(30.45)	(31.06)	(31.88)	(31.99)	(32.57)	(32.87)	(33.09)
PC_AREA_IR	16.18***	20.01***	23.46***	24.99***	18.94***	18.1***	18.43***	17.64***	14.38***	12.91***
	(2.09)	(2.46)	(2.85)	(3.52)	(2.91)	(3.22)	(2.98)	(3.26)	(3.7)	(4.12)
PC_AREA_FARM	1.66***	1.1	0.51	−0.28	−0.27	−1.42	−1.33	−2.48*	−3.21**	−4.17***
	(0.63)	(0.74)	(0.9)	(0.87)	(0.83)	(0.96)	(1.17)	(1.38)	(1.33)	(1.44)

Note: ***, **, and * indicate 1 percent, 5 percent, and 10 percent significance levels, respectively. Robust standard errors are in parentheses, clustered at field level. Farm and crop fixed effects are included but not reported. Sample: 45,256 fields. For ease of reporting, all coefficients are scaled by a factor 10^2.

Table 6.A2 Regression results, soybeans

Variables	ℓ = 0.75 km	ℓ = 1.00 km	ℓ = 1.25 km	ℓ = 1.50 km	ℓ = 1.75 km	ℓ = 2.00 km	ℓ = 2.25 km	ℓ = 2.50 km	ℓ = 2.75 km	ℓ = 3.00 km
H	−0.67	0.52	4.77**	5.74**	8.48***	9.6***	6.83**	6.47***	5.73**	5.47*
	(2.1)	(2.15)	(2.22)	(2.22)	(2.17)	(2.6)	(2.59)	(2.3)	(2.53)	(2.8)
WB	0.46	0.46	0.47	0.5	0.49	0.5	0.49	0.49	0.49	0.48
	(0.45)	(0.44)	(0.45)	(0.46)	(0.45)	(0.46)	(0.46)	(0.45)	(0.45)	(0.45)
WB^2	0.02*	0.02*	0.02*	0.02*	0.02*	0.02*	0.02*	0.02*	0.02*	0.02*
	(0.01)	(0.01)	(0.01)	(0.01)	(0.01)	(0.01)	(0.01)	(0.01)	(0.01)	(0.01)
WB × IR	−0.29	−0.31	−0.32	−0.28	−0.34	−0.29	−0.32	−0.35	−0.36	−0.33
	(0.67)	(0.68)	(0.67)	(0.68)	(0.68)	(0.67)	(0.67)	(0.68)	(0.67)	(0.67)
WB^2 × IR	0.01	0.01	0.01	0.01	0.01	0.01	0.01	0.00	0.00	0.01
	(0.01)	(0.01)	(0.01)	(0.01)	(0.01)	(0.01)	(0.01)	(0.01)	(0.01)	(0.01)
SEAS_LEN	−0.31***	−0.32***	−0.32***	−0.32***	−0.32***	−0.32***	−0.32***	−0.32***	−0.32***	−0.32***
	(0.03)	(0.03)	(0.03)	(0.03)	(0.03)	(0.03)	(0.03)	(0.03)	(0.03)	(0.03)
ln(AREA)	3.41***	3.23***	3.22***	3.11***	3.19***	3.11***	3.07***	3.08***	3.06***	3.05***
	(1.06)	(1.04)	(1.04)	(1.02)	(1.01)	(1.01)	(1.02)	(1.03)	(1.04)	(1.04)
IR	15	14.64	13.87	15.39	14.1	15.01	14.92	14.77	14.51	14.97
	(10.42)	(10.3)	(10.38)	(10.57)	(10.64)	(10.63)	(10.63)	(10.6)	(10.5)	(10.56)
LON	162.75***	163.82***	165.6***	164.95***	164.08***	167.43***	165.77***	165.3***	164.49***	165***
	(47.3)	(46.98)	(46.97)	(46.85)	(46.5)	(46.4)	(47.55)	(47.3)	(47.18)	(47.34)
LAT	−81.62	−85.66	−87.16	−87.27	−89.05	−88.29	−87.28	−85.28	−81.96	−82.61
	(55.94)	(56.42)	(55.8)	(55.55)	(54.97)	(56.05)	(57.28)	(57.78)	(59.72)	(59.12)
PC_AREA_IR	3.93	4.13	6.47	0.25	11.89*	10.59	4.9	13.09*	16.41**	10.6
	(5.19)	(4.65)	(5.24)	(6.27)	(6.46)	(6.84)	(7.24)	(7.12)	(8.22)	(8.97)
PC_AREA_FARM	4.61***	4.28***	2.85*	2.39	3.09	0.99	0.43	1.25	−0.94	−1.25
	(1.68)	(1.37)	(1.67)	(2.27)	(2.3)	(2.8)	(3.14)	(3.07)	(2.95)	(3.54)

Note: ***, **, and * indicate 1 percent, 5 percent, and 10 percent significance levels, respectively. Robust standard errors are in parentheses, clustered at field level. Farm and **crop** fixed effects are included but not reported. Sample: 6,825 fields. For ease of reporting, all coefficients are scaled by a factor 10^2.

Table 6.A3   Regression results, sunflowers

Variables	ℓ = 0.75 km	ℓ = 1.00 km	ℓ = 1.25 km	ℓ = 1.50 km	ℓ = 1.75 km	ℓ = 2.00 km	ℓ = 2.25 km	ℓ = 2.50 km	ℓ = 2.75 km	ℓ = 3.00 km
H	2.91	4.59*	2.57	-1.05	-0.91	-3.08	-6.2**	-9.12***	-11.9***	-15.58***
	(3.32)	(2.72)	(2.41)	(3.14)	(3.3)	(3.62)	(3.11)	(3.13)	(4.44)	(4.59)
WB	1.09***	1.08***	1.07***	1.07***	1.06***	1.06***	1.08***	1.08***	1.09***	1.09***
	(0.31)	(0.31)	(0.31)	(0.31)	(0.31)	(0.31)	(0.32)	(0.31)	(0.31)	(0.31)
WB^2	0.01**	0.01**	0.01**	0.01**	0.01**	0.01**	0.01**	0.01**	0.01**	0.01**
	(0.00)	(0.00)	(0.00)	(0.00)	(0.00)	(0.00)	(0.00)	(0.00)	(0.00)	(0.00)
WB × IR	-2.41**	-2.43**	-2.43**	-2.44**	-2.43**	-2.43**	-2.44**	-2.48**	-2.49**	-2.5**
	(1.06)	(1.08)	(1.09)	(1.1)	(1.1)	(1.11)	(1.11)	(1.09)	(1.08)	(1.07)
WB^2 × IR	-0.03*	-0.03*	-0.03*	-0.03*	-0.03*	-0.03*	-0.03*	-0.03*	-0.03*	-0.03*
	(0.01)	(0.01)	(0.01)	(0.01)	(0.01)	(0.01)	(0.01)	(0.01)	(0.01)	(0.01)
SEAS_LEN	-0.11**	-0.12**	-0.12**	-0.12**	-0.12**	-0.12**	-0.12**	-0.12**	-0.12**	-0.12**
	(0.05)	(0.05)	(0.05)	(0.05)	(0.05)	(0.05)	(0.05)	(0.05)	(0.05)	(0.05)
ln(AREA)	-8.83***	-9.02***	-8.99***	-9.07***	-9.00***	-8.92***	-8.9***	-8.95***	-8.87***	-9.00***
	(1.23)	(1.28)	(1.24)	(1.25)	(1.26)	(1.25)	(1.26)	(1.25)	(1.25)	(1.25)
IR	27.76	26.37	24.03	24.52	24.03	24.05	24.36	23.75	23.35	24.08
	(21.24)	(21.37)	(21.57)	(21.92)	(21.8)	(21.89)	(21.59)	(21.07)	(21.08)	(20.79)
LON	199.61***	198.91***	198.71***	195.38***	194.93***	191.12***	188.4***	187.68***	186.17***	187.15***
	(45.09)	(45.04)	(44.73)	(45.24)	(44.77)	(45.38)	(45.43)	(45.15)	(44.03)	(43.69)
LAT	-227.75***	-227.42***	-227.48***	-225.22***	-227.59***	-229.49***	-224.67***	-221.18***	-218.81***	-213.74***
	(69.58)	(69.82)	(69.95)	(70.78)	(70.51)	(69.39)	(69.36)	(69.26)	(69.12)	(69.74)
PC_AREA_IR	-13.48**	-4.9	6.43	4.53	10.34	14.07	10.17	12.42	20.2**	9.4
	(5.73)	(5.68)	(7.44)	(7.62)	(9.06)	(9.01)	(9.66)	(9.72)	(10.16)	(10.17)
PC_AREA_FARM	3.73*	1.09	0.78	0.43	1.74	4.36	5.35	5.02	6.3	7.09
	(2.12)	(1.89)	(2.8)	(3.46)	(3.51)	(4.19)	(4.52)	(5)	(5.25)	(5.55)

Note: ***, **, and * indicate 1 percent, 5 percent, and 10 percent significance levels, respectively. Robust standard errors are in parentheses, clustered at field level. Farm and crop fixed effects are included but not reported. Sample: 9,441 fields. For ease of reporting, all coefficients are scaled by a factor 10^2.

Table 6.A4 Robustness check: Regression results, all crops pooled, $\alpha = 0.1$

Variables	ℓ = 0.75 km	ℓ = 1.00 km	ℓ = 1.25 km	ℓ = 1.50 km	ℓ = 1.75 km	ℓ = 2.00 km	ℓ = 2.25 km	ℓ = 2.50 km	ℓ = 2.75 km	ℓ = 3.00 km
H	4.03***	3.03***	4.19***	2.24***	2.02**	1.7*	0.32	0.42	−0.35	−1.01
	(1.24)	(1.13)	(1.1)	(0.77)	(0.89)	(0.88)	(0.98)	(0.89)	(1.1)	(1.03)
WB	0.65***	0.64***	0.64***	0.63***	0.64***	0.65***	0.67***	0.67***	0.67***	0.67***
	(0.15)	(0.15)	(0.15)	(0.15)	(0.15)	(0.15)	(0.15)	(0.15)	(0.15)	(0.15)
WB^2	0.01***	0.01***	0.01***	0.01***	0.01***	0.01***	0.01***	0.01***	0.01***	0.01***
	(0.00)	(0.00)	(0.00)	(0.00)	(0.00)	(0.00)	(0.00)	(0.00)	(0.00)	(0.00)
WB × IR	−1.00***	−1.03***	−1.04***	−1.05***	−1.04***	−1.03***	−1.03***	−1.03***	−1.03***	−1.03***
	(0.32)	(0.32)	(0.31)	(0.31)	(0.31)	(0.31)	(0.31)	(0.31)	(0.31)	(0.31)
WB^2 × IR	0.00	0.00	0.00	0.00	0.00	0.00	0.00	0.00	0.00	0.00
	(0.00)	(0.00)	(0.00)	(0.00)	(0.00)	(0.00)	(0.00)	(0.00)	(0.00)	(0.00)
IR	0.00	0.00	0.00	0.00	0.00	0.00	0.00	0.00	0.00	0.00
	(0.00)	(0.00)	(0.00)	(0.00)	(0.00)	(0.00)	(0.00)	(0.00)	(0.00)	(0.00)
SEAS_LEN	−0.29***	−0.29***	−0.29***	−0.29***	−0.29***	−0.29***	−0.29***	−0.29***	−0.29***	−0.29***
	(0.02)	(0.02)	(0.02)	(0.02)	(0.02)	(0.02)	(0.02)	(0.02)	(0.02)	(0.02)
ln(AREA)	−2.67***	−2.82***	−2.86***	−2.94***	−2.94***	−2.99***	−2.99***	−3.01***	−3.02***	−3.04***
	(0.42)	(0.42)	(0.41)	(0.41)	(0.41)	(0.41)	(0.41)	(0.41)	(0.41)	(0.42)
IR	36.71***	36.00***	35.48***	35.96***	36.79***	37.48***	37.92***	38.03***	38.03***	38.2***
	(5.82)	(5.86)	(5.88)	(5.89)	(5.89)	(5.88)	(5.88)	(5.82)	(5.85)	(5.85)
LON	83.27***	83.62***	84.9***	84.55***	84.39***	83.44***	82.66***	82.94***	82.9***	82.57***
	(16.13)	(16.08)	(16.04)	(16.11)	(16.12)	(16.09)	(16.08)	(15.97)	(15.95)	(16.01)
LAT	−27.31	−27.76	−27.97	−27.64	−27.47	−27.54	−27.64	−27.11	−26.62	−26.82
	(28.76)	(28.87)	(29.11)	(30.5)	(30.84)	(31.43)	(31.53)	(32.31)	(32.75)	(32.71)
PC_AREA_IR	13.52***	16.08***	19.91***	21.44***	20.86***	20.42***	17.00***	16.97***	17.24***	14.18***
	(1.76)	(1.96)	(1.76)	(2.00)	(2.32)	(2.17)	(2.58)	(2.39)	(2.97)	(2.9)
PC_AREA_FARM	1.68**	1.16*	0.61	−0.42	−0.17	−0.81	−0.52	−1.51	−2.14	−2.47
	(0.69)	(0.68)	(0.86)	(0.97)	(0.91)	(1.00)	(1.19)	(1.39)	(1.53)	(1.76)

Note: ***, **, and * indicate 1 percent, 5 percent, and 10 percent significance levels, respectively. Robust standard errors are in parentheses, clustered at field level. Farm and crop fixed effects are included but not reported. Sample: 64,862 fields. For ease of reporting, all coefficients are scaled by a factor 10².

References

Bastin, G., P. Scarth, V. Chewings, A. Sparrow, R. Denham, M. Schmidt, P. O'Reagain, R. Shepherd, and B. Abbott. 2012. "Separating Grazing and Rainfall Effects at Regional Scale Using Remote Sensing Imagery: A Dynamic Reference-Cover Method." *Remote Sensing of Environment* 121 (0): 443–57.

Baumgärtner, S. 2006. "Measuring the Diversity of What? And for What Purpose? A Conceptual Comparison of Ecological and Economic Biodiversity Indices." Working Paper, Department of Economics, University of Heidelberg.

Beketov, M. A., B. J. Kefford, R. B. Schafer, and M. Liess. 2013. "Pesticides Reduce Regional Biodiversity of Stream Invertebrates." *Proceedings of the National Academy of Sciences* 110 (27): 11039–43.

Bellora, C., and J.-M. Bourgeon. 2016. "Agricultural Trade, Biodiversity Effects and Food Price Volatility." Working Paper 2016-06, CEPII.

Benedetti, R., and P. Rossini. 1993. "On the Use of NDVI Profiles as a Tool for Agricultural Statistics: The Case Study of Wheat Yield Estimate and Forecast in Emilia Romagna." *Remote Sensing of Environment* 45 (3): 311–26.

Brock, W. A., and A. Xepapadeas. 2003. "Valuing Biodiversity from an Economic Perspective: A Unified Economic, Ecological, and Genetic Approach." *American Economic Review* 93 (5): 1597–1614.

Carew, R., E. G. Smith, and C. Grant. 2009. "Factors Influencing Wheat Yield and Variability: Evidence from Manitoba, Canada." *Journal of Agricultural and Applied Economics* 41 (3): 625–39.

Carlson, T. N., and D. A. Ripley. 1997. "On the Relation between NDVI, Fractional Vegetation Cover and Leaf Area Index." *Remote Sensing of Environment* 62 (3): 241–52.

Chen, J., M. Shiyomi, C. Bonham, T. Yasuda, Y. Hori, and Y. Yamamura. 2008. "Plant Cover Estimation Based on the Beta Distribution in Grassland Vegetation." *Ecological Research* 23 (5): 813–19.

DAFF (Department of Agriculture, Forestry and Fisheries). 2009. *Sunflower*. Production guideline, Department of Agriculture, Forestry and Fisheries, Republic of South Africa, https://www.nda.agric.za/docs/Brochures/prodGuideSunflower.pdf.

DAFF (Department of Agriculture, Forestry and Fisheries). 2014a. *Maize*. Production guideline, Department of Agriculture, Forestry and Fisheries, Republic of South Africa.

DAFF (Department of Agriculture, Forestry and Fisheries). 2014b. *Soybeans*. Production guideline, Department of Agriculture, Forestry and Fisheries, Republic of South Africa.

Das, D. K., K. K. Mishra, and N. Kalra. 1993. "Assessing Growth and Yield of Wheat Using Remotely Sensed Canopy Temperature and Spectral Indices." *International Journal of Remote Sensing* 14 (17): 3081–92.

Di Falco, S., and J. Chavas. 2006. "Crop Genetic Diversity, Farm Productivity and the Management of Environmental Risk in Rainfed Agriculture." *European Review of Agricultural Economics* 33 (3): 289–314.

Di Falco, S., and J. Chavas. 2009. "On Crop Biodiversity, Risk Exposure, and Food Security in the Highlands of Ethiopia." *American Journal of Agricultural Economics* 91 (3): 599–611.

Donaldson, D., and A. Storeygard. 2016. "The View from Above: Applications of Satellite Data in Economics." *Journal of Economic Perspectives* 30 (4): 171–98.

Doraiswamy, P. C., and P. W. Cook. 1995. "Spring Wheat Yield Assessment Using NOAA AVHRR Data." *Canadian Journal of Remote Sensing* 21:43–51.

Eidenshink, J. C. 1992. "The 1990 Conterminous U.S. AVHRR Dataset." *Photogrammetric Engineering and Remote Sensing* 58 (6): 809–13.

Fernandez-Cornejo, J., S. Jans, and M. Smith. 1998. "Issues in the Economics of Pesticide Use in Agriculture: A Review of the Empirical Evidence." *Review of Agricultural Economics* 20 (2): 462–88.

Ferreira, S. L., T. Newby, and E. du Preez. 2006. *Use of Remote Sensing in Support of Crop Area Estimates in South Africa.* ISPRS WG VIII/10 Workshop 2006, Remote Sensing Support to Crop Yield Forecast and Area Estimates.

Foley, J. A., N. Ramankutty, K. A. Brauman, E. S. Cassidy, J. S. Gerber, M. Johnston, N. D. Mueller, C. O'Connell, D. K. Ray, P. C. West, C. Balzer, E. M. Bennett, S. R. Carpenter, J. Hill, C. Monfreda, S. Polasky, J. Rockstrm, J. Sheehan, S. Siebert, D. Tilman, and D. P. M. Zaks. 2011. "Solutions for a Cultivated Planet." *Nature* 478 (7369): 337–42.

Gallai, N., J.-M. Salles, J. Settele, and B. E. Vaissière. 2009. "Economic Valuation of the Vulnerability of World Agriculture Confronted with Pollinator Decline." *Ecological Economics* 68 (3): 810–21.

Gouel, C., and H. Guimbard. 2018. "Nutrition Transition and the Structure of Global Food Demand." Forthcoming in the *American Journal of Agricultural Economics*.

Groten, S. M. E. 1993. "NDVI—Crop Monitoring and Early Yield Assessment of Burkina Faso." *International Journal of Remote Sensing* 14 (8): 1495–1515.

Gupta, R., S. Prasad, G. Rao, and T. Nadham. 1993. "District Level Wheat Yield Estimation Using NOAA/AVHRR NDVI Temporal Profile." *Advances in Space Research* 13 (5): 253–56.

Hayes, M. J., and W. L. Decker. 1996. "Using NOAA AVHRR Data to Estimate Maize Production in the United States Corn Belt." *International Journal of Remote Sensing* 17 (16): 3189–200.

Hochheim, K., and D. G. Barber. 1998. "Spring Wheat Yield Estimation for Western Canada Using NOAA NDVI Data." *Canadian Journal of Remote Sensing* 24:17–27.

Huete, A., K. Didan, T. Miura, E. Rodriguez, X. Gao, and L. Ferreira. 2002. "Overview of the Radiometric and Biophysical Performance of the MODIS Vegetation Indices." *Remote Sensing of Environment* 83 (1–2): 195–213.

Huete, A., H. Q. Liu, K. Batchily, and W. Van Leeuwen. 1997. "A Comparison of Vegetation Indices over a Global Set of TM Images for EOS-MODIS." *Remote Sensing of Environment* 59 (3): 440–51.

Hughes, G., and L. Madden. 1993. "Using the Beta-binomial Distribution to Describe Aggregated Patterns of Disease Incidence." *Phytopathology* 83 (7): 759–63.

Irvine, K. M., and T. J. Rodhouse. 2010. "Power Analysis for Trend in Ordinal Cover Classes: Implications for Long-Term Vegetation Monitoring." *Journal of Vegetation Science* 21 (6): 1152–61.

Jiguet, F., V. Devictor, R. Julliard, and D. Couvet. 2012. "French Citizens Monitoring Ordinary Birds Provide Tools for Conservation and Ecological Sciences." *Acta Oecologica* 44:58–66.

Jönsson, P., and L. Eklundh. 2002. "Seasonality Extraction by Function Fitting to Time-Series of Satellite Sensor Data." *IEEE Transactions on Geoscience and Remote Sensing* 40 (8): 1824–32.

Jönsson, P., and L. Eklundh. 2004. "TIMESAT—a Program for Analyzing Time-Series of Satellite Sensor Data." *Computers and Geosciences* 30 (8): 833–45.

Koller, M., and S. K. Upadhaya. 2005. "Prediction of Processing Tomato Yield Using a Crop Growth Model and Remotely Sensed Aerial Images." *Transactions of the ASAE* 48 (6): 2335–41.

Labus, M. P., G. A. Nielsen, R. L. Lawrence, R. Engel, and D. S. Long. 2002. "Wheat

Yield Estimates Using Multi-temporal NDVI Satellite Imagery." *International Journal of Remote Sensing* 23 (20): 4169–80.

Landis, D. A., M. M. Gardiner, W. van der Werf, and S. M. Swinton. 2008. "Increasing Corn for Biofuel Production Reduces Biocontrol Services in Agricultural Landscapes." *Proceedings of the National Academy of Sciences* 105 (51): 20552–57.

Loreau, M., and A. Hector. 2001. "Partitioning Selection and Complementarity in Biodiversity Experiments." *Nature* 412 (6842): 72–76.

Ma, B. L., L. M. Dwyer, C. Costa, E. R. Cober, and M. J. Morrison. 2001. "Early Prediction of Soybean Yield from Canopy Reflectance Measurements." *Agronomy Journal* 93 (6): 1227–34.

Malézieux, E., Y. Crozat, C. Dupraz, M. Laurans, D. Makowski, H. Ozier-Lafontaine, B. Rapidel, S. Tourdonnet, and M. Valantin-Morison. 2009. "Mixing Plant Species in Cropping Systems: Concepts, Tools and Models. A Review." *Agronomy for Sustainable Development* 29 (1): 43–62.

McDaniel, M. D., L. K. Tiemann, and A. S. Grandy. 2014. "Does Agricultural Crop Diversity Enhance Soil Microbial Biomass and Organic Matter Dynamics? A Meta-analysis." *Ecological Applications* 24 (3): 560–70.

Nuarsa, I. W., F. Nishio, F. Nishio, and C. Hongo. 2011. "Relationship between Rice Spectral and Rice Yield Using MODIS Data." *Journal of Agricultural Science* 3 (2): 80–88.

Oerke, E. 2006. "Crop Losses to Pests." *Journal of Agricultural Science* 144 (1): 31–43.

Oerke, E. 2007. "Crop Losses to Animal Pests, Plant Pathogens and Weeds." In *Encyclopedia of Pest Management*, vol. 2, 116–20. Boca Raton, FL: CRC Press.

Pianka, E. R. 1999. *Evolutionary Ecology*, 6th ed. San Francisco: Benjamin Cummings.

Pimentel, D. 2005. "Environmental and Economic Costs of the Application of Pesticides Primarily in the United States." *Environment, Development and Sustainability* 7 (2): 229–52.

Potdar, M. B. 1993. "Sorghum Yield Modelling Based on Crop Growth Parameters Determined from Visible and Near-IR Channel NOAA AVHRR Data." *International Journal of Remote Sensing* 14 (5): 895–905.

Prasad, A. K., L. Chai, R. P. Singh, and M. Kafatos. 2006. "Crop Yield Estimation Model for Iowa Using Remote Sensing and Surface Parameters." *International Journal of Applied Earth Observation and Geoinformation* 8 (1): 26–33.

Quarmby, N. A., M. Milnes, T. L. Hindle, and N. Silleos. 1993. "The Use of Multi-temporal NDVI Measurements from AVHRR Data for Crop Yield Estimation and Prediction." *International Journal of Remote Sensing* 14 (2): 199–210.

Shannon, C. E. 1948. "A Mathematical Theory of Communication." *Bell System Technical Journal* 27:379–423, 623–56.

Shiyomi, M., S. Takahashi, and J. Yoshimura. 2000. "A Measure for Spatial Heterogeneity of a Grassland Vegetation Based on the Beta-binomial Distribution." *Journal of Vegetation Science* 11 (5): 627–32.

Smale, M., J. Hartell, P. W. Heisey, and B. Senauer. 1998. "The Contribution of Genetic Resources and Diversity to Wheat Production in the Punjab of Pakistan." *American Journal of Agricultural Economics* 80 (3): 482–93.

Sutton, M. A., O. Oenema, J. W. Erisman, A. Leip, H. van Grinsven, and W. Winiwarter. 2011. "Too Much of a Good Thing." *Nature* 472 (7342): 159–61.

Tilman, D., and J. A. Downing. 1994. "Biodiversity and Stability in Grasslands." *Nature* 367 (6461): 363–65.

Tilman, D., S. Polasky, and C. Lehman. 2005. "Diversity, Productivity and Temporal

Stability in the Economies of Humans and Nature." *Journal of Environmental Economics and Management* 49 (3): 405–26.

Tilman, D., D. Wedin, and J. Knops. 1996. "Productivity and Sustainability Influenced by Biodiversity in Grassland Ecosystems." *Nature* 379 (6567): 718–20.

Tscharntke, T., A. M. Klein, A. Kruess, I. Steffan-Dewenter, and C. Thies. 2005. "Landscape Perspectives on Agricultural Intensification and Biodiversity—Ecosystem Service Management." *Ecology Letters* 8 (8): 857–74.

Weissteiner, C. J., and W. Kuhbauch. 2005. "Regional Yield Forecasts of Malting Barley (Hordeum vulgare L.) by NOAA-AVHRR Remote Sensing Data and Ancillary Data." *Journal of Agronomy and Crop Science* 191 (4): 308–20.

Weitzman, M. L. 2000. "Economic Profitability versus Ecological Entropy." *Quarterly Journal of Economics* 115 (1): 237–63.

Zhang, X., M. A. Friedl, and C. B. Schaaf. 2006. "Global Vegetation Phenology from Moderate Resolution Imaging Spectroradiometer (MODIS): Evaluation of Global Patterns and Comparison with in situ Measurements." *Journal of Geophysical Research* 111 (G4), DOI: 10.1029/2006JG000217.

Crop Disease and Agricultural Productivity
Evidence from a Dynamic Structural Model of Verticillium Wilt Management

Christine L. Carroll, Colin A. Carter,
Rachael E. Goodhue, and C.-Y. Cynthia Lin Lawell

7.1 Introduction

Crop diseases can have a large impact on agricultural productivity. Invasive plant pathogens, including fungi, cause an estimated $21 billion in crop losses each year in the United States (Rossman 2009). *Verticillium dahliae* is a soil-borne fungus that is introduced to the soil via infested spinach seeds and that causes subsequent lettuce crops to be afflicted with Verticillium

Christine L. Carroll is an assistant professor at the College of Agriculture at California State University, Chico.

Colin A. Carter is distinguished professor of agricultural and resource economics at the University of California, Davis.

Rachael E. Goodhue is department chair and professor of agricultural and resource economics at the University of California, Davis.

C.-Y. Cynthia Lin Lawell is an associate professor and the Robert Dyson Sesquicentennial Chair in Environmental, Energy and Resource Economics at Cornell University.

We thank Krishna V. Subbarao, Julian Alston, Andre Boik, Colin Cameron, Erich Muehlegger, Kevin Novan, Peter Orazem, John Rust, Wolfram Schlenker, Paul Scott, Dan Sumner, Sofia Villas-Boas, Marca Weinberg, Jim Wilen, and Jinhua Zhao for invaluable discussions and comments. We also received helpful comments from seminar participants at the University of California at Davis and California State University at Chico and from conference participants at the NBER Understanding Productivity Growth in Agriculture Conference, the Heartland Environmental and Resource Economics Workshop, the Association of Environmental and Resource Economists (AERE) Summer Conference, the American Agricultural Economics Association (AAEA) Annual Meeting, the Giannini Agricultural and Resource Economics Student Conference, and the Interdisciplinary Graduate and Professional Student (IGPS) Symposium. We received funding from USDA NIFA (grant # 2010-51181-21069). We also benefited from valuable discussions with Tom Bengard, Bengard Ranch; Kent Bradford, Seed Biotechnology Center UC-Davis; Leslie Crowl, Monterey County Agricultural Commissioner's Office; Rich DeMoura, UC-Davis Cooperative Extension; Gerard Denny, INCOTEC; Lindsey du Toit, Washington State University; Thomas Flewell, Flewell Consulting; Hank Hill, Seed Dynamics, Inc.; Steve Koike, Cooperative Extension Monterey County; Dale Krolikowski, Germains Seed Technology; Chester Kurowski, Monsanto; Donald W. McMoran, WSU Extension; Marc Meyer, Monsanto; Chris Miller, Rijk Zwaan; Augustin Ramos, APHIS; Scott Redlin, APHIS; Richard Smith, Cooperative Extension Monterey County;

wilt (V. wilt). Lettuce is an important crop in California, and the majority of lettuce production in the United States occurs in California. The value of California's lettuce crop was $1.7 billion in 2013 (NASS 2015).

How crop diseases are managed can have a large impact on agricultural productivity as well. V. wilt can be prevented or controlled by the grower by fumigating with methyl bromide, planting broccoli (a low-return crop), or not planting spinach. These control options entail incurring costs or foregoing profit in the current period for future benefit. V. wilt can also be prevented or controlled by the spinach seed company testing and cleaning the spinach seeds. However, seed companies are unwilling to test or clean spinach seeds, as they are not affected by this disease.

This chapter analyzes the effects of V. wilt on agricultural productivity. In particular, we use a dynamic structural econometric model of V. wilt management for lettuce crops in Monterey County, California, to examine the effects of V. wilt on crop-fumigation decisions and grower welfare. We also discuss our research on the externalities that arise with renters and between seed companies and growers due to V. wilt, as these disease-related externalities have important implications for agricultural productivity.

We use a dynamic model for several reasons. First, the control options (fumigation, planting broccoli, and not planting spinach) require incurring costs or foregoing profit in the current period for possible future benefit and are thus are best modeled with a dynamic model.[1] Second, because cropping and fumigation decisions are irreversible (as is the damage from V. wilt), because the rewards from cropping and fumigation decisions are uncertain, and because growers have leeway over the timing of cropping and fumigation decisions, there is an option value to waiting, which requires a dynamic model (Dixit and Pindyck 1994). Third, *Verticillium dahliae* takes time to build up in the soil and, once present, persists for many years.

There are several advantages to using a dynamic structural econometric model to model grower-crop and fumigation decisions. First, unlike reduced-form models, a structural approach explicitly models the dynamics of crop and fumigation decisions by incorporating continuation values that explicitly model how expectations about the future affect current decisions.

A second advantage of the structural model is that we are able to estimate the effect of each state variable on the expected payoffs from different crop

Laura Tourte, UC Cooperative Extension Santa Cruz County; Bill Waycott, Monsanto; and Mary Zischke, California Leafy Greens Research Program. Carter and Goodhue are members, and Lin Lawell is a former member of the Giannini Foundation of Agricultural Economics. All errors are our own. For acknowledgments, sources of research support, and disclosure of the authors' material financial relationships, if any, please see https://www.nber.org/chapters/c13943.ack.

1. Some of these actions may also generate benefits in the current period for the current crop. For example, in addition to being an investment in protecting potential future lettuce crops from V. wilt, methyl bromide can also be beneficial to the current crop of strawberries. However, on net, these control options generally require incurring net costs or foregoing profit in the current period.

and fumigation choices and are therefore able to estimate parameters that have direct economic interpretations. The dynamic model accounts for the continuation value, which is the expected value of the value function next period. With the structural model, we are able to estimate parameters in the payoffs from different crop and fumigation choices, since we are able to structurally model how the continuation values relate to the payoffs from the crop and fumigation choices.

A third advantage of our structural model is that we can use the parameter estimates from our structural model to simulate the effects of crop disease on agricultural productivity. In particular, we run counterfactual simulations to analyze the effects of V. wilt on crop-fumigation decisions and grower welfare.

The dynamic structural econometric modeling approach we use in our research to analyze V. wilt management innovates upon previous methodological approaches to analyzing crop disease and agricultural productivity and can be applied in many other settings, including to other crop diseases and to other issues of agricultural management in other areas of the world.

The balance of this chapter proceeds as follows. Section 7.2 provides background on the California lettuce industry, V. wilt, and options to control the disease. Section 7.3 is a brief review of the relevant literature. Section 7.4 describes our dynamic structural econometric model. Section 7.5 describes our data. We present our results in section 7.6 and our counterfactual simulations in section 7.7. Section 7.8 concludes.

7.2   Background

California, a major agricultural producer and global trader, sustains significant economic damage from invasive plant pathogens. Fungi damage a wide variety of California crops, resulting in yield- and quality-related losses, reduced exportability, and increased fungicide expenditures (Palm 2001).

Measured by value, lettuce ranks in the top 10 agricultural commodities produced in California (NASS 2015). Much of California's lettuce crop is grown in Monterey County, where lettuce production value is 27 percent of the county's agricultural production value (Monterey County Agricultural Commissioner 2015). Approximately 10 to 15,000 acres are planted to lettuce in Monterey County each season (spring, summer, and fall). Spinach, broccoli, and strawberries are also important crops in the region.

Verticillium dahliae is a soil-borne fungus that causes lettuce to be afflicted with V. wilt. No effective treatment exists once plants are infected by the fungus (Xiao and Subbarao 1998; Fradin and Thomma 2006). The fungus can survive in the soil for 14 years as microsclerotia, which are resting structures that are produced as the pathogen colonizes a plant. This system allows the fungus to remain in the soil even without a host plant. When a susceptible host is planted, microsclerotia attack through the roots, enter the water-conducting tissue, and interfere with the water uptake and transport through the plant. If the density of microsclerotia in the soil passes a threshold, a disease known as V. wilt occurs.

V. wilt first killed a lettuce (*Lactuca sativa* L.) crop in California's Parajo Valley in 1995. Prior to 1995, lettuce was believed to be immune. Since then, the disease has spread rapidly through the Salinas Valley, the prime lettuce production region of California. By 2010, more than 150 fields were infected with V. wilt (Atallah, Hayes, and Subbarao 2011),[2] amounting to more than 4,000 acres (Krishna Subbarao, personal communication 2013).[3] Although growers have resisted reporting the extent of the disease since 2010, it is likely that the number of affected acres has increased since then (Krishna Subbarao, personal communication, 2013).

Verticillium dahliae is introduced to the soil in three possible ways. First, V. wilt can be spread locally from field to field by workers or equipment. Local spread is a relatively minor contributor, however, and growers have taken steps to mitigate this issue themselves—for example, by cleaning equipment before moving between fields.

Second, V. wilt is introduced to the soil via infested lettuce seeds. However, studies of commercial lettuce seed lots from around the world show that fewer than 18 percent tested positive for *Verticillium dahliae*, and of those, the maximum incidence of infection was less than 5 percent (Atallah, Hayes, and Subbarao 2011). These relatively low levels do not cause V. wilt in lettuce at an epidemic level. Models of the disease suggest that it would be necessary for lettuce seed to have an incidence of infection of at least 5 percent and be planted back to back for three to five seasons in order for the disease to appear, with at least five subsequent seasons required for the high disease levels currently seen (Atallah, Hayes, and Subarrao 2011).

Third, V. wilt is introduced to the soil via infested spinach seeds. Spinach seeds have been shown to be the main source of the disease (du Toit, Derie, and Hernandez-Perez 2005; Short et al. 2015); 89 percent of spinach seed samples are infected, with an incidence of infected seeds per sample of mean 18.51 percent and range 0.3 percent to 84.8 percent (du Toit, Derie, and Hernandez-Perez 2005). The precise impact of planting infected spinach seeds on V. wilt of lettuce was recently assessed and proven to be the cause of the disease on lettuce (Short et al. 2015). The pathogen isolated from infected lettuce plants is genetically identical to the pathogen carried on spinach seeds (Atallah et al. 2010).

2. As not all the fields that were infected by 2010 were known at the time the study by Atallah, Hayes, and Subbarao (2011) was published, the number of fields affected by 2010 fields was actually even higher, numbering over 175 fields (Krishna Subbarao, personal communication 2013).

3. Krishna Subbarao is a professor of plant pathology and cooperative extension specialist at the University of California at Davis. He has studied V. wilt for many years.

Infected spinach seeds carry an average of 200 to 300 microsclerotia per seed (Maruthachalam et al. 2013). As spinach crops are seeded at up to 9 million seeds per hectare for baby leaf spinach, even a small proportion of infected seeds can introduce many microsclerotia (du Toit and Hernandez-Perez 2005).

One method for controlling V. wilt is to fumigate with methyl bromide. As methyl bromide is an ozone-depleting substance, the Montreal Protocol has eliminated methyl bromide use for fumigation of vegetable crops such as lettuce; however, certain crops such as strawberries have received critical-use exemptions through 2016[4] (California Department of Pesticide Regulation 2010; USEPA 2012b), and the residual effects from strawberry fumigation provide protection for one or two seasons of lettuce before microsclerotia densities rise (Atallah, Hayes, and Subbarao 2011). The long-term availability of this solution is limited and uncertain.

A second method for controlling V. wilt is to plant broccoli. Broccoli is not susceptible to V. wilt, and it also reduces the levels of microsclerotia in the soil (Subbarao and Hubbard 1996; Subbarao, Hubbard, and Koike 1999; Shetty et al. 2000). Some growers have experimented with this solution, but relatively low returns from broccoli in the region prevent this option from becoming a widespread solution. Planting all infected acreage to broccoli may also flood the market, driving down broccoli prices.

A third method for controlling V. wilt is to not plant spinach, since spinach seeds are the vector of pathogen introduction (du Toit, Derie, and Hernandez-Perez 2005). Growers who use this third control method of not planting spinach must forgo any relative profits they may have received if they planted spinach instead of another crop.

In addition to the control measures that the grower can take, V. wilt can also be prevented or controlled by a spinach seed company through testing and cleaning the spinach seeds. Testing or cleaning seeds is an important option for preventing *Verticillium dahliae* from being introduced into a field but can be uncertain and potentially costly. Although *Verticillium dahliae* cannot be completely eliminated by seed cleaning, incidence levels in spinach seed can be significantly reduced (du Toit and Hernandez-Perez 2005). Very recent developments in testing procedures suggest that testing spinach seeds for *Verticillium dahliae* might soon be feasible on a commercial basis. Moreover, a very recent innovation speeds up testing spinach seeds. Previously, testing for *Verticillium dahliae* in spinach seeds took approximately

---

4. Critical-use exemption requests through 2014 specify that up to one-third of the California strawberry crop will be fumigated with methyl bromide, but actual use was much lower. The remainder of the crop is treated with alternatives such as chloropicrin or 1,3-Dichloropropene (1,3-D) (USEPA 2012a). However, these alternatives (unless combined with methyl bromide) tend to be less effective for V. wilt (Atallah, Hayes, and Subbarao 2011). Field trials of other chemical fumigants either have not been widely used due to township caps or are not yet registered and approved.

two weeks and could not accurately distinguish between pathogenic and nonpathogenic species (Duressa et al. 2012). This new method takes only one day to complete, is highly sensitive (as it is able to detect one infected seed out of 100), and can distinguish among species (Duressa et al. 2012).

V. wilt can also be controlled by restricting the imports of spinach seeds infested with *Verticillium dahliae*, but doing so would have trade implications. Currently, the United States has no phytosanitary restrictions on spinach seed imports, but Mexico prohibits the importation of seeds if more than 10 percent are infected (IPC 2003).

V. wilt can therefore be prevented or controlled by the grower by fumigating with methyl bromide, planting broccoli, or not planting spinach. These control options require long-term investment for future gain. V. wilt can also be prevented or controlled by the spinach seed company by testing and cleaning the spinach seeds. However, seed companies are unwilling to test or clean spinach seeds, as they are not affected by this disease.

7.3   Literature Review

The first strand of literature to which our chapter relates is on the economics of pest management (Hueth and Regev 1974; Carlson and Main 1976; Wu 2001; Noailly 2008; McKee et al. 2009), which focuses on pests for which treatment is available after crops are affected. In contrast, V. wilt cannot be treated once crops are affected. Existing work on crop disease, such as Johansson et al. (2006) and Gómez, Nunez, and Onal (2009) on soybean rust and Atallah et al. (2015) on grapevine leafroll disease, focuses on spatial issues regarding the spread of the disease. In contrast, V. wilt has only a limited geographic impact, and thus dynamic considerations are more important than spatial ones for V. wilt.

A second strand of literature to which our chapter relates is on dynamic models in agricultural management. As *Verticillium dahliae* persists in the soil for many years, a static model such as that proposed by Moffitt, Hall, and Osteen (1984) will not properly account for the future benefits of reducing microsclerotia in the soil. The dynamics of V. wilt more closely fit the seed bank management model by Wu (2001).

Dynamic models have been used in agricultural management to analyze many problems. Weisensel and van Kooten (1990) use a dynamic model of growers' choices to plant wheat or to use tillage fallow versus chemicals to store moisture. In a related paper, van Kooten, Weisensel, and Chinthammit (1990) use a dynamic model that explicitly includes soil quality in the grower's utility function and the trade-off between soil quality (which may decline due to erosion) and net returns.

Our chapter builds on the literature on dynamic structural econometric modeling. Rust's (1987, 1988) seminal papers develop a dynamic structural econometric model using nested fixed point maximum likelihood estimation. This model has been adapted for many applications, including bus engine replacement (Rust 1987), nuclear power plant shutdown (Rothwell and Rust 1997), water management (Timmins 2002), agriculture (De Pinto and Nelson 2009; Scott 2013), air conditioner purchases (Rapson 2014), wind turbine shutdowns and upgrades (Cook and Lin Lawell 2019), and copper-mining decisions (Aguirregabiria and Luengo 2016). Carroll et al. (2019a) develop and estimate a dynamic structural model to analyze short-versus long-term decision-making for disease control. Carroll et al. (2019b) develop and estimate a dynamic structural model to analyze the supply-chain externality between growers and spinach seed companies in controlling V. wilt.

7.4 Dynamic Structural Econometric Model

To analyze the effects of V. wilt, we develop and estimate a single-agent dynamic structural econometric model using the econometric methods developed by Rust (1987). Each month t, each grower i chooses an action $d_{it} \in D$. The possible actions for each grower for each month include one of five crops (resistant, susceptible [other than lettuce], lettuce, spinach, and broccoli), combined with the choice to fumigate with methyl bromide. To focus on the crops most relevant to this problem, we group the crops resistant to V. wilt together and the crops (other than lettuce) susceptible to V. wilt together. Lettuce, spinach, and broccoli are included separately, as these crops are most relevant to V. wilt. Susceptible crops include strawberries, artichokes, and cabbage. Resistant crops include cauliflower and celery.

Although the raw data are observations on the day and time any fumigant is applied on a field, we aggregate to monthly observations. Growers are generally only making one crop-fumigation decision each season. The length of the season varies among crops and can be as short as one month for spinach and more than a year for strawberries. For this reason, we choose a month as the time period for each crop-fumigation decision. To cover the case of multimonth seasons, we include a dummy variable for whether the grower continues with the same crop chosen in the previous month. Moreover, because not all crops are harvested in all months, we also include dummy variables for each crop-month indicating whether a particular month is a harvest month for a particular crop. For example, although Monterey County grows crops during a large portion of the year, few crops are harvested in the winter months.

To estimate growers' losses from V. wilt, it would be ideal to observe actual prices, quantities, costs, and levels of microsclerotia for both growers facing losses from V. wilt and those who are not. In theory, profit-maximizing growers make optimal planting and fumigating decisions factoring in planting and input costs as well as the costs of microsclerotia building up in the soil over time and potentially impacting future crops. Unfortunately, data on growers' actual price, quantity, costs, and levels of microsclerotia are not available.[5]

We account for the important factors in a grower's profit-maximizing decision by including in the payoff function state variables that affect revenue, state variables that affect costs, state variables that affect both revenue and costs, and state variables that affect either revenue or cost by affecting the microsclerotia and the spread of V. wilt. The different state variables we include may have effects on price, yield, input costs, or microsclerotia levels. Costs are accounted for by the crop-fumigation dummies and the constant in our model, and we allow these costs to differ between the early and later periods of our data set. The largest cost difference among crops is due to fumigation, so we include a dummy for methyl bromide fumigation to account for the net costs of fumigation and to absorb cost differences among crops.

The per-period payoff to a grower from choosing action d_{it} at time t depends on the values of the state variables $\mathbf{s}_{it}$ at time t as well as the choice-specific shock $\varepsilon_{it}(d_{it})$ at time t. The state variables $\mathbf{s}_{it}$ at time t include crop prices for each crop ($price_{it}(d_{it})$), dummy variables for each crop indicating whether this month is a harvest month for that crop ($harvestmonthdummy_{it}(d_{it})$), dummy variables for each crop indicating whether that crop is the same as the crop chosen in the previous month ($lastcropdummy_{it}(d_{it})$), a variable measuring whether and how much the methyl bromide control option was used in the past ($methylbromidehistory_{it}$), and a variable measuring whether and how much the broccoli control option was used in the past ($broccolihistory_{it}$).

There is a choice-specific shock $\varepsilon_{it}(d_{it})$ associated with each possible action $d_{it} \in D$. Let ε_{it} denote the vector of choice-specific shocks faced by grower i at time t: $\varepsilon_{it} \equiv \{\varepsilon_{it}(d_{it}) | d_{it} \in D\}$. The vector of choice-specific shocks ε_{it} is observed by grower i at time t, before grower i makes his time-t action choice, but is never observed by the econometrician.

The per-period payoff to a grower from choosing action d_{it} at time t is given by[6]

$$U(d_{it}, \mathbf{s}_{it}, \varepsilon_{it}, \theta) = \pi(d_{it}, \mathbf{s}_{it}, \theta) + \varepsilon_{it}(d_{it}),$$

where the deterministic component $\pi(\cdot)$ of the per-period payoff is given by

---

5. The University of California at Davis "Cost and Return Studies" have a limited number of estimates for the revenue and costs, but estimates are not available for all the crops and years in our model.

6. Because the model requires discrete data, we bin the action and state variables. This means that there are no meaningful units associated with the variables, payoffs, or value functions, and the payoff and value functions described in the model do not explicitly measure revenue or profit. However, the payoff function does include action and state variables that affect revenue (such as price), costs (such as the methyl bromide dummy), both revenue and costs, and either revenue and/or costs through their effect on microsclerotia and the spread of V. wilt.

(1) $\pi(d_{it}, \mathbf{s}_{it}, \theta) = \theta_1 \cdot spinachdummy_{it} + \theta_2 \cdot methylbromidedummy_{it}$

$\qquad + \theta_3 \cdot broccolidummy_{it} + \theta_4 \cdot (lettucedummy_{it} * methylbromidehistory_{it})$

$\qquad + \theta_5 \cdot (lettucedummy_{it} * broccolihistory_{it})$

$\qquad + \theta_6 \cdot (spinachdummy_{it} * methylbromidehistory_{it})$

$\qquad + \theta_7 \cdot (spinachdummy_{it} * broccolihistory_{it})$

$\qquad + \theta_8 \cdot lettucedummy_{it} + \theta_9 \cdot (price_{it}(d_{it}) * harvestmonthdummy_{it}(d_{it}))$

$\qquad + \theta_{10} \cdot lastcropdummy_{it}(d_{it}) + \theta_{11},$

where $spinachdummy_{it}$, $methylbromidedummy_{it}$, $broccolidummy_{it}$, and $lettuce$-$dummy_{it}$ are among the possible actions $d_{it} \in D$.

Spinach will tend to increase microsclerotia, thus decreasing the quantity harvested, increasing microsclerotia costs, and potentially increasing input costs as growers need to fumigate more. The coefficient θ_1 on the spinach dummy captures the effects of spinach on payoffs that are not internalized in the spinach price.[7]

Especially in more recent years, methyl bromide fumigation is very expensive and raises input costs dramatically. Fumigation is the largest cost difference among crops. Thus methyl bromide fumigation is a control option that requires incurring costs or forgoing profit in the current period for future benefit. The coefficient θ_2 on the dummy for methyl bromide fumigation accounts for the costs of fumigation and absorbs the cost differences among crops.[8]

Broccoli is not highly profitable but may yield future benefits for lettuce growers. Thus planting broccoli is a control option that requires incurring costs or forgoing profit in the current period for future benefit. The coefficient θ_3 on the broccoli dummy captures the effects of broccoli on payoffs that are not internalized in the broccoli price.

Since the control options require incurring costs or forgoing profit in the

---

7. We do not include spinach history in addition to the spinach dummy in the per-period payoff for several reasons. First, when we include spinach history within the last 12 months, the coefficients on spinach history are not significant. Second, owing to state space constraints, including spinach history would necessitate dropping other state variables, many of which are significant. Third, *Verticillium dahliae* takes several years to build up in the soil and once present, persists for many years. The appropriate length of time for spinach history is therefore likely to be at least as long as the time period of our data set. We therefore unfortunately do not have enough years of data in order to control for spinach history in a relevant manner. Fourth, since *Verticillium dahliae* takes several years to build up in the soil and once present, persists for many years, growers may not necessarily base their decisions on spinach history, since they may not know or recall the entire spinach history over many years.

8. In addition to being an investment in protecting potential future lettuce crops from V. wilt, methyl bromide can also be beneficial to the current crop of strawberries. However, on net, methyl bromide fumigation generally requires incurring net costs or foregoing profit in the current period. A negative sign on the coefficient on the dummy for methyl bromide fumigation would indicate a net cost to methyl bromide fumigation.

current period for future benefit, previous use of control options may affect current payoffs. We therefore include variables indicating the fumigation history with methyl bromide within the last 12 months and the broccoli history within the last 12 months. We expect methyl bromide fumigation history and broccoli history to be closely linked to the presence of microsclerotia in a field. Methyl bromide fumigation history and broccoli history will tend to decrease microsclerotia levels in the soil, leading to increased harvest for susceptible crops, lower microsclerotia costs, and lower input costs.

We interact the variables measuring previous use of control options with a dummy variable for lettuce being planted in the current period because lettuce is the primary susceptible crop. Methyl bromide fumigation history interacted with planting lettuce today would have a positive coefficient θ_4 if having fumigated with methyl bromide is an effective control option. Similarly, broccoli history interacted with planting lettuce today would have a positive coefficient θ_5 if having planted broccoli is an effective control option. These two parameters therefore enable us to assess the effectiveness of these two respective control options.

We also interact the methyl bromide history and broccoli history variables with the dummy variable for spinach being planted in the current period to capture whether the undesirability of spinach is mitigated by having methyl bromide history and/or broccoli history.

Growers continue to plant lettuce even though it is susceptible, and the coefficient θ_8 on the lettuce dummy captures any additional benefit of lettuce beyond its price.

Growers base decisions in part on the price or gross return they expect to receive for their harvested crops (Scott 2013). We interact price with a dummy variable that is equal to one during the harvest season for each crop to capture the fact that although a grower may plant the same crop for multiple months, he only receives revenue during the months of the harvest season for that crop.[9] In particular, the expected gross revenue to harvesting

---

9. On average, the length of the harvest season is less than 2 months in our data set and equal to about 1.5 months on average for most crops. The exception is susceptible crops, including strawberries, which have an average harvest season length of 2.59 months. In the case of strawberries, however, strawberries are an ongoing harvest crop and therefore the more months in the harvest season they are grown, the more product can be harvested, so it is reasonable to assume that a grower may receive revenue each harvest month during which strawberries are grown. We choose not to model the grower as only receiving the revenue for his crop on the first month of the harvest season, as this would not explain why growers may plant the same crop for multiple months in the harvest season. Staying in the harvest season longer sometimes yields higher revenue because it enables the grower to harvest more product or replant the crop for more harvest, both of which are better captured by having the grower receive more revenue if he stays in the harvest season longer. For similar reasons, we choose not to model the grower as only receiving the revenue for his crop on the last month of the harvest season. As seen in Carroll et al. (2018a), we find that the results are robust to whether we divide the marketing year average price for each crop by its average harvest season length and therefore to whether we assume growers who plant the same crop for multiple months receive more revenue than those who plant that crop for only one month.

a crop during nonharvest season months (e.g., during the winter) is zero.[10] Thus by incorporating the expected gross return in the payoff of function and by modeling the dynamic decision-making of growers of when and what to plant and whether and when to fumigate, our model accounts for the biological reality of how long a crop needs to be in the ground because a profit-maximizing grower is unlikely to pull out the crop before it is ready to harvest (and therefore before he would receive the expected return), barring problems such as V. wilt or other issues that meant that crop was unhealthy.

The last crop dummy variable is equal to one if the crop chosen this month is the same as the crop planted in the previous month. The last crop dummy captures both the requirement to grow a particular crop over multiple months as well as any tendency for a grower to choose to replant the same crop over and over again, perhaps harvest after harvest.

The value function for a long-term grower, which gives the present discounted value of the grower's entire stream of per-period payoffs at the optimum, is given by the following Bellman equation,

$$(2) \quad V(\mathbf{s},\varepsilon,\theta) = \max_{d \in D}(\pi(d,\mathbf{s},\theta) + \varepsilon(d) + \beta \int V(\mathbf{s}',\varepsilon';\theta) d\Pr(\mathbf{s}',\varepsilon'|\mathbf{s},\varepsilon,d,\theta)),$$

where β is the discount factor. We set our monthly discount factor to $\beta = 0.999$.

To estimate the unknown parameters $\theta = (\theta_1,...,\theta_{11})$, we use a nested fixed point maximum likelihood estimation technique developed by Rust (1987, 1988). We assume the observed choices are the result of the optimal decision rule $d_t = \gamma(\mathbf{s}_t,\varepsilon_t)$ that solves the Bellman equation.

We assume that the state variables evolve as a first-order Markov process, with a transition density given by $\Pr(\mathbf{s}_{t+1},\varepsilon_{t+1}|\mathbf{s}_t,d_t,\varepsilon_t,\theta)$. Since the price variable we use is the annual county average, we assume that the choice of any one grower would not have a large enough effect to influence prices and therefore that the distribution of price next period does not depend on any single grower's decisions this period; we therefore model crop prices as evolving exogenously. In particular, we estimate the transition density for each crop price as a nonparametric function of lagged values of the crop prices for all crops. The endogenous state variables (methyl bromide fumigation history, broccoli history, and last crop dummy) evolve deterministically as a function of this period's action.

As is standard in many dynamic structural models, we make the following conditional independence assumption on the transition density:

$$\Pr(\mathbf{s}_{t+1},\varepsilon_{t+1}|\mathbf{s}_t,d_t,\varepsilon_t,\theta) = \Pr(\mathbf{s}_{t+1}|\mathbf{s}_t,d_t,\theta)\Pr(\varepsilon_{t+1}|\theta).$$

We also assume that the choice-specific shocks are distributed multivariate extreme value.

---

10. The costs of inputs are included in the constant, which we expect to be negative.

Under these assumptions, the value function for a long-term grower given in equation (2) can be rewritten as

$$V(\mathbf{s},\varepsilon,\theta) = \max_{d \in D(s)}(\pi(d,\mathbf{s},\theta) + \varepsilon(d) + \beta V^c(\mathbf{s},d,\theta)),$$

where $V^c(\cdot)$ is the continuation value, which is the expected value of the value function next period conditional on the state variables and action this period:

(3) $$V^c(\mathbf{s},d,\theta) = \int V(\mathbf{s}',\varepsilon';\theta)d\Pr(\mathbf{s}',\varepsilon'|\mathbf{s},\varepsilon,d,\theta).$$

The choice probability for a long-term grower is given by

$$\Pr(d|\mathbf{s},\theta) = \frac{\exp(\pi(d,s,\theta) + \beta V^c(\mathbf{s},d,\theta))}{\sum_{\tilde{d} \in D(\mathbf{s})}\exp(\pi(\tilde{d},s,\theta) + \beta V^c(\mathbf{s},\tilde{d},\theta))}.$$

After obtaining the model predictions for the choice probabilities as functions of the state variables and the unknown parameters θ, the parameters θ can then be estimated using maximum likelihood. The likelihood function is a function of the choice probabilities and therefore a function of the continuation value $V^c(\cdot)$. Solving for the parameters θ via maximum likelihood thus requires an inner fixed-point algorithm to compute the continuation value $V^c(\cdot)$ as rapidly as possible and an outer optimization algorithm to find the maximizing value of the parameters θ—that is, a fixed point calculation is nested within a maximum likelihood estimation (MLE). From Blackwell's theorem, the fixed point is unique.

Identification of the parameters θ comes from the differences between per-period payoffs across different action choices, which in infinite horizon dynamic discrete choice models are identified when the discount factor β and the distribution of the choice-specific shocks ε_{it} are fixed (Abbring 2010; Magnac and Thesmar 2002; Rust 1994). In particular, the parameters in our model are identified because each term in the deterministic component $\pi(\cdot)$ of the per-period payoff given in equation (1) depends on the action d_{it} being taken at time t and therefore varies based on the action taken; as a consequence, the parameters do not cancel out in the differences between per-period payoffs across different action choices and are therefore identified. For example, the coefficient θ_1 on the spinach dummy is identified in the difference between the per-period payoff from choosing to plant spinach and the per-period payoff from any action choice d_{it} that does not involve planting spinach.[11]

Standard errors are formed by a nonparametric bootstrap. Fields are randomly drawn from the data set with replacement to generate 100 independent panels each with the same number of fields as in the original data set. The structural model is run on each of the new panels. The standard errors

---

11. To identify the constant θ_{11}, we normalize the deterministic component $\pi(\cdot)$ of the per-period payoff from choosing "other" to 0.

are then formed by taking the standard deviation of the parameter estimates from each of the panels.

7.5   Data

We use Pesticide Use Reporting (PUR) data from the California Department of Pesticide Regulation.[12] Our data set is composed of all fields in Monterey County on which any regulated pesticide was applied in the years 1993 to 2011, inclusively.[13] Additional data on prices, yields, and acreage come from the Monterey Agricultural Commissioner's Office. We collapse the data set into monthly observations.

We group the crops into six categories: susceptible (which includes artichoke, strawberries, and cabbage but excludes lettuce, which we represent separately), resistant (cauliflower and celery), lettuce, spinach, broccoli, and other.[14] From these, we form nine action choices: susceptible, susceptible with recent fumigation, resistant, broccoli, broccoli with recent fumigation, lettuce, lettuce with recent fumigation, spinach, and other.[15]

For control options, we use recent histories for broccoli and methyl bromide because their effects on microsclerotia are relatively short-lived. Microsclerotia levels rebound within one to two seasons, or approximately one year. Thus broccoli history is the number of months broccoli was planted in the last 12 months, and methyl bromide history is the number of months methyl bromide was used in the last 12 months.

The vast majority of fields (94 percent of observations) in our data set have only one grower over the entire time period. Of these, we analyze those

12. For more information, see http://www.cdpr.ca.gov/docs/pur/purmain.htm.
13. We use the field identifier as well as the section, township, and range data from the PUR data set to match fields across time. We delete a small number of observations that are nonagricultural uses (golf courses, freeway sidings, etc.).
14. To make the model manageable, we include only the most common crops in Monterey County and those that are most often grown in rotation with lettuce. The crops explicitly included in our model account for nearly 90 percent of the observations. We account for the many rarely planted crops by including an "other" option, which includes various herbs, berries, nursery products, nuts, wine grapes, livestock, and many others.
15. The data contain the crop planted in each field for each recorded pesticide application. Although the focus of our research is on methyl bromide, the other pesticides provide observations regarding which crops are in the ground at which times. Due to the nature of the data, sometimes we do not observe the entire production cycle of a crop. For example, strawberries are often in the ground for a year or more; however, if there is no registered pesticide applied in one of those months, a gap in the production cycle may appear in our data. We account for this issue in several ways. As long as the missing data are missing for exogenous reasons, missing data will not bias the results. Since there are no pesticide treatments for V. wilt once crops are in the ground, we have reason to believe that missing months mid–production cycle due to no pesticide application in that month are exogenous to the impact of V. wilt on crop and methyl bromide fumigation choice. We compared the distribution of these months between short-term and long-term growers and find that they are similar. Finally, in the simulations, we simulate all months in the time period, but only count grower months that are present in the actual data when calculating welfare and other statistics for comparison purposes.

long-term growers who appear in the data from 1994 to 2010, and we model their decision-making as an infinite horizon problem. This data set on long-term growers consists of 615 fields, each over 17 years.

We use a marketing year average price for each crop[16] to represent growers' expectations about prices for each year. The marketing year average price is in units of dollars per acre and therefore measures revenue per acre and incorporates yield.[17] Using the current year's marketing year average price assumes that growers have rational expectations about what the average marketing year price will be that year.[18] The Monterey County Agricultural Commissioner's Office publishes annual crop reports including prices, yields harvest, and acreages for major crops in the county. Monterey County is a major producer of many of the crops included in our model. For most crops, these prices are highly correlated with California-wide price data published by the NASS. We discretize the marketing year average price into six bins; the marketing year average price bins are shown in figure 7.1.

We combine the marketing year average price data with data on the timing of harvests for various crops in Monterey. For each crop, the harvest-month dummy variable for that crop is equal to one in months during which that crop may be harvested and zero in months during which that crop is not harvested (i.e., winter months for most crops).[19] For all crops, we have observations during the winter months, including crops that have just been planted and are not yet ready for harvest, and crops such as strawberries that overwinter for harvest in the coming year.

Summary statistics for the state variables for long-term growers are in table 7.1. The mean discretized price for broccoli is relatively low, affirming that broccoli is a low-return crop. Spinach makes up a relatively small por-

16. For lettuce, we use a weighted average of the prices for head and leaf lettuce. In the early years of the data set, romaine and other types of lettuce were not broken out separately, so gross revenue numbers vary based on this reporting but do not affect the discretized value of the price.

17. We look at gross revenue rather than net revenue due to data limitations. Costs are captured by our crop-fumigation dummies and our constant. Estimating net revenue did not improve the overall model, and cost differences among crops are mainly driven by methyl bromide fumigation, which is explicitly included in the model, and/or the difference between strawberry costs compared to other crops. Strawberry costs are generally an order of magnitude higher than for the vegetable crops, in part due to fumigation cost according to Richard Smith, farm advisor for vegetable crop production and weed science with the University of California Cooperative Extension in Monterey County. We also attempted to incorporate this effect by including dummy variables for the different crop choices and fumigation, with resistant crops as the baseline. Unsurprisingly, the susceptible dummy variable (which includes strawberries) was collinear with the methyl bromide fumigation variable; we therefore do not include the susceptible crop dummy variable in our model. We expect the crop-fumigation dummies to at least partially capture the cost differences among the different crops.

18. Instead of rational expectations about price, another possible assumption is that growers' best guess for this year's price is last year's price. The results are robust to whether we use lagged prices rather than current prices (Carroll et al. 2018a).

19. There is a separate harvest-month dummy variable for each crop month. These data come from Richard Smith.

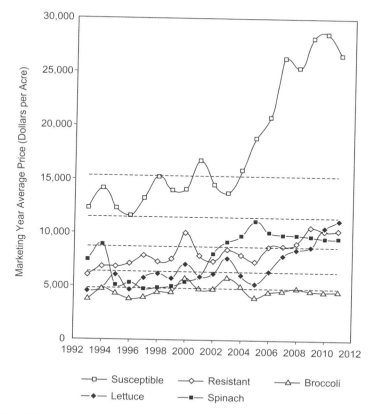

Fig. 7.1   Marketing year average prices per acre

Note: Black dashed lines delineate the bins used to discretize the marketing year average price.

tion of the acreage grown in Monterey County, approximately a tenth of the size of the acreage planted to lettuce according to the most recent Monterey County Crop Report.

Figure 7.2 plots the actual fraction of grower-months in each action type for the long-term growers. As seen in figure 7.2, lettuce accounts for over 60 percent of the grower-months for these long-term growers. Figure 7.3 plots the actual fraction of grower-months in each action by month of the year. The actual fraction of grower-months in each action varies by the month of the year, with lettuce predominant in the spring and summer months and other and susceptible crops having the highest proportion in the winter months. Figure 7.4 plots the actual fraction of grower-months in each action type over the years. The proportions are relatively constant across years.

Table 7.1   Summary statistics for state variables

	Mean	Std. dev.	Minimum	Maximum
Spinach dummy	0.0285	0.1665	0	1
Methyl bromide today dummy	0.0033	0.0577	0	1
Broccoli dummy	0.0606	0.2385	0	1
Lettuce × Methyl bromide history	0.0229	0.1602	0	3
Lettuce × Broccoli history	1.1709	1.8277	0	12
Spinach × Methyl bromide history	0.0015	0.0431	0	2
Spinach × Broccoli history	0.0397	0.3701	0	10
Lettuce today dummy	0.6379	0.4806	0	1
Susceptible price × Susceptible harvest	5.0660	1.4914	0	6
Resistant price × Resistant harvest	1.8748	1.6125	0	4
Broccoli price × Broccoli harvest	1.1742	0.5082	0	2
Lettuce price × Lettuce harvest	1.9552	1.1004	0	4
Spinach price × Spinach harvest	2.5268	1.4709	0	4

Notes: Number of observations: 25,789. For each crop, the harvest month dummy variable for that crop is equal to one in months during which that crop may be harvested and zero in months during which that crop is not harvested (i.e., winter months for most crops).

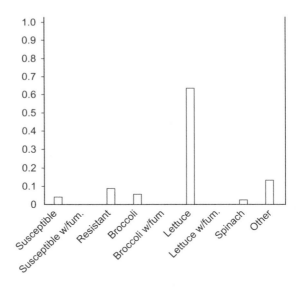

Fig. 7.2   Actual fraction of grower months in each action

7.6   Results

The results for long-term growers are presented in table 7.2. We run our model on three different time periods: the entire time period of our data set ("All"), the early half of the data prior to 2001 ("Early"), and the later half of the data from 2001 to 2011 ("Late"). We report our estimates for the

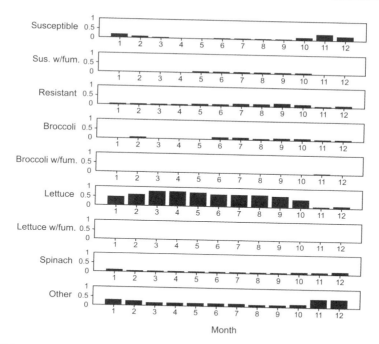

Fig. 7.3   Fraction of grower months in each action type by month of the year

parameters in the per-period payoff function in equation (1). The payoffs do not have units because price is discretized and therefore no longer in dollars. Since we do not have units for payoffs, we can compare only relative payoffs and welfare.

According to the results, the coefficient on the spinach dummy is significant and negative, suggesting that planting spinach is undesirable for reasons that are not fully captured by its price.[20] This coefficient provides evidence that V. wilt is a problem, since it is likely due to the fact that spinach is associated with V. wilt that spinach is undesirable.[21]

The coefficient on methyl bromide in the current period is significant and

---

20. Because price is the discretized marketing average price of spinach per acre, the price measures revenue per acre and therefore incorporates yield as well. Thus the significant negative coefficient on the spinach dummy suggests that spinach is not desirable to plant for reasons that are not fully captured by its price, yield, or revenue per acre.

21. One may worry that the negative coefficient on the spinach dummy is possibly also consistent with a problem in modeling where the other crops with longer crop cycles would potentially be more appealing than spinach. However, even when returns are divided by the length of season, the returns to spinach versus other crops still follow the same order. This result suggests that the season length is not the driving factor behind this coefficient. We confirm in Carroll et al. (2018a) that the significant negative coefficient on the spinach dummy is robust to whether we divide returns by season length.

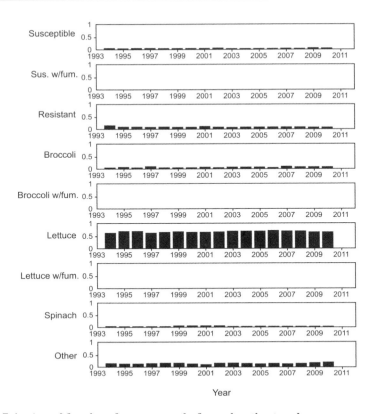

Year

Fig. 7.4   Actual fraction of grower months for each action type by year

negative, which means that there is a cost to methyl bromide that may yield future benefit to either the current crop or a future crop. The coefficient is more negative in the later half of the data, likely because the Montreal Protocol started to limit the legal availability of methyl bromide during this period (California Department of Pesticide Regulation 2010; USEPA 2012b) and also because there is more demand for methyl bromide in the later half of the data set, when V. wilt became more of a problem, resulting in a higher price for using methyl bromide.

The broccoli dummy coefficient is negative but not significant, suggesting that planting broccoli is not as desirable as planting lettuce (since the lettuce dummy has a significant positive coefficient) and requires foregoing current benefits (or incurring current costs) for future gain.

The coefficient on the interaction term between lettuce and methyl bromide history is significant and positive in the later half of the time period, suggesting that methyl bromide is an effective control option in the later period. Similarly, the coefficient on the interaction term between lettuce

Table 7.2   **Results for long-term growers**

	All	Early	Late
Coefficients in the per-period payoff function on:			
Spinach dummy	−1.1311***	−1.1905***	−1.0703***
	(0.2981)	(0.3297)	(0.2419)
Methyl bromide dummy	−6.0705***	−5.6993***	−6.3633***
	(0.064)	(0.1077)	(0.063)
Broccoli dummy	−0.332	−0.5953	−0.1615
	(0.2035)	(0.4956)	(0.18)
Lettuce dummy × Methyl bromide history	0.2717	0.1992	0.8501*
	(0.4648)	(0.4174)	(0.3797)
Lettuce dummy × Broccoli history	0.3682***	0.3674***	0.3707***
	(0.0605)	(0.0632)	(0.0558)
Spinach dummy × Methyl bromide history	0.026	0.0787	0.2734
	(0.1956)	(0.3034)	(0.1949)
Spinach dummy × Broccoli history	0.2643	0.2665	0.2573
	(0.4769)	(0.2598)	(0.6341)
Lettuce dummy	1.4346***	1.3844***	1.4691***
	(0.1817)	(0.1874)	(0.1782)
Price × Harvest month dummy	−0.1585***	−0.1558***	−0.16***
	(0.0414)	(0.0458)	(0.0399)
Last crop dummy	21.2161***	24.2249***	20.0534***
	(1.0463)	(3.8795)	(0.786)
Constant	−1.1482***	−1.0881***	−1.1906***
	(0.3027)	(0.2381)	(0.2592)
Total average effects on per-period payoff of:			
Spinach dummy	−1.1206***	−1.1791***	−1.0603***
	(0.2987)	(0.3299)	(0.2431)
Lettuce dummy	1.4498***	1.4003***	1.4838***
	(0.1817)	(0.1874)	(0.1782)
Methyl bromide history	0.2378	0.1276	0.5554*
	(0.2968)	(0.2630)	(0.2450)
Broccoli history	0.2424***	0.2390***	0.2460***
	(0.0409)	(0.0405)	(0.0400)
Number of observations	25,761	10,833	14,928

Notes: Standard errors are in parentheses. Significance codes: *** 0.1 percent level, ** 1 percent level, * 5 percent level.

and broccoli history is significant and positive, which suggests that planting broccoli is also an effective control option.

Although the coefficient on the spinach dummy and methyl bromide history interaction term is not significant, the point estimate is positive and smaller in magnitude than the spinach dummy coefficient, suggesting that the undesirability of spinach is mitigated by having methyl bromide history. In addition to the significant positive coefficient on the lettuce and methyl bromide interaction in the later period, this further suggests that methyl bromide is an effective control option in the later period.

Similarly, although the coefficient on the spinach dummy and broccoli history interaction term is not significant, the point estimate is positive and smaller in magnitude than the spinach dummy, also suggesting that the undesirability of spinach is mitigated by broccoli history. In addition to the significant positive coefficient on the lettuce and broccoli history interaction, this further suggests that planting broccoli is an effective control option.

The lettuce dummy has a significant positive coefficient, which means that owners derive benefits from planting lettuce beyond its price, such as meeting shipper contract requirements.[22] Thus it is desirable for growers to control V. wilt, since they benefit from planting lettuce.

The coefficient on price at the time of harvest is negative. At first blush, this may appear counterintuitive, as economic theory predicts that price will have a positive effect on return. After looking further into the data, however, the reason for this result becomes more clear. Strawberries have a much higher revenue per acre than any of the vegetable crops included in this data set, on the order of $70,000 for strawberries versus $20,000 or less for some vegetable crops. Most growers concentrate on either strawberry crops or vegetable crops, so there are very few cases in the data of growers switching to strawberries from vegetable crops, even though this is what one would expect based on price alone. When strawberries are removed as an action choice in the analysis, the coefficient for price is then positive. In addition, some strawberry growers are switching to contracts in which the price plays very little role in determining their profit. They are paid a baseline amount for growing the crop and may make more money in a particularly good year but do not bear the downside risk in a poor year.

The negative coefficient on price at the time of harvest therefore suggests that growers may be committed to previous crops and therefore do not respond to price. For example, growers may have connections and contracts that tie them to certain crops. They may have expertise or risk profiles that better suit certain crops. Perhaps some growers consider themselves vegetable growers, and the cost of switching to strawberries is too high. Uncertainty related to the future of methyl bromide and its lack of suitable replacements for treating V. wilt could also play a role. Factors that may make growers less likely to switch crops are at least partially captured in our model by the last crop dummy. We hope to explore these issues further in future work.

The coefficient on the last crop dummy is significant and positive, which suggests that growers are committed to previous crops, which is also consistent with the hypothesis that growers do not switch crops often and therefore are less responsive to price.

The total average effects of the variables that appear in more than one

---

22. In the model, returns are estimated at the county level, so although contracts can and do specify prices, we expect the return used in the model to be exogenous to contracting decisions.

term of the per-period payoff function are reported at the bottom of table 7.2. The spinach dummy has a total average effect that is significant and negative on net, which provides evidence that V. wilt is a problem, even if the undesirability of spinach is mitigated by having methyl bromide history and/or broccoli history.

The lettuce dummy has a significant and positive total average effect, which means that owners derive benefits from planting lettuce beyond its price and that the benefits of lettuce are enhanced in the presence of control options such as methyl bromide history and/or broccoli history.

Methyl bromide history has a positive total average effect that is significant in the later half of the time period, suggesting that methyl bromide is an effective control option in the later period. Similarly, broccoli history has a significant and positive total average effect, suggesting that planting broccoli is an effective control option.

In using a marketing year average price for each crop to represent growers' expectations about prices for each year, we assume that growers have rational expectations about the price. Instead of rational expectations about price, another possible assumption is that a grower's best guess for this year's price is last year's price. The results are robust to whether we use lagged prices rather than current prices (Carroll et al. 2018a).

We choose not to model the grower as only receiving the revenue for his crop the first month of the harvest season, as this would not explain why growers may plant the same crop for multiple months in the harvest season. Staying in the harvest season longer sometimes yields higher revenue because it enables the grower to harvest more product or replant the crop for more harvest, both of which are better captured by having the grower receive more revenue if he stays in the harvest season longer. For similar reasons, we choose not to model the grower as only receiving the revenue for his crop the last month of the harvest season. As seen in Carroll et al. (2018a), we find that the results are robust to whether we divide the marketing year average price for each crop by its average harvest season length and therefore to whether we assume growers who plant the same crop for multiple months in a harvest season receive more revenue than those who plant that crop for only one month in the harvest season.

We calculate the normalized average grower welfare per grower per month for the entire time period ("All"), the early time period ("Early"), and the later time period ("Late"). The welfare is calculated as the present discounted value of the entire stream of payoffs to growers evaluated at the parameter values, summed over all growers in the relevant data set and then divided by the number of grower-months in the relevant data set. The average grower welfare per grower per month is then normalized so that the average welfare per grower per month over the entire time period ("All") is 100.

The standard errors for the welfare values are calculated using the parameter estimates from each of 100 bootstrap samples. For each of the 100

Table 7.3	Normalized average present discounted grower welfare per grower month		
	All	Early	Late
Grower welfare (per grower month)	100	117.3475	92.7063
	(5.0957)	(19.2088)	(3.4884)

Note: The average grower welfare per grower per month is normalized so that the average welfare per grower per month over the entire time period ("all") is 100. Standard errors in parentheses. All welfare values are significant at a 0.1 percent level.

bootstrap samples, we calculate the average welfare per grower per month using the parameter estimates from that bootstrap sample and normalize it. The standard error of the normalized welfare is the standard deviation of the normalized welfare over all 100 bootstrap samples.

The welfare results are presented in table 7.3. According to the welfare results, average grower welfare per grower-month is higher in the earlier time period than in the later time period, perhaps because V. wilt became more of a problem in the later time period.

7.7 Simulations

We use the estimated parameters from our dynamic structural model to simulate the effects of crop disease on agricultural productivity. In particular, we use counterfactual simulations to analyze the effects of V. wilt on crop-fumigation decisions and on grower welfare.

The severity of the crop disease is measured by the coefficient θ_1 on the spinach dummy in the grower's per-period payoff function. The spinach dummy coefficient captures the effects of spinach on payoffs that are not internalized in spinach price. The more negative the spinach dummy coefficient θ_1, the more severe the disease.

To analyze the effects of crop disease on agricultural productivity, we use the estimated parameters from our dynamic structural model in section 7.6 to simulate how different values of the spinach dummy coefficient would affect the choices and payoffs of growers. According to the results of the dynamic structural model for growers in table 7.2, the coefficient θ_1 on the spinach dummy when we use data over the entire time period ("All") is -1.1311.

We consider a set of 21 evenly spaced values of the spinach dummy coefficient θ_1 between -2.00 and 0.00. A spinach dummy coefficient θ_1 of -2.00 represents a scenario in which V. wilt is even more severe than it currently is and therefore one in which spinach seeds have an even greater negative effect on grower payoffs than they currently do. A spinach dummy coefficient θ_1 equal to zero represents a scenario in which V. wilt is no longer an economically damaging disease and therefore one in which the effect of spinach on grower payoffs (aside from price effects) is neutral and not economically significant.

For each possible value of the spinach dummy coefficient θ_1, we run 100 simulations of the choices and payoffs that would arise if the spinach dummy coefficient were equal that values. For each of the 100 simulations, we calculate the average grower welfare per month, which is the total welfare divided by the number of grower-months. Then for each possible value of the spinach dummy coefficient, we average the grower welfare per month over the 100 simulations using that value of the spinach dummy coefficient. We then calculate the average benefits to the grower from mitigating the disease taking the average grower welfare per month at each value of the spinach dummy coefficient and then subtracting the average grower welfare per month when the spinach dummy coefficient θ_1 is an extremely severe -2.00. In other words, we normalize the average grower welfare per month when the spinach dummy coefficient θ_1 is an extremely severe -2.00 to 0.

Standard errors are calculated using a nonparametric bootstrap. In particular, we calculate the standard errors of the grower benefits from disease mitigation using the parameter estimates from each of 25 bootstrap samples. For each of the 25 bootstrap samples, we run 25 simulations using the parameter estimates from that bootstrap sample.[23] The standard error of the grower benefits is the standard deviation of the respective statistic over all 25 bootstrap samples.

Figure 7.5 plots the benefits to a grower per month from mitigating the disease, averaged over 100 simulations, as a function of the coefficient θ_1 on the spinach dummy achieved. According to our results, the benefits to the growers are the highest when the coefficient on spinach is driven up to zero, which represents the scenario in which V. wilt is no longer an economically damaging disease. As the coefficient on spinach becomes more negative (representing scenarios in which V. wilt is more severe a disease), the benefits to growers decline.

To analyze the effects of mitigating V. wilt on crop-fumigation decisions, we simulate the crop choices of long-term growers when the spinach dummy coefficient θ_1 is equal to -1.00, which represents the scenario in which V. wilt is less severe than it currently is, and when the spinach dummy coefficient θ_1 is equal to zero, which represents the scenario in which V. wilt is no longer an economically damaging disease.

Standard errors and 95 percent confidence intervals are calculated using a nonparametric bootstrap. In particular, we calculate the standard errors of the simulation statistics (e.g., mean fraction of grower-months in each action) using the parameter estimates from each of 25 bootstrap samples. For each of the 25 bootstrap samples, we run 25 simulations using the parameter

23. Constraints on computational time preclude us from running the 25 simulations per bootstrap sample for more than 25 bootstrap samples per scenario. When we calculated the standard error for welfare for scenario one using 100 bootstrap samples instead of 25 bootstrap samples, the value of the standard errors were similar using both 25 bootstrap samples and 100 bootstrap samples.

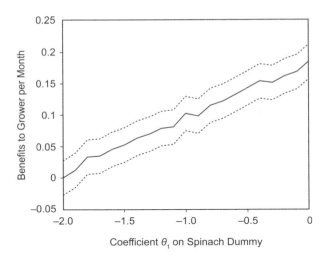

Fig. 7.5 Normalized average per-month (per-period) grower benefits from disease mitigation

Notes: The less negative the spinach dummy coefficient , the less severe the disease. We calculate the average benefits to the grower from mitigating the disease by subtracting the average grower welfare per month when the spinach dummy coefficient θ_1 is an extremely severe -2.00 from the average grower welfare per month at each value of the spinach dummy coefficient. In other words, we normalize the average grower welfare per month when the spinach dummy coefficient θ_1 is an extremely severe -2.00 to 0. Benefits are averaged over 100 simulations. Dotted lines indicate the 95 percent confidence interval, which is calculated using a nonparametric bootstrap.

estimates from that bootstrap sample.[24] The standard error of the simulation statistics (e.g., mean fraction of grower-months in each action) is the standard deviation of the respective statistic over all 25 bootstrap samples.

Figures 6 and 7 simulate growers crop choices when V. wilt is no longer an economically damaging disease ($\theta_1 = 0$) and when V. wilt is less severe than it currently is ($\theta_1 = -1.00$), respectively. The fraction of grower-months planted to lettuce is higher under both scenarios than they are in the actual data in figure 7.2. Thus when V. wilt is less severe, growers plant more lettuce, likely because V. wilt then becomes less of a problem.

Figures 8 and 9 show the fraction of grower-months in each action type by month of year when V. wilt is no longer an economically damaging disease ($\theta_1 = 0$) and when V. wilt is less severe than it currently is ($\theta_1 = -1.00$), respectively. Compared to figure 7.3, which shows the actual data, the results of the simulations of less-severe disease show more grower-months planted

24. Constraints on computational time preclude us from running the 25 simulations per bootstrap sample for more than 25 bootstrap samples per scenario. When we calculated the standard error for welfare for scenario one using 100 bootstrap samples instead of 25 bootstrap samples, the value of the standard errors were similar using both 25 bootstrap samples and 100 bootstrap samples.

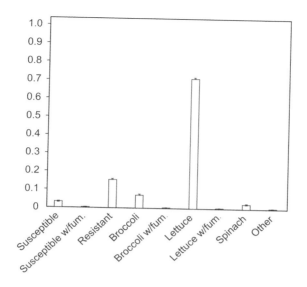

Fig. 7.6 Simulated mean fraction of grower months in each action when spinach dummy coefficient θ_1 equals 0

Notes: The fraction of grower months in each action is averaged over 25 simulations. Error bars represent the 95-percent confidence interval, which is calculated using a nonparametric bootstrap.

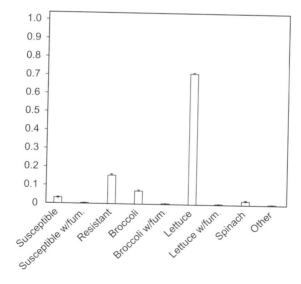

Fig. 7.7 Simulated mean fraction of grower months in each action when spinach dummy coefficient θ_1 equals -1.00

Notes: The fraction of grower months in each action is averaged over 25 simulations. Error bars represent the 95-percent confidence interval, which is calculated using a nonparametric bootstrap.

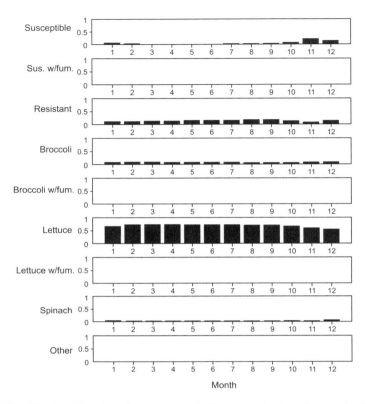

Fig. 7.8   Simulated fraction of grower months in each action type by month of year when spinach dummy coefficient θ_1 equals 0

Notes: The fraction of grower months in each action by month of year is averaged over 25 simulations. Error bars represent the 95-percent confidence interval, which is calculated using a nonparametric bootstrap.

to lettuce, especially in the last months of the year, when the actual data consists more of susceptible and other crops.

Figures 10 and 11 show the fraction of grower months in each action type by year when V. wilt is no longer an economically damaging disease ($\theta_1 = 0$) and when V. wilt is less severe than it currently is ($\theta_1 = -1.00$), respectively. Compared to figure 7.4, which shows the actual data, the results of the simulations of less-severe disease show more grower-months planted to lettuce and fewer grower months planted to other crops. Thus when the disease is less severe, growers plant more lettuce, likely because V. wilt then becomes less of a problem.

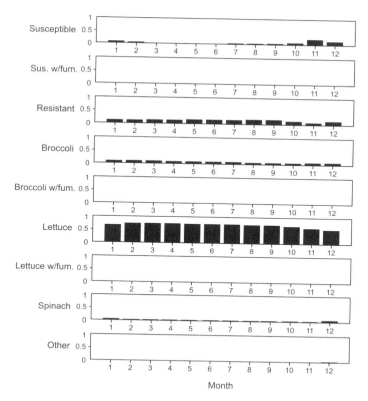

Fig. 7.9   **Simulated fraction of grower-months in each action type by month of year when spinach dummy coefficient θ_1 equals −1.00**

Notes: The fraction of grower months in each action by month of year is averaged over 25 simulations. Error bars represent the 95-percent confidence interval, which is calculated using a nonparametric bootstrap.

7.8   Conclusion

This chapter discusses the effects on agricultural productivity of *Verticillium dahliae*, a soil-borne fungus that is introduced to the soil via infested spinach seeds and causes lettuce to be afflicted with V. wilt. We use a dynamic structural econometric model of V. wilt management for lettuce crops in Monterey County, California, to examine the effects of V. wilt on crop-fumigation decisions and on grower welfare.

According to our results, planting spinach is undesirable for reasons that are not fully captured by its price, which is consistent with the conclusion that V. wilt is a problem. Fumigating with methyl bromide and planting broccoli are both effective control options but involve incurring costs or foregoing profit in the current period for future benefit. We find that average

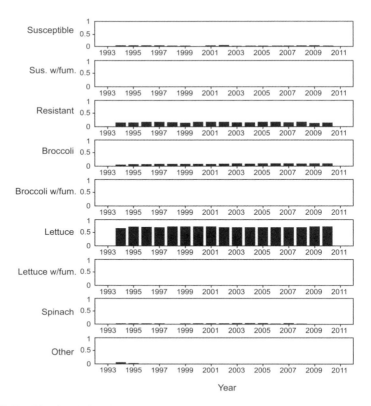

Fig. 7.10   Simulated fraction of grower-months in each action type by year when spinach dummy coefficient θ_1 equals 0

Notes: The fraction of grower-months in each action by year is averaged over 25 simulations. Error bars represent the 95-percent confidence interval, which is calculated using a nonparametric bootstrap.

grower welfare per grower-month is higher in the earlier time period than in the later time period, perhaps because V. wilt became more of a problem in the later time period.

According to the results of our counterfactual simulations of the effects of V. wilt on agricultural productivity, the benefits to the growers are the highest when the coefficient on spinach is equal to zero, which represents the scenario in which V. wilt is no longer an economically damaging disease. As the coefficient on spinach becomes more negative (representing scenarios in which V. wilt is more severe a disease), the benefits to growers decline. When the disease is less severe, growers plant more lettuce, likely because V. wilt then becomes less of a problem. Thus V. wilt has important effects on crop-fumigation decisions, grower welfare, and agricultural productivity.

There are two main externalities that arise due to V. wilt and that have

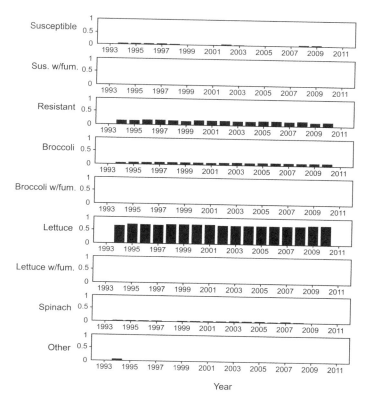

Fig. 7.11   **Simulated fraction of grower-months in each action type by year when spinach dummy coefficient θ_1 equals -1.00**

Notes: The fraction of grower-months in each action by year is averaged over 25 simulations. Error bars represent the 95-percent confidence interval, which is calculated using a nonparametric bootstrap.

important implications for agricultural productivity. The first externality is an intertemporal externality. When faced with managing a disease that requires future investment, short- and long-term decision-makers may have different incentives and choose to manage the disease differently. In the case of V. wilt, because the options for controlling V. wilt require long-term investments for future gain, an intertemporal externality arises with short-term growers, who are likely to rent the land for only a short period of time. Renters, therefore, might not make the long-term investments needed to control V. wilt. As a consequence, future renters and the landowner may suffer from decisions of previous renters not to invest in control options. Thus decisions made by current renters impose an intertemporal externality on future renters and the landowner.

In Carroll et al. (2018a), we analyze the factors that affect crop choice and fumigation decisions made by growers and consider how the decisions of long-term growers (whom we call "owners") differ from those of short-term growers (whom we call "renters"). We examine whether existing renter contracts internalize the intertemporal externality that a renter's decisions today impose on future renters and the landowner and analyze the implications of renting versus owning land on welfare.

Although contracts can be a potential method for internalizing an externality between different parties, our empirical results in Carroll et al. (2018a) show that existing rental contracts do not fully internalize the intertemporal externality imposed by renters on future renters and the landowner. This outcome may be because of the relatively recent development of the disease and knowledge of its causes, more restrictive contracts not being the norm, the possibility of land unknowingly being contaminated before rental, or difficulty in enforcing or monitoring aspects of the contract, such as whether boots and equipment are washed between fields.

In addition to the intertemporal externality, a second externality that arises due to V. wilt is a supply-chain externality between companies selling spinach seed and growers who may sell lettuce. Growers wish to protect their fields from V. wilt, but they cannot easily prevent introduction of the disease by spinach seeds when spinach is planted without incurring testing costs and cleaning fees. Currently, seed companies are unwilling to test or clean spinach seeds, especially as spinach producers are not affected by this disease. Thus decisions made by seed companies regarding whether and how much to test or clean spinach seeds impose a supply-chain externality on growers.

In Carroll et al. (2018b), we analyze the supply-chain externality between growers and seed companies. We calculate the benefits to growers from testing and cleaning spinach seeds by simulating growers' optimal decisions and welfare under different levels of seed testing and cleaning. We then estimate the spinach seed company's cost to test and clean spinach seeds in order to reduce the level of microsclerotia and compare the spinach seed company's cost to the grower's benefits. Because seed cleaning cost data are not available, we use several functional forms and parameters to estimate potential cost functions. We then use the benefits and costs to determine the welfare maximizing level of seed testing and cleaning.

According to our results in Carroll et al. (2018b), using data over the entire time period, we find that a cooperative solution would increase welfare, and in most cases, a cooperative solution would require that the spinach seed company engage in more spinach seed testing and cleaning than in the status quo. Our work regarding the supply-chain externality between seed companies and growers sheds light on how treatment of spinach seeds could potentially reduce externalities between seed companies and growers.

Crop diseases and how they are managed can have a large impact on agricultural productivity. Externalities due to V. wilt that arise with renters and between seed companies and growers have important implications for the management of V. wilt in particular and also for the management of diseases in agriculture in general.

References

Abbring, J. 2010. "Identification of Dynamic Discrete Choice Models." *Annual Review of Economics* 2:367–94.

Aguirregabiria, V., and A. Luengo. 2016. "A Microeconometric Dynamic Structural Model of Copper Mining Decisions." Working Paper, University of Toronto.

Atallah, S., M. Gómez, J. Conrad, and J. P. Nyrop. 2015. "A Plant-Level, Spatial, Bioeconomic Model of Plant Disease, Diffusion, and Control: Grapevine Leafroll Disease." *American Journal of Agricultural Economics* 97:199–218.

Atallah, Z., R. Hayes, and K. Subbarao. 2011. "Fifteen Years of Verticillium Wilt of Lettuce in America's Salad Bowl: A Tale of Immigration, Subjugation, and Abatement." *Plant Disease* 95:784–92.

Atallah, Z., K. Maruthachalam, L. Toit, S. Koike, R. Michael Davis, S. Klosterman, R. Hayes, and K. Subbarao. 2010. "Population Analyses of the Vascular Plant Pathogen *Verticillium dahliae* Detect Recombination and Transcontinental Gene Flow." *Fungal Genetics and Biology* 47:416–22.

California Department of Pesticide Regulation. 2010. "Department of Pesticide Regulation Announces Work Group to Identify Ways to Grow Strawberries without Fumigants." http://www.cdpr.ca.gov/docs/pressrls/2012/120424.htm.

Carlson, G. A., and C. E. Main. 1976. "Economics of Disease-Loss Management." *Annual Review of Phytopathology* 14:381–403.

Carroll, C. L., C. A. Carter, R. E. Goodhue, and C.-Y. C. Lin Lawell. 2019a. "The Economics of Decision-Making for Crop Disease Control." Working Paper.

Carroll, C. L., C. A. Carter, R. E. Goodhue, and C.-Y. C. Lin Lawell. 2019b. "Supply Chain Externalities and Agricultural Disease." Working Paper.

Cook, J. A., and C.-Y. C. Lin Lawell. 2019. "Wind Turbine Shutdowns and Upgrades in Denmark: Timing Decisions and the Impact of Government Policy." Working Paper, Cornell University.

De Pinto, A., and G. C. Nelson. 2009. "Land Use Change with Spatially Explicit Data: A Dynamic Approach." *Environmental and Resource Economics* 43:209–29.

Duressa, D., G. Rauscher, S. T. Koike, B. Mou, R. J. Hayes, K. Maruthachalam, K. V. Subbarao, and S. J. Klosterman. 2012. "A Real-Time PCR Assay for Detection and Quantification of Verticillium Dahliae in Spinach Seed." *Phytopathology* 102:443–51.

du Toit, L., M. Derie, and P. Hernandez-Perez. 2005. "Verticillium Wilt in Spinach Seed Production." *Plant Disease* 89:4–11.

du Toit, L., and P. Hernandez-Perez. 2005. "Efficacy of Hot Water and Chlorine for Eradication of *Cladosporium Variabile, Stemphylium Botryosum*, and *Verticillium Dahliae* from Spinach Seed." *Plant Disease* 89:1305–12.

Fradin, E. F., and B. P. H. J. Thomma. 2006. "Physiology and Molecular Aspects of Verticillium Wilt Diseases Caused by *V. Dahliae* and *V. Albo-Atrum*." *Molecular Plant Pathology* 7:71–86.

Gómez, M. I., H. M. Nunez, and H. Onal. 2009. "Economic Impacts of Soybean Rust on the US Soybean Sector." 2009 Annual Meeting, July 26–28, Milwaukee, Wisconsin, no. 49595, Agricultural and Applied Economics Association.

Hueth, D., and U. Regev. 1974. "Optimal Agricultural Pest Management with

Increasing Pest Resistance." *American Journal of Agricultural Economics* 56: 543–52.

IPC (International Phytosanitary Certificate). 2003. International Phytosanitary Certificate No. 4051.

Johansson, R. C., M. Livingston, J. Westra, and K. M. Guidry. 2006. "Simulating the U.S. Impacts of Alternative Asian Soybean Rust Treatment Regimes." *Agricultural and Resource Economics Review* 35:116–27.

Magnac, T., and D. Thesmar. 2002. "Identifying Dynamic Discrete Decision Processes." *Econometrica* 70:801–16.

Maruthachalam, K., S. J. Klosterman, A. Anchieta, B. Mou, and K. V. Subbarao. 2013. "Colonization of Spinach by *Verticillium Dahliae* and Effects of Pathogen Localization on the Efficacy of Seed Treatments." *Phytopathology* 103:268–80.

McKee, G. J., R. E. Goodhue, F. G. Zalom, C. A. Carter, and J. A. Chalfant. 2009. "Population Dynamics and the Economics of Invasive Species Management: The Greenhouse Whitefly in California-Grown Strawberries." *Journal of Environmental Management* 90:561–70.

Moffitt, L., D. Hall, and C. Osteen. 1984. "Economic Thresholds under Uncertainty with Application to Corn Nematode Management." *Southern Journal of Agricultural Economics* 16:151–57.

Monterey County Agricultural Commissioner. 2015. "Crop Reports and Economic Contributions." http://www.co.monterey.ca.us/home/showdocument?id=12607.

NASS (National Agricultural Statistics Service). 2015. "California Agricultural Statistics: 2013 Crop Year." http://www.nass.usda.gov/Statistics_by_State/California /Publications/California_Ag_Statistics/Reports/index.php.

Noailly, J. 2008. "Coevolution of Economic and Ecological Systems." *Journal of Evolutionary Economics* 18:1–29.

Palm, M. E. 2001. "Systematics and the Impact of Invasive Fungi on Agriculture in the United States." *BioScience* 51:141–47.

Rapson, D. 2014. "Durable Goods and Long-Run Electricity Demand: Evidence from Air Conditioner Purchase Behavior." *Journal of Environmental Economics and Management* 68:141–60.

Rossman, A. 2009. "The Impact of Invasive Fungi on Agricultural Ecosystems in the United States." *Biological Invasions* 11:97–107.

Rothwell, G., and J. Rust. 1997. "On the Optimal Lifetime of Nuclear Power Plants." *Journal of Business and Economic Statistics* 15:195–208.

Rust, J. 1987. "Optimal Replacement of GMC Bus Engines: An Empirical Model of Harold Zurcher." *Econometrica: Journal of the Econometric Society* 55:999–1033.

Rust, J. 1988. "Maximum Likelihood Estimation of Discrete Control Processes." *SIAM Journal on Control and Optimization* 26:1006–24.

Rust, J. 1994. "Structural Estimation of Markov Decision Processes." In *Handbook of Econometrics*, vol. 4, edited by R. Engle and D. McFadden, 3081–3143. Amsterdam: North Holland.

Scott, P. T. 2013. "Dynamic Discrete Choice Estimation of Agricultural Land Use." Working Paper. http://www.ptscott.com.

Shetty, K., K. Subbarao, O. Huisman, and J. Hubbard. 2000. "Mechanism of Broccoli-Mediated Verticillium Wilt Reduction in Cauliflower." *Phytopathology* 90:305–10.

Short, D. P. G., S. Gurung, S. T. Koike, S. J. Klosterman, and K. V. Subbarao. 2015. "Frequency of *Verticillium* Species in Commercial Spinach Fields and Transmission of *V. Dahliae* from Spinach to Subsequent Lettuce Crops." *Phytopathology* 105:80–90.

Subbarao, K. V., and J. C. Hubbard. 1996. "Interactive Effects of Broccoli Residue and Temperature on *Verticillium Dahliae* Microsclerotia in Soil and on Wilt in Cauliflower." *Phytopathology* 86:1303–10.

Subbarao, K. V., J. C. Hubbard, and S. T. Koike. 1999. "Evaluation of Broccoli Residue Incorporation into Field Soil for Verticillium Wilt Control in Cauliflower." *Plant Disease* 83:124–29.

Timmins, C. 2002. "Measuring the Dynamic Efficiency Costs of Regulators' Preferences: Municipal Water Utilities in the Arid West." *Econometrica* 70:603–29.

USEPA (United States Environmental Protection Agency). 2012a. "Critical Use Exemption Information." https://www.regulations.gov/document?D=EPA-HQ-OAR-2013-0369-0032.

USEPA (United States Environmental Protection Agency). 2012b. "The Phaseout of Methyl Bromide." https://www.epa.gov/ods-phaseout/methyl-bromide.

van Kooten, G. C., W. P. Weisensel, and D. Chinthammit. 1990. "Valuing Tradeoffs between Net Returns and Stewardship Practices: The Case of Soil Conservation in Saskatchewan." *American Journal of Agricultural Economics* 72:104–13.

Weisensel, W. P., and G. C. van Kooten. 1990. "Estimation of Soil Erosion Time Paths: The Value of Soil Moisture and Topsoil Depth Information." *Western Journal of Agricultural Economics* 15:63–72.

Wu, J. 2001. "Optimal Weed Control under Static and Dynamic Decision Rules." *Agricultural Economics* 25:119–30.

Xiao, C., and K. Subbarao. 1998. "Relationships between *Verticillium Dahliae* Inoculum Density and Wilt Incidence, Severity, and Growth of Cauliflower." *Phytopathology* 88:1108–15.

8

Willingness to Pay for Low Water Footprint Foods during Drought

Hannah Krovetz, Rebecca Taylor, and Sofia B. Villas-Boas

8.1 Introduction

In January 2014, the governor of California declared a Drought State of Emergency, asking all Californians to reduce water consumption by 20 percent.[1] While droughts are a recurring feature of California's climate, the drought beginning in late 2011 was the driest and warmest drought on record, putting California agriculture under stress (Hanak et al. 2015).[2] California—a major producer of dairy, tree nuts, fruits, and vegetables—relies heavily on irrigation, much of which is supplied by the state's extensive system of water supply infrastructure—reservoirs, managed groundwater basins, and interregional conveyance facilities.[3] Farmers have taken measures to adapt to drought conditions, such as by shifting toward less

Hannah Krovetz is an analyst at Analysis Group.

Rebecca Taylor is an assistant professor in the School of Economics at the University of Sydney.

Sofia B. Villas-Boas is a professor of agricultural and resource economics at the University of California, Berkeley.

We thank Peter Berck and participants at the NBER Understanding Productivity Growth in Agriculture Conference and especially Dmitri Taubinsky, Wolfram Schlenker, Christine Carroll, and Marca Weinberg for their discussion and suggestions. We thank the Giannini Foundation and the College of Natural Resources' Sponsored Program for Undergraduate Research for financial support in the survey implementation. For acknowledgments, sources of research support, and disclosure of the authors' material financial relationships, if any, please see https://www.nber.org/chapters/c13949.ack.

1. Source: California Department of Water Resources, "Governor's Drought Declaration," accessed April 28, 2017, http://www.water.ca.gov/waterconditions/declaration.cfm.

2. In 2015, the drought caused crop revenue losses of up to $902 million, with losses of $250 million in the dairy industry and $100 million in the feedlot industry (Howitt et al. 2015). There was also an increased fallowing of cropland due to lack of water, which led to rising food prices (Howitt et al. 2015).

3. California Department of Water Resources, "Drought in California," accessed April 28, 2017, http://www.water.ca.gov/wateruseefficiency/docs/2014/021114_Kent_Drought2012.pdf.

water-intensive crop varietals and by adopting more water-efficient irrigation methods (Hanak et al. 2015).[4] Given that the region may increasingly experience high temperatures and low precipitation flows (Mann and Gleick 2015), is there a market for consumers to compensate farmers for adopting more water-efficient production practices?

The rise of eco-labels has created a market for sustainable food options; however, currently a "low water footprint" label is not available to guide consumers who want to decrease the water footprint of their food consumption. Virtual water of an item—defined as the amount of water used during the entire production process, from planting to processing to distribution—varies greatly across California's top-grossing agricultural commodities (Mekonnen and Hoekstra 2011).[5] Changing consumers' dietary habits may have a significant impact on the sustainability of agriculture with regard to water constraints if consumers choose to purchase more water-efficient options. This chapter empirically assesses whether consumers respond to information on the water footprint of the food they choose and tests whether providing additional information on drought severity sways consumers to choose low water footprint (LWF) food options.

We investigate whether consumers are willing to pay for LWF agricultural products by designing and implementing a choice experiment via an online distributed survey of California consumers.[6] Before the choice experiment, we collect data on respondents' demographic characteristics and stated environmental concern. For the choice experiment, we present the respondents with four food products: avocados, almonds, lettuce, and tomatoes. Within each food product, survey respondents are asked their purchase choice among options that vary by production method (conventional or organic), water footprint (average or LWF), and price. In addition, we implement an information treatment in the survey design. Half of the respondents are randomly assigned to a treatment group, where they are briefed before the choice experiment about the drought severity in California. The control group is instead taken directly to the choice experiment, without additional information on the drought.

Using the survey data, we estimate a discrete choice model for consumer preferences, where a choice is defined as a bundle of attributes: product type, price, an organic indicator, and an LWF indicator. From the structural demand model parameters, we obtain estimates of the willingness to

---

4. Climate change and the resulting drought are leading to a new, lower baseline to which the agricultural sector is already adapting.

5. While nuts and tree fruit are more water intensive than lettuce, animal products such as milk, eggs, and beef are more water intensive than plant crops (Mekonnen and Hoekstra 2011). Thus it is not surprising that a diet high in animal products (mainly in Europe and the United States) uses about 1,321 gallons of water per capita per day, while diets low in animal products require about half that amount (Renault 2002).

6. Given that water usage labels currently are not implemented in the retail setting, we cannot use scanner data to measure actual consumer responses.

pay (WTP) for the various specified product attributes. In addition, we test whether revealing information on the drought matters for the WTP estimates. We are able to present novel findings in terms of heterogeneity of WTP along the respondents' demographics and their environmental scores and the role of drought information on WTP. Finally, by simulating a variety of changes in the choice set facing consumers, we obtain estimates of counterfactual choices under alternative policy scenarios and calculate the resulting welfare changes, measured as changes in the distribution of consumer surplus. We also relate the individual-level changes in consumer surplus to the demographic characteristics of the respondents.

We find that, on average, consumers have a significant positive marginal utility toward water efficiency and estimate that there is an implied positive willingness to pay for water efficiency of about 11 dollars. This positive WTP means that respondents are on average willing to pay 12 cents for each gallon of water saved. Moreover, informing consumers about the drought severity increases consumers' WTP for the LWF options, albeit not significantly. We additionally explore heterogeneity in WTP based on crop type and consumer characteristics. We find differences in the WTP along respondents' stated environmental concern, which is measured by level of agreement with statements pertaining the environmental issues and policies. There is also significant heterogeneity with respect to education and race. Using counterfactual simulations of removing LWF labels and drought information from the choice set attributes, we estimate changes in choices that imply significant consumer surplus losses, especially for the subgroup of respondents who are white, have attained higher levels of education, and have higher environmental scores.

The contribution of our chapter is twofold: (1) to estimate stated preferences and corresponding WTP for water efficiency in the production of crops and (2) to investigate whether consumers respond to information about drought severity and the water footprints of products in their choice sets. The availability of information about a product's attribute, such as water footprint, does not necessarily mean consumers will incorporate it into their decisions and alter their behavior. Our study provides a distribution of WTP estimates for LWF food options during drought years and an empirical test of whether consumers directly incorporate available information. In so doing, we equip resource managers with important information on the efficacy of LWF labels as well as a barometer reading on consumer stated preferences.

The rest of the chapter proceeds as follows. Section 8.2 reviews the related literature. Section 8.3 describes the empirical setting and the research design (i.e., the choice experiment and identification strategies) and summarizes the data. Section 8.4 outlines the model to estimate consumer choices and willingness to pay for product attributes. Section 8.5 presents the results of the choice model and discusses the findings in terms of the average WTP and the distribution of WTP in the sample. Section 8.6 derives the method to perform simulations and discusses the choice and welfare changes due to a counterfactual policy scenario. Finally, section 8.7 concludes and presents avenues of future research.

8.2   Literature Review

Related literature investigates consumer knowledge and market mechanisms to nudge consumers toward sustainable food products. With respect to consumer knowledge, Macdiarmid (2012) finds that fewer than 20 percent of respondents believe they would know how to make the necessary changes to create a sustainable diet. Smith (2008) also discusses how consumers often lack the knowledge or ability to discriminate between what is sustainable and what is not. However, Tait et al. (2011) find that, when evaluating consumer attitudes toward sustainability attributes, water efficiency is among the most important attributes of a food item, behind price and carbon footprint. With respect to market mechanisms, numerous studies have shown that providing consumers with information about product sustainability through "eco-labels" impacts consumer choices, such as the USDA organic seal (Kiesel and Villas-Boas 2007), sustainable seafood advisories (Hallstein and Villas-Boas 2013), dolphin-free tuna labels (Teisl, Roe, and Hicks 2002), and environmentally certified wood products (Aguilar and Vlosky 2007). Therefore, given consumers' stated lack of knowledge on the sustainability of their diets and the effectiveness of eco-labels in other settings, this chapter contributes to the literature by estimating how much consumers would value a water footprint label.

We follow closely and expand the existing revealed and stated preference literature, which uses a variety of reduced form and structural approaches to infer the value consumers place on product attributes that are not observable or tasteable by consumers at the point of purchase (such as organic, vitamin-fortified, dolphin-safe, free-range, rBGH-free). In the reduced-form context, hedonic price model approaches have been used to estimate relative values for food product attributes (Asche and Guillen 2012; Roheim, Gardiner, and Asche 2007; Roheim, Asche, and Santos 2011; Jaffry et al. 2004; McConnell and Strand 2000). Structurally, demand-system approaches are estimated to place a willingness to pay for product attributes (Alfnes et al. 2006; Teisl, Roe, and Hicks 2002). Our work is more closely related to this second literature stream and is the first to use these methods to place a value on water efficiency in the production of food and to ask whether consumers might be willing to pay for reduced environmental disamenities associated with food production.

While there are several means of agricultural adaptation in the context of water constraints and droughts—such as the observed increase in fallowing of irrigated acres, regional crop shifting, and groundwater depletion

(Howitt et al. 2015)—this chapter investigates whether there is willingness to pay for fewer gallons of water used within crop types. Changing food habits through information and labeling may have a significant impact on the water requirements of agriculture if consumers react to signals in the marketplace. A higher WTP supports an increase in price for a specific attribute, such as decreased virtual water footprint, because of the additional benefit to the consumer (Abidoye et al. 2011). There is very little, if any, empirical evidence on consumer reactions to information on water use in food production, and this chapter fills this gap in the literature. Being able to distinguish food products in the market will enable consumers to act on their values when presented with a choice between a conventional and a sustainable good. Such changes in demand and consumer awareness could spark a major production shift, just as organic agriculture did in the 2000s (Dimitri and Greene 2002).

8.3   Empirical Setting, Survey Design, and Data

We designed and implemented a choice experiment, with an information treatment, via an online survey of California consumers.[7] We collected survey responses from 193 California residents. For each of the respondents, we first asked for information on their demographic characteristics (i.e., gender, age, education, and race). Second, we asked respondents to answer whether they agreed or disagreed with 10 environmentally related statements in order to construct a measure of each respondent's environmental score. Finally, we collected data on the respondents' choices among options to purchase four food products: avocados, almonds, lettuce, and tomatoes. These four crops are highly ranked in terms of California's agricultural value and represent approximately 5 percent of California's 25.5 million operated farm acres.[8] In 2015, California produced more than a third of the country's vegetables and two-thirds of the country's fruits and nuts.[9] Moreover, in 2015, almonds were California's second most valued commodity ($5.33 billion), lettuce was fifth ($2.25 billion), and tomatoes were seventh (1.71 billion).[10]

In addition, we implemented an information treatment in the survey

---

7. The survey company ensured that there is no monetary prize to cause its audience to rush through to complete a survey. Rather, respondents decide which charity they want the survey company to donate for their response.

8. Source: National Agricultural Statistics Service, United States Department of Agriculture, "2015 State Agriculture Overview," accessed December 21, 2016, https://www.nass.usda.gov /Quick_Stats/Ag_Overview/stateOverview.php?state=CALIFORNIA.

9. Source: California Department of Food and Agriculture, "California Agricultural Production Statistics—2015 Crop Year Report," accessed April 28, 2017, https://www.cdfa.ca.gov /statistics/.

10. Source: California Department of Food and Agriculture, "California Agricultural Production Statistics—2015 Crop Year Report," accessed April 28, 2017, https://www.cdfa.ca.gov /statistics/.

design. Half of respondents were randomly assigned to a treatment group, where they were briefed about the drought severity in California before the choice experiment. The remaining half in the control group got taken directly to the choice experiment, without information on the drought.

To base the choice experiment on realistic numbers, we collect industry estimates on the virtual water used in avocado, almonds, lettuce, and tomatoes. Recall that virtual water is defined as the amount of water used per unit of food during its production (Renault 2002). The average water footprint displayed to survey respondents in our study—in terms of gallons per pound of product produced—is 157 gallons per pound for avocados, 1,715 gallons per pound of almonds, 14.8 gallons per pound for lettuce, and 16.9 gallons per pound of tomatoes.

The experiment asked respondents to choose, for each of a set of horticultural crops, between organic and conventional methods, with average water footprint and low water footprint. This 2 × 2 matrix gives rise to variation, which allows us to distinguish between organic methods and water efficiency—a specific environmental amenity. What we do not allow is for respondents to switch between different horticultural crops directly, while indirectly they may stop buying a crop and start buying a new one after receiving information on water usage.

8.3.1   Experimental Choice Design

This study uses a discrete choice experiment (1) to evaluate consumer preferences for water footprint as an attribute of food choices and (2) to calculate the difference in WTP between a treatment group with additional drought information and a control group.[11] Discrete choice experiments are among the most common methods for gathering stated preference and are rooted in Random Utility Models. The first step is to define a product as being made up of a set of attributes. Then respondents are asked to choose a single option, simulating the context that consumers are normally presented with in the marketplace (Tait et al. 2011). There is also an "I would not purchase any of these" option to allow for identification and counterfactual simulations (Gao and Schroeder 2009; Alfnes et al. 2006).[12]

We asked survey respondents to reveal their preferences for five different options within each of four food items—Haas avocados, almonds, head lettuce, and tomatoes—as can be seen in table 8.1. These items were chosen

---

11. See figure 8A.1 for the survey instrument. The information concerning the drought acts as the treatment, preceding the questions concerning preferences toward water footprint and organic production in food choices (i.e., the treatment information about the drought preceded the avocado first-choice question for the treatment group in figure 8A.1). The control group performed the choice experiment in figure 8A.1 without any additional information.

12. If we do not include an outside option, simulations that increase attributes in a way that the relative ratio of such attributes remains unchanged (such as all prices doubling) will imply that the relative probabilities of choosing the options also remains unchanged, and this is not reasonable if, for example, consumers are budget constrained.

Table 8.1   **Choice set design: Production method, water footprint, and price**

Product	Production method	Water footprint (gal/lb)	Price ($/lb)
Hass avocado			
	Conventional	Average (157)	0.98
	Organic	Average (157)	2.00
	Organic	Efficient (80)	2.40
	Conventional	Efficient (80)	1.18
Almond			
	Conventional	Average (1,715)	5.99
	Organic	Average (1,715)	11.59
	Organic	Efficient (1,450)	13.90
	Conventional	Efficient (1,450)	7.19
Lettuce (head)			
	Conventional	Average (14.8)	2.17
	Organic	Average (14.8)	5.00
	Organic	Efficient (5.9)	6.00
	Conventional	Efficient (5.9)	2.60
Tomatoes (fresh)			
	Conventional	Average (16.9)	1.56
	Organic	Average (16.9)	1.99
	Organic	Efficient (6.5)	2.39
	Conventional	Efficient (6.5)	1.87

Note: For each item there are two levels of variety (conventional or organic), two levels of water footprint (average and efficient), and four price levels to portray the four combinations of production method and water footprint. For all products, an option "I would not purchase any of these" was also given to respondents.

because avocados and almonds are high-value tree crops that are less adaptable to yearly environmental factors. They require more water than many field crops because the trees need to be maintained and watered year-round. Tomatoes and lettuce represent less permanent, more adaptable crops with lower water footprints. Each food item has three attributes: water footprint, price, and production method (either conventional or organic). Water footprint has two levels, average and low (or "efficient"). Since the production method and water footprint attributes both have two levels, there are 2 × 2 = 4 possible attribute-combinations per item, not counting price. Finally, we use the average price for conventional and organic versions of the products. In the choice options presented in the experiment, we add an invented 20 percent price premium if the item has efficient water use.

For a random subset of the respondents, additional information on the California drought and its impact on agriculture came before the choice experiment. This information was given to respondents in the form of a short summary statement and an infographic highlighting how much water goes into producing different foods. The information concerning the drought acts as a primer, or treatment, preceding the choice experiment questions. The control group performed the choice experiment without any additional

Table 8.2   Summary statistics

		California population*	Treated group respondents	Control group respondents	Total respondents
Panel A. Demographics					
Gender	Male	49.7	53.06	52.29	52.66
	Female	50.3	46.94	47.71	47.34
Age	17 or younger	24.4	1.83	2.04	1.93
	18–59	59.3	66.06	66.33	66.18
	60 or older	16.3	32.11	31.63	31.88
Education	Less than some college	60.4	27.78	37.76	32.52
	Associate degree, bachelor degree	27.8	31.48	29.59	30.58
	Graduate degree or more	11.8	40.74	32.65	36.89
HH income	$49,000 or less	41.5	26.42	31.25	28.71
	$50,000–$99,999	28.9	30.19	29.17	29.70
	$100,000 or more	29.4	43.40	39.58	41.58
Race	White (including Hispanic)	57.6	83.64	76.53	80.29
	Black, Asian, and other minorities	42.4	16.36	23.47	19.71
Number of observations		38.8 million	110	98	208
Panel B. Summary statistics of survey responses					
	Organic (share)		25.26	30.45	28.00
	LWF (share)		65.56	62.50	63.94
	None of the options (share)		20.92	17.05	18.87
	Average price of chosen options		2.86	3.14	3.01

Source for the California Data: 2014 CA Census Fact Finder Database.

information. By comparing average responses in the treatment and control groups, we can test the role of information on food choices and on the estimates of WTP inferred via the structural choice model. This is done under the assumption that the control group is a good counterfactual to the treatment group. The next subsection analyzes the balance of treatment and control groups and presents the summary statistics of the data used in the analysis.

8.3.2   Survey Data Summary Statistics

The survey instrument was sent to a total of 208 respondents, where the sample size was determined by financial constraints. Summary statistics of our data set are presented in table 8.2. This table is organized in two panels. In panel A, the demographic makeup of survey respondents in the treatment and control groups is compared to the total California population. In panel

B, we present the share of respondents choosing the organic and low water footprint attributes in the treatment and control groups.

In panel A of table 8.2, ages "17 or younger" in the survey sample are underrepresented compared to the California population. Furthermore, the "50–59" and "60 or older" age groups were overrepresented in the survey sample, suggesting that the sample data are skewed toward older populations. Similarly, panel A shows that education attainment levels of "Less than high school degree" and "High school degree or equivalent" are underrepresented in the survey sample and "Graduate degree" is overrepresented. Income levels in the sample overall are fairly representative of the California population, as is race and gender. When comparing the treatment and control groups to each other, we have balance across the demographic variables, with the makeup of the control and treatment groups similar for all rows in panel A.[13]

Turning now to the bottom panel B of table 8.2, we present survey response summary statistics for the share of respondents choosing organic and low water footprint (LWF) options and the average price of the alternative chosen. The row titled "Organic (share)" represents the fraction of events where a respondent chooses an organic option. A mean of 28 for the total means that survey respondents overall chose organic products 28 percent of the time. "LWF (share)" is the fraction of events in which a respondent chooses the lower water footprint option. For the total survey population, respondents choose a water-efficient option 64 percent of the time. Average price is the average of all prices of items chosen, which is $3.01. If a respondent chooses "I would not purchase any of these," the price is defined as zero. The treatment group has a lower average organic choice share than the control group (25 percent versus 30 percent) and a higher average LWF choice share (66 percent versus 63 percent). The treatment group has a lower average price paid for the chosen alternatives than the control group ($2.86 versus $3.14), which aligns with the treatment group choosing the $0 outside option more often (21 percent versus 17 percent).

Next we use the survey data to construct a measure of environmental concern of each respondent based on the degree of agreement/disagreement with a series of 10 statements regarding environmental issues and policies. Table 8.3 lists each of 10 statements and reports average survey responses. For each statement, we assign a value of 5 if the response is "Strongly agree" and 1 if the response is "Strongly disagree." The measure of environmental concern of each respondent, henceforth called environmental score, is the

---

13. An illustration of the balance of demographics in the control and treated group is presented in figures 8A.2 and 8A.3. We cannot reject that the average is similar between control and treated groups for any of the demographic variables. Moreover, we cannot reject the null in a Kolmogorov Smirnov test for equality of distributions between treatment and control groups for education (p-value = 0.936) and income (p-value = 0.481).

Table 8.3   **Response summary statistics for ten statements underlying environmental score**

Statement	Average (standard error)
1. Climate change is a result of human activities and is already affecting people worldwide.	4.05 (0.089)
2. Protecting the environment should be given utmost priority, even if it causes slower economic growth and some loss of jobs.	3.81 (0.084)
3. It is the government's responsibility to impose high taxes(on fossil fuels.	3.45 (0.097)
4. The US government should impose stricter laws on pollution.	3.97 (0.087)
5. People should pay higher prices to address climate change.	3.19 (0.096)
6. There should be more investment using tax dollars in alternative fuels.	3.80 (0.092)
7. People should make lifestyle changes to reduce environmental damage.	4.20 (0.074)
8. It is important to purchase things that are more environmentally friendly, even at a greater cost.	3.74 (0.083)
9. The current generation has a responsibility to protect the environment for future generations, even if it leaves them less well off.	3.83 (0.085)
10. Personal food choices can affect the environmental impact of agriculture.	3.96 (0.081)
Environmental score	38.01 (0.720)

sum of assigned values for all statements. This way, the environmental score has a minimum value of 10 if a respondent strongly disagrees with all 10 of the environmental statements and a maximum of 50 if the respondent strongly agrees with all of the same 10 statements. Table 8.3 shows that the average environmental score among all respondents is 38.01.[14]

8.4   Empirical Strategy to Estimate Willingness to Pay for Product Attributes

To analyze the impact of information on consumer choice, we define information provision via labels as an additional or differentiated product attribute. Recognizing that products can be defined as a bundle of perceived attributes provides the framework to compute consumers' willingness to pay for product attributes in a discrete choice model. Starting from a random utility framework (as in McFadden 1974, McFadden and Train 2000, and

14. The bottom right panel of figure 8A.2 shows that the average environmental score is balanced for the treatment and control groups, and given the confidence intervals, we cannot reject that the averages are similar. Furthermore, when comparing the full distributions in the top left panel of figure 8A.3 using kernel density estimates and in a Kolmogorov Smirnov equality of distributions test, a p-value of 0.943 implies that we cannot reject the null of equal distributions for the environmental score of respondents in the treatment and control groups.

Train 2003), where both the product attributes as well as the random term are assumed to enter linearly, the utility from consuming a certain product can be described as

$$(1) \qquad U_{ji} = X_j\beta_i + \varepsilon_{ji}.$$

The matrix X_j indicates the attributes of product j, the vector β_i indicates the marginal utility that individual i places on these attributes, and ε_{ji} indicates the error term.

Distributional assumptions about β_i and ε_{ij} drive the econometric model decision. If we assume that ε_{ij} is independently and identically distributed extreme value (type I), then we have a logit choice model. If we also specify

$$(2) \qquad \beta_i = \beta_0 + \beta_1 D_i,$$

then we have a mixed logit model, where the marginal utility coefficients vary according to the respondent's observed demographics D_i. This implies that different decision-makers may have different preferences. If instead we allow decision-makers to have different preferences due to a more general unobserved heterogeneity structure, and not just due to observable demographics, then we define the coefficients β_i to vary as

$$(3) \qquad \beta_i = \beta_0 + \beta_2 v_i,$$

where v_i is a normal random variable capturing any heterogeneity. If there is no heterogeneity in individual preferences relative to the average, then β_2 will be zero. If, however, there is heterogeneity in preferences relative to the average, then β_2 will be different from zero. If β_i is specified as (3), then we have a random coefficient logit model. This offers flexibility in incorporating consumer heterogeneity with regard to food choice attributes, such as organic and low water footprint.[15]

Third, if we define the coefficients β_i to be combination of the two previous heterogeneity specifications as

$$(4) \qquad \beta_i = \beta_0 + \beta_1 D_i + \beta_2 v_i,$$

we have a random coefficients mixed logit model with demographics as mixing parameters. If there is no heterogeneity in individual preferences relative to the average, then β_1 and β_2 will be zero. If, however, there is heterogeneity in preferences due to demographics relative to the average, then β_1 will be different from zero, and if there is additional random heterogeneity, then β_2 will be different from zero as well. This choice model offers flexibility in incorporating consumer heterogeneity with regard to food attributes as a function of D_i directly as well as allowing for random determinants of heterogeneity via v_i. This modeling approach combined with the unique choice experimental

---

15. To recover how D_i affects the departure from mean valuations, we project estimated β_i on observed demographics D_i in a second step.

setting and resulting data variation for agricultural food choices allows us to estimate consumers' valuation for water efficiency on average together with the complete distribution of valuation of survey respondents (as in Revelt and Train 2000 and Huber and Train 2001).[16]

Assuming that consumers choose one unit of product j among all the possible products available at a certain time that maximizes their indirect utility, then the probability that good j is chosen is the probability that good j maximizes consumer i's utility

(5) $\Pr(\text{Choice}_j) = \Pr(U_{ji} > U_{ki}) = \Pr(X_j\beta_i + \varepsilon_{ji} > X_k\beta_i + \varepsilon_{ki}), \forall k \neq j.$

Then the following closed-form solution can be derived for the probability that a respondent's product choice corresponds to product j as

(6) $$Prob_{ji} = \frac{e^{X_j\beta_i + \alpha \text{Price}_j}}{\sum_{k=0}^{N} e^{X_k\beta_i + \alpha \text{Price}_k}},$$

where $\alpha = \alpha_0$ is the marginal utility with respect to price, which is constant for all respondents, and β_i contains the marginal utilities relative to the remaining attributes X for respondent i. The mean utility of the option "I would not purchase any of these" presented to a respondent in the choice experiments is normalized to zero. In other words, the organic, LWF, and price variables for the outside option is set equal to zero in all the experimental choice cases. This implies that equation (6) becomes

(7) $$Prob_{ji} = \frac{e^{X_j\beta_i + \alpha \text{Price}_j}}{1 + \sum_{k=1}^{N} e^{X_k\beta_i + \alpha \text{Price}_k}}.$$

Finally, given that each respondent makes decisions for the four different products, defining $T = 4$ products and defining the distribution of the $\theta = (\alpha,\beta)$ parameters in general form as $f(\theta | \alpha_0, \beta_0, \beta_1, \beta_2)$, where β is specified in equations (2), (3), or (4) and $\alpha = \alpha_0$ for all respondents, then the probability of individual i making a sequence of choices among the five alternatives $(j = 0, \ldots 4)$ is given as

(8) $$S_i = \int \prod_{t=1}^{T} \prod_{j=0}^{4} \left[\frac{e^{X_{ijt}\beta_i + \alpha \text{Price}_{jt}}}{1 + \sum_{k=1}^{N} e^{X_{ikt}\beta_i + \alpha \text{Price}_{kt}}} \right]^{Y_{ijt}} f(\theta | \alpha 0, \beta_0, \beta_1, \beta_2) d\theta,$$

where $Y_{ijt} = 1$ if the respondent i chooses alternative j for situation t and 0 otherwise. Given a total of I respondents, the parameters $(\alpha = \alpha_0, \beta_0, \beta_1, \beta_2)$ are estimated by maximizing the simulated log-likelihood function

(9) $$SLL = \sum_{i=1}^{I} \ln \left(\frac{1}{R} \sum_{r=1}^{R} \prod_{t=1}^{T} \prod_{j=0}^{4} \left[\frac{e^{X_{ijt}\beta_i^{[r]} + \alpha \text{Price}_{jt}}}{1 + \sum_{k=1}^{N} e^{X_{ikt}\beta_i^{[r]} + \alpha \text{Price}_{kt}}} \right]^{Y_{ijt}} \right),$$

where $\beta_i^{[r]}$ is the r-th draw for respondent i from the distribution of β.

---

16. To recover how D_i affects the departure from mean valuations, we project estimated β_i on observed demographics D_i in a second step.

8.4.1   Estimating Average and Heterogeneous Marginal Utility and Willingness to Pay

To estimate β_i, we proceed as follows. Given that the expected value of β, conditional on a given response Y_i of individual i and a set of alternatives characterized by X_i for product t, is given by

$$(10) \quad E[\beta | Y_i, X_i] = \frac{\int \beta \prod_{t=1}^{T} \prod_{j=0}^{4} \left[\left(e^{X_{ijt}\beta + \alpha \text{Price}_{jt}} \right) \Big/ \left(1 + \sum_{k=1}^{N} e^{X_{ikt}\beta + \alpha \text{Price}_{kt}} \right) \right]^{Y_{ijt}} f(\beta | \beta_0, \beta_1, \beta_2) d\beta}{\int \beta \prod_{t=1}^{T} \prod_{j=0}^{4} \left[\left(e^{X_{ijt}\beta + \alpha \text{Price}_{jt}} \right) \Big/ \left(1 + \sum_{k=1}^{N} e^{X_{ikt}\beta + \alpha \text{Price}_{kt}} \right) \right]^{Y_{ijt}} f(\beta | \beta_0, \beta_1, \beta_2) d\beta},$$

then equation (9) can be thought of as the conditional average of the coefficient for the subgroup of individuals who face the same alternatives and make the same choices. For each individual i, we estimate a certain attribute's β_i, following Revelt and Train (2000), by simulation according to the following

$$(11) \quad \hat{\beta}_i = \frac{(1/R) \sum_{r=1}^{R} \beta_i^{[r]} \prod_{t=1}^{T} \prod_{j=0}^{4} \left[\left(e^{X_{ijt}\beta_i^{[r]} + \alpha \text{Price}_{jt}} \right) \Big/ \left(1 + \sum_{k=1}^{N} e^{X_{ikt}\beta_i^{[r]} + \alpha \text{Price}_{kt}} \right) \right]^{Y_{ijt}}}{(1/R) \sum_{r=1}^{R} \prod_{t=1}^{T} \prod_{j=0}^{4} \left[\left(e^{X_{ijt}\beta_i^{[r]} + \alpha \text{Price}_{jt}} \right) \Big/ \left(1 + \sum_{k=1}^{N} e^{X_{ikt}\beta_i^{[r]} + \alpha \text{Price}_{kt}} \right) \right]^{Y_{ijt}}},$$

where $\beta[r]$ is the r-th draw for individual i from the estimated i's distribution of β.

The resulting estimates of each respondent's WTP for a particular attribute x are obtained as the ratio of β_i and the marginal utility with respect to price α. We can therefore recover not just the average WTP but also the distribution of the WTP in the sample of respondents, and standard errors are obtained using the Delta Method. Finally, we relate the estimated willingness to pay (WTP_i) to each respondent's demographics and environmental scores by estimating the equation

$$(12) \qquad\qquad WTP_i = \gamma_0 + \gamma_1 D_i + \varepsilon_i^w,$$

where WTP_i is a vector of all respondents' individually estimated willingness to pay for the LWF alternatives, D_i are the demographic characteristics (including the environmental score) of respondent i, and γ_0, γ_1 are parameters to be estimated.

8.5   Results

First we present the results from the choice estimates originating from a conditional logit specification. In this first step, we investigate whether there is significant average stated marginal utility for LWF options as well as stated heterogeneity in the marginal utility as a function of observable characteristics of the respondents in terms of demographics and environmental score. Second, we explore a more flexible random coefficients choice model, allowing the heterogeneity to vary from the average marginal utility in a random fashion. Third, we include D_i as mixing parameters directly and estimate the random coefficients mixed logit model. Given that the conditional logit, as well as the random coefficient logit and the random coefficient mixed logit models, is estimated by maximizing the likelihood and simulated likelihood, respectively, we perform model comparisons using the Akaike information criterion (AIC) among the estimated specifications and discuss the best specification used moving forward.

The average marginal utility as well as each respondents' marginal utility are estimated using simulated maximum likelihood (Revelt and Train 2000). The intuition behind the estimation is that each respondent's β_i is computed as a conditional average of the βs of respondents similar to them, in that they make similar sequences of choices when presented with the same options in the experimental design and have similar demographics D_i. Each respondent's WTP for the LWF attribute is then obtained as the ratio between the β_i and the marginal utility of price α.

The variation in estimated individual departures from the average WTP can be either purely random or due to the fact that respondents have similar characteristics. This is investigated by correlating the estimated WTP_i with respondents' demographics and environmental scores.

8.5.1   Conditional Logit Estimates

In table 8.4, we present the estimates of the conditional logit choice model specification, where β_i are given by equation (2). The dependent variable in all of the columns is an indicator variable that is equal to one if an individual chose that alternative and equal to zero otherwise. There are five alternatives to choose from in each of four product groups. All specifications include individual fixed effects controlling for constant characteristics that may affect their choice behavior on average as well as product fixed effects to control constant characteristics of each agricultural product.

In column (1), the right-hand-side variables are the price, an "Organic" dummy that is equal to one if the alternative is organic and equal to zero otherwise, an indicator *LWF* equal to one for if the alternative has a low water footprint and equal to zero otherwise, and interactions *Treat* × *Organic* and *Treat* × *LWF*, where Treat is equal to one if the respondent was in the information treatment group. From the estimates in column (1), we see that the coefficient on price is negative and significant, meaning that a high price lowers the marginal utility of purchasing an alternative. The marginal utility of the organic attribute is negative but not significantly different from zero. The LWF attribute has an average marginal utility of 1.272, which is positive and significant. Finally, while being in the treatment group does not imply a higher marginal utility for the LWF attribute, given the nonsignificant coefficient of the interaction *Treat* × *LWF*, being in the treatment group implies a significantly lower marginal utility for the organic attribute, given the negative and significant coefficient of the interaction *Treat* × *Organic*.

Table 8.4   **Conditional logit choice estimates**

	Condit. logit (1)	Condit. logit (2)
Price	–0.139***	–0.146***
	(0.019)	(0.020)
Organic	–0.164	–0.152
	(0.120)	(0.123)
LWF	1.272***	–2.382***
	(0.109)	(0.440)
Treat × LWF	0.179	0.297*
	(0.148)	(0.161)
Treat × Organic	–0.297*	–0.285*
	(0.160)	(0.164)
Env × LWF		0.053***
		(0.008)
Edu × LWF		0.430***
		(0.108)
White × LWF		0.690***
		(0.188)
No. of obs.	4160	3,960
Log likelihood	–1,168.959	–1,074.598
AIC	2,347.919	2,165.195
Product FE	Yes	Yes
Respondent FE	Yes	Yes

Note: Robust standard errors in parentheses. * $p < 0.10$, ** $p < 0.05$, *** $p < 0.01$. The table displays the estimates of conditional logit regressions where the dependent variable is equal to one if an alternative out of 5 is chosen and equal to zero otherwise. *Organic* = 1 for organic choices. *LWF* = 1 for low water footprint choices—that is, the more efficient characteristic. *Treat* = 1 if the respondent received the information treatment. Specification (2) also includes the interaction of *LWF* and respondent characteristics. Only the significant coefficients are reported due to space in column (2). Respondents' AIC reports the Akaike's information criterion for model specification testing.

In column (2), we further interact demographic characteristics such as age, income, education, gender, and environmental score with the variables in column (1). This specification in column (2) allows us to estimate the average marginal utility for all variables in column (1) as well as departures from those averages with respect to the observable characteristics of the respondents. Even though all the lower-order terms of triple interactions are included in the specification in column (2), they are not all reported in table 8.4 due to space limitations. The number of observations drops in column (2) because not all respondents gave us complete demographic information.

First, we find that the log likelihood increases to –1075, relative to –1169 in column (1), implying that we explain more of the variation in choices with this specification. Moreover, when comparing models, the second specification is preferred, given its lower AIC estimate. Second, the marginal utility of price remains negative and significant. Third, there is heterogeneity for the LWF attribute in specification (2) that the averages in (1) mask, given that several coefficients associated with the interaction of demographics and product attributes are statistically different from zero. In particular, the marginal utility for the LWF attribute increases significantly with the environmental score (given the positive and significant coefficient of 0.053), increases with education (coefficient of 0.430), and increases for white respondents (coefficient of 0.690). None of the other demographics significantly affect the marginal utility with respect to the LWF attribute. Fourth, there is no organic marginal utility heterogeneity. Finally, none of the triple interactions terms, such as $Treat \times LWF \times D_i$, are significant for any D_i. This implies that there is no differential heterogeneity in the treatment group and in the control group in the way respondents value organic or low water footprint options depending on their observable demographics and environmental score.

We next turn to a mixed logit specification—a more flexible choice specification where we allow the average taste parameters to vary randomly for the respondents and not just as a function of a set of observable respondents' characteristics. We also compare the log likelihood of these nested model specifications and test whether conditioning on demographics or allowing for random heterogeneity explains more of the observed variation in the choices of different consumers when faced with the choice experiment design.

8.5.2   Random Coefficients Logit Choice Estimates

In the first two columns of table 8.5, we present the estimates of the random coefficients logit choice model specification, where β_i are given by equation (3). The dependent variable in all of the columns is an indicator variable that is equal to one if an individual chose that alternative and equal to zero otherwise. There are five alternatives to choose from in each of four product groups. All specifications include respondent fixed effects controlling for constant characteristics that may affect their choice behavior on average. In columns (1) and (2), the right-hand-side variables are the same as in column (1) of table 8.4; however, in column (1), we allow for unobserved random heterogeneity in the two product attributes LWF and $Organic$, and in column (2), we additionally allow the information treatment parameters to have random unobserved heterogeneity by estimating a random coefficient for $Treat \times LWF$ and $Treat \times Organic$.

The top half of table 8.5 (labeled "Mean") reports the average estimated marginal utilities. The price coefficient is negative and significant in columns (1) and (2) of table 8.5 and in the same magnitude of the marginal utility estimates of price for the conditional logit specifications in table 8.4. From the estimates in column (1), we see that the coefficient of price is negative and

Table 8.5	Random coefficient and mixed logit choice estimates		
	Random coeff. logit (1)	Random coeff. logit (2)	Mixed logit (3)
Mean			
Price	−0.191***	−0.191***	−0.194***
	(0.023)	(0.023)	(0.024)
Organic	−0.683**	−0.637**	−0.685**
	(0.305)	(0.301)	(0.317)
LWF	1.546***	1.516***	−2.735***
	(0.191)	(0.179)	(0.674)
Treat × Organic	−0.518	−0.646	−0.665
	(0.421)	(0.492)	(0.505)
Treat × LWF	0.252	0.325	0.391
	(0.267)	(0.281)	(0.255)
Env × LWF			0.058***
			(0.013)
Edu × LWF			0.521***
			(0.169)
White × LWF		a	0.822***
			(0.299)
SD			
LWF	1.427***	1.250***	0.998***
	(0.174)	(0.223)	(0.212)
Organic	2.409***	2.270***	2.362***
	(0.279)	(0.345)	(0.349)
Treat × Organic		1.197	1.316
		(1.014)	(0.957)
Treat × LWF		1.088**	0.841*
		(0.513)	(0.465)
No. of obs.	4,160	4,160	3,960
Log likelihood	−1,059.665	−1,058.920	−983.592
AIC	2,133.329	2,135.841	1,991.184
Respondent FE	Yes	Yes	

Note: Robust standard errors in parentheses. * $p < 0.10$, ** $p < 0.05$, *** $p < 0.01$. The table displays the estimates of mixed logit regressions where the dependent variable is equal to one if an alternative out of 5 is chosen and equal to zero otherwise. *Organic* = 1 for organic choices. *LWF* = 1 for low water footprint choices. *Treat* = 1 if the respondent received the information treatment. AIC reports the Akaike's information criterion for model specification testing.

significant, meaning that a high price lowers the marginal utility of purchasing an alternative. The average marginal utility of the organic attribute is negative and significant. The LWF attribute has an average marginal utility that is positive and significant. Finally, being in the treatment group does not imply a higher marginal utility for the LWF attribute nor for the organic attribute, given the nonsignificant coefficients of the interactions *Treat* × *LWF* and *Treat* × *Organic*.

The bottom half of table 8.5 (labeled "SD") reports the standard errors of estimated marginal utilities. There is significant heterogeneity in the marginal utility of the two attributes, given the significant and positive coefficients for the standard errors of the LWF and organic marginal utilities.

8.5.3   Random Coefficients Mixed Logit Choice Estimates

Next, we investigate whether a random coefficient mixed logit presents itself as the preferred specification to move forward in estimating WTP and performing policy simulations. In the third column of table 8.5, we present the estimates of the random coefficients mixed logit choice model specification, where β_i are given by equation (4). In addition to the random coefficients in column (2), in column (3) we additionally allow the demographic characteristics and environmental score to interact with the *LWF*, choosing the interactions that yielded significant coefficients in the conditional logit specification in table 8.4.

For the mean marginal utilities in column (3), the price coefficient is negative and significant and in the same magnitude of the marginal utility estimates of price for the random coefficients logit in columns (1) and (2) as well as in the same magnitude as the conditional logit specifications in table 8.4. As we would expect, this means that a higher price lowers the marginal utility of purchasing an alternative. The mean marginal utility of the organic attribute is negative and significant. The *LWF* attribute has an average marginal utility of −2.735, which is negative and significant and is different from the point estimates in column (1) and (2), since now the *LWF* attribute is interacted with demographics. To get the average marginal utility for the *LWF* attribute we need to add the mean coefficient of −2.735 to the coefficient of the demographic interactions times the average demographics, which we do later.

Finally, being in the treatment group does not imply a higher mean marginal utility for the LWF or Organic attribute, given the nonsignificant coefficients of the interactions *Treat × LWF* and *Treat × Organic.* One possible reason the information treatment about the drought was ineffective is that California residents were already aware of the severity of the highly publicized drought. According to Google trends, web searches for the phrase "California drought" in California have been high since the beginning of 2014.[17] Providing additional information that consumers already consider when faced with a low water footprint label would not lead to a behavioral response.

Looking at the deviations from the mean marginal utilities, reported in the bottom of table 8.5 under the label "SD," there is significant heterogeneity in the marginal utility of the two attributes. This is evidenced by the positive and significant estimates of standard deviations of the LWF and organic marginal utilities.

---

17. Source: Google Trends, "California Drought" web searches, accessed April 28, 2017, https://www.google.com/trends/explore?geo=US-CA q=california%20drought.

To interpret the point estimates for the attribute of interest, we obtain the mean marginal utility for the LWF attribute by adding up the mean marginal utility of −2.735 with the heterogeneous marginal utilities estimated by interactions with demographics.[18] The sum of the average marginal utility and all the heterogeneity terms equals 1.78, an estimate that is larger but in the ballpark of the estimates in columns (1) and (2) of table 8.5.

Moving forward, we choose the model that better predicts the choices made by respondents in our sample using the AIC. The AIC is like a log likelihood ratio test with an extra adjustment in terms of number of regressors in the specifications for different models. When testing between models, we choose the model that has the lowest absolute value of the AIC. We compare all columns of tables 8.4 and 8.5 using the reported AIC. We choose column (3) of table 8.5 because it is the model that has the lowest AIC, equal to 984. In the remainder of this chapter, we will use this random coefficient mixed logit as the specification to estimate respondents' distribution of marginal utilities and the distribution of WTP and to perform counterfactual policy simulations.

8.5.4 Willingness to Pay for Low Water Footprint Attribute and Willingness to Pay for Gallons of Water Saved

Given the estimated model parameters in column (3) of table 8.5, we start by estimating the distribution of the respondents' individual marginal utilities and resulting WTP_i with respect to the attribute of interest.

Each individual β_i is estimated using equation (11) and then divided by the marginal utility of price α to obtain each WTP_i. The top left panel of figure 8.1 displays the kernel density of the distribution of WTP_i for the LWF attribute, and the top right panel breaks up the average estimated WTP for the white subgroup and the nonwhite subgroup. The two bottom panels relate estimated WTP to two demographic characteristics of the respondents.

We estimate that the average WTP is 11.02 dollars for the LWF attribute. Given that this attribute is associated with an average saving of 90.4 gallons, then the average WTP per gallon saved is 11.02/90.4, which is equal to 12 cents per gallon of water saved. In particular, we estimate the WTP to be 5.4 cents per gallon saved in the production of avocados, 9.3 cents per gallon saved in the production of almonds, 48 cents per gallon saved in the production of tomatoes, and 1.3 cents for one gallon of water saved in the production of lettuce.

Furthermore, the estimated distribution of WTP in the top left panel of figure 8.1 is not concentrated at the average WTP, suggesting that there

---

18. The heterogeneity part is equal to the marginal utility with respect to environmental score and LWF interaction (0.058) times the average environmental score (35.6) plus the marginal utility with respect to low water footprint and education (0.52) times the average education (3.5, recall that education is classified in increasing levels of school attained, from 1 to 4), plus the marginal utility for white and LWF (0.058) times the share of white respondents (77 percent).

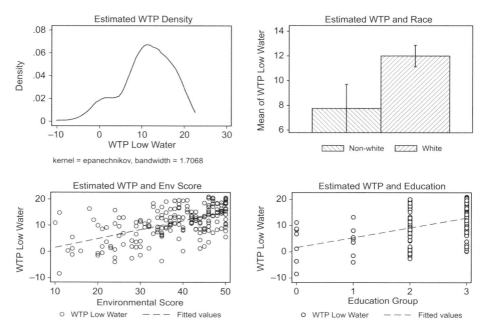

Fig. 8.1   Estimated WTP for low water attribute, for entire sample and by respondent characteristics

Notes: The figure displays the kernel density of the distribution of estimated WTP for the LWF attribute and then relates the estimated WTP for respondents to the respondents' demographics. Estimates are based on mixed logit choice specification with demographics and random coefficients. Education is considered in four ranges: education = 1 if "less than high school degree," education = 2 if "high school degree or equivalent (e.g., GED)," education = 3 if "some college but no degree or associate degree," and finally, education = 4 if "bachelor degree or graduate degree."

is heterogeneity in the value of the LWF attribute. Looking first into race, breaking up the WTP by white and nonwhite subgroups of respondents, does render significant differences in WTP, as we can see in the right panel of figure 8.1, where the average for white respondents is higher than for nonwhite respondents. Illustrative evidence in the two bottom panels of figure 8.1 suggests that there is a positive relationship between the respondents' estimated WTP and the environmental score of respondents as well as a positive relationship between the estimated WTP and the respondents' increasing degree of education attained. When sorting individuals by increasing environmental score on the horizontal axis, we fit an upward sloping linear OLS model estimate from regressing WTP and environmental score, as depicted by the fitted values in the upward sloping line in the bottom left panel of figure 8.1. The same happens for the scatter plot of WTP and education levels as shown in the bottom right panel data scatter plot and upward sloping linear fitted values.

Heterogeneity in the WTP is formally investigated by estimating equation

Table 8.6	Regression of respondents' mixed logit WTP estimates on demographics
	WTP for LWF characteristic
	(1)
Env.	0.304***
	(0.037)
Income	0.195
	(0.289)
Educ.	2.403***
	(0.465)
Age	−0.078
	(0.218)
Female	0.709
	(0.623)
White	4.277***
	(0.739)
Constant	−12.814***
	(1.610)
No. of obs.	193
R-squared	0.530

Note: Robust standard errors in parentheses. * $p < 0.10$, ** $p < 0.05$, *** $p < 0.01$.

(12), a linear regression of the estimated individual WTP, and the characteristics of the respondents. The estimates are reported in table 8.6. While income, age, and gender are not significantly correlated with the WTP for the low water option, a respondent's stated level of education and environmental score are both positively correlated with WTP. The white subgroup of the respondents also has a significantly higher WTP than their nonwhite counterparts.

8.6   Choice Changes and Welfare Changes in Counterfactual Policy Simulations

Finally, we ask the counterfactual question of what would happen to respondents' choices and consumer welfare, ceteris paribus, were there to be no water footprint information revealed to consumers. To answer this question, we perform simulations and compute the maximizing utility choices for each respondent in this counterfactual scenario. With that, we are able to simulate respondents' new choices and estimate the distribution of changes in respondents' consumer surplus. To assess who loses and who wins, we project the changes in consumer surplus on respondents' demographics and environmental scores in the final step.

8.6.1   Simulating Respondents Counterfactual Choices

For each counterfactual scenario, we keep respondents' preferences unchanged, which in practice means that the marginal utility parameters are not changing from the baseline model presimulation. To estimate choices given the model parameters, we estimate the probabilities of each attribute being chosen in each product (avocados, almonds, lettuce, and tomatoes) by all respondents, given the data on the attributes presimulation as in equation (7). In so doing, we obtain the predicted presimulation baseline choices for all respondents. Then we change the vector or vectors of attributes under the counterfactual scenario considered, defined as $\tilde{X}$, and recompute the probabilities that each respondent would make under this scenario for all cases, using the new attributes in equation (7). For example, simulating no low water footprint labels means that all products are indistinguishable in this counterfactual scenario along the LWF attribute, which means in practice that $X_{ij,LWF} = 0, \forall i, j$, which also implies that all interactions with that attribute are zero in the scenario.

8.6.2   Estimating Consumer Welfare Changes in Policy Simulations

Estimates of changes in consumer surplus (CS) are derived through simulation of consumer choices under counterfactual compositions of their attribute choice sets. These correspond to a respondent's compensating variation for a change in product attributes (Small and Rosen 1981). The expected consumer surplus, CS_i, is defined as

$$(13) \qquad CS_i = \frac{1}{\alpha} \ln \sum_j e^{X_j \beta_i - \alpha Price_j},$$

where α denotes the marginal utility of price. We estimate the consumer surplus for the choices as they are and for the best alternative when the LWF attribute is removed and when there is no longer a drought information treatment. Changes in consumer surplus are then obtained for each respondent. We estimate the average change in consumer surplus as well as how changes in consumer surplus are related to respondents' individual demographic characteristics and environmental score by estimating the following equation

$$(14) \qquad \Delta(CS)_i = \delta_0 + \delta_1 D_i + \varepsilon_i^{cs},$$

where $\Delta(CS)_i$ is a vector of all the respondents' individually estimated changes in CS for the policy simulation of no drought information and no LWF label, D_i are the demographic characteristics (including the environmental score) of respondent i, and δ_0, δ_1 are parameters to be estimated.

8.6.3   Policy Simulation of Removing Low Water Footprint and Drought Information

First, we estimate the predicted average probabilities of the choices for each of the five alternatives given the estimated parameters of column (3) in table 8.5. These are depicted in the left panel of figure 8.2 with the confidence intervals for each alternative. Recall that alternative 1 (A1) is the conventional and average water footprint option, alternative 2 (A2) is conventional and low water footprint, alternative 3 (A3) is organic and average water footprint, alternative 4 (A4) is organic and low water footprint, and alternative 5 (A5) is none of the above.

In the baseline, all the average predicted probabilities are statistically significantly different from each as given by the confidence intervals in figure 8.2. The option most chosen, as predicted by the model, is A2 (conventional and LWF). The next option is A4 (organic and LWF). The third most chosen is the outside option, A5 (none of the above). The least chosen option is A3 (organic and average water footprint).

When simulating the counterfactual choices of removing the LWF labels from the information set of the respondents, the average predicted probabilities change significantly relative to the baseline, as given by the right panel of figure 8.2. Now the most chosen option is not to select any of the four options—namely, A5. A2 and A4 (the LWF options) drop significantly relative to baseline. A3's probability of being chosen is now significantly different from zero, as respondents switched from A4 toward A3. This is because both A3 and A4 are organic, A3 is cheaper than A4, and now there is no reason to buy A4, given that the LWF label is not available as differentiation. The same happens for A1 and A2—A2 drops relative to baseline and A1 increases, as A1 is cheaper than A2 and both are conventional products. In terms of welfare, since the outside option increases so much and its utility is normalized to zero, it is expected that those consumers who switch to A5 have a lower utility than before.[19] We investigate formally the changes in respondents' consumer surplus by comparing the baseline and the counterfactual scenario's compensated variation for all respondents.

Figure 8.3 presents the estimated changes in consumer surplus for the respondents when they are faced with the same five options, but A2 and A4 are no longer identified as low water footprint, and they are no longer given an information treatment on the drought. The top left panel of this figure depicts the kernel density of the distribution of changes in consumer surplus for all respondents. Most of the consumers lose, given that most of the mass is below 0, some respondents stay the same, while a small proportion of the distribution covers positive welfare changes. Overall, the visual evidence suggests that this policy experiment has a net welfare loss.

In the remaining panels of figure 8.3, we relate the changes in simulated consumer surplus to respondents' characteristics. The top right panel shows an almost flat but slightly negative fitted linear regression of changes in consumer surplus with respondents' environmental scores. In the left bottom panel, it appears that the average change in consumer surplus is more negative for lower educated subgroups than for higher educated subgroups, although those differences are not statistically different from each other. In

19. All products exhibit similar changes in probabilities.

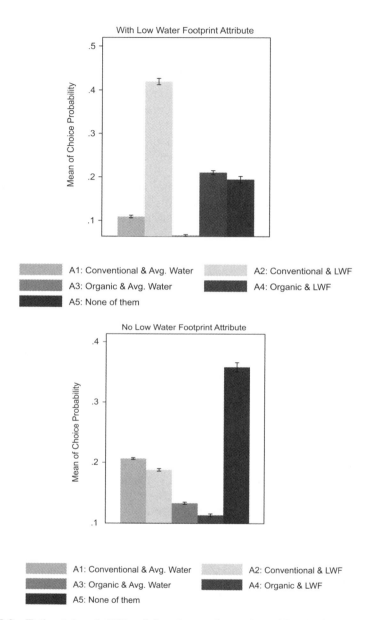

Fig. 8.2 Estimated probability of choosing an alternative, with and without a low water footprint attribute

Notes: The figure displays the average estimated probabilities, and confidence intervals, of choosing the five alternatives with and without an LWF attribute. Estimates are based on the random coefficients mixed logit choice specification with demographics and random coefficients. The five alternatives are (1) conventional and average water, (2) conventional and low water, (3) organic and average water, (4) organic and low water, and (5) none of them.

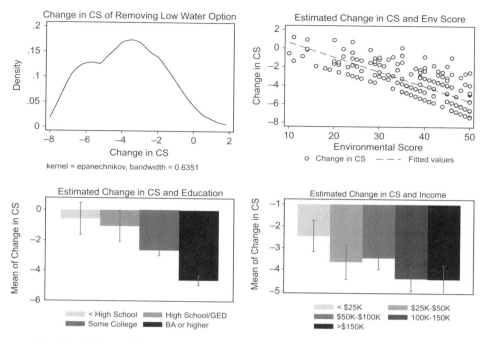

Fig. 8.3   Estimated change in consumer surplus with and without a low water attribute

Notes: The figure displays the kernel density of the distribution of changes in CS with and without the LWF attribute. Estimates are based on mixed logit choice specification. Education is considered in four ranges: less than high school degree, high school degree or equivalent (e.g., GED), some college or associate degree, and bachelor degree or graduate degree. Income is classified into five ranges: less than $25,000, $25,000–49,999, $50,000–$99,999, $100,000–149,999, and $150,000 or more.

the bottom right, we also see a nonlinear relationship between respondents' income and respondents' average change in consumer surplus.

We test whether there are significant heterogeneous changes in consumer surplus by estimating equation (12). These estimates are reported in table 8.7. On average, respondents lose 3.35 dollars in terms of surplus from this policy experiment. Given that the average price of the chosen option is about 3 dollars, this is a large loss and corresponds to the most action being driven by consumers who switch to the outside option of not consuming anything. The findings in table 8.7 are consistent with the graphical correlations in the top right and bottom panels of figure 8.3. Higher education and being white are negatively and significantly correlated with consumer surplus losses. A higher environmental score is correlated with a larger consumer surplus loss, although the negative point estimate is economically very small and not significant. Respondents' income is uncorrelated with consumer surplus losses, given the insignificant coefficient associated with increases in income.

Table 8.7   Regression of change in consumer surplus estimates on demographics

	Change in CS (1)
Env.	−0.142***
	(0.005)
Income	−0.012
	(0.032)
Educ.	−1.057***
	(0.091)
Age	−0.042
	(0.034)
Female	−0.036
	(0.097)
White	−1.933***
	(0.128)
Constant	7.045***
	(0.470)
Num. of obs.	193
R-squared	0.929

Note: Change in consumer estimates from simulation of removing LWF option. Robust standard errors in parentheses. * $p < 0.10$, ** $p < 0.05$, *** $p < 0.01$.

From the top left panel of figure 8.3, we identify a large proportion of respondents who lose and also a smaller proportion of respondents who do not lose in this policy experiment. To understand this heterogeneity, figure 8.4 breaks up the baseline choices (top panels) and simulated predicted choices (bottom panels) for those who have a net loss (left panels) and for those who do not (right panels). We can now see that the ones who have no welfare losses (right panels) were those respondents whose preferred alternative was A5 (i.e., none of them), then A1 and A3, and lastly A2 and A4, which are the LWF options. It is therefore not surprising that welfare does not drop for these consumers due to the policy. Welfare actually increases slightly for these respondents due to random factors affecting utility. In the left panels, the net losers were those consumers who preferred A2 and A4 and due to the policy had the largest inconvenience and had to make significantly different choices from the top left to the bottom left panel.

Finally, we estimate that total welfare drops, given that the sum of changes in consumer surplus is −749.2 for the losers and 3.77 for the nonlosers in the survey sample. Given that the sample is more educated, has higher income, and is more white than the California average, and because we find greater consumer surplus losses for those who are white, educated, and wealthier, we may be overestimating the welfare losses in California. We reweight each consumer surplus change estimate to reflect the California distribution of income, race, and education and recompute the total change in the reweighted change in consumer surplus. The histogram of changes in consumer surplus for the survey sample (dark bars) and the histogram of

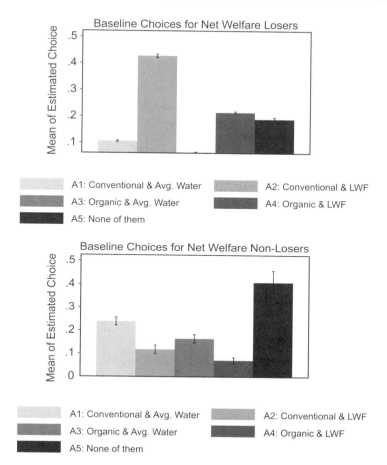

Fig. 8.4   Estimated probability of choosing alternatives, with and without a low water attribute and for net welfare losers and nonlosers

Notes: The figure displays the average estimated probabilities, and confidence intervals, of choosing the five alternatives with the LWF attribute (baseline top panels) and without LWF attribute (simulated bottom panels). Estimates are based on the random coefficients mixed logit choice specification for net welfare losers (left panels) and nonlosers (right panels). The five alternatives are (1) conventional and average water, (2) conventional and low water, (3) organic and average water, (4) organic and low water, and (5) none of them.

changes in consumer surplus for the reweighted California (light bars) are depicted in figure 8.5. We see that most of the mass of the reweighted histograms for income (top left), education (top right), age (bottom left), and race (bottom right) shifts to the right, meaning that the sample was indeed overstating the welfare losses relative to the CA population. We obtain a total net loss of −237 dollars when reweighting by income, −268 when reweighting by education, −323 when reweighting by age, and −415 when reweighting to match the race distribution in California. While these are all lower estimates

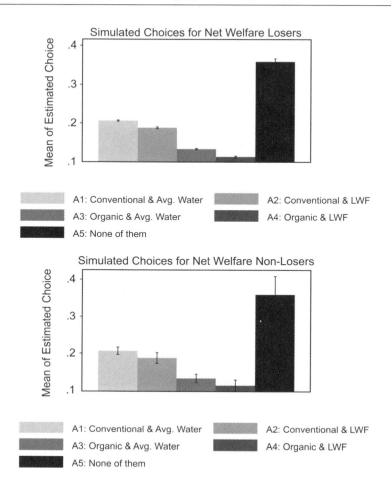

Fig. 8.4   (cont.)

of welfare losses than the sample estimate of −745, they are significantly different than zero.

8.7   Conclusion

In the context of recent California drought years, we investigate empirically whether consumers are willing to pay for more efficient water usage in the production of four California agricultural products. We implement an Internet survey choice experiment for avocados, almonds, lettuce, and tomatoes to elicit consumer valuation for water efficiency via revealed choices. We estimate a model of consumer demand where a product is defined as a bundle of three attributes: price, production method (conventional or

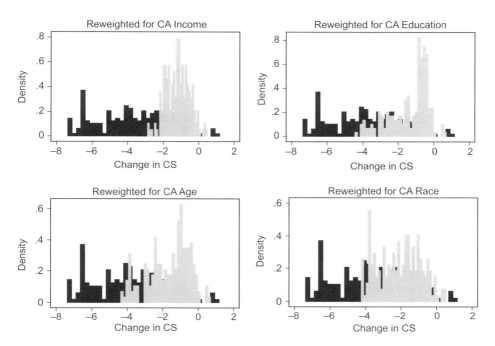

Fig. 8.5   Histograms of changes in consumer surplus for the survey sample (dark bars) and for the survey sample reweighted to the California distribution of demographics (light bars)

Notes: The figure displays the sample histogram of the respondents' changes in consumer surplus due to the counterfactual simulation of removing the LWF option, depicted with dark bars. In the light bars, we overlap the histogram of the estimated changes in consumer surplus where we reweight the sample to match the California distribution of income (top left), education (top right), age (bottom left), and race (bottom right), based on the random coefficients mixed logit choice specification. Estimates are based on mixed logit choice specification.

organic), and water usage (average or efficient). Varying the attribute space presented to consumers in the experimental choice design gives us the data variation to estimate a discrete choice model based on a conditional logit specification and a random coefficient mixed logit specification. In so doing, this chapter provides researchers and policymakers with the first estimates of the distribution of WTP for low water footprint food options during drought years. In addition, we test whether revealing information on the drought matters for the WTP.

We find that, on average, there is an implied positive willingness to pay for water efficiency of about 11 dollars. In terms of gallons of water saved, this means that respondents are on average willing to pay 12 cents for each gallon of water saved in the production of food. Moreover, when informing consumers about the drought severity, this increases consumer's WTP for the LWF options, albeit not significantly. Having additional information on consumer demographic characteristics, we find that there is heterogeneity in the WTP along respondents' stated environmental concern. There is also significant heterogeneity with respect to education and race. Using counterfactual simulations of removing water footprint and drought information from the attribute choice set, we estimate changes in choices that imply significant consumer surplus losses, especially for respondents reporting higher levels of attained education and environmental score and for white respondents.

The consumer valuation estimates provide insights into the policy debate regarding how to label and present food products (Lee and Hatcher 2001) in California and in a future of water scarcity. The WTP far exceeds the cost of one gallon of water sold to agriculture, which ranges from 0.5 cents to 0.3 cents in California during drought years, 10 times as much as during nondrought years.[20] While a comprehensive cost-benefit analysis also requires data on the cost (possibly involving technological changes) of saving one gallon of water used in production, our findings have policy implications in that they suggest there to be at least a demand-side, market-based potential to nudge consumers who want to decrease their water footprint and follow a more sustainable diet.

Our present chapter offers valuable insights into the effectiveness of revealing information on a product's water footprint in a form of a label and on educating consumers about water constraints in the production of the food they buy (i.e., drought severity). However, there are three potential weaknesses: (1) we have captured consumers' stated preferences and not actual behaviors, (2) there is a small sample size, and (3) there is nonrepresentation of the sample for the California population. Following field studies and methodologies implemented in our own previous work (Hilger, Rafert, and Villas-Boas 2011), and given that there can be disparities between consumers' stated preferences and their actual purchases (Hensher and Bradley 1993; Batte et al. 2007), future work should extend the experimental approach into a retail-level consumer field study—using actual choices rather than survey choices to assess consumer responses and valuations for water efficiency and based on a larger and more representative sample. Furthermore, future work should repeat the survey during nondrought years, given that the WTP estimates may be different if the analysis is performed in years when water is perceived to be more plentiful.

20. Estimates obtained by using the reported costs to farmers ranging from $1,000 to $1,800 per cubic acre, given that one cubic acre corresponds to 325,851 gallons. Source: Bloomberg, "California Water Prices Soar for Farmers as Drought Grows," accessed April 28, 2017, http:// www.bloomberg.com/news/articles/2014-07-24/california-water-prices-soar-for-farmers-as -drought-grows.

Appendix

Survey for CA Choices

thank you for participating in this survey.

* Required

1. **What is your gender** *
   Mark only one oval.

   ◯ male

   ◯ female

2. **What is your age** *
   Mark only one oval.

   ◯ 18-20

   ◯ 21-29

   ◯ 30-39

   ◯ 40-49

   ◯ 50-59

   ◯ 60 or older

3. **What is your highest level of education** *
   Mark only one oval.

   ◯ Less than high school degree

   ◯ High School degree or equivalent (e.g. GED)

   ◯ Some college but no degree

   ◯ Bachelor degree

   ◯ graduate degree

4. **What is your household income** *
   Mark only one oval.

   ◯ less than $25,000

   ◯ $25,000 to $49,000

   ◯ $50,000 to 75,000

   ◯ $75,000 to $100,000

   ◯ $100,000 to $125,000

   ◯ $125,000 to $150,000

   ◯ $150,000 or more

Fig. 8A.1   Survey instrument

5. **How many people live in your household?** *

Mark only one oval.

- ○ 1
- ○ 2
- ○ 3
- ○ 4
- ○ 5 or more

6. **What is your race** *

Mark only one oval.

- ○ White
- ○ Hispanic
- ○ Black or African American
- ○ Asian
- ○ American Indian
- ○ Other: _____

7. **Climate change is a result of human activities and is already affecting people worldwide.** *

Mark only one oval.

	1	2	3	4	5	
Strongly Disagree	○	○	○	○	○	Strongly Agree

8. **Protecting the environment should be given utmost priority, even if it causes slower economic growth and some loss of jobs.** *

Mark only one oval.

	1	2	3	4	5	
Strongly Disagree	○	○	○	○	○	Strongly Agree

9. **It is the government's responsibility to impose high taxes on fossil fuels.** *

Mark only one oval.

	1	2	3	4	5	
Strongly Disagree	○	○	○	○	○	Strongly Agree

Fig. 8A.1   (cont.)

10. **The U.S. government should impose stricter laws on pollution.** *
Mark only one oval.

	1	2	3	4	5	
Strongly Disagree	◯	◯	◯	◯	◯	Strongly Agree

11. **People should pay higher prices to address climate change.** *
Mark only one oval.

	1	2	3	4	5	
Strongly Disagree	◯	◯	◯	◯	◯	Strongly Agree

12. **There should be more investment using tax dollars in alternative fuels.** *
Mark only one oval.

	1	2	3	4	5	
Strongly Disagree	◯	◯	◯	◯	◯	Strongly Agree

13. **People should make lifestyle changes to reduce environmental damage.** *
Mark only one oval.

	1	2	3	4	5	
Strongly Disagree	◯	◯	◯	◯	◯	Strongly Agree

14. **It is important to purchase things that are more environmentally friendly, even at a greater cost.**
*
Mark only one oval.

	1	2	3	4	5	
Strongly Disagree	◯	◯	◯	◯	◯	Strongly Agree

15. **The current generation has a responsibility to protect the environment for future generations, even if it leaves them less well off.** *
Mark only one oval.

	1	2	3	4	5	
Strongly Disagree	◯	◯	◯	◯	◯	Strongly Agree

Fig. 8A.1 (cont.)

16. **Personal food choices can affect the environmental impact of agriculture** *
Mark only one oval.

	1	2	3	4	5	
Strongly Disagree	◯	◯	◯	◯	◯	Strongly Agree

Choices
Which of the products would you choose for your household?

17. **Avocados**

Mark only one oval.

◯ $0.98 Lb, conventional, Average Water footprint of 157 gallons per Lb

◯ $2.00/Lb organic, Average Water Footprint of 157 gallons per Lb

◯ $1.18/ Lb Conventional, Efficient Water Footprint, 80 gallons per Lb

◯ $2.40 Lb, Organic Efficient Water Footprint , 80 gallons per Lb

◯ I would not purchase any of these

Fig. 8A.1 (cont.)

18. **Almonds**

Mark only one oval.

- ◯ $5.99 Lb, conventional, Average Water footprint of 1,715 gallons per Lb
- ◯ $11.59 Lb organic, Average Water Footprint of 1,715 gallons per Lb
- ◯ $7.19 Lb Conventional, Efficient Water Footprint, 1,450 gallons per Lb
- ◯ $13.90 Lb, Organic Efficient Water Footprint , 1,450 gallons per Lb
- ◯ I would not purchase any of these

Fig. 8A.1   (cont.)

19. **Lettuce**

Mark only one oval.

- ◯ $2.17 Lb, conventional, Average Water footprint of 14.8 gallons per Lb
- ◯ $5.00 Lb organic, Average Water Footprint of 14.8 gallons per Lb
- ◯ $2.60 Lb Conventional, Efficient Water Footprint, 5.9 gallons per Lb
- ◯ $6.00 Lb, Organic Efficient Water Footprint , 5.9 gallons per Lb
- ◯ I would not purchase any of these

Fig. 8A.1   (cont.)

20. **Tomato**

Mark only one oval.

◯ $1.56 Lb, conventional, Average Water footprint of 16.9 gallons per Lb

◯ $1.99 Lb organic, Average Water Footprint of 16.9 gallons per Lb

◯ $1.87 Lb, Conventional Efficient Water Footprint , 6.5 gallons per Lb

◯ $2.39 Lb Organic, Efficient Water Footprint, 6.5 gallons per Lb

◯ I would not purchase any of these

Fig. 8A.1   (cont.)

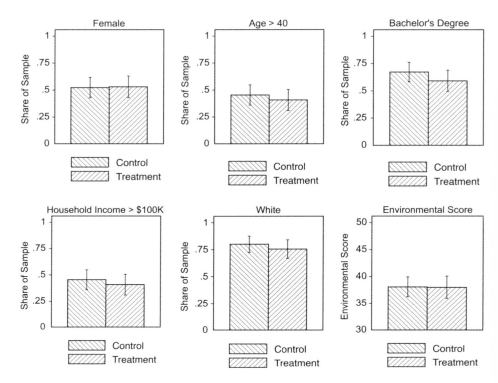

Fig. 8A.2 Average respondent characteristics for treatment and control groups

Notes: The figure displays the average demographic characteristics of respondents for the control and for the treatment groups separately. Environmental score has a minimum value of 10 if a respondent strongly disagreed with all 10 of the environmental statements and a maximum of 50 if the respondent strongly agreed with all of the same 10 statements.

Source: Survey. N = 208 observations.

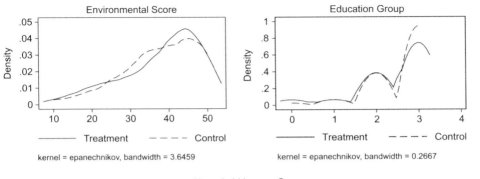

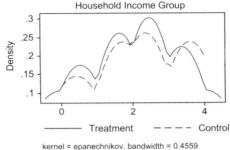

Fig. 8A.3   Kernel density estimates and test of distribution equality

Notes: The figure displays the kernel density estimates of characteristics of respondents for the control and for the treatment groups separately and tests for equality using the Kolmogorov-Smirnov test. Kolmogorov-Smirnov test for equal distribution (*p*-values in parentheses): environmental score = 0.075 (0.943), education = 0.0748 (0.936), income = 0.1183 (0.481).

Source: Survey. N = 208 observations.

References

Abidoye, B. O., H. Bulut, J. Lawrence, B. Mennecke, and A. M. Townsend. 2011. "US Consumers' Valuation of Quality Attributes in Beef Products." *Journal of Agricultural and Applied Economics* 43 (1): 1–12.

Aguilar, F., and R. P. Vlosky. 2007. "Consumer Willingness to Pay Price Premiums for Environmentally Certified Wood Products in the US." *Forest Policy and Economics* 9:1100–12.

Alfnes, F., A. Guttormensen, G. Steine, and K. Kolstad. 2006. "Consumer's Willingness to Pay for the Color of Salmon: A Choice Experiment with Real Economic Incentives." *American Journal of Agricultural Economics* 88 (4): 1050–61.

Asche, F., and J. Guillen. 2012. "The Importance of Fishing Method, Gear and Origin: The Spanish Hake Market." *Marine Policy* 36 (2): 365–69.

Batte, M., N. Hooker, T. Haab, and J. Beaverson. 2007. "Putting Their Money Where Their Mouths Are: Consumer Willingness to Pay for Multi-ingredient, Processed Organic Food Products." *Food Policy* 32 (2): 145–49.

Dimitri, C., and C. Greene. 2002. "Recent Growth Patterns in the US Organic Foods Market." *Agriculture Information Bulletin* 777. Washington, DC: US Department of Agriculture Economic Research Service.

Gao, Z., and T. Schroeder. 2009. "Effects of Label Information on Consumer Willingness-to-Pay for Food Attributes." *American Journal of Agricultural Economics* 91 (3): 795–809.

Hallstein, E., and S. B. Villas-Boas. 2013. "Can Household Consumers Save the Wild Fish? Lessons from a Sustainable Seafood Advisory." *Journal of Environmental Economics and Management* 66 (1): 52–71.

Hanak, E., J. Mount, C. Chappelle, J. Lund, J. Medellin-Azuara, P. Moyle, and N. Seavy. 2015. "What If California's Drought Continues?" Public Policy Institute of California, August. Accessed April 28, 2017. http://www.ppic.org/content/pubs/report/R_815EHR.pdf.

Hensher, D., and M. Bradley. 1993. "Using Stated Response Data to Enrich Revealed Preference Discrete Choice Models." *Marketing Letters* 4 (2): 139–52.

Hilger, J., G. Rafert, and S. Villas-Boas. 2011. "Expert Opinion and the Demand for Experience Goods: An Experimental Approach in the Retail Wine Market." *Review of Economics and Statistics* 93 (4): 1289–96.

Howitt, R., J. Medellín-Azuara, D. MacEwan, J. Lund, and D. Sumner. 2015. "Economic Analysis of the 2015 Drought for California Agriculture." UC Davis Center for Watershed Sciences.

Huber, J., and K. Train. 2001. "On the Similarity of Classical and Bayesian Estimates of Individual Mean Partworths." *Marketing Letters* 12 (3): 259–69.

Jaffry, S., H. Pickering, Y. Ghulam, D. Whitmarsh, and P. Wattage. 2004. "Consumer Choices for Quality and Sustainability Labelled Seafood Products in the UK." *Food Policy* 29 (3): 215–28.

Kiesel, K., and S. B. Villas-Boas. 2007. "Got Organic Milk? Consumer Valuations of Milk Labels after the Implementation of the USDA Organic Seal." *Journal of Agricultural and Food Industrial Organization* 5 (1): 1–38.

Lee, K. H., and C. B. Hatcher. 2001. "Willingness to Pay for Information: An Analyst's Guide." *Journal of Consumer Affairs* 35 (1): 120–39.

Macdiarmid, J. 2012. "Is a Healthy Diet an Environmentally Sustainable Diet?" *Proceedings of the Nutrition Society* 72 (1): 13–20.

Mann, M., and P. Gleick. 2015. "Climate Change and California Drought in the 21st Century." *Proceedings of the National Academy of Sciences* 112 (3): 3858–59.

McConnell, K. E., and I. E. Strand. 2000. "Hedonic Prices for Fish: Tuna Prices in Hawaii." *American Journal of Agricultural Economics* 82 (1): 133–44.

McFadden, D. 1974. "The Measurement of Urban Travel Demand." *Journal of Public Economics* 3 (4): 303–28.

McFadden, D., and K. Train. 2000. "Mixed MNL Models for Discrete Response." *Journal of Applied Econometrics* 15 (5): 447–70.

Mekonnen, M. M., and A. Y. Hoekstra. 2011. "The Green, Blue and Grey Water Footprints of Crops and Derived Crop Products." *Hydrology and Earth System Sciences* 15 (5): 1577–1600.

Renault, D. 2002. "Value of Virtual Water in Food: Principles and Virtues." Paper presented at the UNESCO-IHE Workshop on Virtual Water Trade, December 12–13, Delft, Netherlands.

Revelt, D., and K. Train. 2000. "Customer-Specific Taste Parameters and Mixed Logit: Households' Choice of Electricity Supplier." Working Paper no. E00-274, Department of Economics, University of California, Berkley.

Roheim, C. A., F. Asche, and J. I. Santos. 2011. "The Elusive Price Premium for Eco-Labelled Products: Evidence from Seafood in the UK Market." *Journal of Agricultural Economics* 62 (3): 655–68.

Roheim, C. A., L. Gardiner, and F. Asche. 2007. "Value of Brands and Other Attributes: Hedonic Analysis of Retail Frozen Fish in the UK." *Marine Resource Economics* 22 (3): 239–53.

Small, K., and H. Rosen. 1981. "Applied Welfare Economics with Discrete Choice Models." *Econometrica* 49 (1): 105–30.

Smith, B. G. 2008. "Developing Sustainable Food Supply Chains." *Philosophical Transactions of the Royal Society: Biological Sciences* 363 (1492): 849–61.

Tait, P., S. Miller, W. Abell, W. Kaye-Blake, M. Guenther, and C. Saunders. 2011. "Consumer Attitudes towards Sustainability Attributes on Food Labels." Paper presented at the 55th Annual AARES National Conference, Melbourne, Victoria.

Teisl, M., B. Roe, and R. Hicks. 2002. "Can Eco-Labels Tune a Market? Evidence from Dolphin Safe Labeling." *Journal of Environmental Economics and Management* 43 (3): 339–59.

Train, K. 2003. *Discrete Choice Methods with Simulation*. New York: Cambridge University Press.

Contributors

Reena Badiani-Magnusson
The World Bank
1818 H Street NW
Washington, DC 20433

Eldon Ball
Department of Agricultural and
    Resource Economics
University of Maryland
College Park, MD 20742

Cecilia Bellora
CEPII
20 avenue de Segur
TSA 10726
75334 Paris cedex 07 France

Élodie Blanc
Center for Global Change Science
Massachusetts Institute of Technology
77 Massachusetts Avenue, E19-411D
Cambridge, MA 02139-4307

Jean-Marc Bourgeon
Department of Economics
École Polytechnique
91126 Palaiseau Cedex France

Mark Brown
Statistics Canada
150 Tunney's Pasture Driveway
Ottawa, Ontario K1A 0T6 Canada

Christine L. Carroll
California State University, Chico
221 Plumas Hall, 400 West First Street
Chico, CA 95929-0310

Colin A. Carter
Agricultural and Resource Economics
University of California, Davis
One Shield Avenue
Davis, CA 95616

Truong Chau
Public Service Commission of the
    District of Columbia
1325 G Street NW, Suite 800
Washington, DC 20005

Shon M. Ferguson
Research Institute of Industrial
    Economics
Grevgatan 34
Box 55665
SE-102 15 Stockholm, Sweden

Rachael E. Goodhue
Agricultural and Resource Economics
University of California at Davis
One Shields Avenue
Davis, CA 95616

Nathan P. Hendricks
Department of Agricultural
    Economics
Kansas State University
342 Waters Hall
Manhattan, KS 66506

Hsing-Hsiang Huang
School for Environment and
    Sustainability
University of Michigan
Ann Arbor, MI 48109-1041

Katrina Jessoe
Department of Agricultural and
    Resource Economics
University of California, Davis
One Shields Avenue
Davis, CA 95616

Hannah Krovetz
Analysis Group
650 California Street
San Francisco, CA 94108

C.-Y. Cynthia Lin Lawell
Charles H. Dyson School of Applied
    Economics and Management
Cornell University
407 Warren Hall
Ithaca, NY 14853-4203

Jayson L. Lusk
Department of Agricultural
    Economics
Purdue University
403 West State St.
West Lafayette, IN 47907

Michael R. Moore
School for Environment and
    Sustainability
University of Michigan
Ann Arbor, MI 48109-1041

Richard Nehring
Economic Research Service
United States Department of
    Agriculture
355 E Street SW
Washington, DC 20024-3221

Wolfram Schlenker
School of International and Public
    Affairs (SIPA)
Columbia University
420 West 118th Street
New York, NY 10027

Eric Strobl
Department of Economics
University of Bern
Hochschulstrasse 6
3012 Bern Switzerland

Jesse Tack
Department of Agricultural
    Economics
Kansas State University
218 Waters Hall
Manhattan, KS 66506

Rebecca Taylor
School of Economics
University of Sydney
Room 370, Merewether Building (H04)
NSW, 2006, Australia

Crina Viju-Miljusevic
Institute of European, Russian, and
    Eurasian Studies
Carleton University
1125 Colonel By Drive
Ottawa, Ontario K1S 5B6 Canada

Sofia B. Villas-Boas
Department of Agricultural and
    Resource Economics
232 Giannini Hall #3310
University of California, Berkeley
Berkeley, CA 94720-3310

Sun Ling Wang
Economic Research Service
United States Department of
    Agriculture
355 E Street SW, 6-235B
Washington, DC 20024-3221

Ryan Williams
Economic Research Service
United States Department of
    Agriculture
355 E Street SW
Washington, DC 20024-3221

Author Index

Abbring, J., 228
Abidoye, B. O., 255
Adamopolous, T., 127
Aguilar, F., 254
Aguirregabiria, V., 223
Aigner, D., 46
Alchian, A. A., 139
Alfnes, F. A., 254, 256
Al-Kaisi, M., 84
Allan, W. R., 139
Allen, R. C., 1
Alston, J. J., 11, 48
Alston, J. M., 11
Amsler, C. A., 56n6
Andersen, J., 114
Andersen, M. A., 11
Anderson, S., 78, 83, 84n13
Annan, F., 78, 79, 81n7, 82, 82n11, 89, 90, 91n17, 95n20
Antle, J., 23
Anyamba, A., 43
Apple, J. W., 15, 26
Aréchiga, C. F., 43
Arritt, R. W., 114
Arrow, K., 82n10
Asche, F., 254
Asner, G. P., 43
Atallah, S., 222
Atallah, Z., 220, 220n2, 221n4
Awada, L., 127, 131n11

Babcock, B. A., 43
Badiani-Magnusson, R., 7, 158n1
Baldwin, J. R., 136n23, 137
Ball, V. E., 48
Banerji, J., 158, 158n3, 169
Barber, D. G., 195
Barkley, A., 11, 17
Barreca, A., 81n8
Barrows, G., 13
Bastn, G., 188
Bateman, I., 95n20
Batte, M., 280
Battese, G., 46
Baumgärtner, S., 197
Beatty, P. H., 28
Beck, S. D., 15, 26
Becker, G. S., 113
Beckie, H. J., 130
Beddow, J. M., 11
Behrens, K., 134n15
Beketov, M. A., 186
Bekkerman, A., 86
Bellemare, M. F., 11
Bellora, C., 7, 187
Below, F. E., 16
Bernard, J. K., 43
Besley, T., 161
Birner, R., 157, 158n1, 169
Bloom, N., 127
Bourgeon, J.-M., 187

Bradley, M., 280
Bravo-Ureta, B. E., 42, 43
Briscoe, J., 158
Brock, W. A., 187
Brooks, H. E., 77
Brown, J. F., 92n18
Brown, M., 7
Brown, W. M., 134n15
Burke, M., 42, 79, 89, 114n31
Burt, O., 160
Bustos, P., 127

Cameron, A. C., 19, 27
Carew, R., 186
Carlson, G. A., 222
Carlson, T. N., 195
Carroll, C. L., 8, 223, 226n9, 230n18,
    233n21, 237, 245, 246
Carter, C. A., 44, 50
Carter, T. R., 43
Cassman, K. G., 27
Chapagain, A. K., 169
Chaudhuri, K., 164
Chavas, J. P., 13, 15, 16, 42, 186, 187, 207
Chen, J., 188
Chinthammit, D., 222
Chite, R. M., 84, 85, 85n16
Christensen, J. H., 77
Cobanov, B., 42, 43, 49, 49n3
Coelli, T., 46
Cole, S., 81n9, 164
Collard-Wexler, A., 127, 148
Collins, K. J., 84
Cook, J. A., 223
Cook, P. W., 195
Costa-Roberts, J., 42

Das, D. K., 195
Dasgupta, S., 164
Davey, K., 127
Davis, L. W., 81n8
Day-Rubenstein, K., 62, 64
Decker, W. L., 195
Dell, M., 42, 43, 64, 78, 114n31
De Loecker, J., 127, 148
De Pinto, A., 223
Derie, M., 220
Deryugina, T., 79, 82, 84n14, 91n17
Deschênes, O., 42, 48, 77, 81n8
Devine, D. G., 128
Di Falco, S., 42, 186, 187, 207
Dimitri, C., 255

Doan, D., 128n3, 130
Doiran, J., 129n8
Donaldson, D., 92n19, 187
Doraiswamy, P.C., 195
Downng, J. A., 185
Draca, M., 127
Du, X., 83
Dubash, N. K., 159, 161, 164n6
Duke, S. O., 12, 13
Du Preez, E., 192, 196
Duressa, D., 222
Du Toit, L., 220, 221
Dyer, J., 128, 130

Ehrlich, I., 113
Einav, L., 79, 82, 82n10, 83, 83n12, 108n29
Eklundh, L., 196
Ellis, C. R., 15, 26
Emerick, K., 42, 79, 89

Fan, S., 157, 158n1
Feng, H., 83
Feng, S., 114n31
Ferguson, S. M., 7, 126, 128, 133n14, 140,
    147n27
Fernandez-Cornejo, J., 11, 13, 27, 188n3
Ferreira, S. L., 192, 196
Ferris, R., 43
Fezzi, C., 95n20
Field, C. B., 27
Finkelstein, A., 82
Fisher, A. C., 43, 77, 81n8, 95, 117
Fishman, R., 158n3
Foley, J., 11, 186
Foster, L., 127, 136, 137, 137n24, 138, 146
Fradin, E. F., 219
Fraumeni, B., 11
Frengley, G. A. G., 127, 148
Friedl, M. A., 196
Fuquay, J. W., 43
Furtan, W. H., 127

Galdon-Sanchez, J. E., 127
Gallai, N., 186
Gandhi, V. P., 157, 158n1, 163
Gao, Z., 256
Gardiner, L., 254
Geene, C., 255
Gelbach, J. B., 19, 27
Gentry, L. F., 16
Gertler, P. J., 81n8
Ghosh, A., 164

Ghosh, S., 46
Gisser, M., 160
Glauber, J. W., 78, 84, 86
Gleick, P., 252
Gollop, F., 11
Gómez, M. I., 222
Good, A. G., 28
Gouel, C., 186
Goyari, P., 42
Grandy, A. S., 186
Grant, C., 186
Greenstone, M., 42, 48, 77, 81n8
Griliches, Z., 17
Groten, S. M. E., 195
Gu, W., 136n23, 137
Guillen, J., 254
Guimbard, H., 186
Gulati, A., 157, 162
Gupta, R., 195
Gurian-Sherman, D., 11

Haigh, T., 78
Hakim, D., 11
Hall, D., 222
Hallstein, E., 254
Haltiwanger, J. C., 127, 136, 137, 138, 146
Hanak, E., 251, 252
Hanemann, M., 43
Hansen, P. J., 43
Hatcher, C. B., 280
Hatfield, J., 41, 42
Hayes, M. J., 195, 220n2, 221n4
Hayes, R., 220
Hector, A., 185
Heinemann, J. A., 12
Heisey, P., 62, 64
Helmberger, P., 160
Hendricks, N. P., 6, 16, 17, 173
Hennessy, D. A., 13, 83
Hensher, D., 280
Hernandez-Perez, P., 220, 221
Hicks, R., 254
Highmoor, T., 129
Hilberg, S., 114
Hilger, J., 280
Hochheim, K., 195
Hoekstra, A. Y., 169, 252, 252n5
Holmes, T. J., 80, 90
Hornbeck, R., 114n31, 160
Howitt, R., 255
Hsiang, S. M., 114n31
Huang, C. J., 46

Huang, H.-H., 7
Huang, J., 62
Huang, Q., 159
Hubbard, J. C., 221
Huber, J., 262
Huber, L. L., 15, 26
Huete, A., 195
Hueth, D., 222
Huffman, W., 48, 50
Hughes, G., 188
Hutchison, W. D., 26

Irvine, K. M., 188

Jaffry, S., 254
Jessoe, K., 7, 158n1
Jiguet, F., 186
Jin, Y., 48, 50
Johansson, R. C., 222
Johnston, W. E., 127, 148
Jones, B. F., 42, 43, 64
Jönsson, P., 196
Jorgenson, D., 11
Just, R. E., 23

Kala, N., 81n9
Kalra, N., 195
Kanwar, S., 160
Karlan, D., 81n9
Kerr, W. A., 128
Keskin, P., 160
Key, N., 42, 43, 45, 46, 49, 61, 62n10, 82, 102
Khanal, A. R., 81n9
Khanna, G., 158
Khemani, S., 164
Kiesel, K., 254
Kim, K., 42
Kirwan, B., 79, 82, 84n14, 91n17
Klein, K., 126
Klein,K. K., 128
Klümper, W., 11, 13, 27
Kluver, D. B., 84
Knops, J., 185
Koike, S. T., 221
Koller, M., 195
Kraft, D. F., 129n8
Krizan, C. J., 127, 136, 137, 138, 146
Kromdijk, J., 28
Krovetz, H., 8
Kuhbauch, W., 195
Kulshreshtha, S. N., 128
Kumar, D. M., 158, 158n1

Kumbhakar, S. C., 46
Kunkel, K., 114

Labus, M. P., 195
Lahiri, A. K., 160
Lamb, P. M., 161, 162
Landis, D. A., 186
Lauer, J., 13, 15, 16
Lee, K. H., 280
Lee, S., 80, 90
Lehman, C., 185
Leibman, M., 13
Levin, J., 82
Levinsohn, J., 56n6
Liang, X., 42
Lileeva, A., 127
Lin Lawell, C.-Y. C., 223
Liu, J. W., 46
Lobell, D. B., 27, 42, 43, 77, 81, 99n24
Loomis, J., 159, 171, 173
Loreau, M., 185
Lovell, C., 46
Luengo, A., 223
Lusk, J. L., 6

Ma, B. L., 15, 196n8
Macdiarmid, J., 254
MacDonald, P. J., 15, 26
Madden, L., 188
Magnac, T., 228
Main, C. E., 222
Malézieux, E., 188n4
Malik, R. P. S., 158
Mann, M., 252
Mansur, E. T., 81n8
Maruthachalam, K., 221
McAllister, C. H., 28
McCarl, B. A., 43
McConnell, K. E., 254
McDaniel, M. D., 186
McFadden, D., 260
McGuckin, J. T., 46
McIntosh, C. T., 89
McKee, G. J., 222
Mearns, L. O., 95n20
Meenakshi, V., 158
Meeusen, W., 46
Mekonnen, M. M., 252, 252n5
Melitz, M. J., 126, 148
Meloche, F., 15
Mendelsohn, R., 42, 62n10, 77, 83

Miguel, E., 114n31
Miller, B. M., 81n9
Miller, D. L., 19, 27
Min, B., 159, 161
Mishra, K. K., 195
Mishra, R. K., 42
Mobarak, A. M., 81n9
Modi, V., 158
Moffitt, L., 222
Monari, L., 162
Moore, F. C., 77
Moore, M. R., 7
Morrison, S. R., 43
Moschini, G., 13
Mukherjee, D., 42, 43
Mukherji, A., 158, 158n1, 169n9
Mullen, K., 162
Mullinix, B. G., 43
Murgai, R., 158

Nagelschmitz, K., 135n19
Nalley, L. L., 11, 17
Namboodiri, N. V., 158, 158n1, 163
Neild, R. E., 84
Neiswander, C. R., 15, 26
Nelson, G. C., 223
New, M., 134
Newby, T., 192, 196
Newman, J. E., 84
Noailly, J., 222
Nolan, E., 14, 15
Nordhaus, W. D., 42, 62n10, 77
Nuarsa, I. W., 195
Nunez, H. M., 222

O'Donoghue, E., 82, 102
Oerke, E., 188n3, 203
Olfert, M. R., 126, 128, 133n14, 140, 147n27
Olken, B. A., 42, 43, 64
Olmstead, A. L., 127, 127n2
Onal, H., 222
Orden, D., 162
Osteen, C., 222
Ostrom, E., 160
Oury, B., 44, 49, 50

Pachauri, R., 161
Paddock, B., 128, 130
Palm, M. E., 219
Paltasingh, K. R., 42
Pardey, P. G., 11

Parry, M. L., 41
Paul, C. J. M., 127, 148
Pavcnik, N., 127
Perry, E. D., 13
Pervez, M. S., 92n18
Peters, D. C., 15, 26
Peterson, J., 173
Petrin, A., 56n6
Pianka, E. R., 185, 188
Pimentel, D., 186
Plant, S., 158n1
Polasky, S., 185
Pope, R. D., 23
Porter, J. R., 43
Potdar, M. B., 195
Prasad, A. K., 195
Prokhorov, A., 56n6
Provencher, B., 160
Pryor, S. C., 114

Qaim, M., 11, 13, 27
Quarmby, N. A., 195
Quiring, S. M., 84

Rafert, G., 280
Rajan, S. C., 15, 161
Ramankutty, N., 133n14
Rapson, D., 223
Ravindranath, R., 158, 158n3
Ray, D. K., 11
Ray, I., 158
Regev, U., 222
Reifschneider, D., 46
Renault, D., 252n5, 256
Restuccia, D., 127
Revelt, D., 262, 264
Rhode, P. W., 127, 127n2
Ringler, C., 158
Ripley, D. A., 195
Roberts, M. J., 2, 11, 17, 42, 43, 48, 77, 79,
    81n8, 89, 93, 94, 99n24, 102, 116, 120
Rodhouse, T. J., 188
Roe, B., 254
Roheim, C. A., 254
Rosegrant, M., 158
Rosenzweig, C., 43
Rosenzweig, M. R., 81n9
Rosine, J., 160
Rossman, A., 217
Rothwell, G., 223
Roy, P., 160

Ruffo, M. L., 16
Rust, J., 222, 228

Sachs, J. D., 42
Salter, R. M., 15, 26
Santos, J. I., 254
Santos, P., 14, 15
Schaaf, C. B., 196
Scheierling, S., 159, 171, 173
Schimmelpfennig, D., 42
Schlenker, W., 2, 11, 17, 42, 43, 48, 77, 78, 79,
    81, 81n7, 81n8, 82, 82n11, 89, 90, 91n17,
    92, 93, 94, 95n20, 99n24, 116, 120
Schmidt, P., 46, 56n6
Schmitz, A., 129
Schmitz, J. A., Jr., 127
Schmitz, T. G., 129
Schnitkey, G., 42, 43, 49, 49n3
Schoengold, K., 158n2, 160
Schroeder, T., 256
Scott, C. A., 158, 158n1
Scott, P. T., 223, 226
Sekhri, S., 160
Semenov, M. A., 43
Sesmero, J. P., 159
Sexton, S., 13
Shah, T., 158, 158n1
Shannon, C. E., 187
Shaw, D., 42, 62n10, 77
Shi, G., 13, 15, 16
Shields, D. A., 78, 85, 85n15, 86, 113n30
Shiyomi, M., 188
Short, D. P. G., 220
Shumway, C. R., 42, 62
Smale, M., 186
Smith, A., 16
Smith, B. G., 254
Smith, E. G., 186
Smith, V. H., 78, 86
Sneeringer, S., 42, 43, 45, 46, 49, 61, 62n10
Somanathan, E., 158, 158n3
St-Pierre, N. R., 42, 43, 49, 49n3
Steduto, P., 83, 84
Stevenson, R., 46
Stiegert, K., 13
Storeygard, A., 92n19, 187
Strand, I. E., 254
Subbarao, K., 219, 220, 220n2, 221, 221n4
Sukhadeo, T., 157
Sumner, D. A., 16, 127
Sun, S., 159

Sunding, D., 127n2
Sutton, M. A., 186
Syverson, C., 127

Tack, J., 6, 11, 17
Tait, P., 254, 256
Takahashi, S., 188
Taylor, R., 8
Teisl, M., 254
Thesmar, D., 228
Thom, E. C., 49
Thomma, B. P. H. J., 219
Tiemann, L. K., 186
Tilman, D., 185
Timmins, C., 223
Tongia, R., 158, 161, 162
Train, K., 260, 261, 262, 264
Trefler, D., 127
Tscharntke, T., 187
Tubiello, F. N., 43
Turpin, F. T., 15, 26

Udry, C., 81n9
Upadhaya, S. K., 195
Urban, D. W., 77, 81, 81n8, 84, 99n24, 120

Van den Broeck, J., 46
Van Kooten, G. C., 222
Van Reenen, J., 127
Varian, H. R., 78n1
Vercammen, J., 128n4, 129n9
Veronesi, M., 42
Viju-Miljusevic, C., 7
Villas-Boas, S. B., 8, 254, 280
Villaviencio, X., 43
Vlosky, R. P., 254
Vries, A. D., 42, 43

Wang, C., 78, 83, 84n13
Wang, H. J., 46
Wang, J., 62
Wang, S. L., 6, 41, 48, 52
Wang, Y., 62
Warner, A. M., 42
Watts, M. J., 78, 86
We, L., 15
Weber, J., 82
Wedin, D., 185
Weisenel, W. P., 222
Weissteiner, C. J., 195
Weitzman, M. L., 187
West, J. W., 43
Williams, J., 158
Williamson, L., 3
Williamson, P., 3
Winkler, J. A., 114
Wu, J., 222
Wu, X., 43

Xepapadeas, A., 187
Xiao, C., 219
Xu, Z., 15, 16, 17

Yang, S., 42, 62
Yoshimura, J., 188
Young, R., 159, 171, 173
Yu, T., 43

Zhang, B., 44, 50
Zhang, X., 196
Zhao, J., 78, 84, 84n13
Zhu, T., 158
Zilberman, D., 13, 127n2, 158n2
Zimbelman, R. B., 49

Subject Index

Note: Page numbers followed by "f" or "t" refer to figures or tables, respectively.

adaptation, land use and, 100–106
agricultural output, 157
agricultural production: crop diseases and, 218; estimation results for Indian, 174–76; potential impacts of future climate change on US, 60–65
agricultural productivity. See productivity, agricultural
agriculture, historical employment in, 1
almonds, 8, 252, 256
avocados, 8, 252, 256

biodiversity, 185–87; data, 191–97; empirical results of model, 197–204; empirical strategy for, 190–91; model for, 187–90
Borlaug, Norman, 6

California: agricultural production in, 219; droughts in, 251–52. See also lettuce crops
caloric conversion factors, for crops, 3–4, 3t
Canada: advent of zero tillage in Western, 130–31; Western Grain Transportation Act, 128–30
climate change: agricultural productivity and, 6; literature on impact of, on crop production, 43; literature studying relationship between weather events and, 42–43; potential impacts of future,

on US agricultural production, 60–65; weather events vs., 42
commodity prices, 5–6, 5f
corn (maize), 5f; global production, 2–3, 3f; yield, US, 13–14, 14f. See also GE (genetically engineered); GE (genetically engineered) corn
corn (maize) yield, trend in US, 13–14, 14f
corn yields, US, 1–2, 2f
crop choice, of farmers, 78
crop diseases, 217–19. See also Verticillium wilt
crop diversity, 185–86; agricultural productivity and, 8; comeback of, 186; contributions of study of, to existing literature, 186–87; data for model of, 191–97; empirical analysis of model results, 197–204; empirical results of model of, 190–91; model of, 187–90
crop insurance, 78, 84–85
crop insurance program, US, farmer response to, 7
cropping pattern, 78; in North Dakota, 104
crop production, literature on impact of climate change on, 43. See also productivity, agricultural
crop yield, preplant precipitation and, 97–99

dairy production, study of climatic effects on US, 45

deductibles, crop insurance, 78, 78n1
diseases, crop, 217–19
diversity, crop, 185–86; agricultural productivity and, 8; comeback of, 16; contribution of study of, to existing literature, 186–87; data for model of, 191–97; empirical analysis of model results, 197–204; empirical results of model of, 190–91; model of, 187–90

eco-labels, 252, 254
economic activities, literature on relationship between climate change/weather effect and, 42–43
economic growth, temperature shocks and, 43
electricity subsidies, Indian agricultural, 157; empirical strategy for study of groundwater demand and, 163–65; expenditures on, 158; impact of, 1558; outline of study of, 159–61; welfare costs of, 178–80

farms, defining, for data use, 134–37
freight rate data, Canadian, 131–34

GE (genetically engineered) corn, 6; data for, 16–18; empirical model for, 18–20; heterogeneity in effects of adopting, 15; results of model, 20–26; studies of, 14–16; trend in adoption of, 14–15, 14f. *See also* corn (maize)
GE (genetically engineered) crops: benefits associated with adoption of, 12–13; factors explaining divergence in views about yield effects of, 12; weather-related factors and, 12; yield effects of, 11; yields of current, 13
grassland acres, 104–5; land-use estimation results for, 107t
Green Revolution, 1, 5–6
groundwater usage, 157; empirical strategy for study of agricultural electricity subsidies and, 163–65; in India, 7, 166, 166f, 170–74. *See also* water usage

India: electricity prices in, 161–63, 168–69; electricity subsidies in, 158; groundwater irrigation in, 158; impact of agricultural subsidies in, 159; water usage in, 7, 166, 166f, 170–74. *See also* electricity subsidies, Indian agricultural

insurance take-up, selection on moral hazard in, 106–11

land use: adaptation and moral hazard in, 100–106; data for, 92–97
lettuce crops, 8, 252, 256; diseases and, 218–19. *See also Verticillium dahliade*; Verticillium wilt
Longitudinal Census of Agriculture File (L-CEAG), 131
low water footprint (LWF), 252; empirical setting, survey design, and data for study of, 255–60; willingness to pay (WTP) and, 252–53

maize. *See* corn (maize)
moral hazard, 78–79, 81–83, 82n10; in land use, 100–106; selection on, in insurance take-up, 106–11

North Dakota: cropping pattern in, 104; land-use estimation for, 105t

Oury index, 44

pest control, benefits of, on agricultural productivity, 8
preplant precipitation, effect of, on corn acres, 100–104
production, day, study of climatic effects on US, 45
production shocks, importance of trade in smoothing, 4–5, 4f
productivity, agricultural, 2–3, 3f; climate change and, 6; crop diversity and, 8; decline in growth of, 11; pest control and, 8; total factor productivity and, 41–42; trade subsidies and, 7. *See also* crop production

railway transportation subsidy, Canadian, 125–26. *See also* Western Grain Transportation Act (WGTA, Canada)
rice: commodity prices, 5f; global production, 2–3, 3f

"shallow loss" provision, 78
Shannon index, 187
South Africa, 185–207
soybeans, 3f; commodity prices, 5f; global production, 2–4; preplant precipitation and, 105–6, 108t

stochastic frontier approach, 46–48; agricultural output and inputs, 48; empirical results of, 54–60; irrigation-ready land density variable, 51; R&D, extension, and roads variables, 51; state productivity growth and climate change patterns, 51–54; weather variables, 48–51

Supplemental Revenue Assistance program (2008), 7

SURE (Supplemental Revenue Assistance Payments) program, 78–79, 85–86

sustainable food products, literature review of, 254

technical change, 126–27

technology adoption, 137–41

temperature shocks, economic growth and, 43

THI load, study of, 43–44

tomatoes, 8, 252, 256

total factor productivity (TFP), growth in agricultural productivity and, 41–42

trade, importance of, in smoothing production shocks, 4–5, 4f

trade liberalization, 125, 126–27

trade subsidies, agricultural productivity and, 7

transportation costs, regression analysis for, 141–47

Verticillium dahliade, 8, 217–18, 219–22; literature review, 222–23

Verticillium wilt, 217–18, 219–22; conclusions, 243–47; data for model of, 229–32; dynamic structural econometric model of, 223–29; literature review, 222–23; results of model, 232–38; simulations for, 238–43

water-saving technologies, willingness to pay for, 8

water usage: in India, 7; precipitation and crop growth in Midwest, 83–84. *See also* groundwater usage

weather events: adaptation and, 77–78; adverse, effects of, 41; climate change vs., 42; literature studying relationship between climate change and, 42–43

weather risk: data, 92–97; empirical strategy for, 87–92

Western Grain Transportation Act (WGTA, Canada), 128–30

wheat: commodity prices, 5f; global production, 2–3, 3f

willingness to pay (WTP): counterfactual policy simulations and, 271–78; empirical strategy to estimate, 260–63; low water footprint (LWF) and, 252–53; results of strategy, 263–71; survey design for, 258–60, 281–87

zero tillage, advent of, in Western Canada, 130–31